jane's world

VOLUME TWO

SPECIAL THANKS TO

Robyn and Terry Moore
Kristy and Brian Miller
Lorrie Myers, for mailing lots of **Jane** stuff.

Jean Schulz, for giving me a "day job" that
supports my cartooning habit

Note to self:
The next time I need someone to
write a foreward, try and find someone
who's not such an egotistical ass.

JANE'S WORLD © PAIGE BRADDOCK 2004
DISTRIBUTED BY UNITED FEATURE SYNDICATE, INC.

Jane's World, Vol. 2
ISBN 0-9742450-1-1

Jane's World
P.O. Box 88
Sebastopol, CA 95472

janetoon@mindspring.com

http://www.JanesWorldComics.com

Material in this book was previously published online,
and in single issues, numbered 7 through 12.

Proofreading done by Stephan Pastis,
creator of Pearls Before Swine (www.Comics.com)

Printed in Canada

jane's world
VOLUME TWO

Paige Braddock
Story and art

Brian Miller
Cover color

Terry Moore
Guest cover, chapter two

Foreward:

Paige Braddock is a thief.

If you are her "friend," and you say something amusing, or do something odd, or tell her a story from your personal life, she will make a mental note of it.

And three weeks later, it will turn up in her comic strip.

She will not ask permission. She will not give you forewarning. It will just be there, for millions to see.

Maybe that's why so many people relate to her comic strip. Because it comes from real life. Which is all fine and good when its somebody else's life she's parading around for everyone to see. But when it's yours, it's grating.

But that's not all. If you're one of the really fortunate few, she will actually make you a character in her strip and use your name.

This occurred to me when she introduced "Stephan Pastis" into the Jane cast. Let me tell you what a nice surprise it is to have two dozen "Pearls Before Swine" fans write to me and ask if I knew that some cartoonist named Paige Braddock had introduced me into her comic strip as a shallow, egotistical ass who was obsessed by women's breasts. I even got a cute nickname, "shallow breast guy."

So if you are one of the many who enjoy Jane's World and appreciate Paige Braddock's work, continue to enjoy it from a distance. Because once you get in Paige Braddock's little circle of friends, it's all over.

Stephan Pastis
(aka Shallow Breast Guy)
Pearls Before Swine

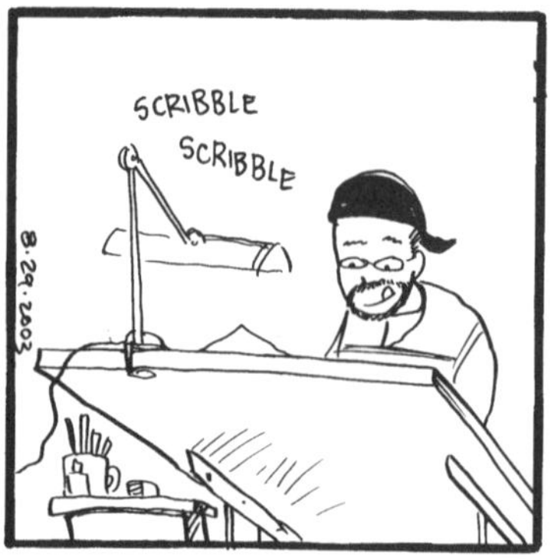
SCRIBBLE
SCRIBBLE
8.29.2003

Stephan Pastis, as he appears in Jane's World, Issue 14

Chapter one

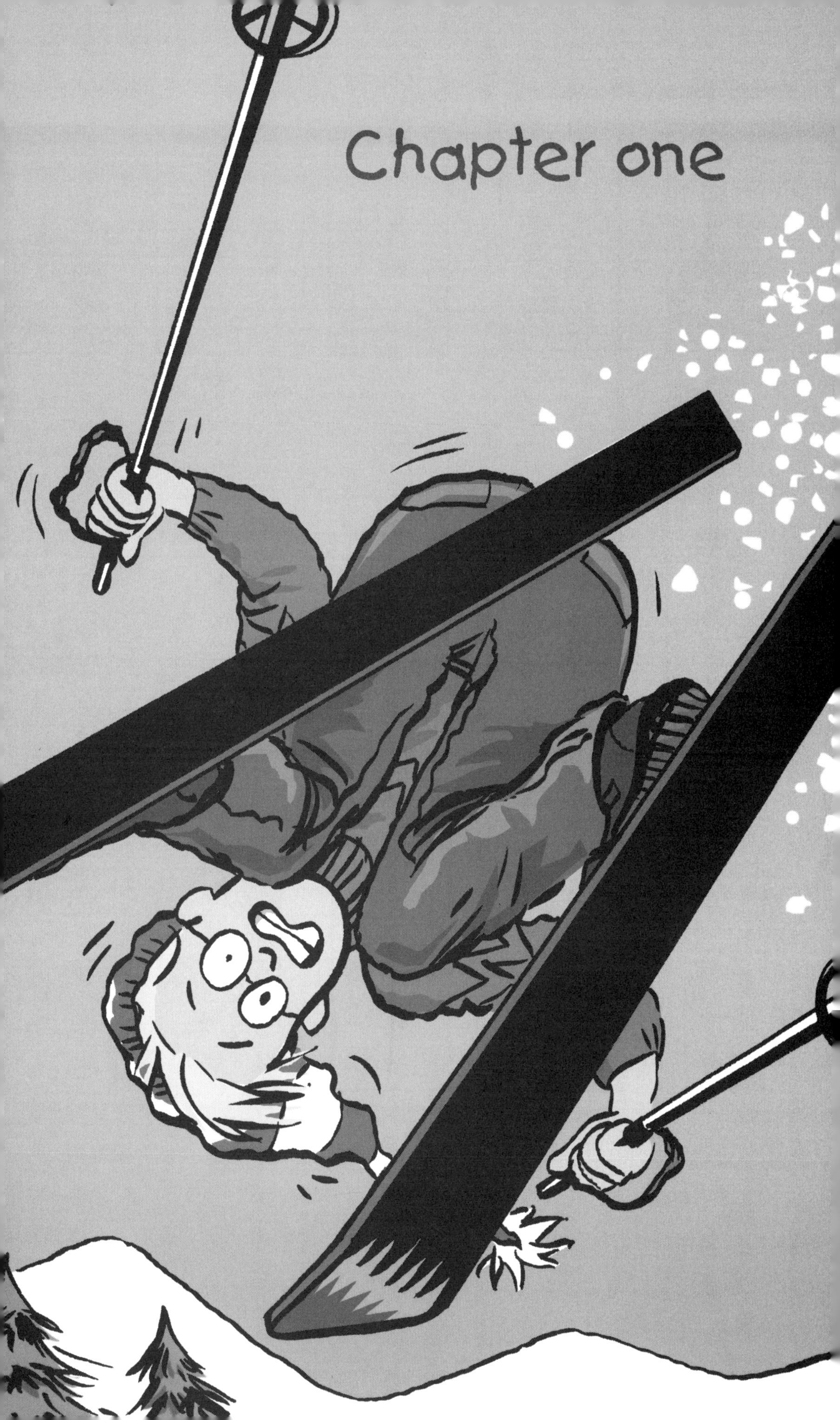

Who's who in Jane's World...

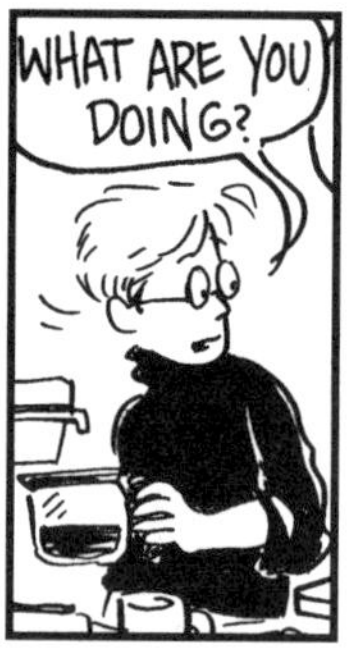
WHAT ARE YOU DOING?

Jane
It's her comic!

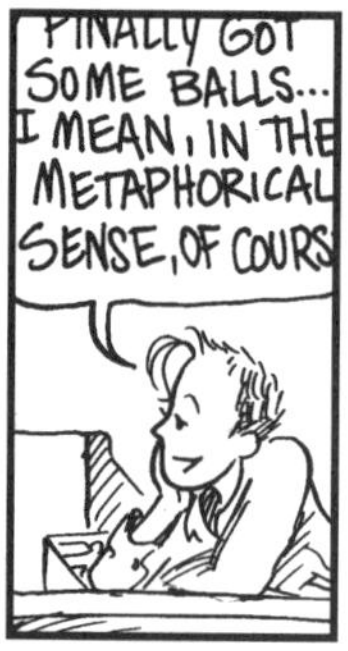
SOME BALLS... I MEAN, IN THE METAPHORICAL SENSE, OF COURS

Natalie
Lethal trainee

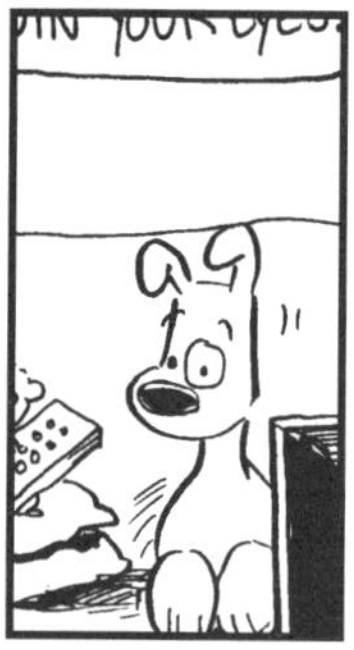

Rusty
Jane's dog

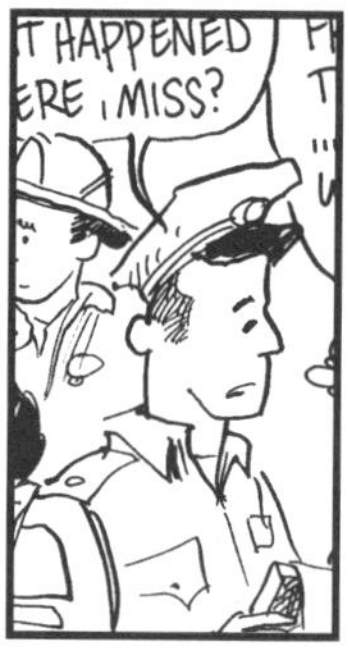
T HAPPENED ERE, MISS?

Rick
Local gay cop

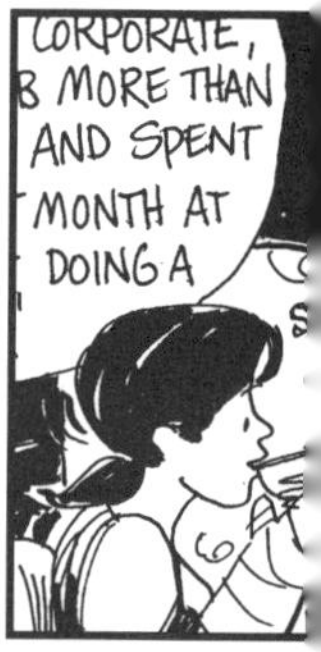
CORPORATE, B MORE THAN AND SPENT MONTH AT DOING A

Maggie
Jane had a crush on her in college

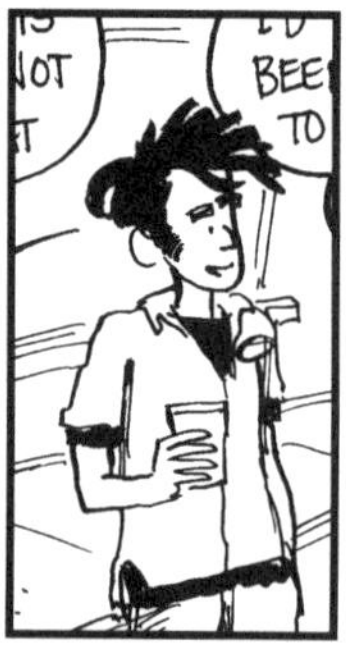

Bud
Jane's cousin

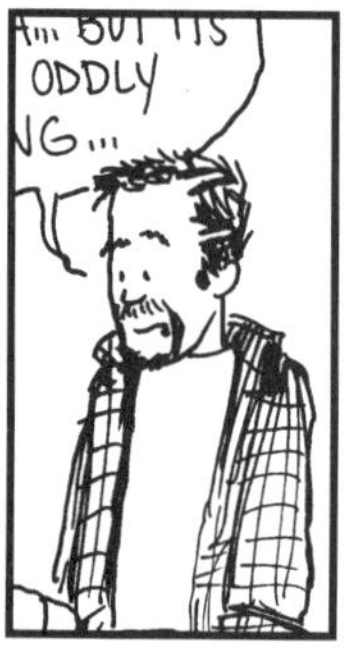
ODDLY

Ethan
Jane's roommate

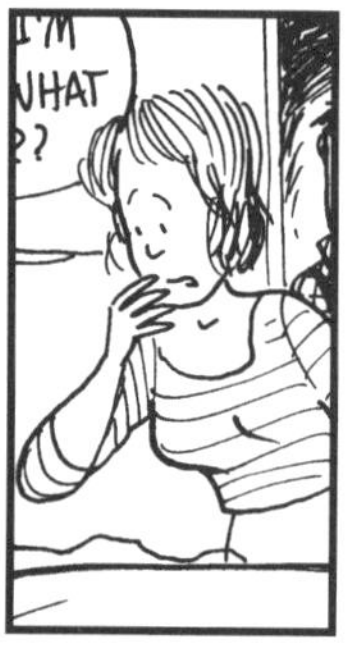

Dorothy
Jane's best friend

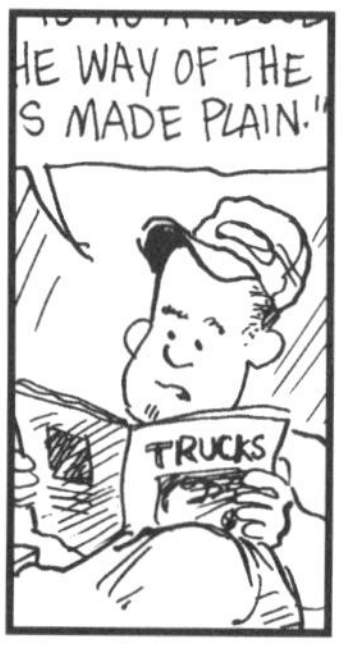
HE WAY OF THE S MADE PLAIN."
TRUCKS

Lowell
Works with Bud at the gas station

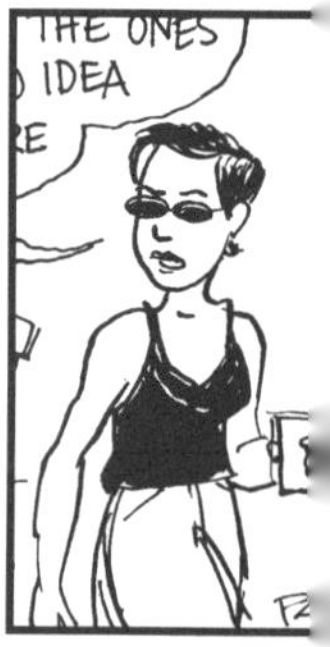
IDEA

Chelle
Needs no introduction

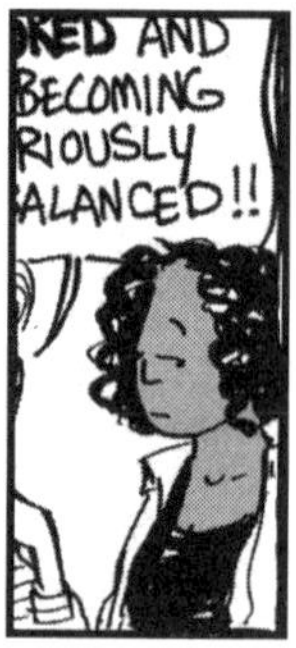
BECOMING RIOUSLY ALANCED!!

Dorrie
Jane's pal and general advice-giver

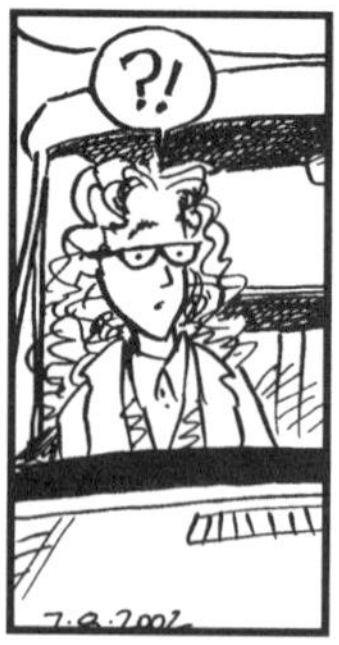
?!

Evelyn
Therapist turned dental student

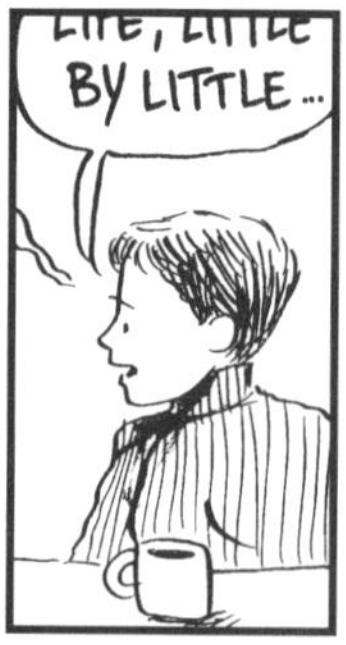
BY LITTLE...

Sarah
Jane's ex-girlfriend

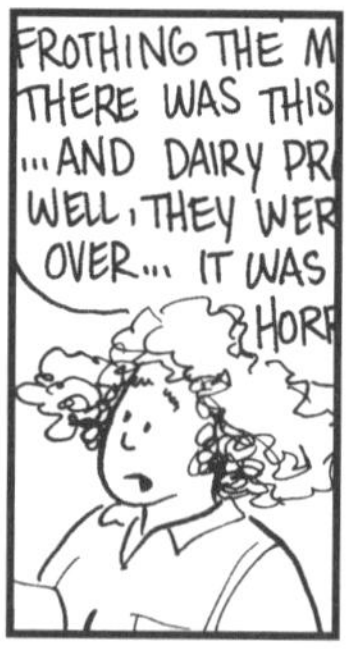
FROTHING THE M THERE WAS THIS ...AND DAIRY PR WELL, THEY WER OVER... IT WAS

Doris
Wannabe cop

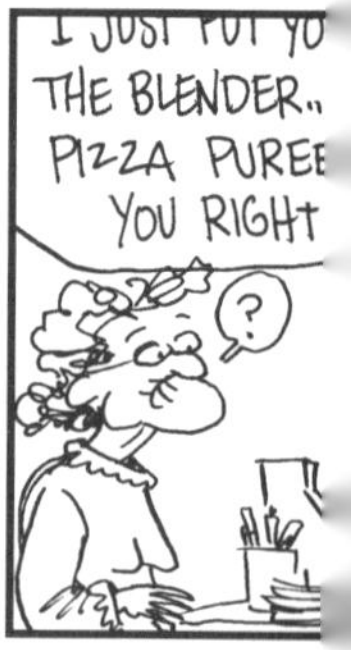
THE BLENDER.. PIZZA PUREE YOU RIGHT
?

Mrs. Beeman
Jane's neighbor

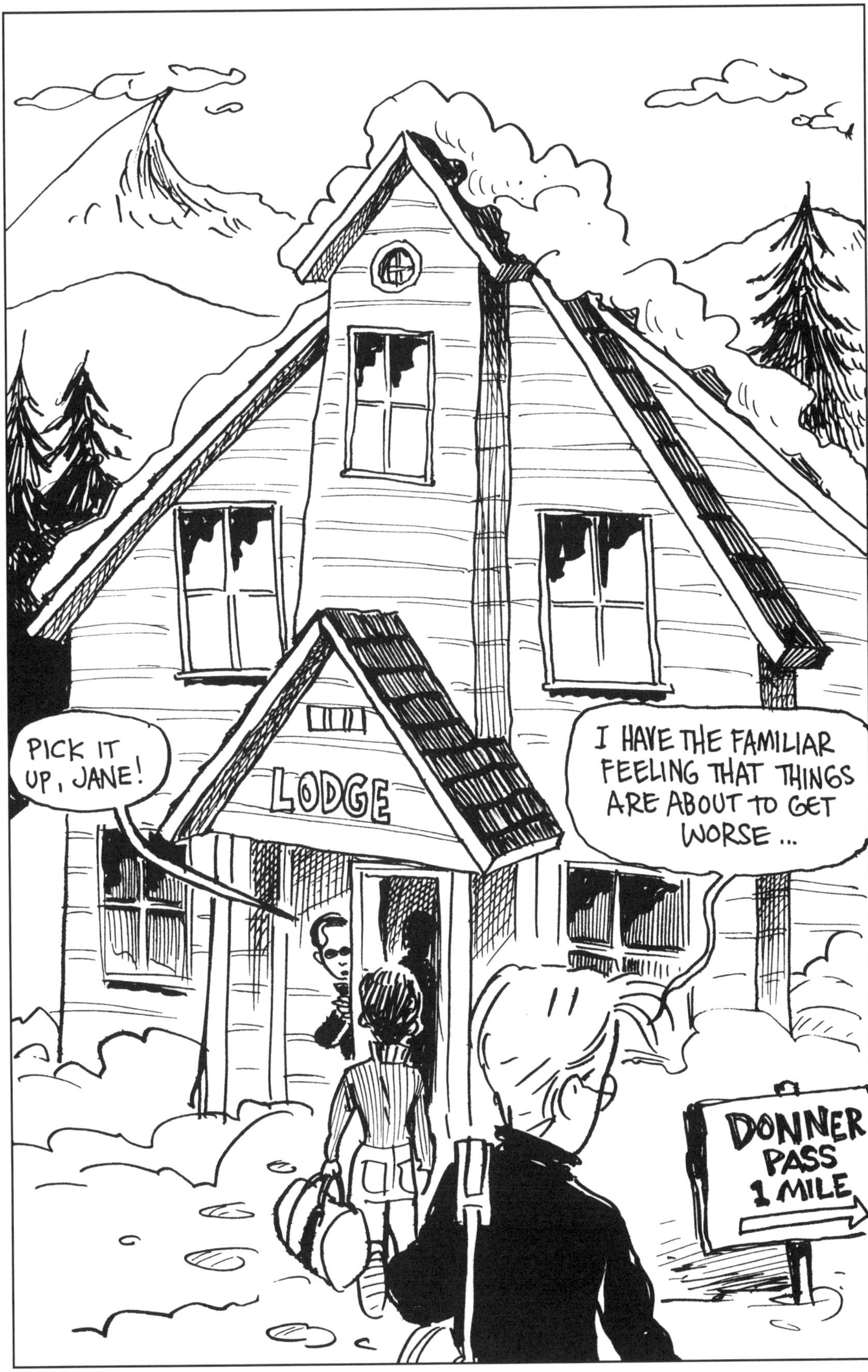
PICK IT UP, JANE!
LODGE
I HAVE THE FAMILIAR FEELING THAT THINGS ARE ABOUT TO GET WORSE ...
DONNER PASS 1 MILE

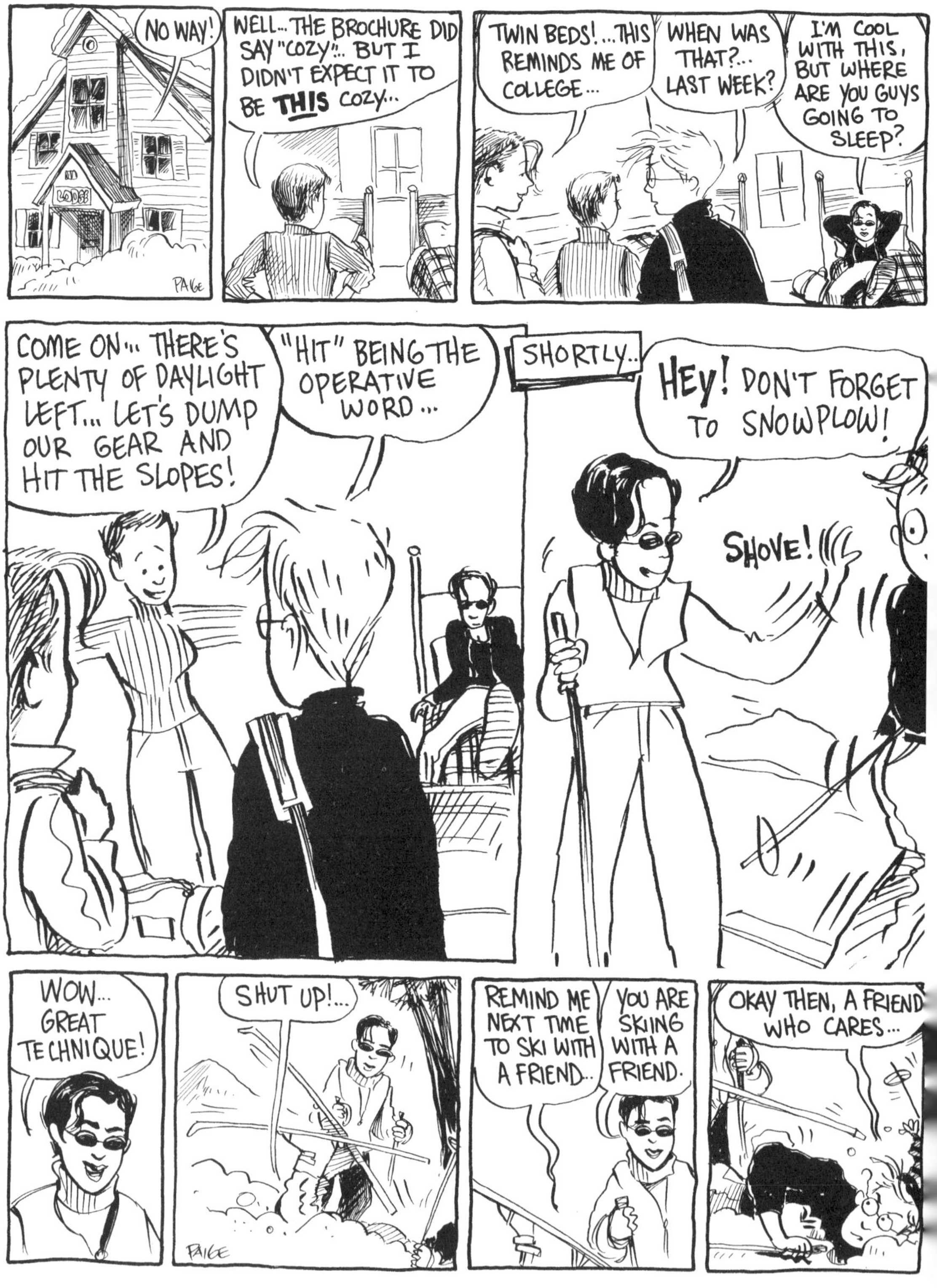
NO WAY!
LODGE
PAIGE
WELL... THE BROCHURE DID SAY "COZY"... BUT I DIDN'T EXPECT IT TO BE THIS COZY...
TWIN BEDS! ...THIS REMINDS ME OF COLLEGE...
WHEN WAS THAT?... LAST WEEK?
I'M COOL WITH THIS, BUT WHERE ARE YOU GUYS GOING TO SLEEP?
COME ON... THERE'S PLENTY OF DAYLIGHT LEFT... LET'S DUMP OUR GEAR AND HIT THE SLOPES!
"HIT" BEING THE OPERATIVE WORD...
SHORTLY..
HEY! DON'T FORGET TO SNOWPLOW!
SHOVE!
WOW... GREAT TECHNIQUE!
SHUT UP!...
PAIGE
REMIND ME NEXT TIME TO SKI WITH A FRIEND..
YOU ARE SKIING WITH A FRIEND.
OKAY THEN, A FRIEND WHO CARES...

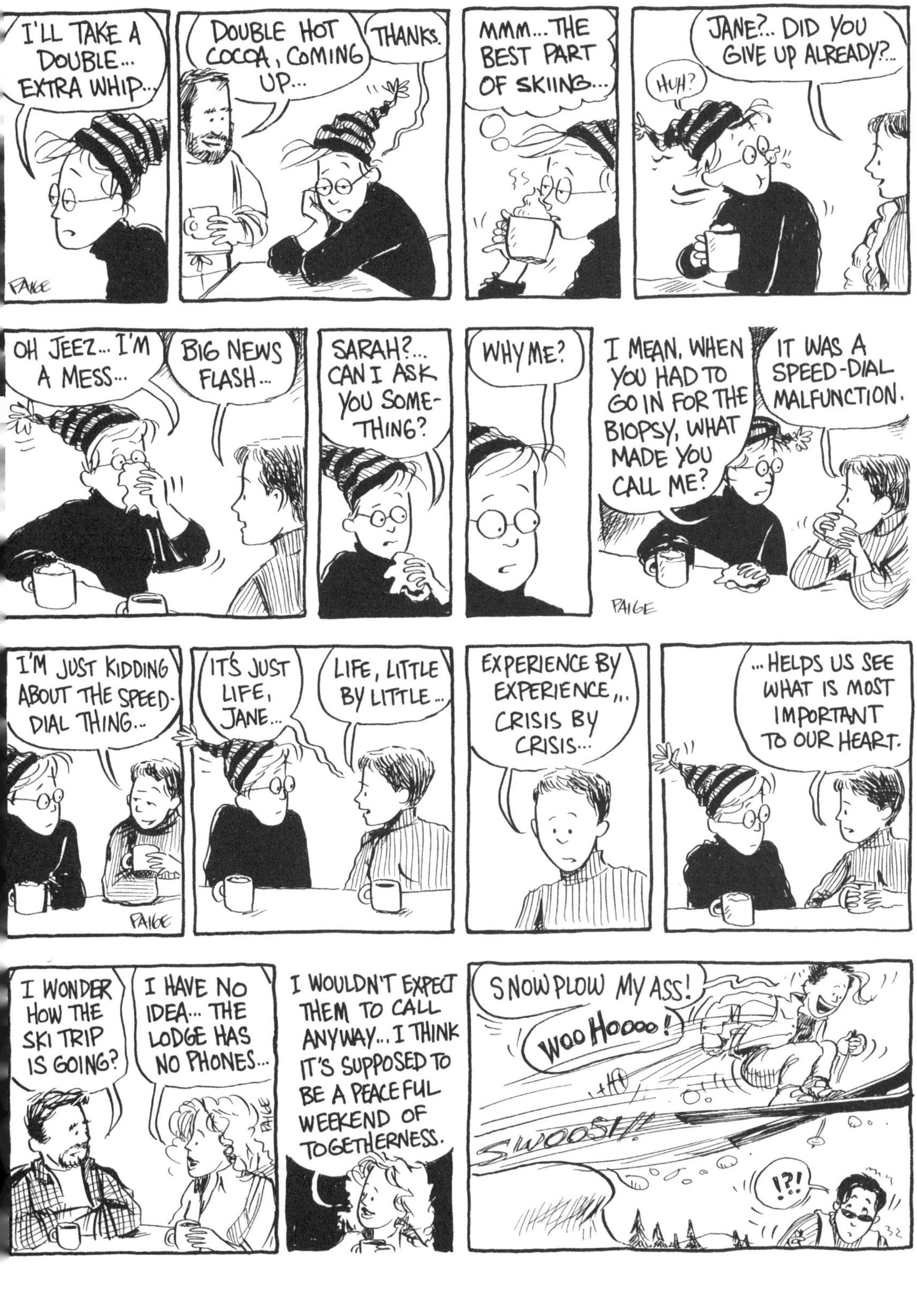
I'LL TAKE A DOUBLE... EXTRA WHIP...
PAIGE
DOUBLE HOT COCOA, COMING UP...
THANKS.
MMM... THE BEST PART OF SKIING...
HUH?
JANE?.. DID YOU GIVE UP ALREADY?...
OH JEEZ... I'M A MESS...
BIG NEWS FLASH...
SARAH?... CAN I ASK YOU SOMETHING?
WHY ME?
I MEAN, WHEN YOU HAD TO GO IN FOR THE BIOPSY, WHAT MADE YOU CALL ME?
IT WAS A SPEED-DIAL MALFUNCTION.
PAIGE
I'M JUST KIDDING ABOUT THE SPEED-DIAL THING...
PAIGE
IT'S JUST LIFE, JANE...
LIFE, LITTLE BY LITTLE...
EXPERIENCE BY EXPERIENCE,.. CRISIS BY CRISIS...
...HELPS US SEE WHAT IS MOST IMPORTANT TO OUR HEART.
I WONDER HOW THE SKI TRIP IS GOING?
I HAVE NO IDEA... THE LODGE HAS NO PHONES...
PAIGE
I WOULDN'T EXPECT THEM TO CALL ANYWAY... I THINK IT'S SUPPOSED TO BE A PEACEFUL WEEKEND OF TOGETHERNESS.
SNOWPLOW MY ASS!
WOO HOOOO!
SWOOSH!!
!?!

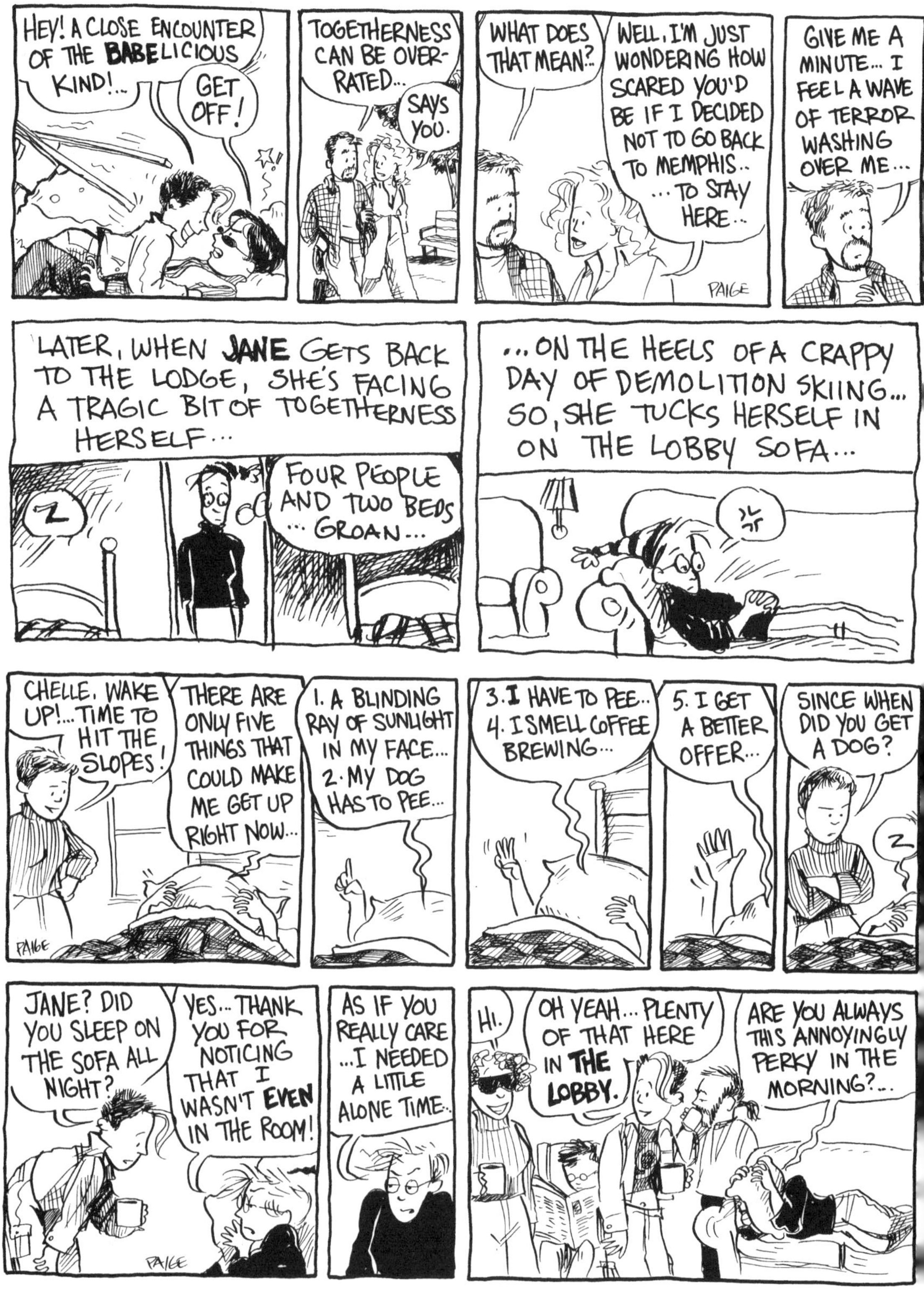
HEY! A CLOSE ENCOUNTER OF THE BABELICIOUS KIND!...
GET OFF!
TOGETHERNESS CAN BE OVER-RATED...
SAYS YOU.
WHAT DOES THAT MEAN?..
WELL, I'M JUST WONDERING HOW SCARED YOU'D BE IF I DECIDED NOT TO GO BACK TO MEMPHIS.. ...TO STAY HERE..
PAIGE
GIVE ME A MINUTE... I FEEL A WAVE OF TERROR WASHING OVER ME...
LATER, WHEN JANE GETS BACK TO THE LODGE, SHE'S FACING A TRAGIC BIT OF TOGETHERNESS HERSELF...
Z
FOUR PEOPLE AND TWO BEDS ...GROAN...
...ON THE HEELS OF A CRAPPY DAY OF DEMOLITION SKIING... SO, SHE TUCKS HERSELF IN ON THE LOBBY SOFA...
CHELLE, WAKE UP!...TIME TO HIT THE SLOPES!
THERE ARE ONLY FIVE THINGS THAT COULD MAKE ME GET UP RIGHT NOW...
1. A BLINDING RAY OF SUNLIGHT IN MY FACE... 2. MY DOG HAS TO PEE...
PAIGE
3. I HAVE TO PEE.. 4. I SMELL COFFEE BREWING...
5. I GET A BETTER OFFER...
SINCE WHEN DID YOU GET A DOG?
Z
JANE? DID YOU SLEEP ON THE SOFA ALL NIGHT?
YES... THANK YOU FOR NOTICING THAT I WASN'T EVEN IN THE ROOM!
PAIGE
AS IF YOU REALLY CARE ...I NEEDED A LITTLE ALONE TIME..
HI.
OH YEAH... PLENTY OF THAT HERE IN THE LOBBY.
ARE YOU ALWAYS THIS ANNOYINGLY PERKY IN THE MORNING?...

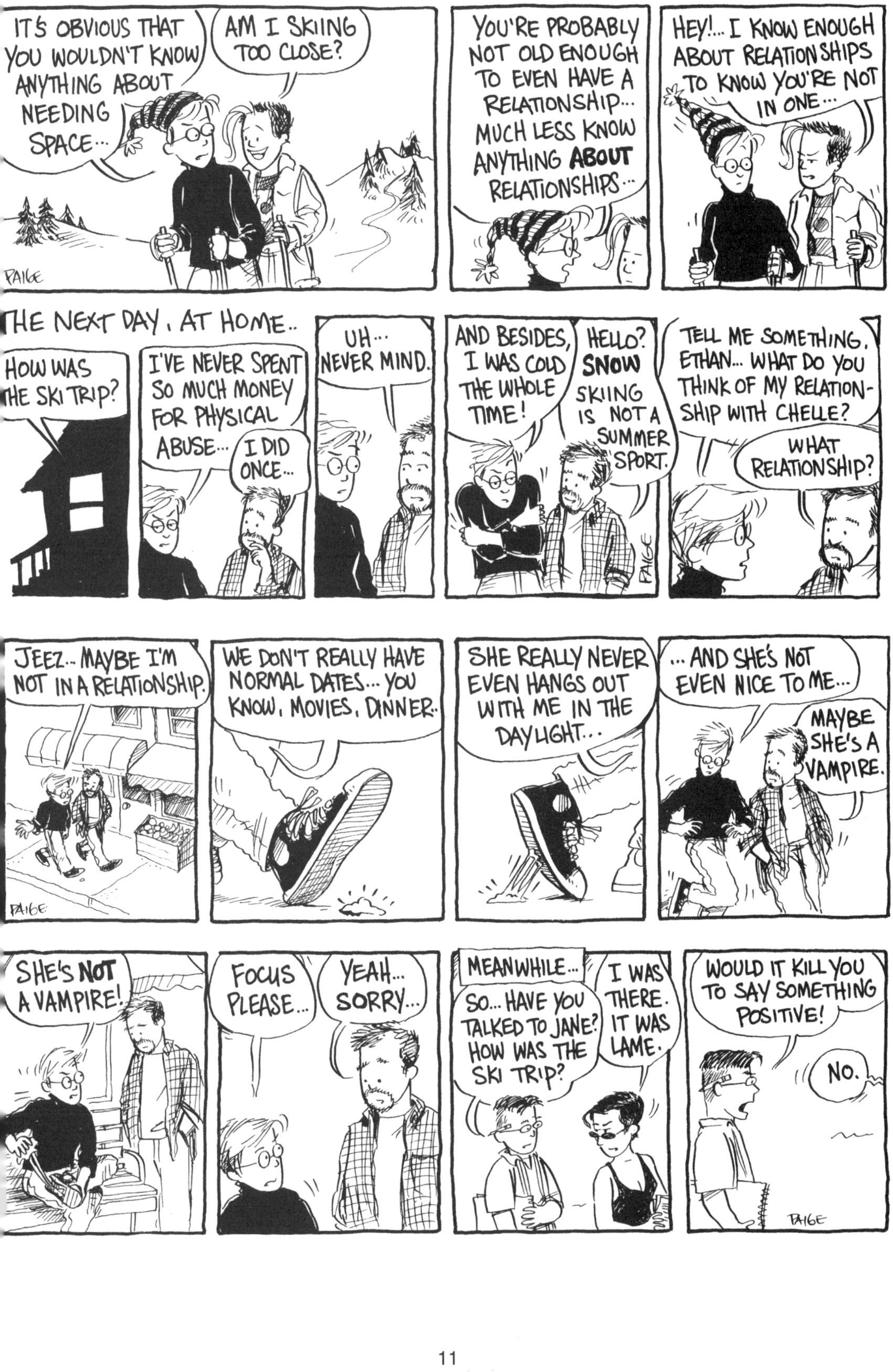
IT'S OBVIOUS THAT YOU WOULDN'T KNOW ANYTHING ABOUT NEEDING SPACE...
AM I SKIING TOO CLOSE?
PAIGE
YOU'RE PROBABLY NOT OLD ENOUGH TO EVEN HAVE A RELATIONSHIP... MUCH LESS KNOW ANYTHING **ABOUT** RELATIONSHIPS...
HEY!... I KNOW ENOUGH ABOUT RELATIONSHIPS TO KNOW YOU'RE NOT IN ONE...
THE NEXT DAY, AT HOME..
HOW WAS THE SKI TRIP?
I'VE NEVER SPENT SO MUCH MONEY FOR PHYSICAL ABUSE...
I DID ONCE...
UH... NEVER MIND.
AND BESIDES, I WAS COLD THE WHOLE TIME!
HELLO? **SNOW** SKIING IS NOT A SUMMER SPORT.
PAIGE
TELL ME SOMETHING, ETHAN... WHAT DO YOU THINK OF MY RELATIONSHIP WITH CHELLE?
WHAT RELATIONSHIP?
JEEZ.. MAYBE I'M NOT IN A RELATIONSHIP.
PAIGE
WE DON'T REALLY HAVE NORMAL DATES... YOU KNOW, MOVIES, DINNER..
SHE REALLY NEVER EVEN HANGS OUT WITH ME IN THE DAYLIGHT...
... AND SHE'S NOT EVEN NICE TO ME...
MAYBE SHE'S A VAMPIRE.
SHE'S **NOT** A VAMPIRE!
FOCUS PLEASE...
YEAH... SORRY...
MEANWHILE...
SO... HAVE YOU TALKED TO JANE? HOW WAS THE SKI TRIP?
I WAS THERE. IT WAS LAME.
WOULD IT KILL YOU TO SAY SOMETHING POSITIVE!
NO.
PAIGE

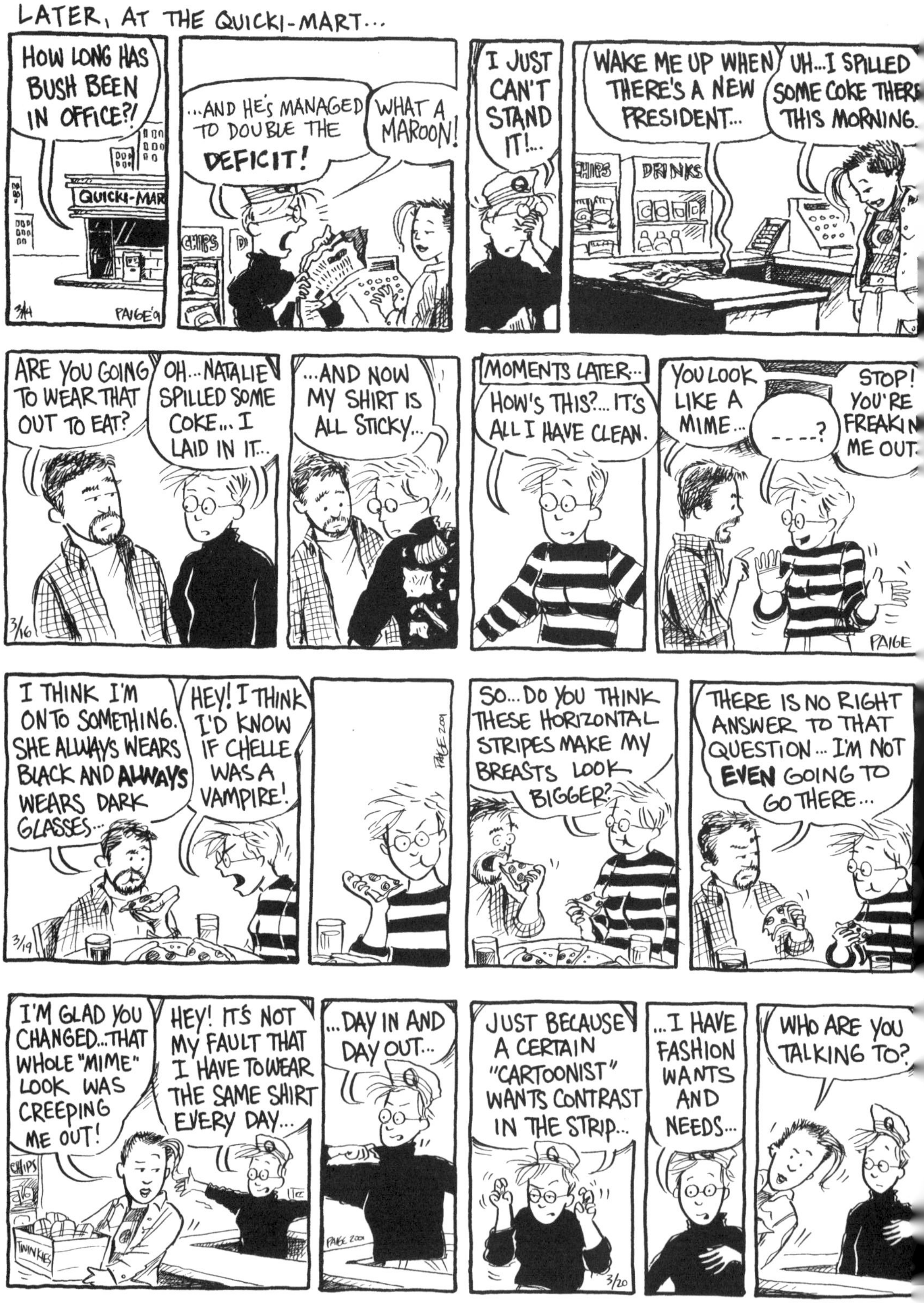
LATER, AT THE QUICKI-MART...
HOW LONG HAS BUSH BEEN IN OFFICE?!
QUICKI-MAR
3/14
PAIGE '01
...AND HE'S MANAGED TO DOUBLE THE DEFICIT!
WHAT A MAROON!
CHIPS
I JUST CAN'T STAND IT!...
WAKE ME UP WHEN THERE'S A NEW PRESIDENT...
UH...I SPILLED SOME COKE THERE THIS MORNING.
CHIPS
DRINKS
ARE YOU GOING TO WEAR THAT OUT TO EAT?
OH...NATALIE SPILLED SOME COKE... I LAID IN IT...
3/16
...AND NOW MY SHIRT IS ALL STICKY...
MOMENTS LATER...
HOW'S THIS?... IT'S ALL I HAVE CLEAN.
YOU LOOK LIKE A MIME...
- - - -?
STOP! YOU'RE FREAKIN ME OUT.
PAIGE
I THINK I'M ONTO SOMETHING. SHE ALWAYS WEARS BLACK AND ALWAYS WEARS DARK GLASSES...
HEY! I THINK I'D KNOW IF CHELLE WAS A VAMPIRE!
3/19
PAIGE 2001
SO... DO YOU THINK THESE HORIZONTAL STRIPES MAKE MY BREASTS LOOK BIGGER?
THERE IS NO RIGHT ANSWER TO THAT QUESTION... I'M NOT EVEN GOING TO GO THERE...
I'M GLAD YOU CHANGED...THAT WHOLE "MIME" LOOK WAS CREEPING ME OUT!
CHIPS
TWINKIES
HEY! IT'S NOT MY FAULT THAT I HAVE TO WEAR THE SAME SHIRT EVERY DAY...
...DAY IN AND DAY OUT...
PAIGE 2001
JUST BECAUSE A CERTAIN "CARTOONIST" WANTS CONTRAST IN THE STRIP...
3/20
...I HAVE FASHION WANTS AND NEEDS...
WHO ARE YOU TALKING TO?

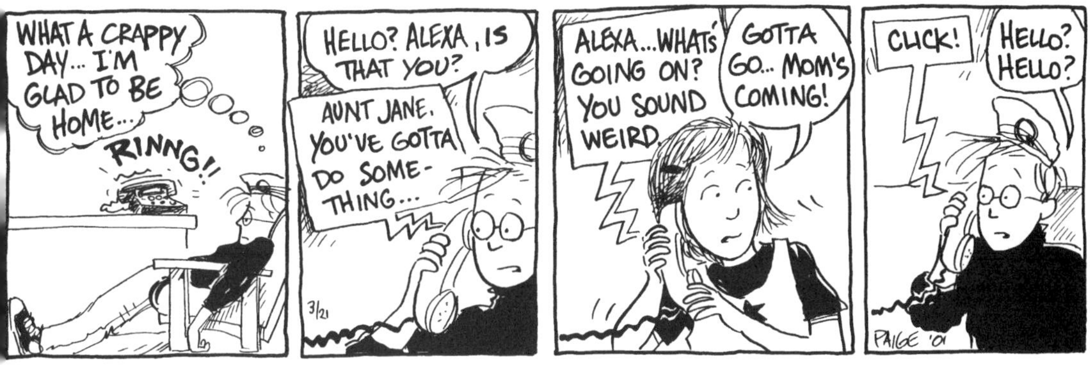
WHAT A CRAPPY DAY... I'M GLAD TO BE HOME...
RINNG!!
3/21
HELLO? ALEXA, IS THAT YOU?
AUNT JANE, YOU'VE GOTTA DO SOMETHING...
ALEXA...WHAT'S GOING ON? YOU SOUND WEIRD
GOTTA GO... MOM'S COMING!
CLICK!
HELLO? HELLO?
PAIGE '01

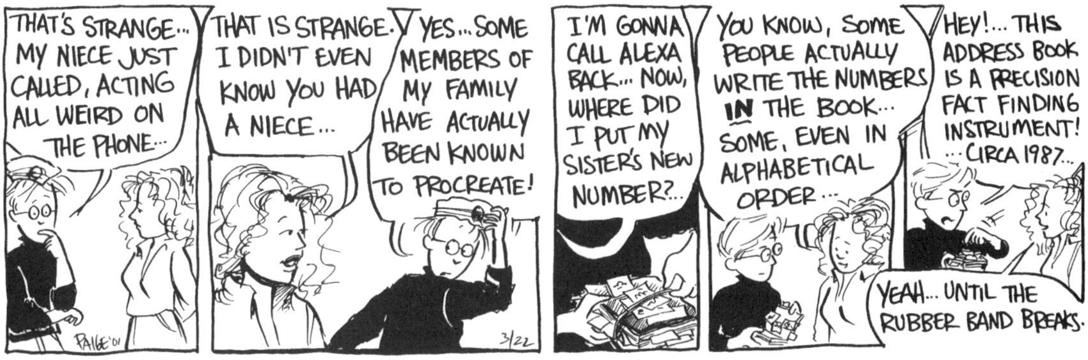
THAT'S STRANGE... MY NIECE JUST CALLED, ACTING ALL WEIRD ON THE PHONE...
PAIGE '01
THAT IS STRANGE. I DIDN'T EVEN KNOW YOU HAD A NIECE...
YES... SOME MEMBERS OF MY FAMILY HAVE ACTUALLY BEEN KNOWN TO PROCREATE!
3/22
I'M GONNA CALL ALEXA BACK... NOW, WHERE DID I PUT MY SISTER'S NEW NUMBER?...
YOU KNOW, SOME PEOPLE ACTUALLY WRITE THE NUMBERS IN THE BOOK... SOME, EVEN IN ALPHABETICAL ORDER...
HEY!... THIS ADDRESS BOOK IS A PRECISION FACT FINDING INSTRUMENT! ...CIRCA 1987...
YEAH... UNTIL THE RUBBER BAND BREAKS.

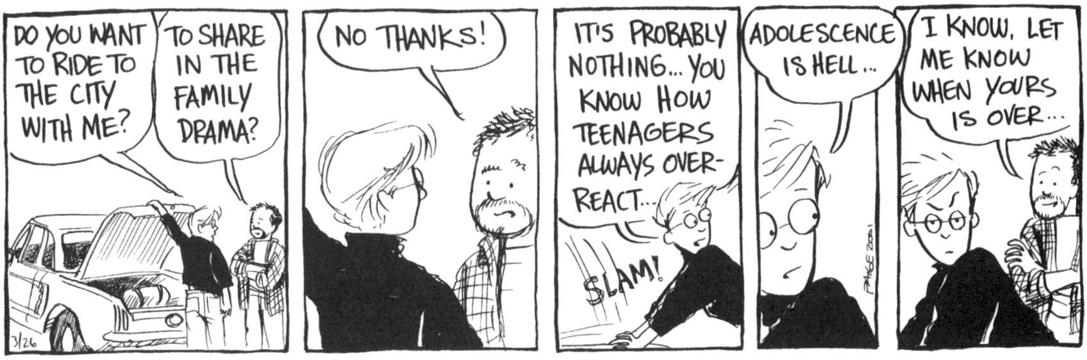
DO YOU WANT TO RIDE TO THE CITY WITH ME?
TO SHARE IN THE FAMILY DRAMA?
3/26
NO THANKS!
IT'S PROBABLY NOTHING... YOU KNOW HOW TEENAGERS ALWAYS OVER-REACT...
SLAM!
ADOLESCENCE IS HELL...
PAIGE 2001
I KNOW, LET ME KNOW WHEN YOURS IS OVER...

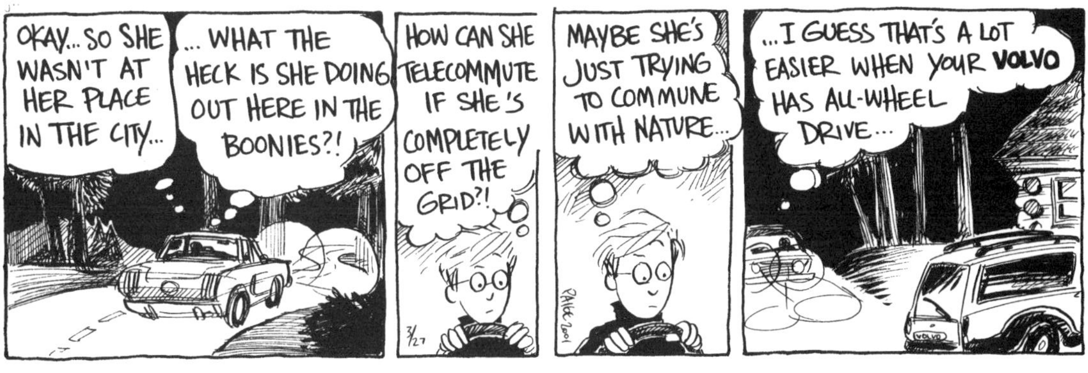
OKAY... SO SHE WASN'T AT HER PLACE IN THE CITY...
... WHAT THE HECK IS SHE DOING OUT HERE IN THE BOONIES?!
HOW CAN SHE TELECOMMUTE IF SHE'S COMPLETELY OFF THE GRID?!
3/27
MAYBE SHE'S JUST TRYING TO COMMUNE WITH NATURE...
PAIGE 2001
...I GUESS THAT'S A LOT EASIER WHEN YOUR VOLVO HAS ALL-WHEEL DRIVE...
VOLVO

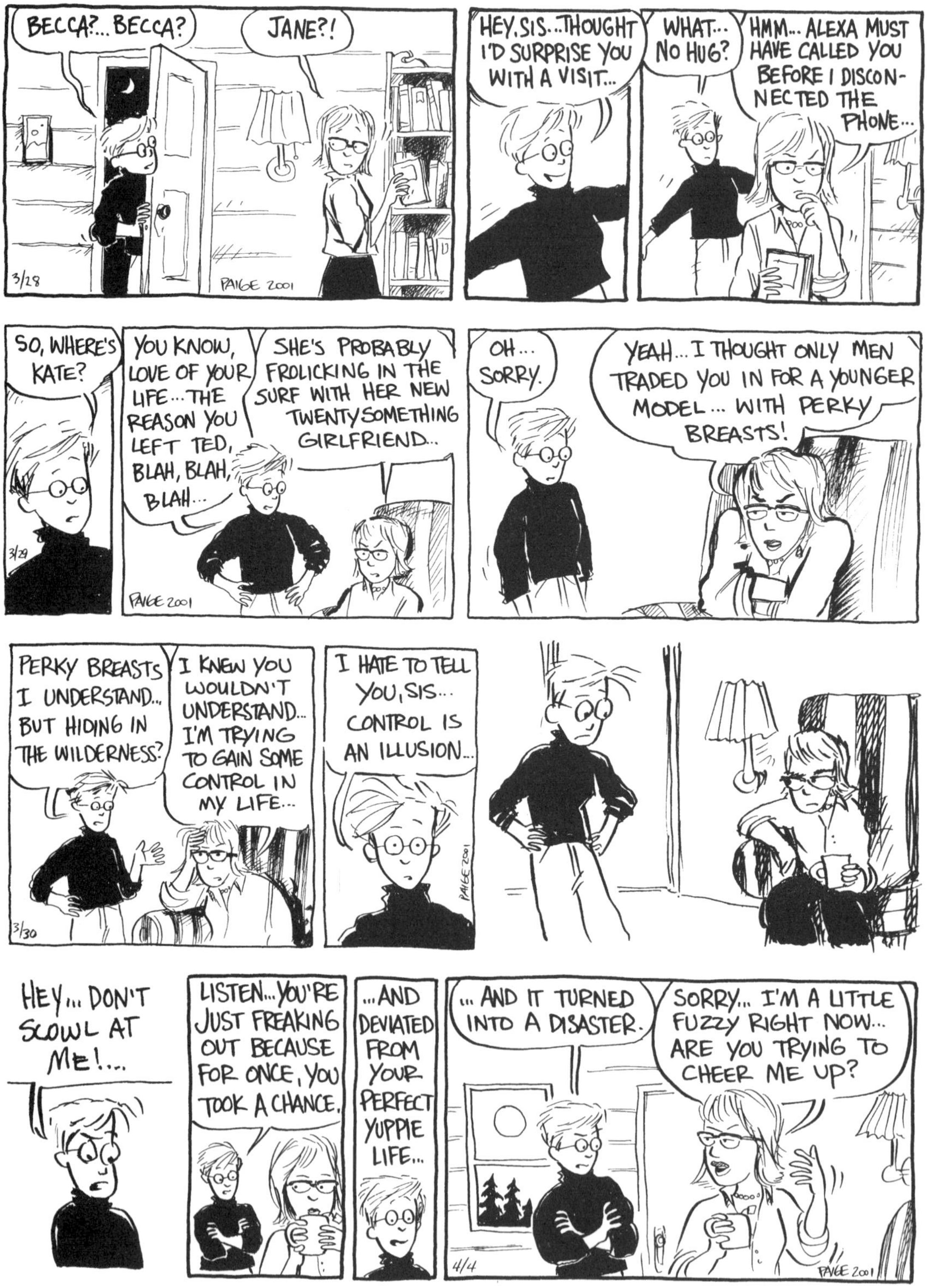
BECCA?... BECCA?
JANE?!
3/28
PAIGE 2001
HEY, SIS... THOUGHT I'D SURPRISE YOU WITH A VISIT...
WHAT... NO HUG?
HMM... ALEXA MUST HAVE CALLED YOU BEFORE I DISCONNECTED THE PHONE...
SO, WHERE'S KATE?
3/29
YOU KNOW, LOVE OF YOUR LIFE... THE REASON YOU LEFT TED, BLAH, BLAH, BLAH...
SHE'S PROBABLY FROLICKING IN THE SURF WITH HER NEW TWENTYSOMETHING GIRLFRIEND...
PAIGE 2001
OH... SORRY.
YEAH... I THOUGHT ONLY MEN TRADED YOU IN FOR A YOUNGER MODEL... WITH PERKY BREASTS!
PERKY BREASTS I UNDERSTAND... BUT HIDING IN THE WILDERNESS?
I KNEW YOU WOULDN'T UNDERSTAND... I'M TRYING TO GAIN SOME CONTROL IN MY LIFE...
3/30
I HATE TO TELL YOU, SIS... CONTROL IS AN ILLUSION...
PAIGE 2001
HEY... DON'T SCOWL AT ME!...
LISTEN... YOU'RE JUST FREAKING OUT BECAUSE FOR ONCE, YOU TOOK A CHANCE.
...AND DEVIATED FROM YOUR PERFECT YUPPIE LIFE...
... AND IT TURNED INTO A DISASTER.
SORRY... I'M A LITTLE FUZZY RIGHT NOW... ARE YOU TRYING TO CHEER ME UP?
4/4
PAIGE 2001

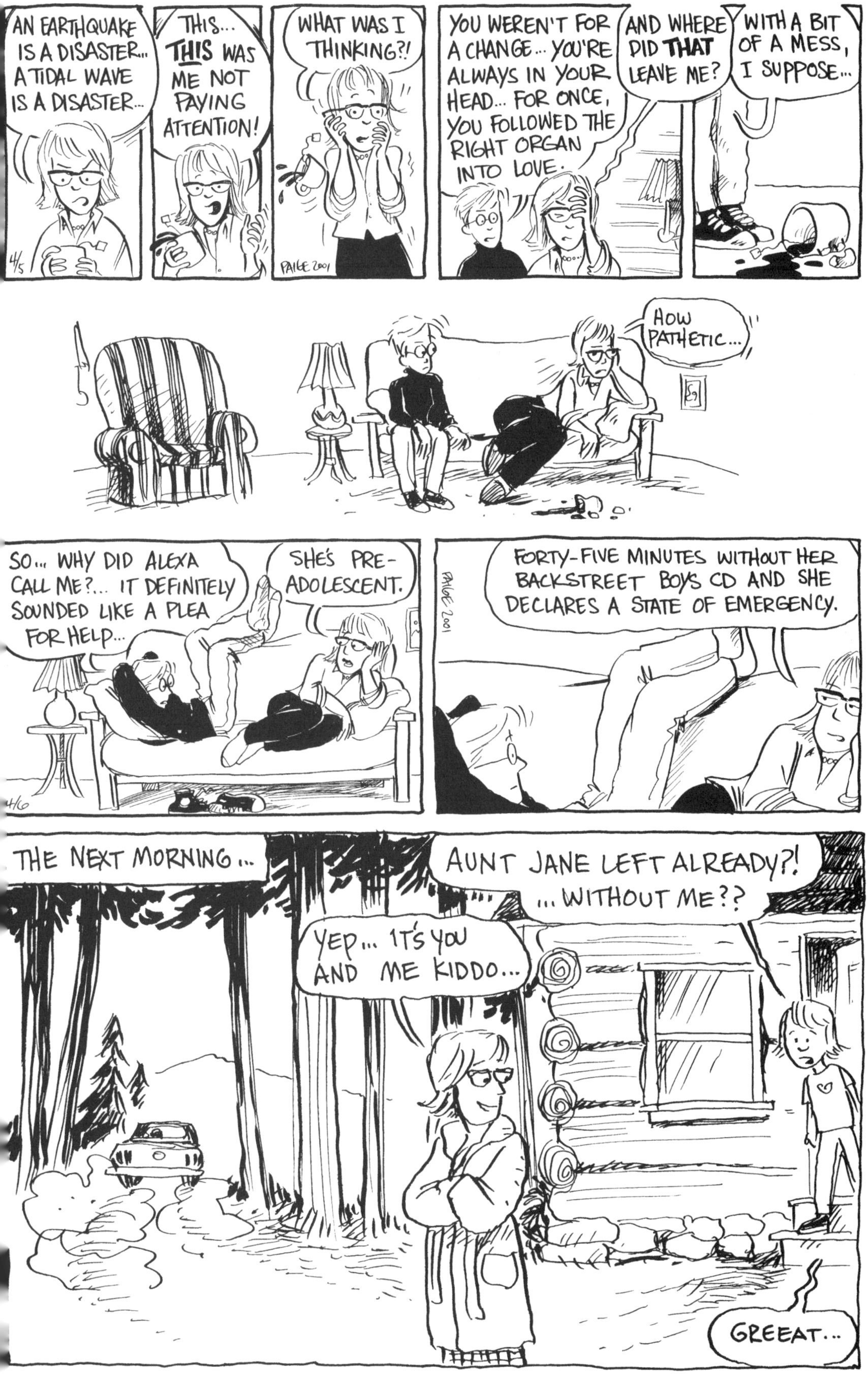
AN EARTHQUAKE IS A DISASTER... A TIDAL WAVE IS A DISASTER...
THIS... THIS WAS ME NOT PAYING ATTENTION!
WHAT WAS I THINKING?!
YOU WEREN'T FOR A CHANGE... YOU'RE ALWAYS IN YOUR HEAD... FOR ONCE, YOU FOLLOWED THE RIGHT ORGAN INTO LOVE.
AND WHERE DID THAT LEAVE ME?
WITH A BIT OF A MESS, I SUPPOSE...
HOW PATHETIC...
SO... WHY DID ALEXA CALL ME?... IT DEFINITELY SOUNDED LIKE A PLEA FOR HELP...
SHE'S PRE-ADOLESCENT.
FORTY-FIVE MINUTES WITHOUT HER BACKSTREET BOYS CD AND SHE DECLARES A STATE OF EMERGENCY.
THE NEXT MORNING...
AUNT JANE LEFT ALREADY?! ...WITHOUT ME??
YEP... IT'S YOU AND ME KIDDO...
GREEAT...

BACK ON THE HOME FRONT, BUD DECIDES TO HOST A YARD SALE...

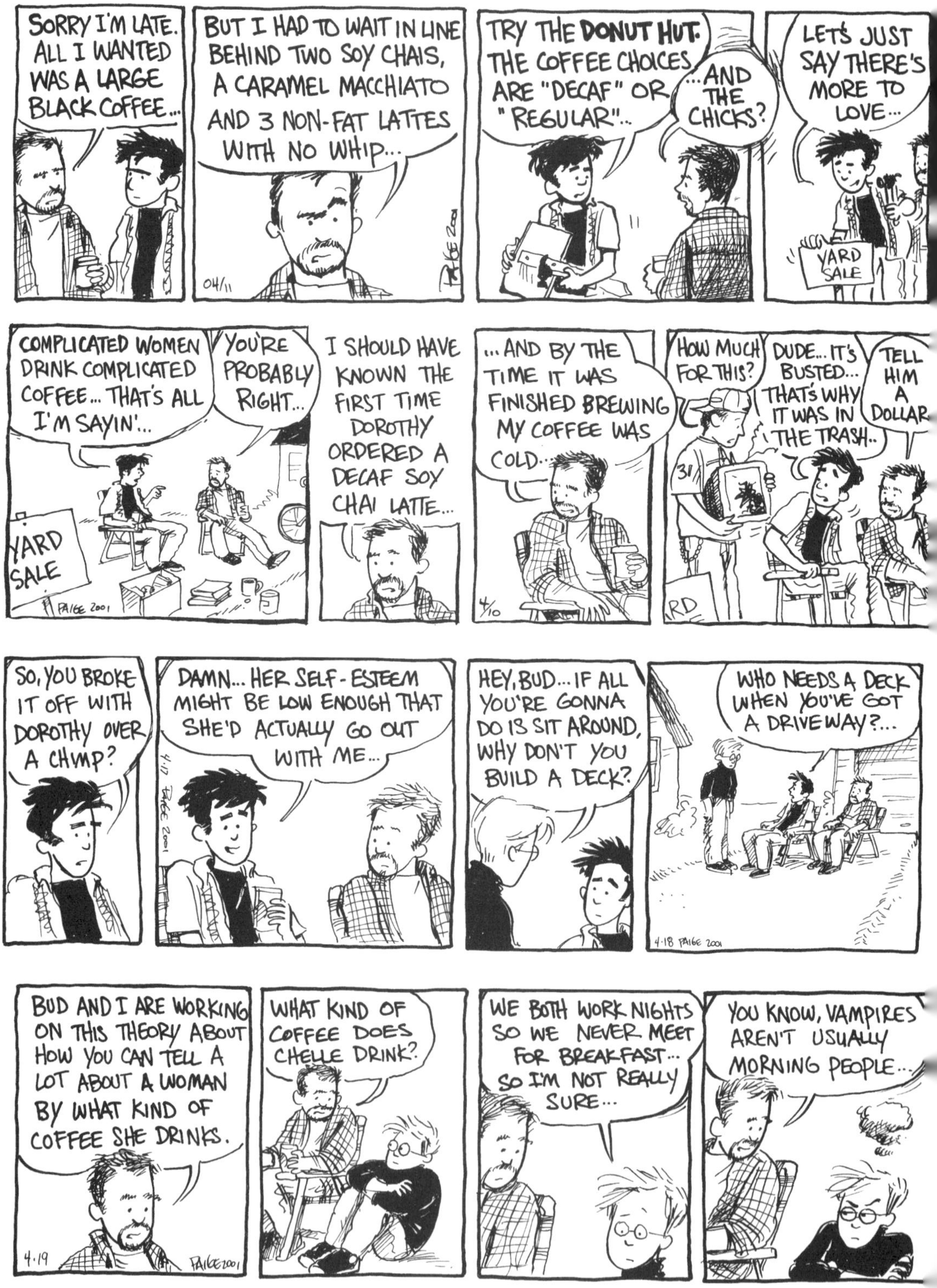
SORRY I'M LATE. ALL I WANTED WAS A LARGE BLACK COFFEE...
BUT I HAD TO WAIT IN LINE BEHIND TWO SOY CHAIS, A CARAMEL MACCHIATO AND 3 NON-FAT LATTES WITH NO WHIP...
04/11
PAIGE 2001
TRY THE DONUT HUT. THE COFFEE CHOICES ARE "DECAF" OR "REGULAR"...
...AND THE CHICKS?
LET'S JUST SAY THERE'S MORE TO LOVE...
YARD SALE
COMPLICATED WOMEN DRINK COMPLICATED COFFEE... THAT'S ALL I'M SAYIN'...
YOU'RE PROBABLY RIGHT...
YARD SALE
PAIGE 2001
I SHOULD HAVE KNOWN THE FIRST TIME DOROTHY ORDERED A DECAF SOY CHAI LATTE...
...AND BY THE TIME IT WAS FINISHED BREWING MY COFFEE WAS COLD...
4/10
HOW MUCH FOR THIS?
DUDE... IT'S BUSTED... THAT'S WHY IT WAS IN THE TRASH..
TELL HIM A DOLLAR
SO, YOU BROKE IT OFF WITH DOROTHY OVER A CHIMP?
4.17 PAIGE 2001
DAMN... HER SELF-ESTEEM MIGHT BE LOW ENOUGH THAT SHE'D ACTUALLY GO OUT WITH ME...
HEY, BUD... IF ALL YOU'RE GONNA DO IS SIT AROUND, WHY DON'T YOU BUILD A DECK?
WHO NEEDS A DECK WHEN YOU'VE GOT A DRIVEWAY?...
4.18 PAIGE 2001
BUD AND I ARE WORKING ON THIS THEORY ABOUT HOW YOU CAN TELL A LOT ABOUT A WOMAN BY WHAT KIND OF COFFEE SHE DRINKS.
4.19
PAIGE 2001
WHAT KIND OF COFFEE DOES CHELLE DRINK?
WE BOTH WORK NIGHTS SO WE NEVER MEET FOR BREAKFAST... SO I'M NOT REALLY SURE...
YOU KNOW, VAMPIRES AREN'T USUALLY MORNING PEOPLE...

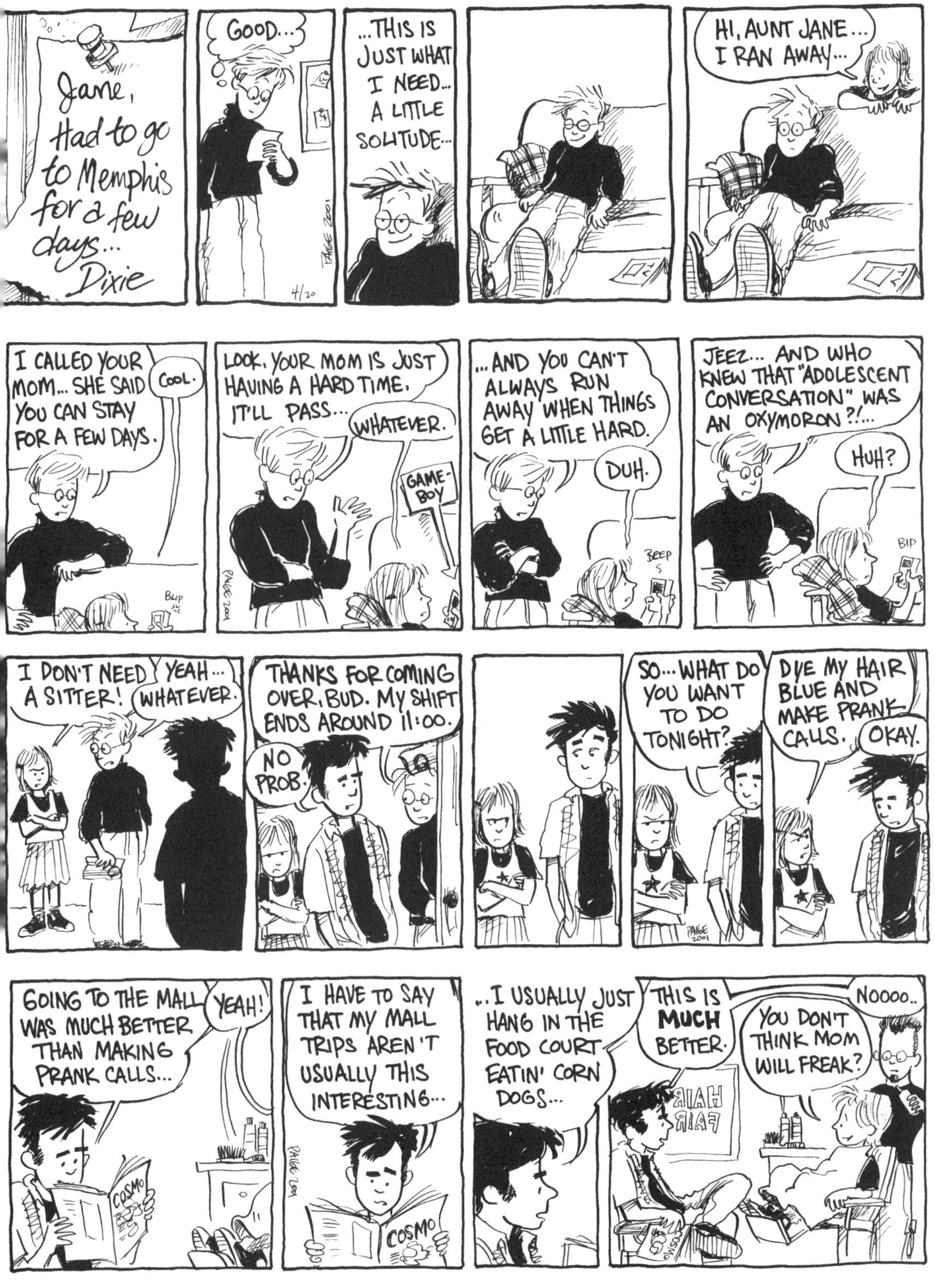
Jane,
Had to go to Memphis for a few days...
Dixie
GOOD...
...THIS IS JUST WHAT I NEED... A LITTLE SOLITUDE...
PAIGE 2001
4/20
HI, AUNT JANE... I RAN AWAY...
I CALLED YOUR MOM... SHE SAID YOU CAN STAY FOR A FEW DAYS.
COOL.
BLIP
LOOK, YOUR MOM IS JUST HAVING A HARD TIME. IT'LL PASS...
WHATEVER.
GAME-BOY
PAIGE 2001
...AND YOU CAN'T ALWAYS RUN AWAY WHEN THINGS GET A LITTLE HARD.
DUH.
BEEP
JEEZ... AND WHO KNEW THAT "ADOLESCENT CONVERSATION" WAS AN OXYMORON ?!...
HUH?
BIP
I DON'T NEED A SITTER!
YEAH... WHATEVER.
THANKS FOR COMING OVER, BUD. MY SHIFT ENDS AROUND 11:00.
NO PROB.
SO... WHAT DO YOU WANT TO DO TONIGHT?
PAIGE 2001
DYE MY HAIR BLUE AND MAKE PRANK CALLS.
OKAY.
GOING TO THE MALL WAS MUCH BETTER THAN MAKING PRANK CALLS...
YEAH!
COSMO
I HAVE TO SAY THAT MY MALL TRIPS AREN'T USUALLY THIS INTERESTING...
PAIGE 2001
COSMO
...I USUALLY JUST HANG IN THE FOOD COURT EATIN' CORN DOGS...
THIS IS MUCH BETTER.
NOOOO..
YOU DON'T THINK MOM WILL FREAK?

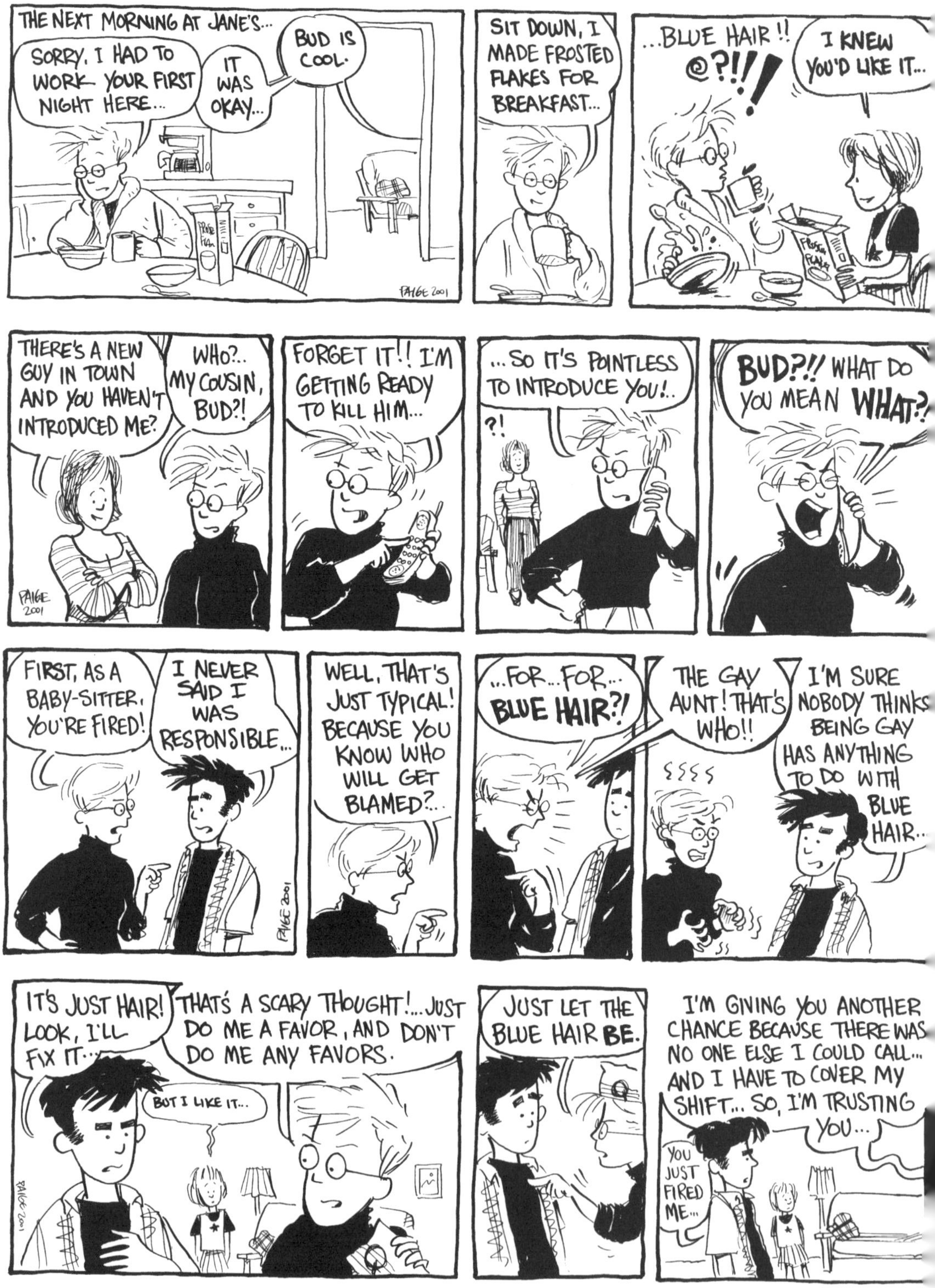
THE NEXT MORNING AT JANE'S...
SORRY, I HAD TO WORK YOUR FIRST NIGHT HERE...
IT WAS OKAY...
BUD IS COOL.
PAIGE 2001
SIT DOWN, I MADE FROSTED FLAKES FOR BREAKFAST...
...BLUE HAIR!!
@?!!!
I KNEW YOU'D LIKE IT...
THERE'S A NEW GUY IN TOWN AND YOU HAVEN'T INTRODUCED ME?
WHO?.. MY COUSIN, BUD?!
PAIGE 2001
FORGET IT!! I'M GETTING READY TO KILL HIM...
...SO IT'S POINTLESS TO INTRODUCE YOU!..
?!
BUD?!! WHAT DO YOU MEAN WHAT?!
FIRST, AS A BABY-SITTER, YOU'RE FIRED!
I NEVER SAID I WAS RESPONSIBLE...
PAIGE 2001
WELL, THAT'S JUST TYPICAL! BECAUSE YOU KNOW WHO WILL GET BLAMED?...
...FOR...FOR... BLUE HAIR?!
THE GAY AUNT! THAT'S WHO!!
I'M SURE NOBODY THINKS BEING GAY HAS ANYTHING TO DO WITH BLUE HAIR...
IT'S JUST HAIR! LOOK, I'LL FIX IT...
THAT'S A SCARY THOUGHT!...JUST DO ME A FAVOR, AND DON'T DO ME ANY FAVORS.
BUT I LIKE IT...
PAIGE 2001
JUST LET THE BLUE HAIR BE.
I'M GIVING YOU ANOTHER CHANCE BECAUSE THERE WAS NO ONE ELSE I COULD CALL... AND I HAVE TO COVER MY SHIFT... SO, I'M TRUSTING YOU...
YOU JUST FIRED ME...

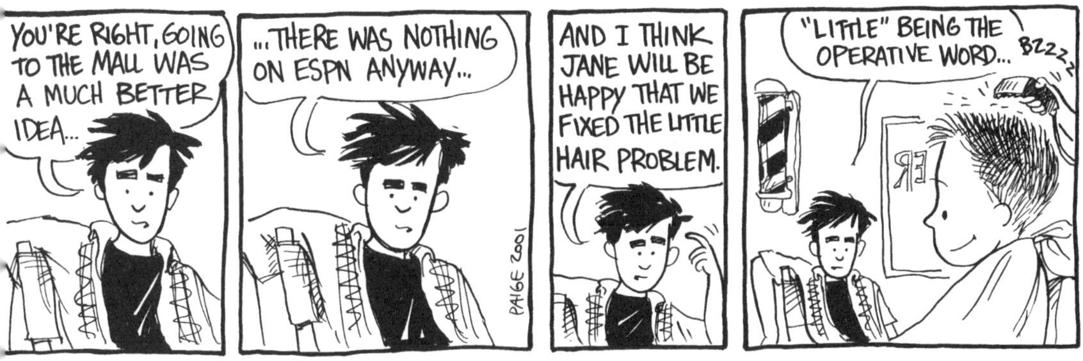
YOU'RE RIGHT, GOING TO THE MALL WAS A MUCH BETTER IDEA...
...THERE WAS NOTHING ON ESPN ANYWAY...
AND I THINK JANE WILL BE HAPPY THAT WE FIXED THE LITTLE HAIR PROBLEM.
PAIGE 2001
"LITTLE" BEING THE OPERATIVE WORD...
BZZZZ

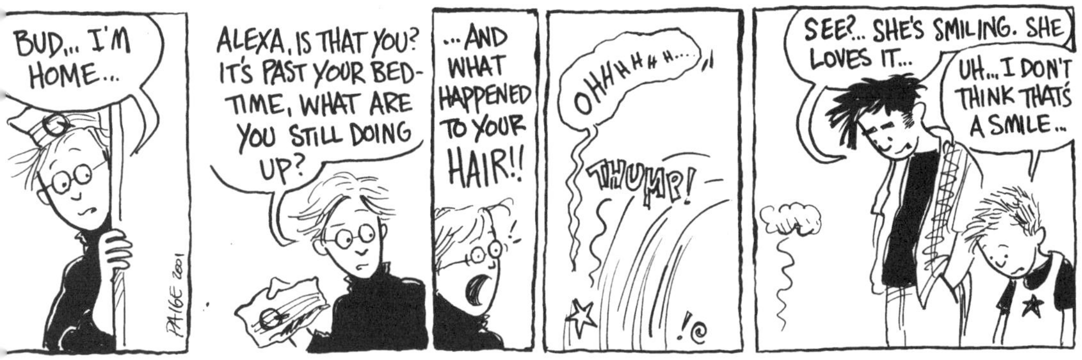
BUD,... I'M HOME...
PAIGE 2001
ALEXA, IS THAT YOU? IT'S PAST YOUR BED-TIME, WHAT ARE YOU STILL DOING UP?
...AND WHAT HAPPENED TO YOUR HAIR!!
OHHHHHH....
THUMP!
SEE?... SHE'S SMILING. SHE LOVES IT...
UH... I DON'T THINK THAT'S A SMILE...

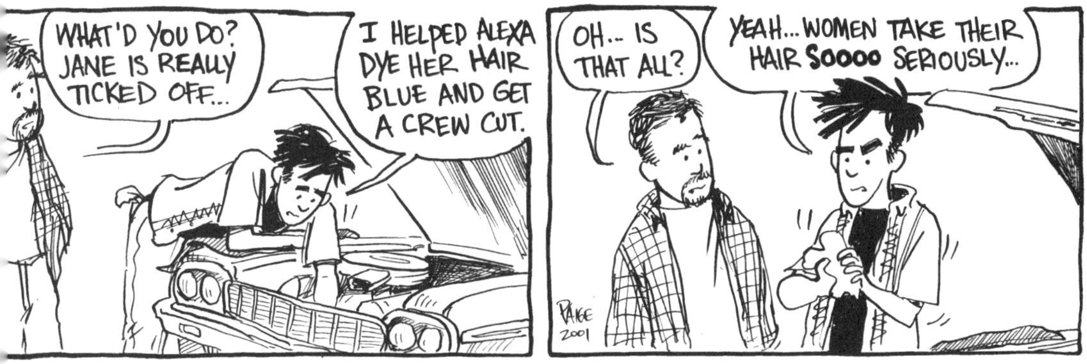
WHAT'D YOU DO? JANE IS REALLY TICKED OFF...
I HELPED ALEXA DYE HER HAIR BLUE AND GET A CREW CUT.
OH... IS THAT ALL?
YEAH... WOMEN TAKE THEIR HAIR SOOOO SERIOUSLY...
PAIGE 2001

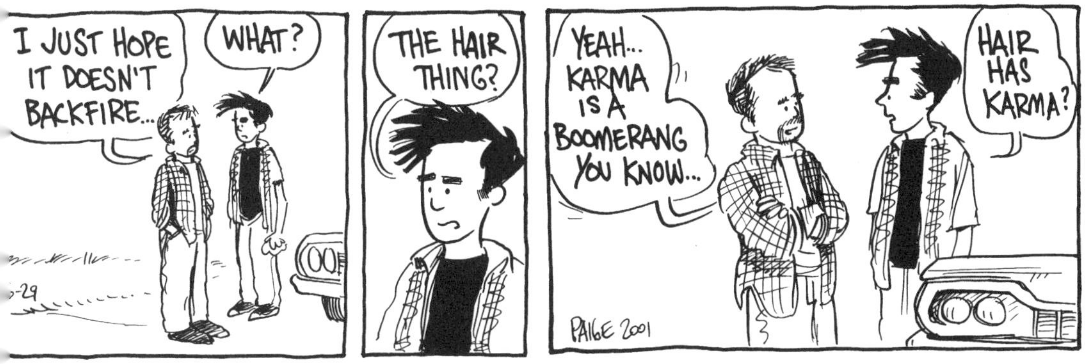
I JUST HOPE IT DOESN'T BACKFIRE...
WHAT?
THE HAIR THING?
YEAH... KARMA IS A BOOMERANG YOU KNOW...
HAIR HAS KARMA?
PAIGE 2001

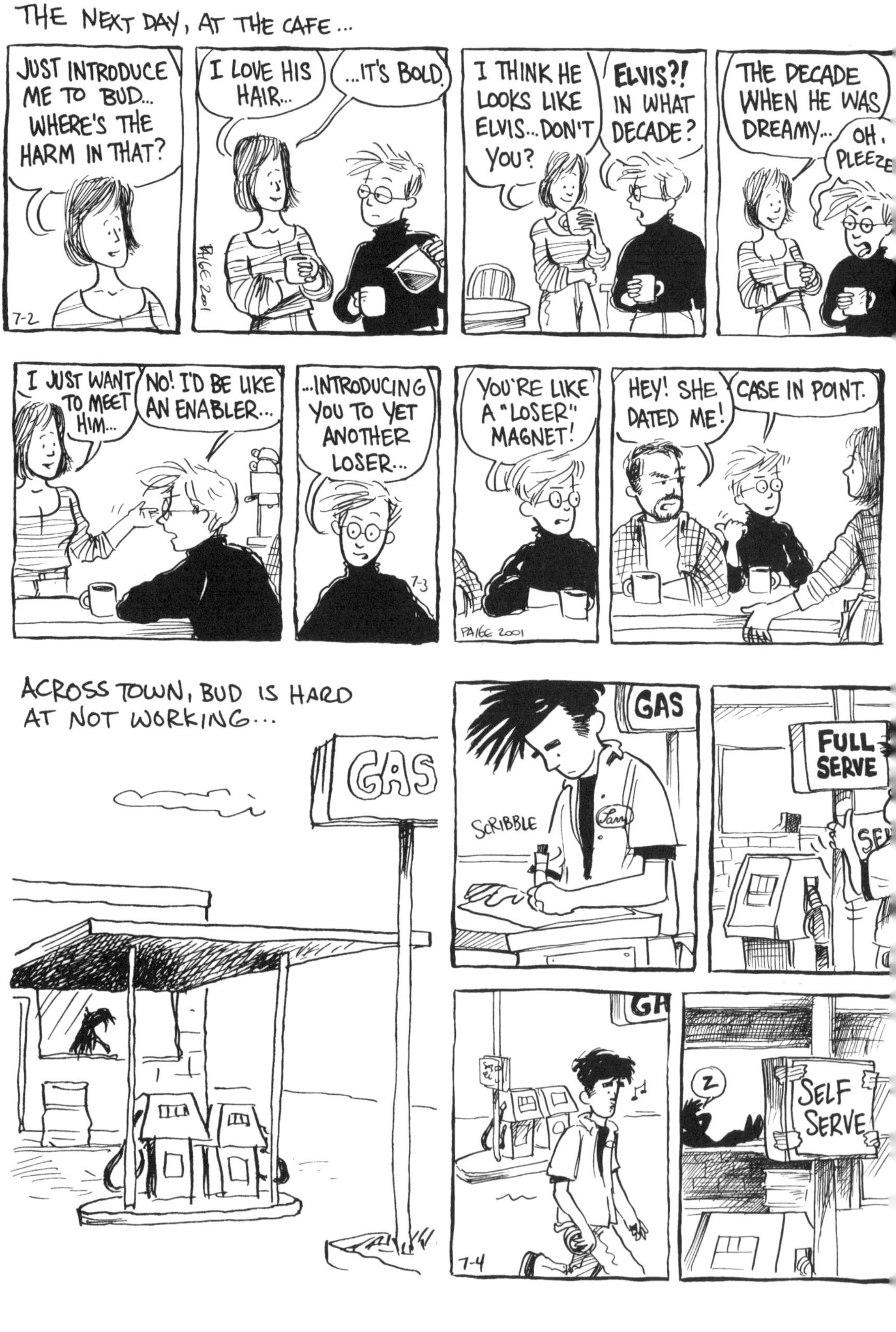
THE NEXT DAY, AT THE CAFE...
JUST INTRODUCE ME TO BUD... WHERE'S THE HARM IN THAT?
7-2
I LOVE HIS HAIR...
...IT'S BOLD.
PAIGE 2001
I THINK HE LOOKS LIKE ELVIS... DON'T YOU?
ELVIS?! IN WHAT DECADE?
THE DECADE WHEN HE WAS DREAMY...
OH, PLEEZE
I JUST WANT TO MEET HIM...
NO! I'D BE LIKE AN ENABLER...
...INTRODUCING YOU TO YET ANOTHER LOSER...
7-3
YOU'RE LIKE A "LOSER" MAGNET!
PAIGE 2001
HEY! SHE DATED ME!
CASE IN POINT.
ACROSS TOWN, BUD IS HARD AT NOT WORKING...
GAS
GAS
SCRIBBLE
FULL SERVE
GA
7-4
Z
SELF SERVE

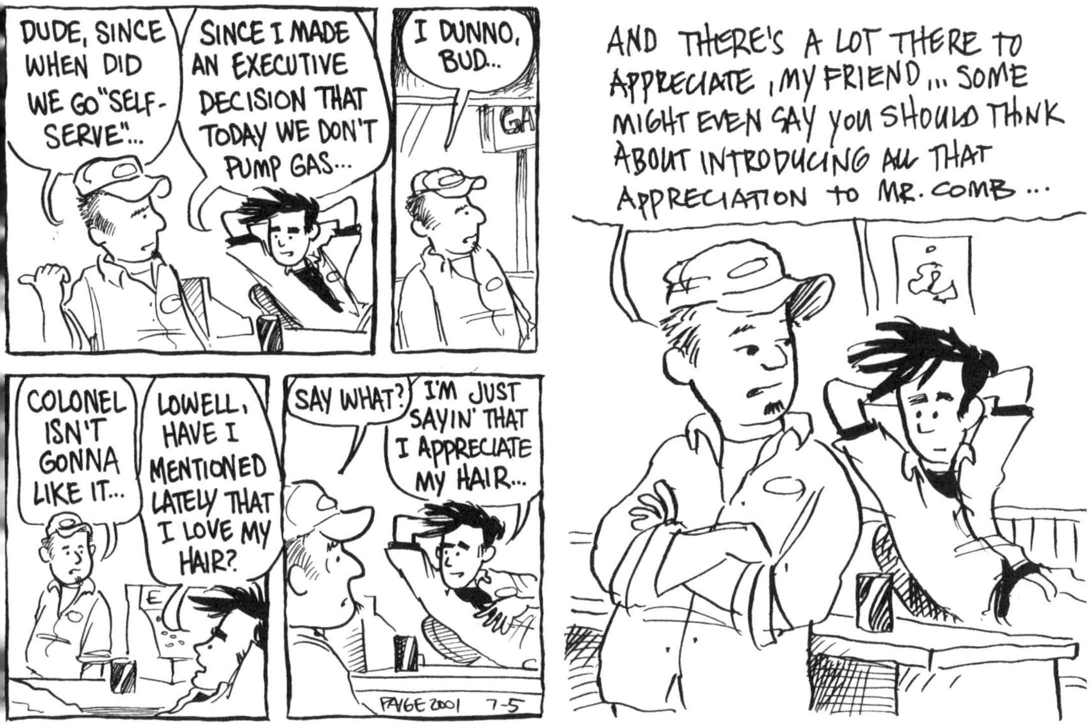
DUDE, SINCE WHEN DID WE GO "SELF-SERVE"...
SINCE I MADE AN EXECUTIVE DECISION THAT TODAY WE DON'T PUMP GAS...
I DUNNO, BUD...
COLONEL ISN'T GONNA LIKE IT...
LOWELL, HAVE I MENTIONED LATELY THAT I LOVE MY HAIR?
SAY WHAT?
I'M JUST SAYIN' THAT I APPRECIATE MY HAIR...
PAIGE 2001 7-5
AND THERE'S A LOT THERE TO APPRECIATE, MY FRIEND... SOME MIGHT EVEN SAY YOU SHOULD THINK ABOUT INTRODUCING ALL THAT APPRECIATION TO MR. COMB...

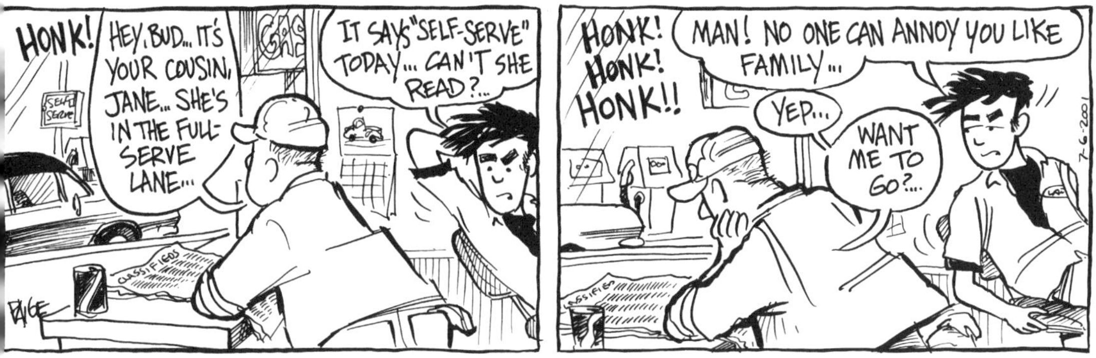
HONK!
HEY, BUD... IT'S YOUR COUSIN, JANE... SHE'S IN THE FULL-SERVE LANE...
IT SAYS "SELF-SERVE" TODAY... CAN'T SHE READ?...
SELF SERVE
CLASSIFIEDS
PAIGE
HONK! HONK! HONK!!
MAN! NO ONE CAN ANNOY YOU LIKE FAMILY...
YEP...
WANT ME TO GO?...
7-6-2001

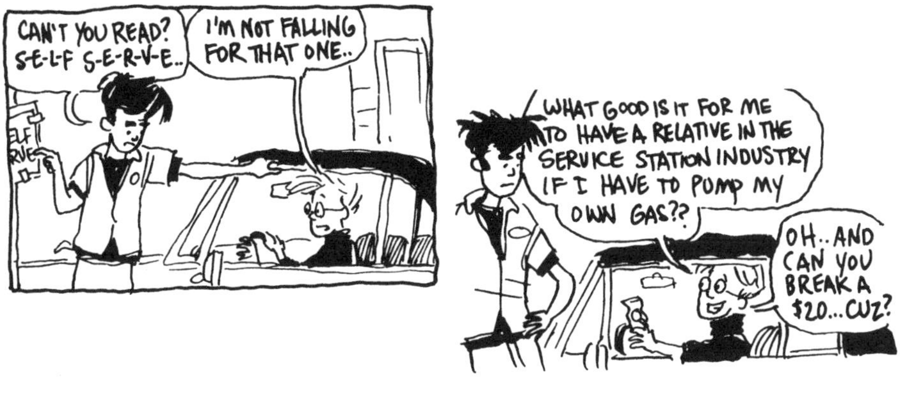
CAN'T YOU READ? S-E-L-F S-E-R-V-E...
I'M NOT FALLING FOR THAT ONE..
WHAT GOOD IS IT FOR ME TO HAVE A RELATIVE IN THE SERVICE STATION INDUSTRY IF I HAVE TO PUMP MY OWN GAS??
OH.. AND CAN YOU BREAK A $20... CUZ?

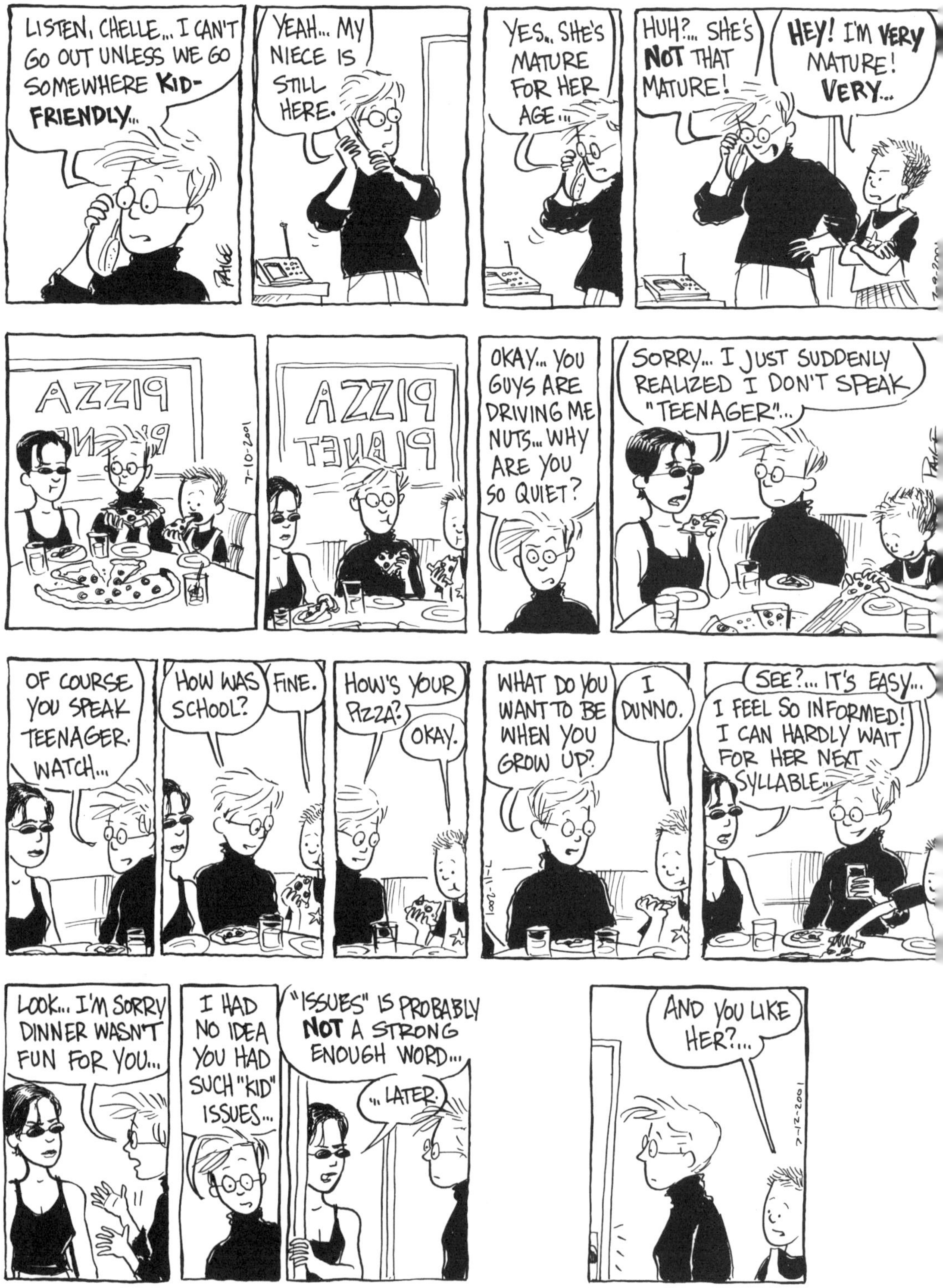
LISTEN, CHELLE... I CAN'T GO OUT UNLESS WE GO SOMEWHERE **KID-FRIENDLY**...
PAIGE
YEAH... MY NIECE IS STILL HERE.
YES... SHE'S MATURE FOR HER AGE...
HUH?... SHE'S **NOT** THAT MATURE!
HEY! I'M **VERY** MATURE! **VERY**...
7-10-2001
OKAY... YOU GUYS ARE DRIVING ME NUTS... WHY ARE YOU SO QUIET?
SORRY... I JUST SUDDENLY REALIZED I DON'T SPEAK "TEENAGER"...
PAIGE
OF COURSE YOU SPEAK TEENAGER. WATCH...
HOW WAS SCHOOL?
FINE.
HOW'S YOUR PIZZA?
OKAY.
7-11-2001
WHAT DO YOU WANT TO BE WHEN YOU GROW UP?
I DUNNO.
SEE?... IT'S EASY...
I FEEL SO INFORMED! I CAN HARDLY WAIT FOR HER NEXT SYLLABLE...
LOOK... I'M SORRY DINNER WASN'T FUN FOR YOU...
I HAD NO IDEA YOU HAD SUCH "KID" ISSUES...
"ISSUES" IS PROBABLY **NOT** A STRONG ENOUGH WORD...
... LATER.
7-12-2001
AND YOU LIKE HER?...

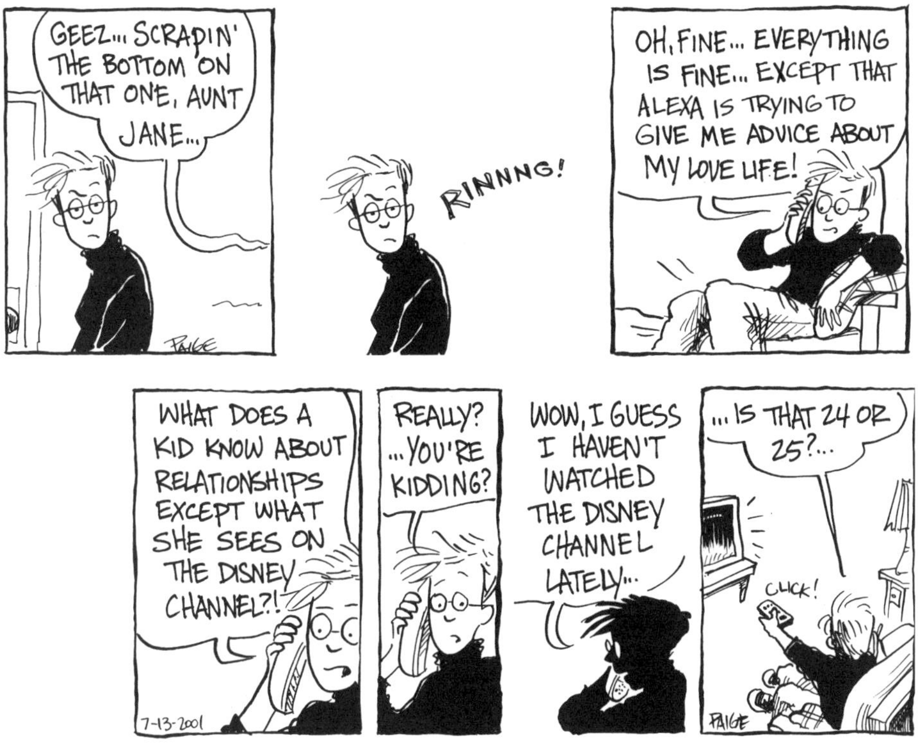
GEEZ... SCRAPIN' THE BOTTOM ON THAT ONE, AUNT JANE...
RINNNG!
OH, FINE... EVERYTHING IS FINE... EXCEPT THAT ALEXA IS TRYING TO GIVE ME ADVICE ABOUT MY LOVE LIFE!
WHAT DOES A KID KNOW ABOUT RELATIONSHIPS EXCEPT WHAT SHE SEES ON THE DISNEY CHANNEL?!
REALLY? ...YOU'RE KIDDING?
WOW, I GUESS I HAVEN'T WATCHED THE DISNEY CHANNEL LATELY...
...IS THAT 24 OR 25?...
CLICK!
7-13-2001
PAIGE

THE NEXT DAY..

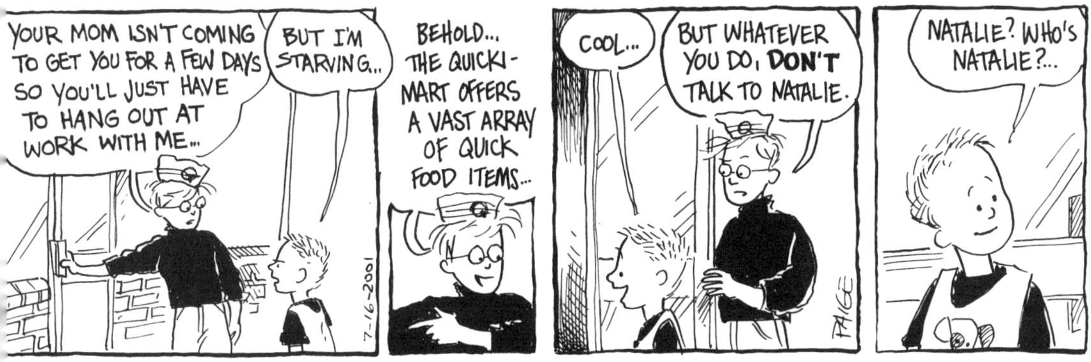
YOUR MOM ISN'T COMING TO GET YOU FOR A FEW DAYS SO YOU'LL JUST HAVE TO HANG OUT AT WORK WITH ME...
BUT I'M STARVING...
BEHOLD... THE QUICKI-MART OFFERS A VAST ARRAY OF QUICK FOOD ITEMS...
COOL...
BUT WHATEVER YOU DO, **DON'T** TALK TO NATALIE.
NATALIE? WHO'S NATALIE?...
7-16-2001
PAIGE

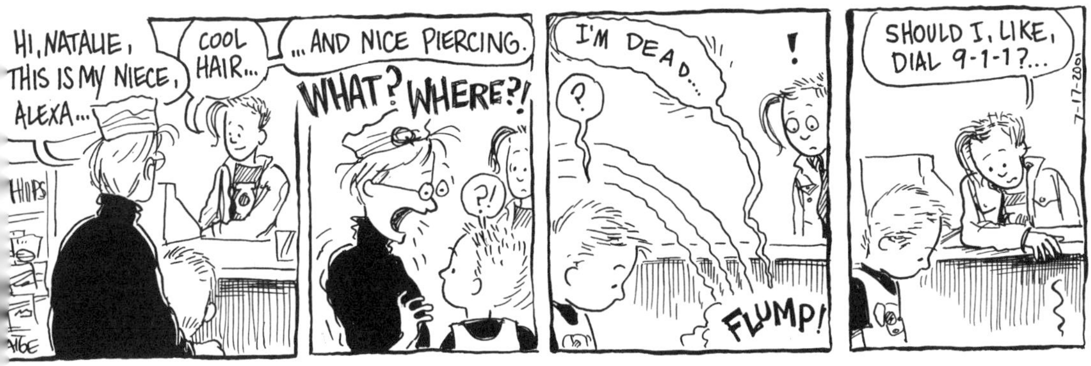
HI, NATALIE, THIS IS MY NIECE, ALEXA...
COOL HAIR...
...AND NICE PIERCING.
WHAT? WHERE?!
?!
I'M DEAD....
?
!
FLUMP!
SHOULD I, LIKE, DIAL 9-1-1?...
7-17-2001

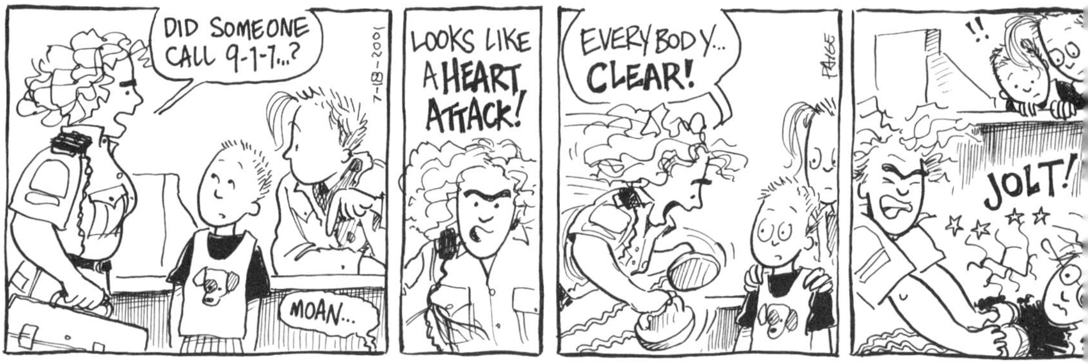
DID SOMEONE CALL 9-1-1...?
7-18-2001
MOAN...
LOOKS LIKE A HEART ATTACK!
EVERYBODY... CLEAR!
PAIGE
!!
JOLT!

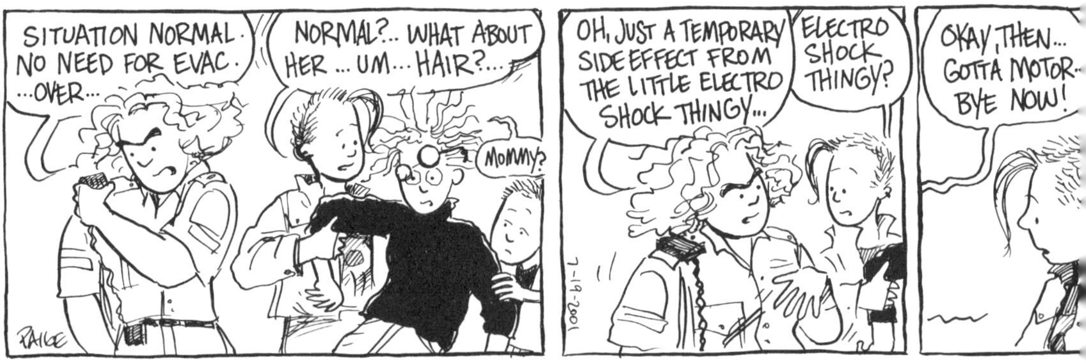
SITUATION NORMAL. NO NEED FOR EVAC. ...OVER...
NORMAL?... WHAT ABOUT HER ... UM... HAIR?...
MOMMY?
PAIGE
OH, JUST A TEMPORARY SIDE EFFECT FROM THE LITTLE ELECTRO SHOCK THINGY...
ELECTRO SHOCK THINGY?
7-19-2001
OKAY, THEN... GOTTA MOTOR-BYE NOW!

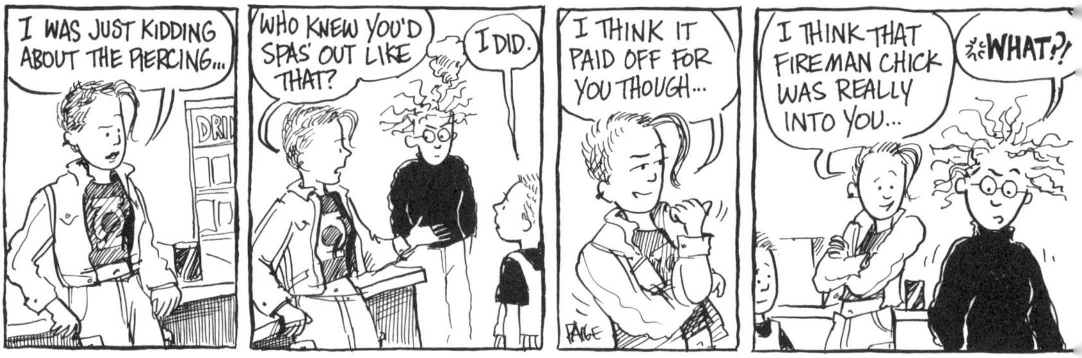
I WAS JUST KIDDING ABOUT THE PIERCING...
DRI
WHO KNEW YOU'D SPAS' OUT LIKE THAT?
I DID.
I THINK IT PAID OFF FOR YOU THOUGH...
PAIGE
I THINK THAT FIREMAN CHICK WAS REALLY INTO YOU...
WHAT?!

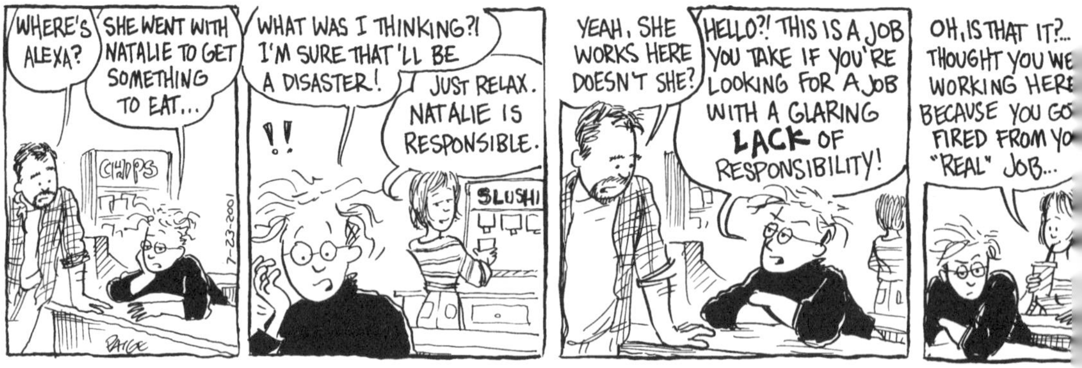
WHERE'S ALEXA?
SHE WENT WITH NATALIE TO GET SOMETHING TO EAT...
CHIPS
7-23-2001
PAIGE
WHAT WAS I THINKING?! I'M SURE THAT'LL BE A DISASTER!
!!
JUST RELAX. NATALIE IS RESPONSIBLE.
SLUSHI
YEAH, SHE WORKS HERE DOESN'T SHE?
HELLO?! THIS IS A JOB YOU TAKE IF YOU'RE LOOKING FOR A JOB WITH A GLARING LACK OF RESPONSIBILITY!
OH, IS THAT IT?... THOUGHT YOU WE WORKING HERE BECAUSE YOU GO FIRED FROM YO "REAL" JOB...

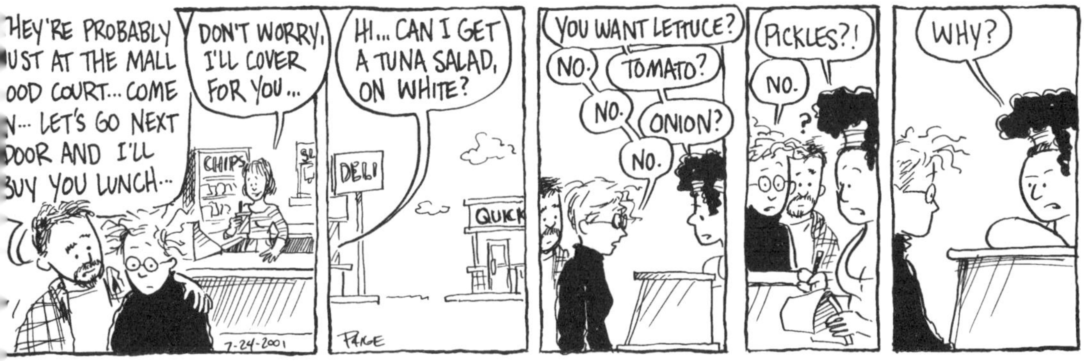
HEY'RE PROBABLY UST AT THE MALL OOD COURT... COME N... LET'S GO NEXT DOOR AND I'LL BUY YOU LUNCH...
DON'T WORRY, I'LL COVER FOR YOU...
CHIPS
7-24-2001
HI... CAN I GET A TUNA SALAD, ON WHITE?
DELI
QUICK
PAIGE
YOU WANT LETTUCE?
NO.
TOMATO?
NO.
ONION?
NO.
PICKLES?!
NO.
?
WHY?

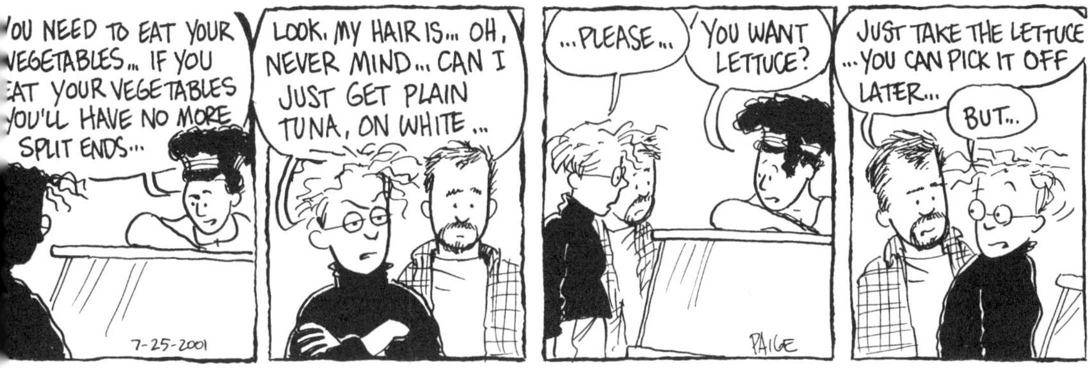
OU NEED TO EAT YOUR VEGETABLES... IF YOU EAT YOUR VEGETABLES YOU'LL HAVE NO MORE SPLIT ENDS...
7-25-2001
LOOK, MY HAIR IS... OH, NEVER MIND... CAN I JUST GET PLAIN TUNA, ON WHITE...
...PLEASE...
YOU WANT LETTUCE?
PAIGE
JUST TAKE THE LETTUCE ...YOU CAN PICK IT OFF LATER...
BUT...

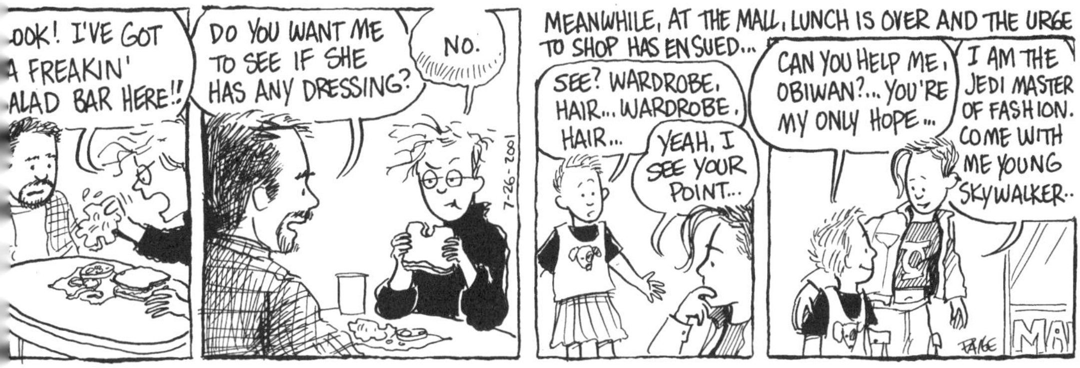
OOK! I'VE GOT A FREAKIN' ALAD BAR HERE!!
DO YOU WANT ME TO SEE IF SHE HAS ANY DRESSING?
NO.
7-26-2001
MEANWHILE, AT THE MALL, LUNCH IS OVER AND THE URGE TO SHOP HAS ENSUED...
SEE? WARDROBE, HAIR... WARDROBE, HAIR...
YEAH, I SEE YOUR POINT...
CAN YOU HELP ME, OBIWAN?... YOU'RE MY ONLY HOPE...
I AM THE JEDI MASTER OF FASHION. COME WITH ME YOUNG SKYWALKER...
PAIGE
MA

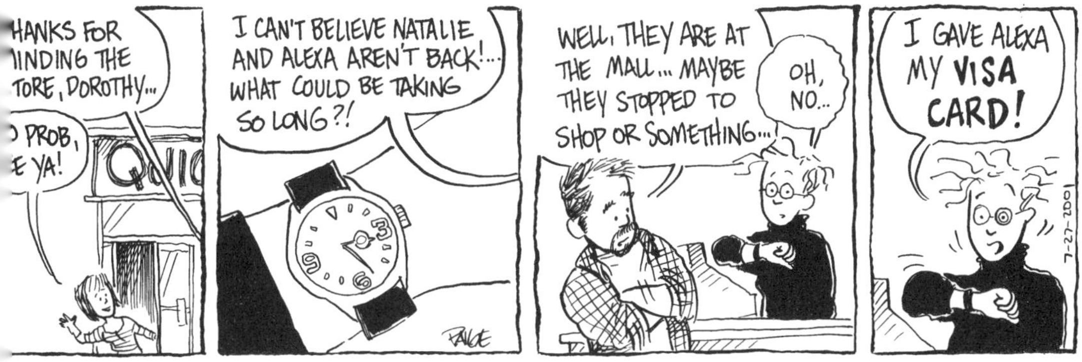
HANKS FOR MINDING THE TORE, DOROTHY...
PROB, E YA!
QUIC
I CAN'T BELIEVE NATALIE AND ALEXA AREN'T BACK!... WHAT COULD BE TAKING SO LONG?!
PAIGE
WELL, THEY ARE AT THE MALL... MAYBE THEY STOPPED TO SHOP OR SOMETHING...
OH, NO...
I GAVE ALEXA MY VISA CARD!
7-27-2001

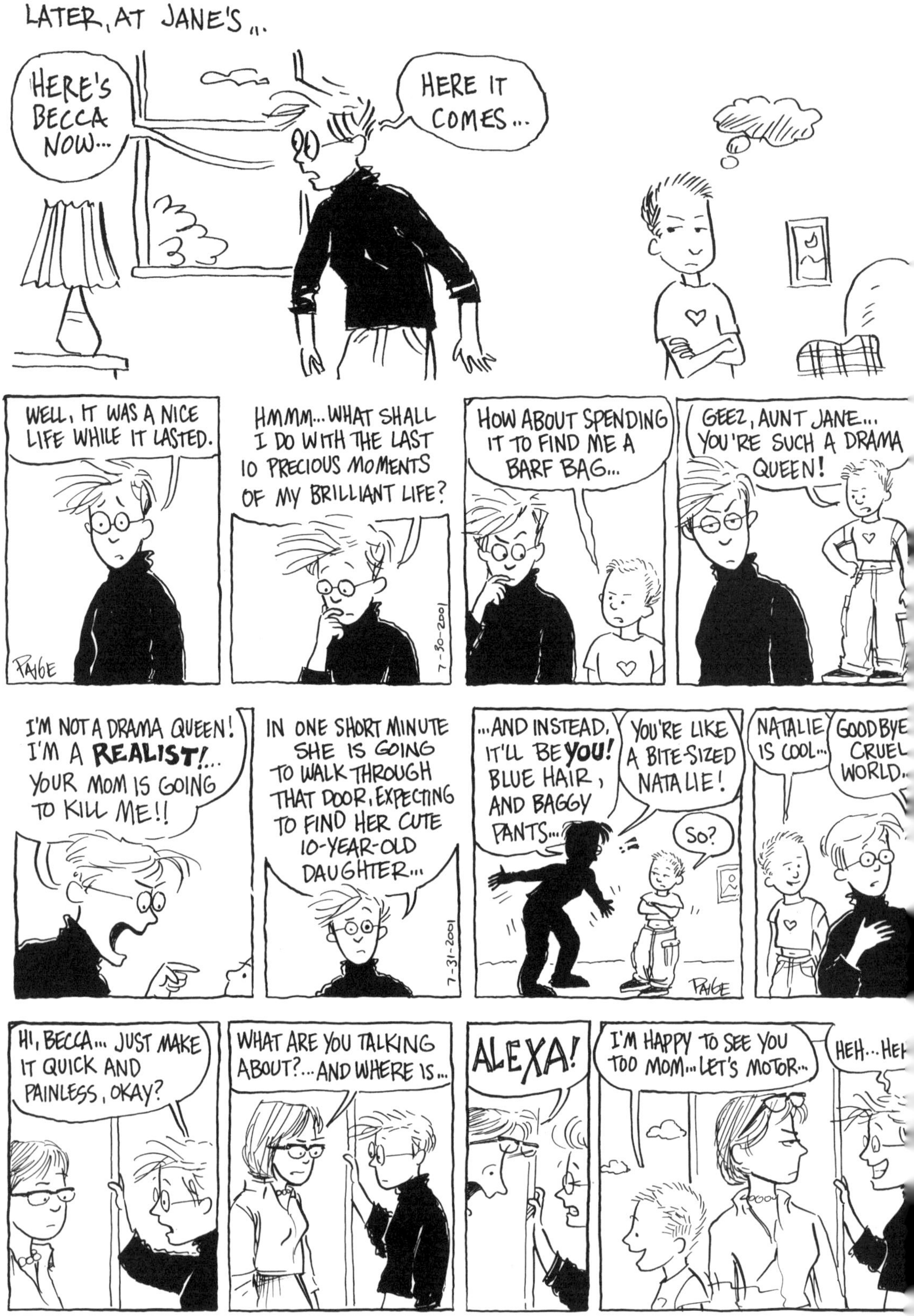
LATER, AT JANE'S...
HERE'S BECCA NOW...
HERE IT COMES...
WELL, IT WAS A NICE LIFE WHILE IT LASTED.
PAIGE
HMMM... WHAT SHALL I DO WITH THE LAST 10 PRECIOUS MOMENTS OF MY BRILLIANT LIFE?
7-30-2001
HOW ABOUT SPENDING IT TO FIND ME A BARF BAG...
GEEZ, AUNT JANE... YOU'RE SUCH A DRAMA QUEEN!
I'M NOT A DRAMA QUEEN! I'M A **REALIST!**... YOUR MOM IS GOING TO KILL ME!!
IN ONE SHORT MINUTE SHE IS GOING TO WALK THROUGH THAT DOOR, EXPECTING TO FIND HER CUTE 10-YEAR-OLD DAUGHTER...
7-31-2001
...AND INSTEAD, IT'LL BE **YOU!** BLUE HAIR, AND BAGGY PANTS...
YOU'RE LIKE A BITE-SIZED NATALIE!
SO?
PAIGE
NATALIE IS COOL...
GOODBYE CRUEL WORLD..
HI, BECCA... JUST MAKE IT QUICK AND PAINLESS, OKAY?
WHAT ARE YOU TALKING ABOUT?... AND WHERE IS...
ALEXA!
I'M HAPPY TO SEE YOU TOO MOM... LET'S MOTOR...
HEH...

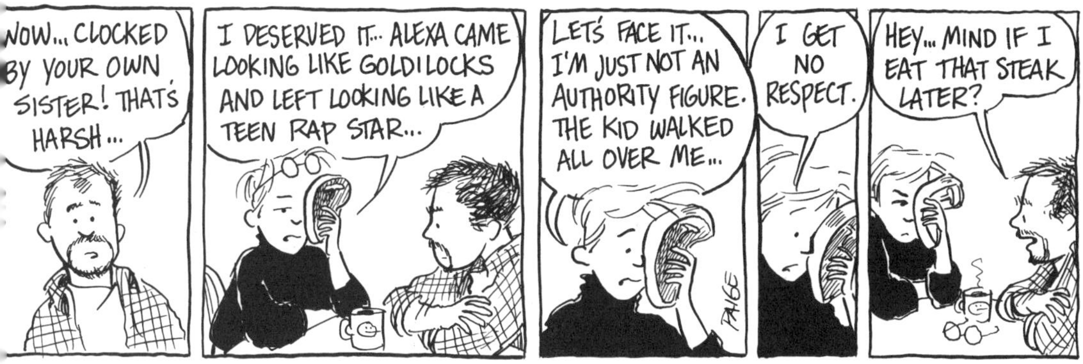
NOW... CLOCKED BY YOUR OWN SISTER! THAT'S HARSH...
I DESERVED IT... ALEXA CAME LOOKING LIKE GOLDILOCKS AND LEFT LOOKING LIKE A TEEN RAP STAR...
LET'S FACE IT... I'M JUST NOT AN AUTHORITY FIGURE. THE KID WALKED ALL OVER ME...
PAIGE
I GET NO RESPECT.
HEY... MIND IF I EAT THAT STEAK LATER?

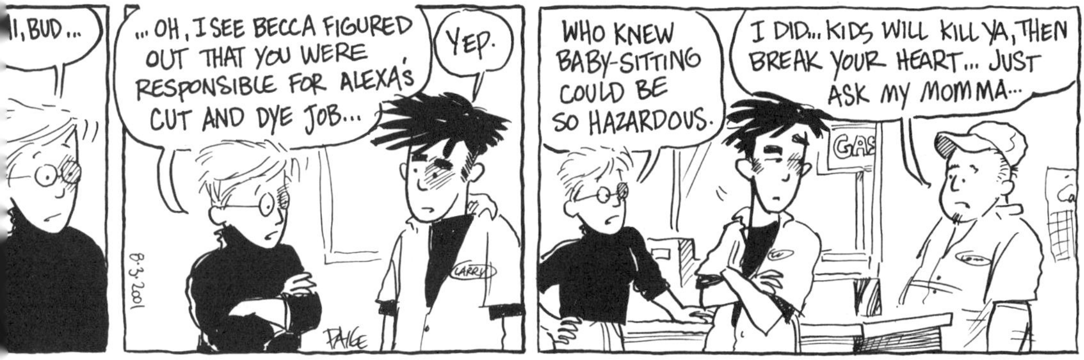
I, BUD...
...OH, I SEE BECCA FIGURED OUT THAT YOU WERE RESPONSIBLE FOR ALEXA'S CUT AND DYE JOB...
YEP.
8-3-2001
LARRY
PAIGE
WHO KNEW BABY-SITTING COULD BE SO HAZARDOUS.
I DID... KIDS WILL KILL YA, THEN BREAK YOUR HEART... JUST ASK MY MOMMA...
GAS

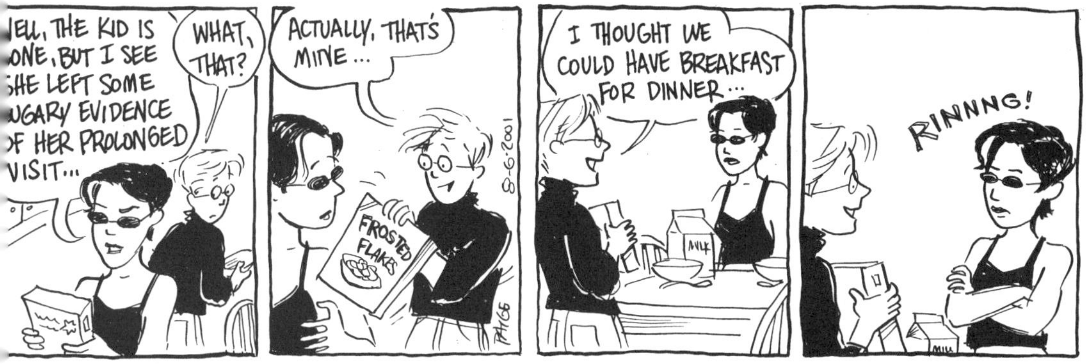
ELL, THE KID IS ONE, BUT I SEE HE LEFT SOME UGARY EVIDENCE F HER PROLONGED VISIT...
WHAT, THAT?
ACTUALLY, THAT'S MINE...
FROSTED FLAKES
8-6-2001
PAIGE
I THOUGHT WE COULD HAVE BREAKFAST FOR DINNER...
MILK
RINNNG!

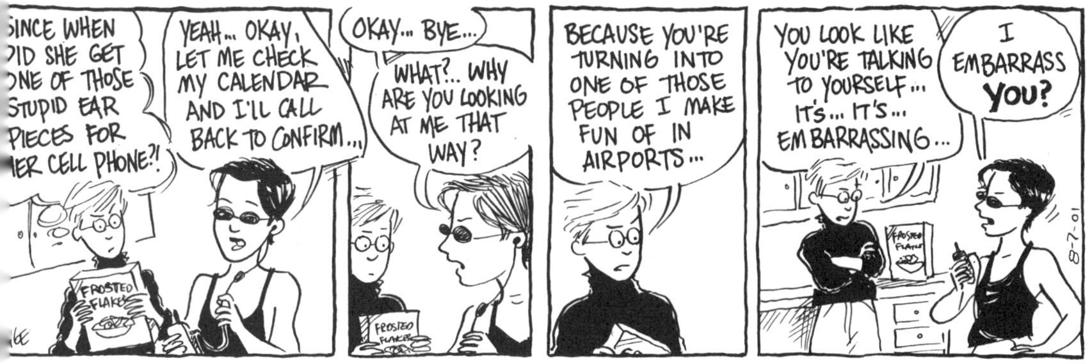
INCE WHEN ID SHE GET NE OF THOSE STUPID EAR PIECES FOR ER CELL PHONE?!
YEAH... OKAY, LET ME CHECK MY CALENDAR AND I'LL CALL BACK TO CONFIRM...
FROSTED FLAKES
OKAY... BYE...
WHAT?.. WHY ARE YOU LOOKING AT ME THAT WAY?
FROSTED FLAKES
BECAUSE YOU'RE TURNING INTO ONE OF THOSE PEOPLE I MAKE FUN OF IN AIRPORTS...
YOU LOOK LIKE YOU'RE TALKING TO YOURSELF... IT'S... IT'S... EMBARRASSING...
I EMBARRASS **YOU?**
FROSTED FLAKES
8-7-01

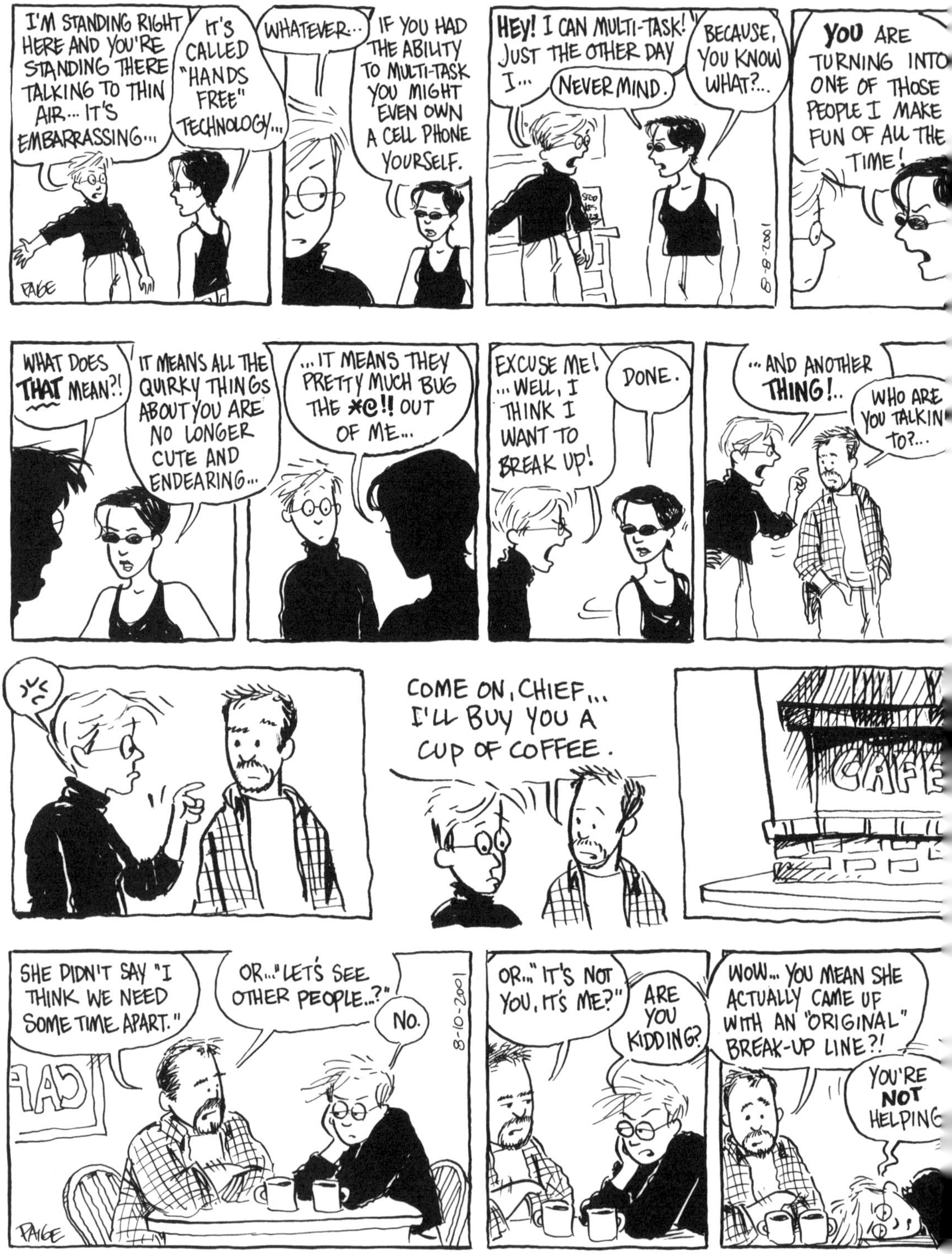
I'M STANDING RIGHT HERE AND YOU'RE STANDING THERE TALKING TO THIN AIR... IT'S EMBARRASSING...
IT'S CALLED "HANDS FREE" TECHNOLOGY...
PAIGE
WHATEVER...
IF YOU HAD THE ABILITY TO MULTI-TASK YOU MIGHT EVEN OWN A CELL PHONE YOURSELF.
HEY! I CAN MULTI-TASK! JUST THE OTHER DAY I...
NEVER MIND.
BECAUSE, YOU KNOW WHAT?...
8-8-2001
YOU ARE TURNING INTO ONE OF THOSE PEOPLE I MAKE FUN OF ALL THE TIME!
WHAT DOES THAT MEAN?!
IT MEANS ALL THE QUIRKY THINGS ABOUT YOU ARE NO LONGER CUTE AND ENDEARING...
...IT MEANS THEY PRETTY MUCH BUG THE *@!! OUT OF ME...
EXCUSE ME! ...WELL, I THINK I WANT TO BREAK UP!
DONE.
...AND ANOTHER THING!...
WHO ARE YOU TALKIN TO?...
COME ON, CHIEF... I'LL BUY YOU A CUP OF COFFEE.
CAFE
SHE DIDN'T SAY "I THINK WE NEED SOME TIME APART."
OR..."LET'S SEE OTHER PEOPLE..?"
NO.
8-10-2001
PAIGE
OR..."IT'S NOT YOU, IT'S ME?"
ARE YOU KIDDING?
WOW... YOU MEAN SHE ACTUALLY CAME UP WITH AN "ORIGINAL" BREAK-UP LINE?!
YOU'RE NOT HELPING

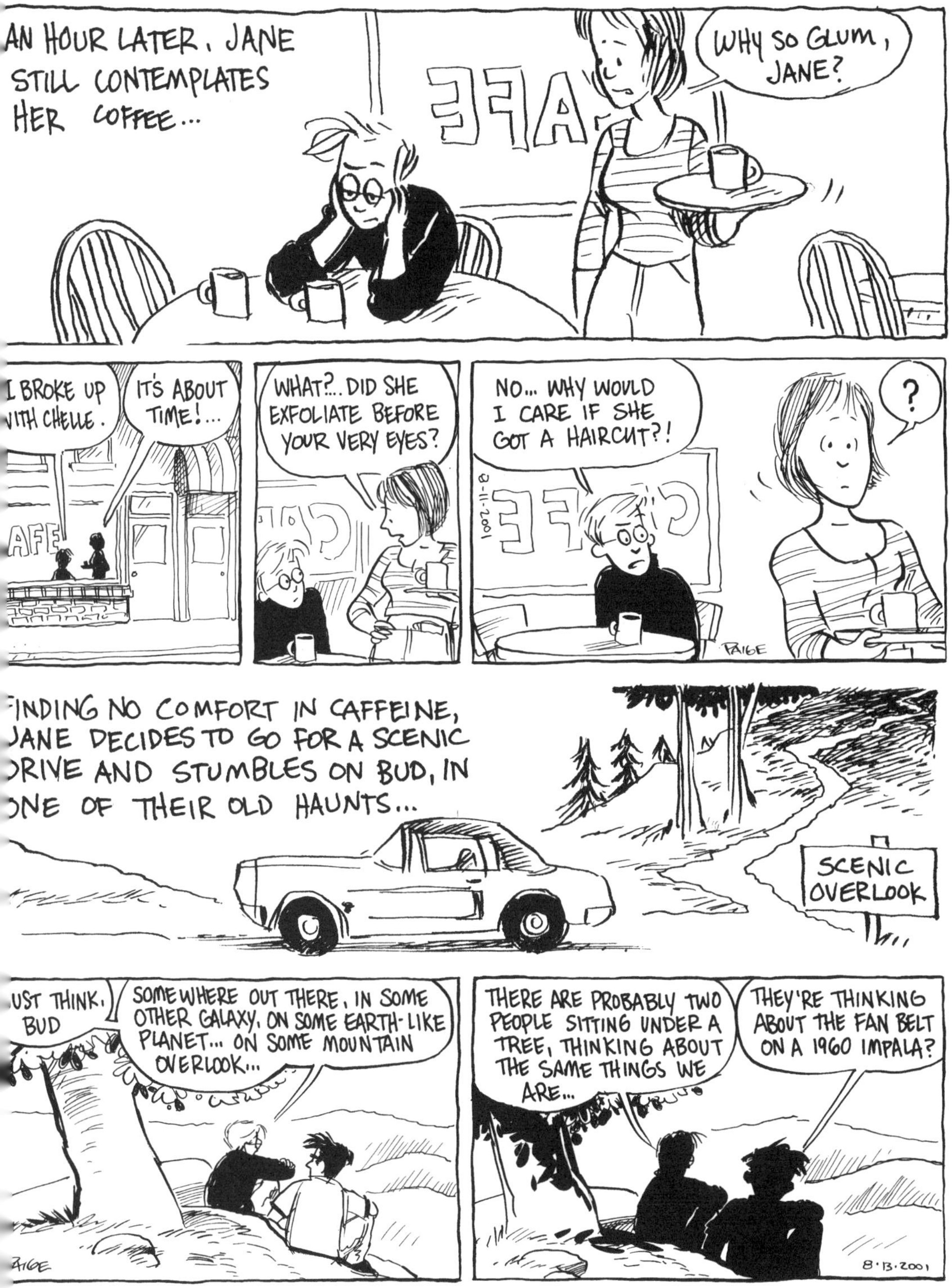
AN HOUR LATER, JANE STILL CONTEMPLATES HER COFFEE...
WHY SO GLUM, JANE?
I BROKE UP WITH CHELLE.
IT'S ABOUT TIME!...
WHAT?... DID SHE EXFOLIATE BEFORE YOUR VERY EYES?
NO... WHY WOULD I CARE IF SHE GOT A HAIRCUT?!
?
8-11-2001
PAIGE
FINDING NO COMFORT IN CAFFEINE, JANE DECIDES TO GO FOR A SCENIC DRIVE AND STUMBLES ON BUD, IN ONE OF THEIR OLD HAUNTS...
SCENIC OVERLOOK
JUST THINK, BUD
SOMEWHERE OUT THERE, IN SOME OTHER GALAXY, ON SOME EARTH-LIKE PLANET... ON SOME MOUNTAIN OVERLOOK...
THERE ARE PROBABLY TWO PEOPLE SITTING UNDER A TREE, THINKING ABOUT THE SAME THINGS WE ARE...
THEY'RE THINKING ABOUT THE FAN BELT ON A 1960 IMPALA?
PAIGE
8·13·2001

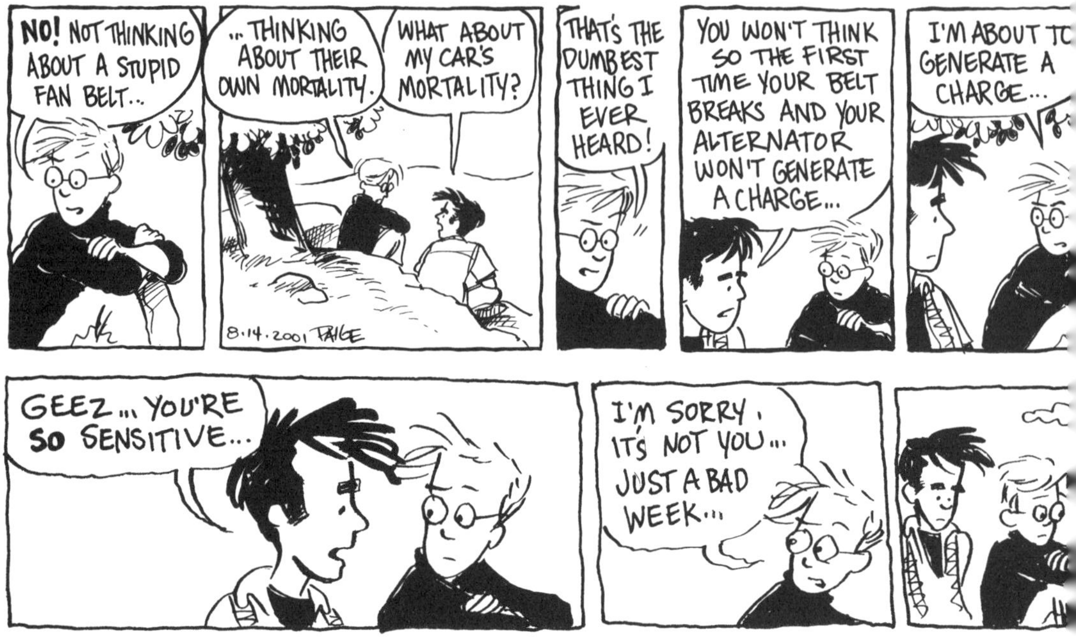
NO! NOT THINKING ABOUT A STUPID FAN BELT...
...THINKING ABOUT THEIR OWN MORTALITY.
WHAT ABOUT MY CAR'S MORTALITY?
8·14·2001 PAIGE
THAT'S THE DUMBEST THING I EVER HEARD!
YOU WON'T THINK SO THE FIRST TIME YOUR BELT BREAKS AND YOUR ALTERNATOR WON'T GENERATE A CHARGE...
I'M ABOUT TO GENERATE A CHARGE...
GEEZ... YOU'RE SO SENSITIVE...
I'M SORRY. IT'S NOT YOU... JUST A BAD WEEK...

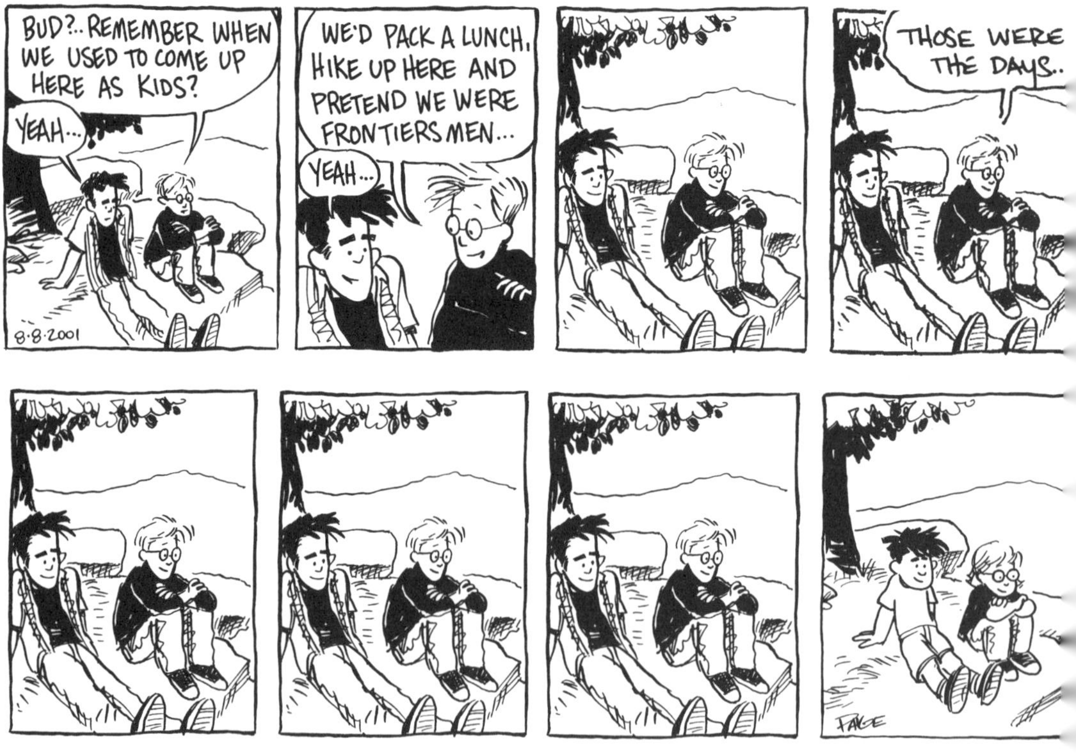
BUD?.. REMEMBER WHEN WE USED TO COME UP HERE AS KIDS?
YEAH...
8·8·2001
WE'D PACK A LUNCH, HIKE UP HERE AND PRETEND WE WERE FRONTIERSMEN...
YEAH...
THOSE WERE THE DAYS..
PAIGE

Chapter two

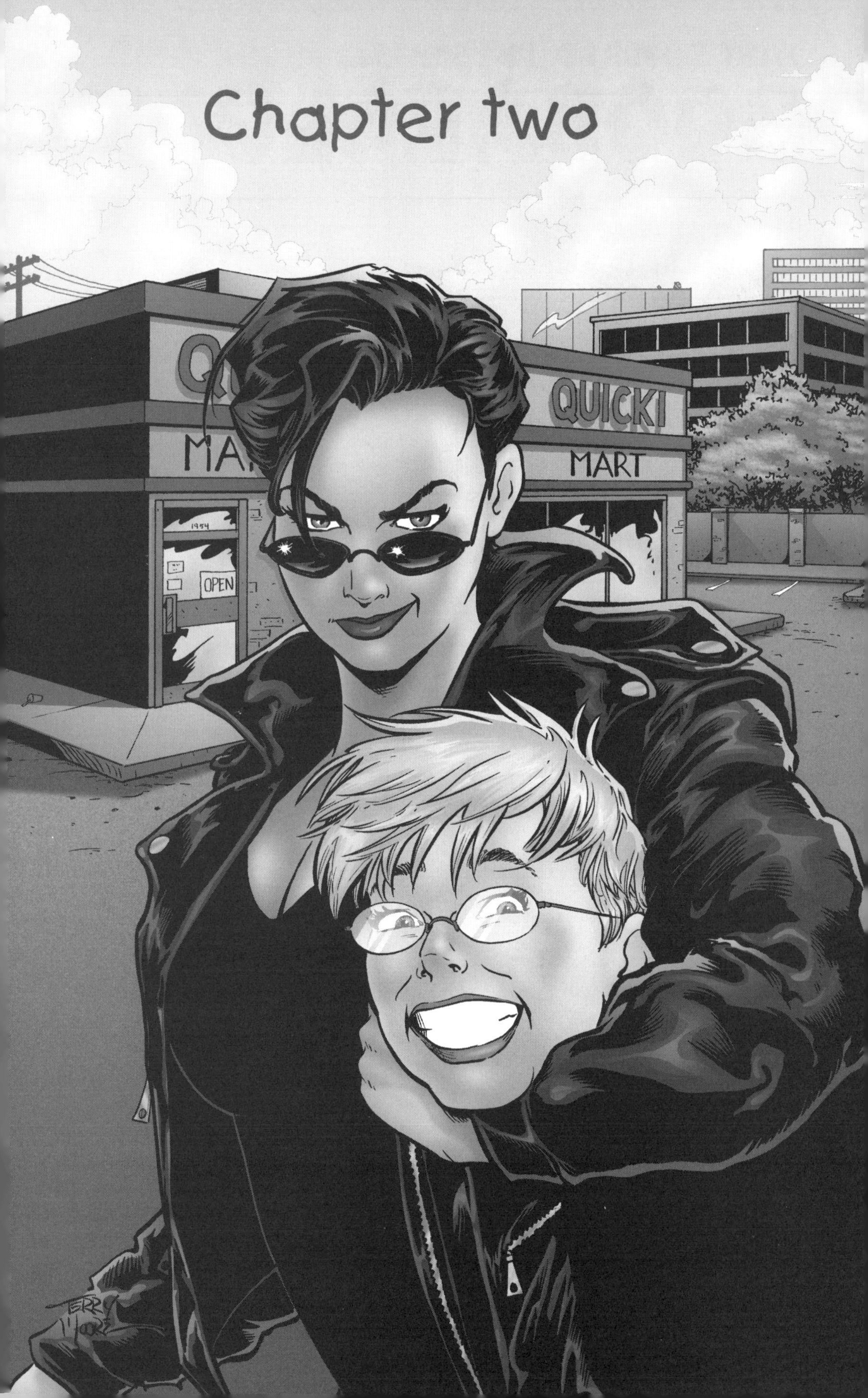
QUICKI
MART
1954
OPEN

JANE'S WORLD PRESENTS...

BOOBAPALOOZA

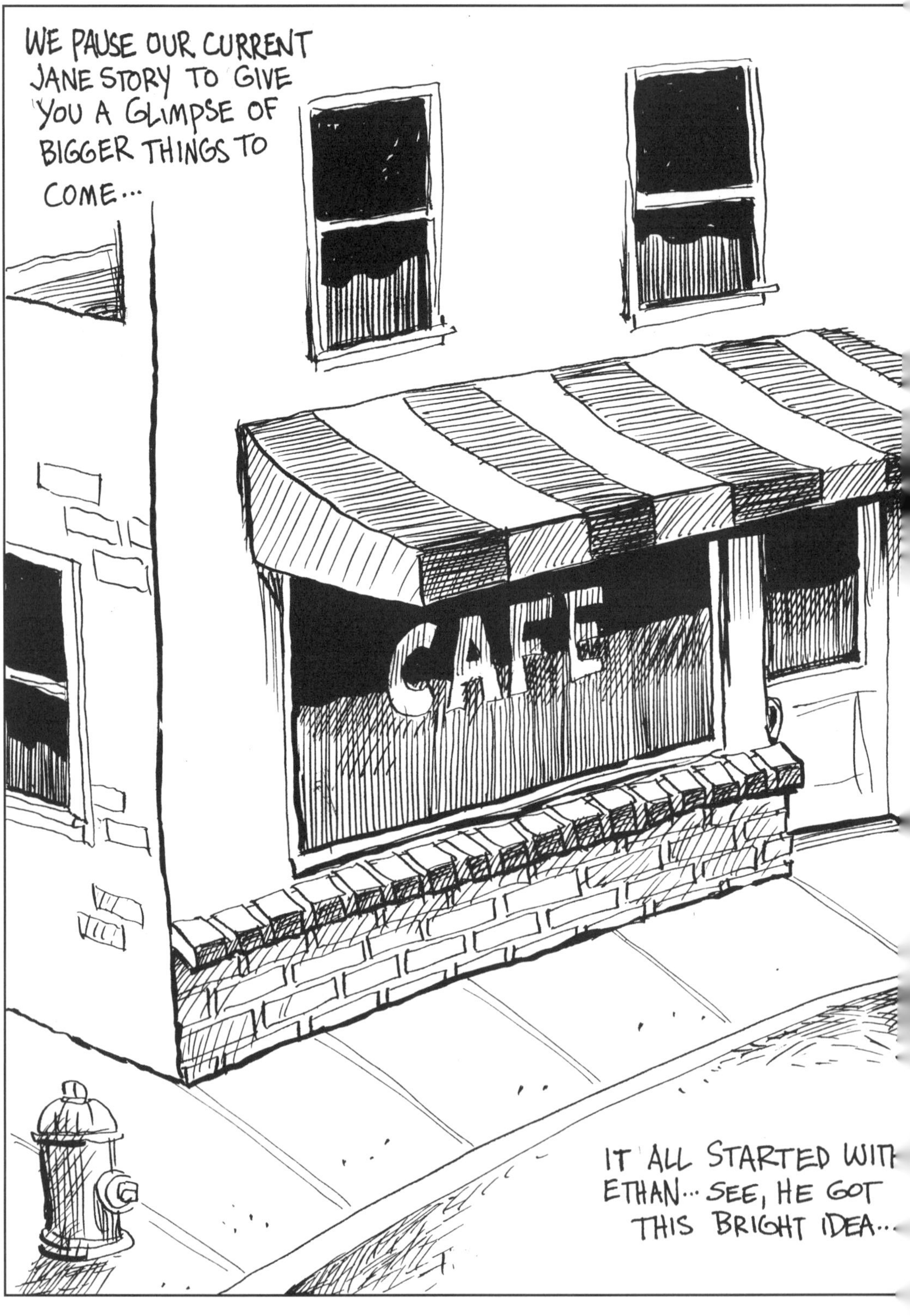
WE PAUSE OUR CURRENT JANE STORY TO GIVE YOU A GLIMPSE OF BIGGER THINGS TO COME...
CAFE
IT ALL STARTED WITH ETHAN... SEE, HE GOT THIS BRIGHT IDEA...

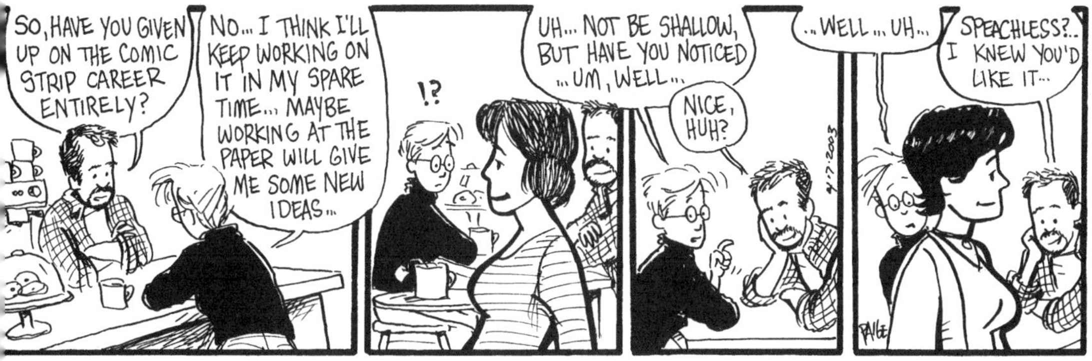
SO, HAVE YOU GIVEN UP ON THE COMIC STRIP CAREER ENTIRELY?
NO... I THINK I'LL KEEP WORKING ON IT IN MY SPARE TIME... MAYBE WORKING AT THE PAPER WILL GIVE ME SOME NEW IDEAS...
!?
UH... NOT BE SHALLOW, BUT HAVE YOU NOTICED ...UM, WELL...
NICE, HUH?
4.7.2003
...WELL... UH...
SPEACHLESS?.. I KNEW YOU'D LIKE IT...
PAIGE

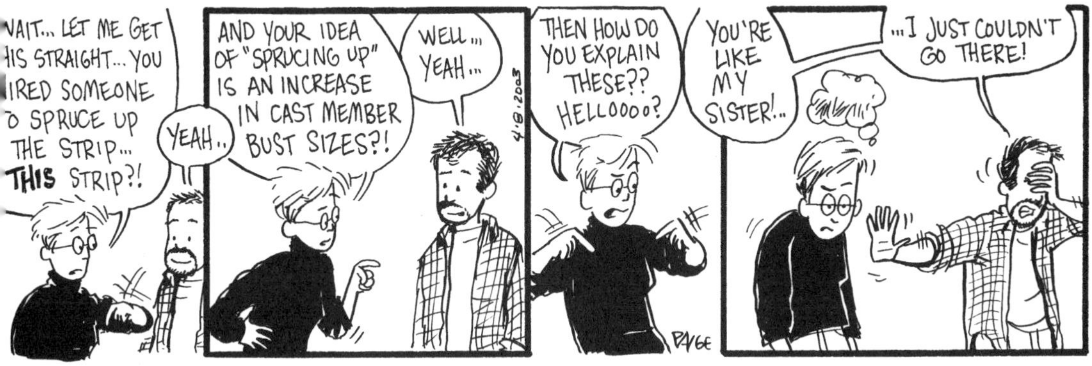
VAIT... LET ME GET HIS STRAIGHT... YOU IRED SOMEONE O SPRUCE UP THE STRIP... THIS STRIP?!
YEAH..
AND YOUR IDEA OF "SPRUCING UP" IS AN INCREASE IN CAST MEMBER BUST SIZES?!
WELL... YEAH...
4.8.2003
THEN HOW DO YOU EXPLAIN THESE?? HELLOOOO?
PAIGE
YOU'RE LIKE MY SISTER!..
...I JUST COULDN'T GO THERE!

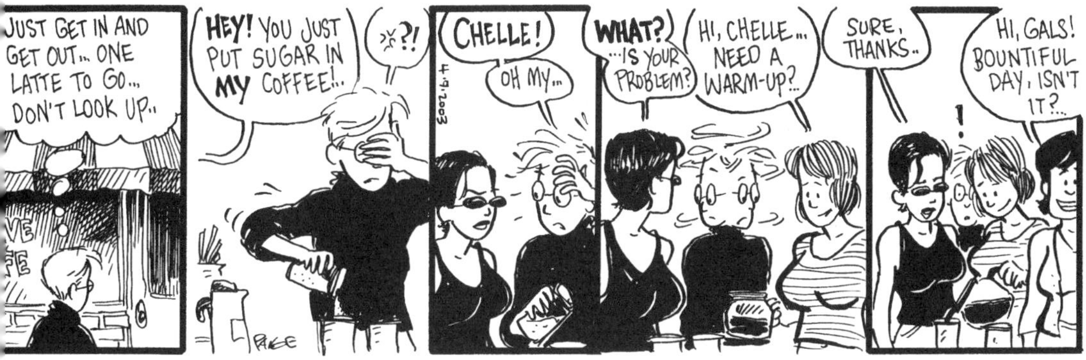
JUST GET IN AND GET OUT... ONE LATTE TO GO... DON'T LOOK UP..
HEY! YOU JUST PUT SUGAR IN MY COFFEE!..
?!
PAIGE
CHELLE!
OH MY...
4.9.2003
WHAT? ...IS YOUR PROBLEM?
HI, CHELLE... NEED A WARM-UP?..
SURE, THANKS..
!
HI, GALS! BOUNTIFUL DAY, ISN'T IT?...

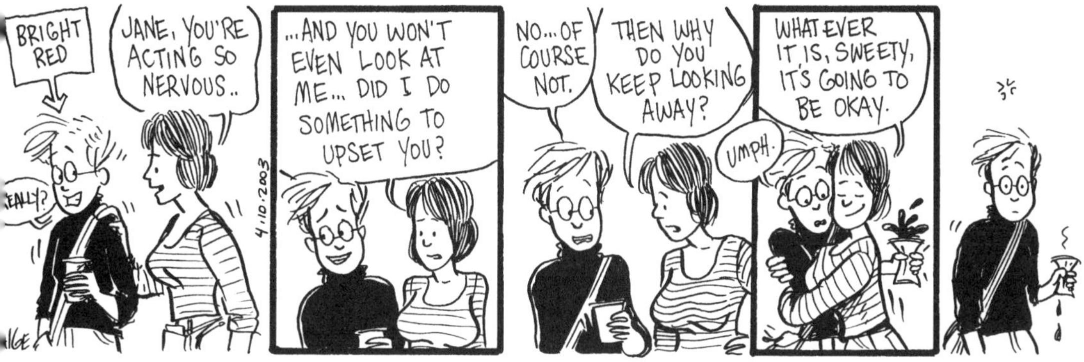
BRIGHT RED
JANE, YOU'RE ACTING SO NERVOUS..
4.10.2003
...AND YOU WON'T EVEN LOOK AT ME... DID I DO SOMETHING TO UPSET YOU?
NO... OF COURSE NOT.
THEN WHY DO YOU KEEP LOOKING AWAY?
WHATEVER IT IS, SWEETY, IT'S GOING TO BE OKAY.
UMPH.

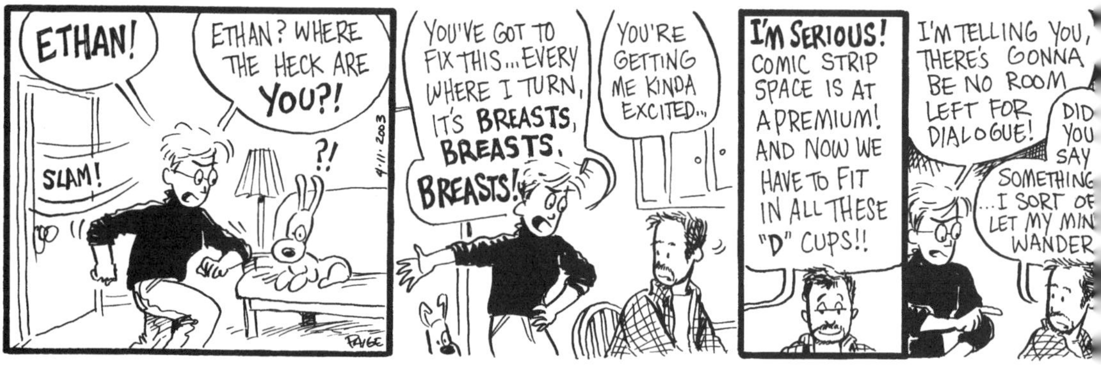
ETHAN!
ETHAN? WHERE THE HECK ARE YOU?!
SLAM!
?!
4·11·2003
PAIGE
YOU'VE GOT TO FIX THIS... EVERY WHERE I TURN, IT'S BREASTS, BREASTS, BREASTS!
YOU'RE GETTING ME KINDA EXCITED...
I'M SERIOUS! COMIC STRIP SPACE IS AT A PREMIUM! AND NOW WE HAVE TO FIT IN ALL THESE "D" CUPS!!
I'M TELLING YOU, THERE'S GONNA BE NO ROOM LEFT FOR DIALOGUE!
DID YOU SAY SOMETHING ...I SORT OF LET MY MIN WANDER

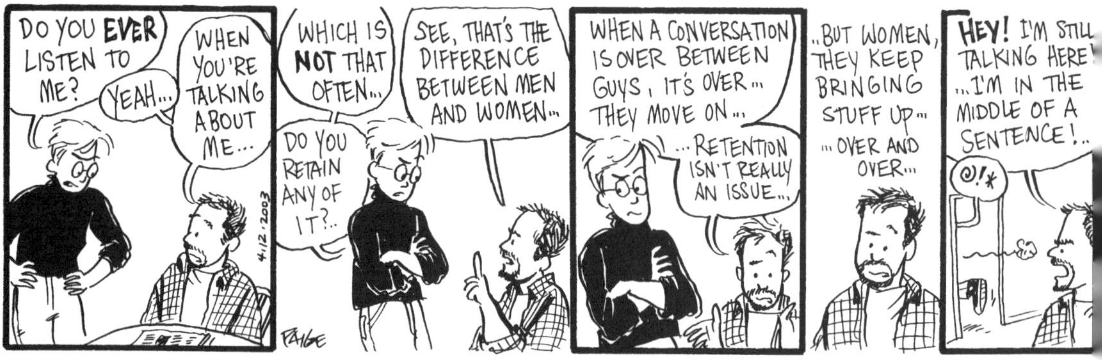
DO YOU EVER LISTEN TO ME?
YEAH...
WHEN YOU'RE TALKING ABOUT ME...
4·12·2003
PAIGE
WHICH IS NOT THAT OFTEN...
DO YOU RETAIN ANY OF IT?..
SEE, THAT'S THE DIFFERENCE BETWEEN MEN AND WOMEN...
WHEN A CONVERSATION IS OVER BETWEEN GUYS, IT'S OVER... THEY MOVE ON...
...RETENTION ISN'T REALLY AN ISSUE...
..BUT WOMEN, THEY KEEP BRINGING STUFF UP...
...OVER AND OVER...
HEY! I'M STILL TALKING HERE! ...I'M IN THE MIDDLE OF A SENTENCE!..
@!*

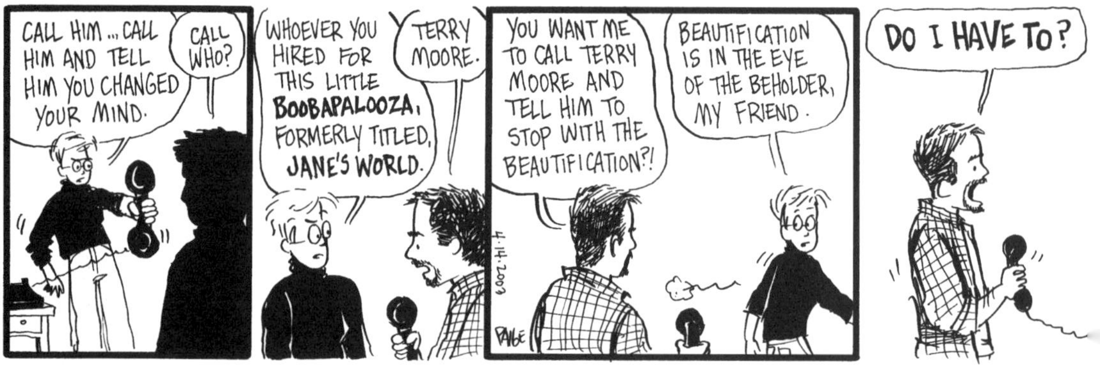
CALL HIM... CALL HIM AND TELL HIM YOU CHANGED YOUR MIND.
CALL WHO?
WHOEVER YOU HIRED FOR THIS LITTLE BOOBAPALOOZA, FORMERLY TITLED, JANE'S WORLD.
TERRY MOORE.
YOU WANT ME TO CALL TERRY MOORE AND TELL HIM TO STOP WITH THE BEAUTIFICATION?!
4·14·2003
PAIGE
BEAUTIFICATION IS IN THE EYE OF THE BEHOLDER, MY FRIEND.
DO I HAVE TO?

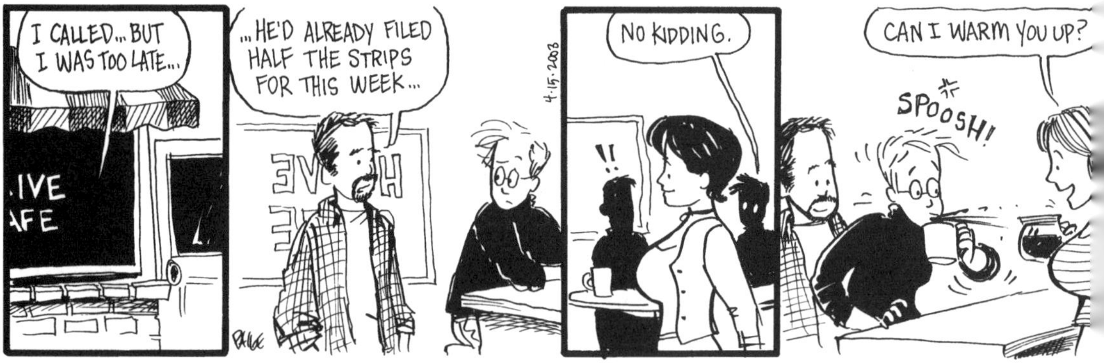
I CALLED... BUT I WAS TOO LATE...
PAIGE
...HE'D ALREADY FILED HALF THE STRIPS FOR THIS WEEK...
4·15·2003
NO KIDDING.
!!
SPOOSH!
CAN I WARM YOU UP?

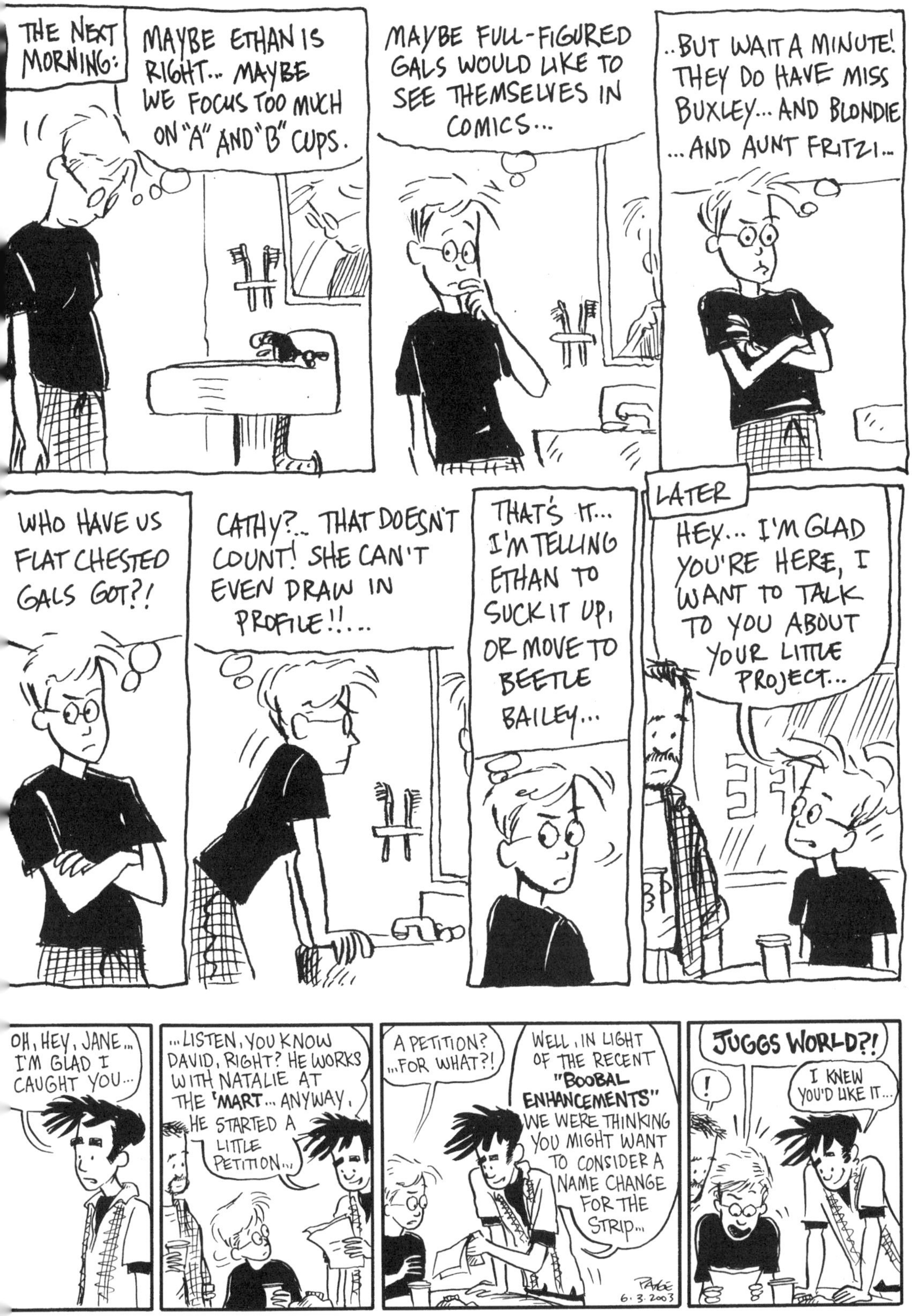
THE NEXT MORNING:
MAYBE ETHAN IS RIGHT... MAYBE WE FOCUS TOO MUCH ON "A" AND "B" CUPS.
MAYBE FULL-FIGURED GALS WOULD LIKE TO SEE THEMSELVES IN COMICS...
..BUT WAIT A MINUTE! THEY DO HAVE MISS BUXLEY... AND BLONDIE ...AND AUNT FRITZI...
WHO HAVE US FLAT CHESTED GALS GOT?!
CATHY?.. THAT DOESN'T COUNT! SHE CAN'T EVEN DRAW IN PROFILE!!...
THAT'S IT... I'M TELLING ETHAN TO SUCK IT UP, OR MOVE TO BEETLE BAILEY...
LATER
HEY... I'M GLAD YOU'RE HERE, I WANT TO TALK TO YOU ABOUT YOUR LITTLE PROJECT...
OH, HEY, JANE... I'M GLAD I CAUGHT YOU...
...LISTEN, YOU KNOW DAVID, RIGHT? HE WORKS WITH NATALIE AT THE 'MART... ANYWAY, HE STARTED A LITTLE PETITION...
A PETITION? ...FOR WHAT?!
WELL, IN LIGHT OF THE RECENT "BOOBAL ENHANCEMENTS" WE WERE THINKING YOU MIGHT WANT TO CONSIDER A NAME CHANGE FOR THE STRIP...
PAIGE 6.3.2003
JUGGS WORLD?!
!
I KNEW YOU'D LIKE IT...

THE END, FOR NOW

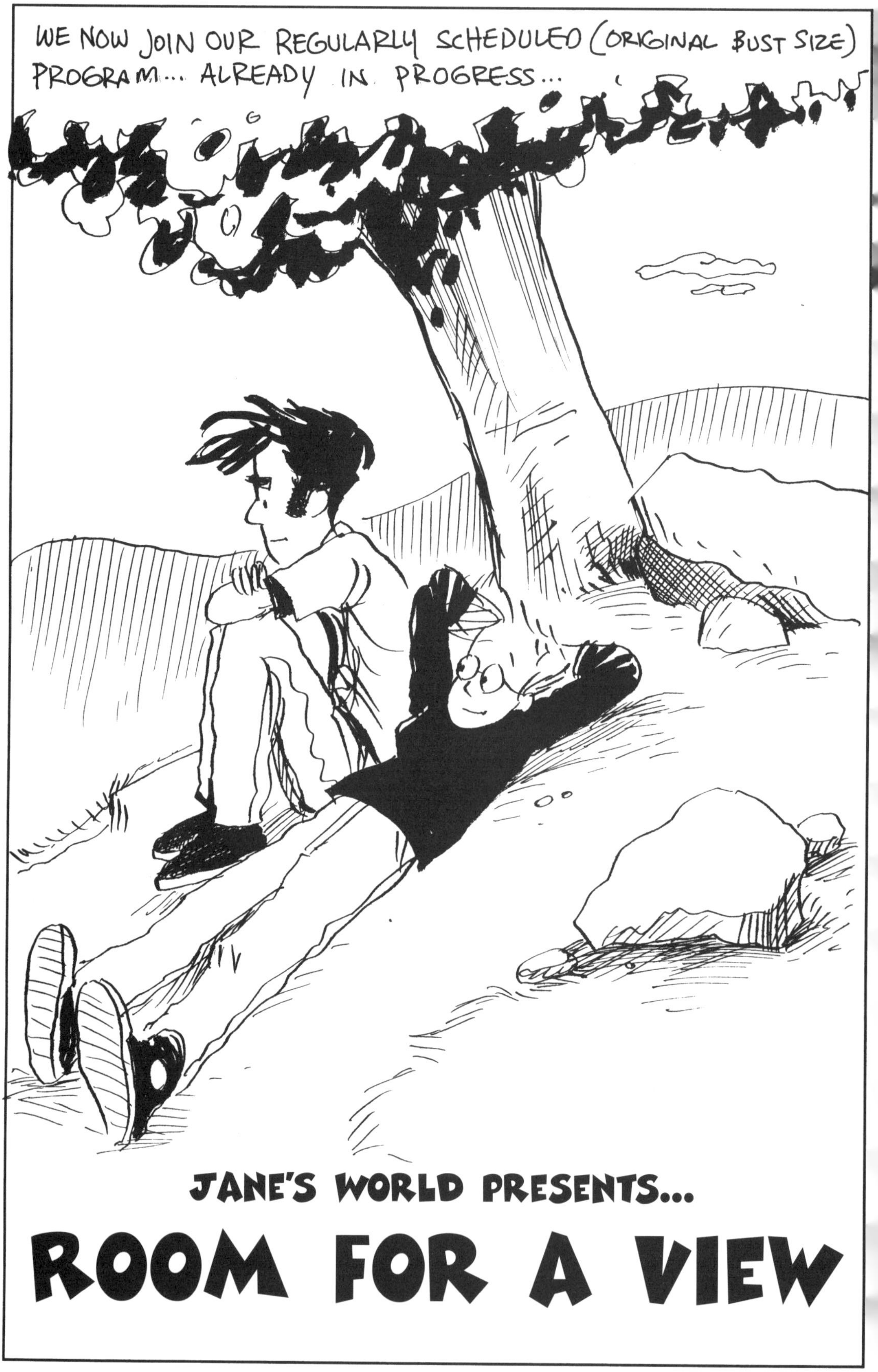
WE NOW JOIN OUR REGULARLY SCHEDULED (ORIGINAL BUST SIZE) PROGRAM... ALREADY IN PROGRESS...
JANE'S WORLD PRESENTS...
ROOM FOR A VIEW

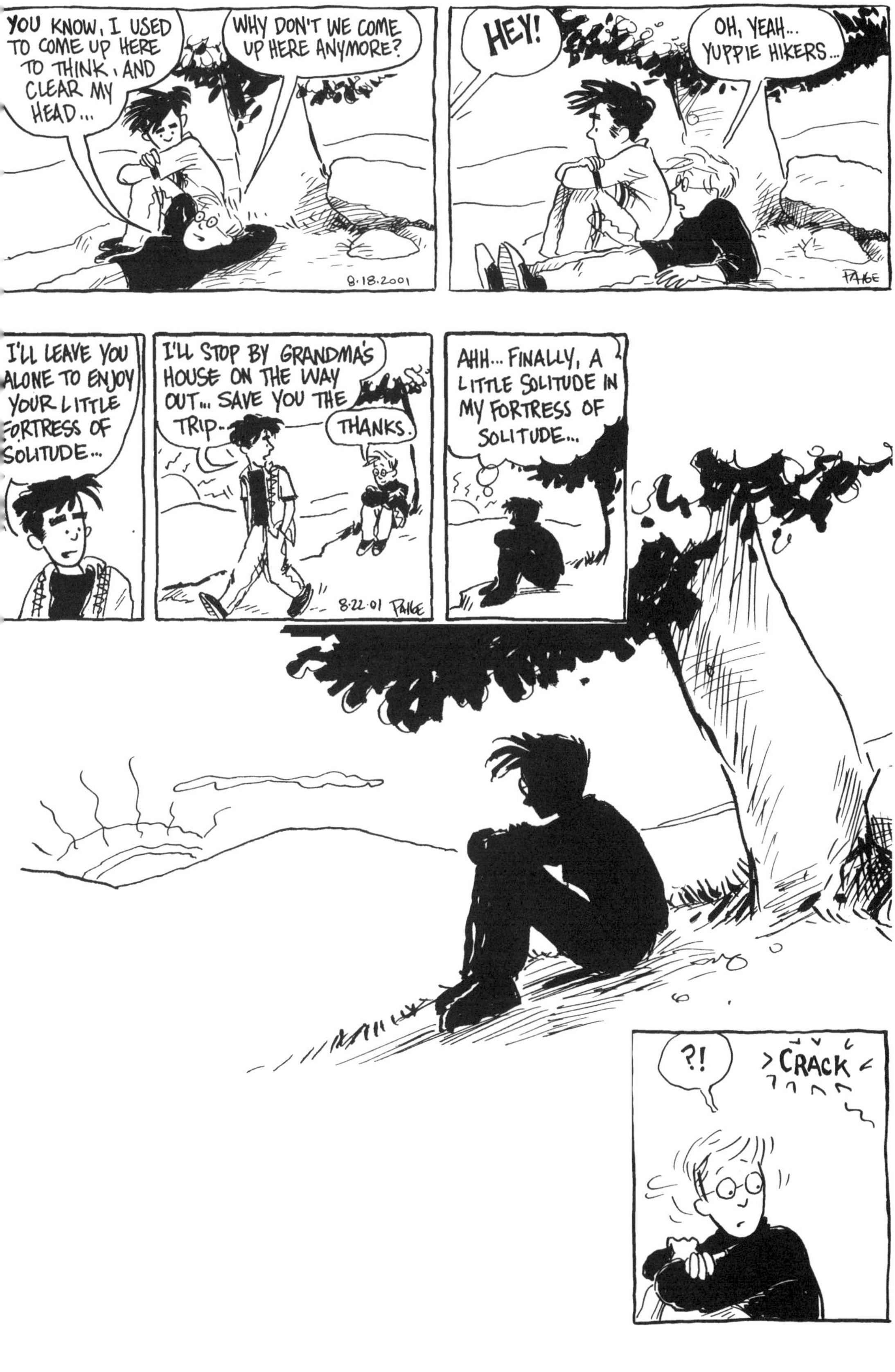
YOU KNOW, I USED TO COME UP HERE TO THINK, AND CLEAR MY HEAD...
WHY DON'T WE COME UP HERE ANYMORE?
8.18.2001
HEY!
OH, YEAH... YUPPIE HIKERS...
PAIGE
I'LL LEAVE YOU ALONE TO ENJOY YOUR LITTLE FORTRESS OF SOLITUDE...
I'LL STOP BY GRANDMA'S HOUSE ON THE WAY OUT... SAVE YOU THE TRIP...
THANKS.
8.22.01 PAIGE
AHH... FINALLY, A LITTLE SOLITUDE IN MY FORTRESS OF SOLITUDE...
?!
CRACK

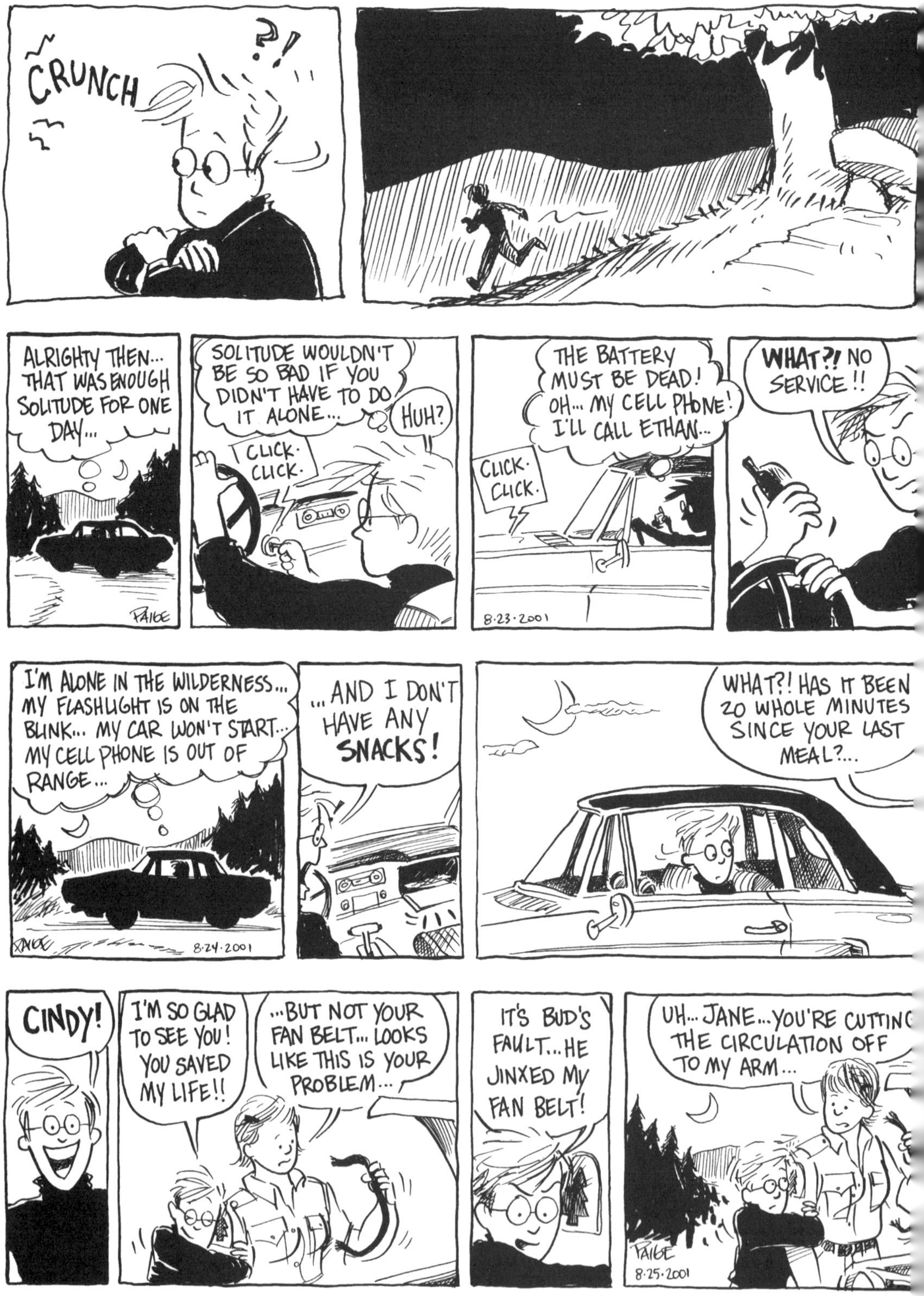
CRUNCH
?!
ALRIGHTY THEN... THAT WAS ENOUGH SOLITUDE FOR ONE DAY...
PAIGE
SOLITUDE WOULDN'T BE SO BAD IF YOU DIDN'T HAVE TO DO IT ALONE...
CLICK· CLICK·
HUH?
THE BATTERY MUST BE DEAD! OH... MY CELL PHONE! I'LL CALL ETHAN...
CLICK· CLICK.
8·23·2001
WHAT?! NO SERVICE!!
I'M ALONE IN THE WILDERNESS... MY FLASHLIGHT IS ON THE BLINK... MY CAR WON'T START... MY CELL PHONE IS OUT OF RANGE...
PAIGE
8·24·2001
...AND I DON'T HAVE ANY SNACKS!
WHAT?! HAS IT BEEN 20 WHOLE MINUTES SINCE YOUR LAST MEAL?...
CINDY!
I'M SO GLAD TO SEE YOU! YOU SAVED MY LIFE!!
...BUT NOT YOUR FAN BELT... LOOKS LIKE THIS IS YOUR PROBLEM...
IT'S BUD'S FAULT... HE JINXED MY FAN BELT!
UH... JANE... YOU'RE CUTTING THE CIRCULATION OFF TO MY ARM...
PAIGE
8·25·2001

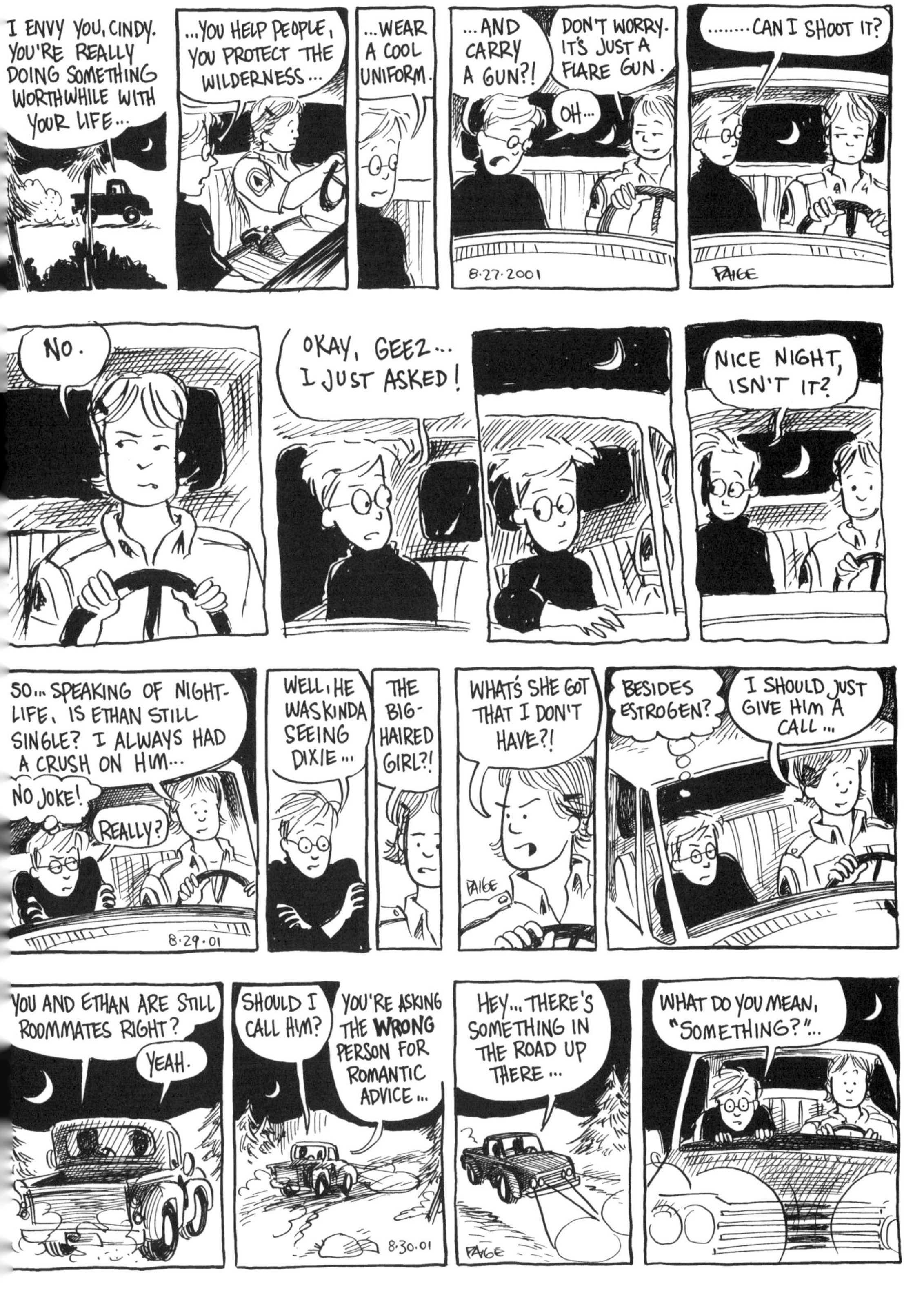
I ENVY YOU, CINDY. YOU'RE REALLY DOING SOMETHING WORTHWHILE WITH YOUR LIFE...
...YOU HELP PEOPLE, YOU PROTECT THE WILDERNESS...
...WEAR A COOL UNIFORM.
...AND CARRY A GUN?!
DON'T WORRY. IT'S JUST A FLARE GUN.
OH...
8·27·2001
........CAN I SHOOT IT?
PAIGE
NO.
OKAY, GEEZ... I JUST ASKED!
NICE NIGHT, ISN'T IT?
SO... SPEAKING OF NIGHT-LIFE, IS ETHAN STILL SINGLE? I ALWAYS HAD A CRUSH ON HIM...
NO JOKE!
REALLY?
8·29·01
WELL, HE WAS KINDA SEEING DIXIE...
THE BIG-HAIRED GIRL?!
WHAT'S SHE GOT THAT I DON'T HAVE?!
PAIGE
BESIDES ESTROGEN?
I SHOULD JUST GIVE HIM A CALL...
YOU AND ETHAN ARE STILL ROOMMATES RIGHT?
YEAH.
SHOULD I CALL HIM?
YOU'RE ASKING THE WRONG PERSON FOR ROMANTIC ADVICE...
8·30·01
HEY... THERE'S SOMETHING IN THE ROAD UP THERE...
PAIGE
WHAT DO YOU MEAN, "SOMETHING?"...

WHAT IS IT?! IS IT DEAD?! ...OR ALIVE??
WELL... IT'S STANDING, SO I ASSUME IT'S ALIVE...
8·31·2001

SEND UP A FLARE!
NO... DON'T PULL THE...
FFFZZZ
POP!
PAIGE

FFZZZ
9·3·2001
I CAN'T SEE!!

VARROOM!!
*@☆!!
?
PAIGE

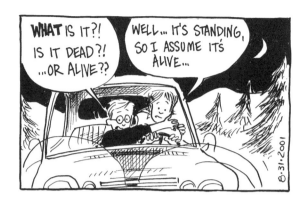

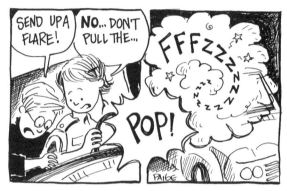

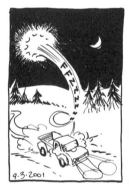

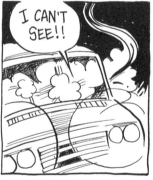

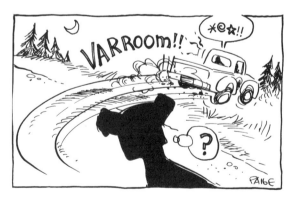

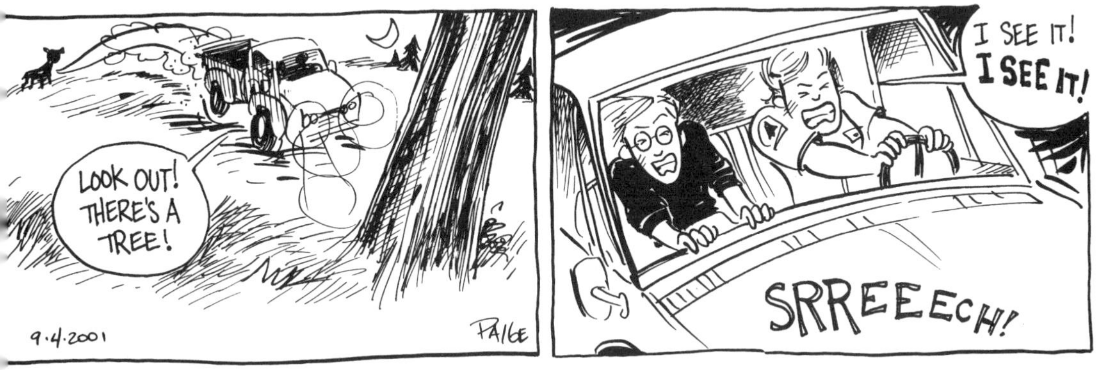
LOOK OUT! THERE'S A TREE!
9.4.2001
PAIGE
I SEE IT! I SEE IT!
SRREEECH!

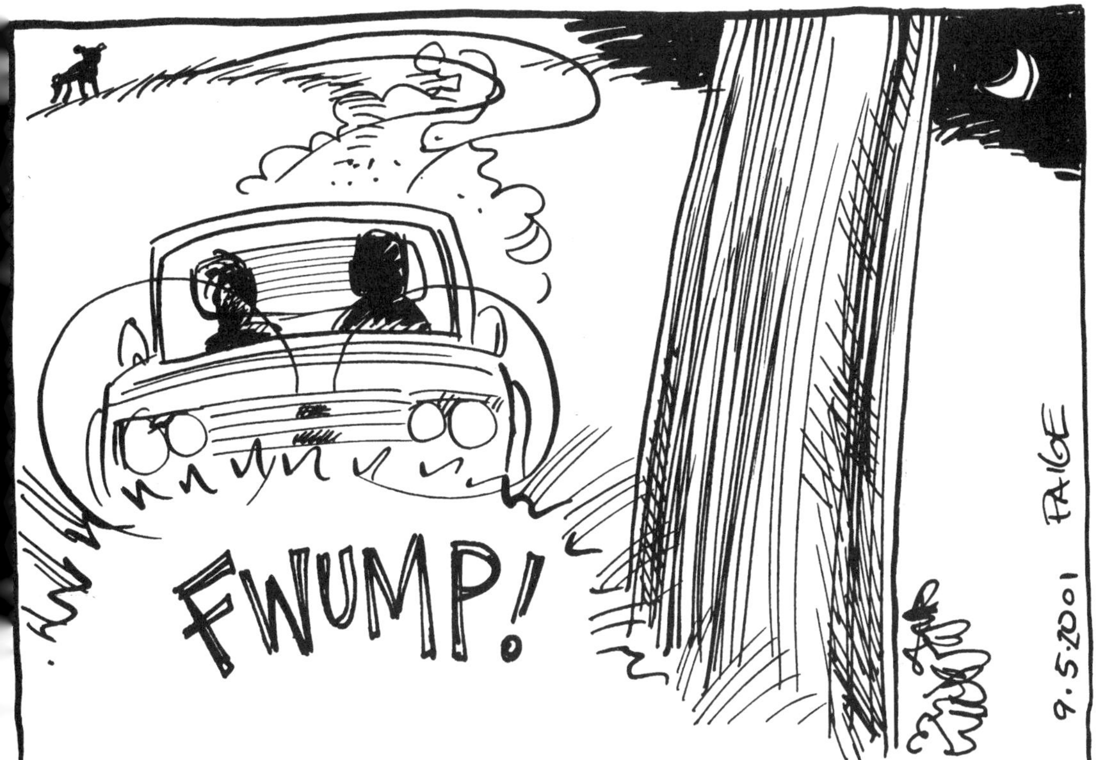
FWUMP!
9.5.2001
PAIGE

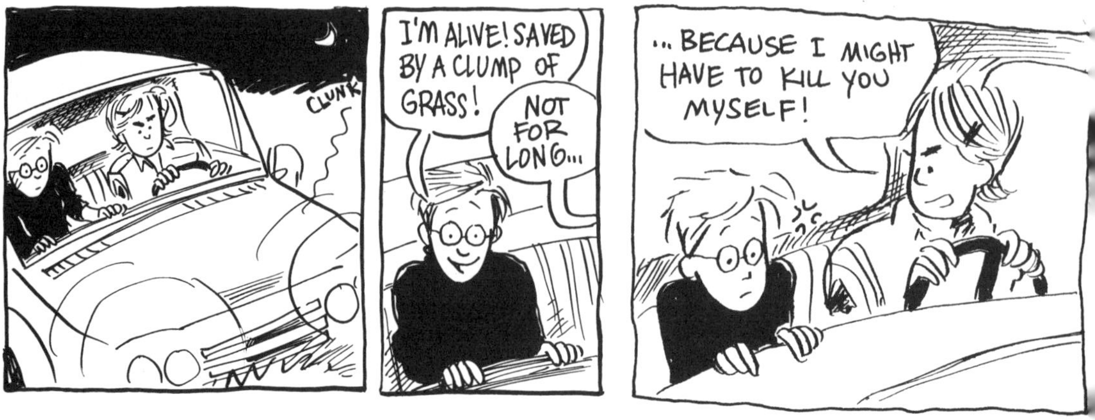
CLUNK
I'M ALIVE! SAVED BY A CLUMP OF GRASS!
NOT FOR LONG...
... BECAUSE I MIGHT HAVE TO KILL YOU MYSELF!

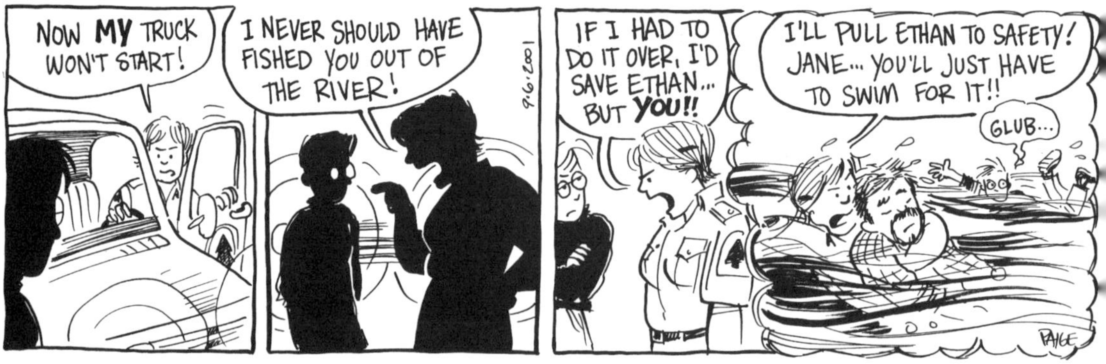
NOW **MY** TRUCK WON'T START!
I NEVER SHOULD HAVE FISHED YOU OUT OF THE RIVER!
9·6·2001
IF I HAD TO DO IT OVER, I'D SAVE ETHAN... BUT **YOU!!**
I'LL PULL ETHAN TO SAFETY! JANE... YOU'LL JUST HAVE TO SWIM FOR IT!!
GLUB...
PAIGE

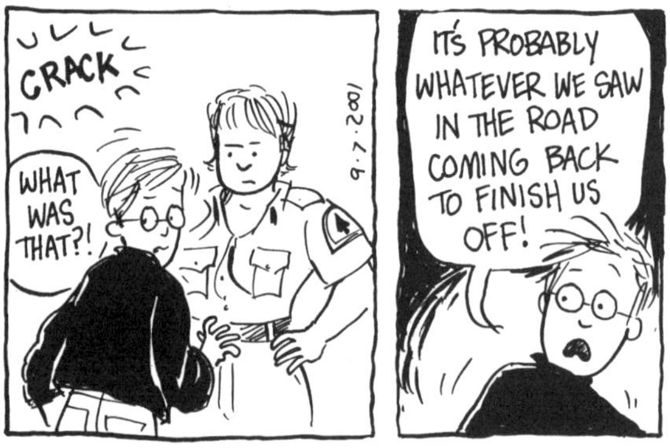
CRACK
WHAT WAS THAT?!
9·7·2001
IT'S PROBABLY WHATEVER WE SAW IN THE ROAD COMING BACK TO FINISH US OFF!

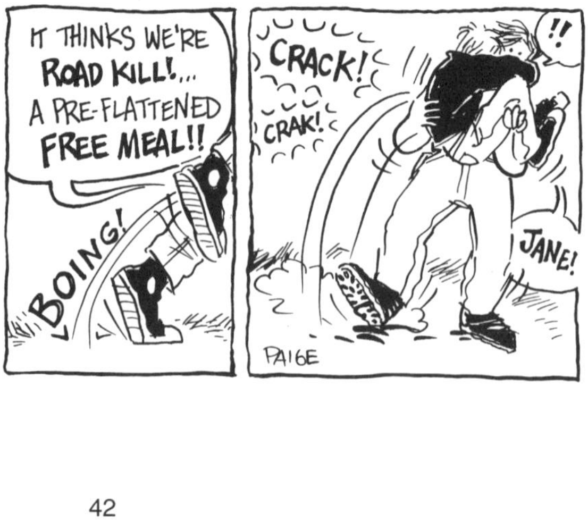
IT THINKS WE'RE **ROAD KILL!**... A PRE-FLATTENED **FREE MEAL!!**
BOING!
CRACK!
CRAK!
!!
JANE!
PAIGE

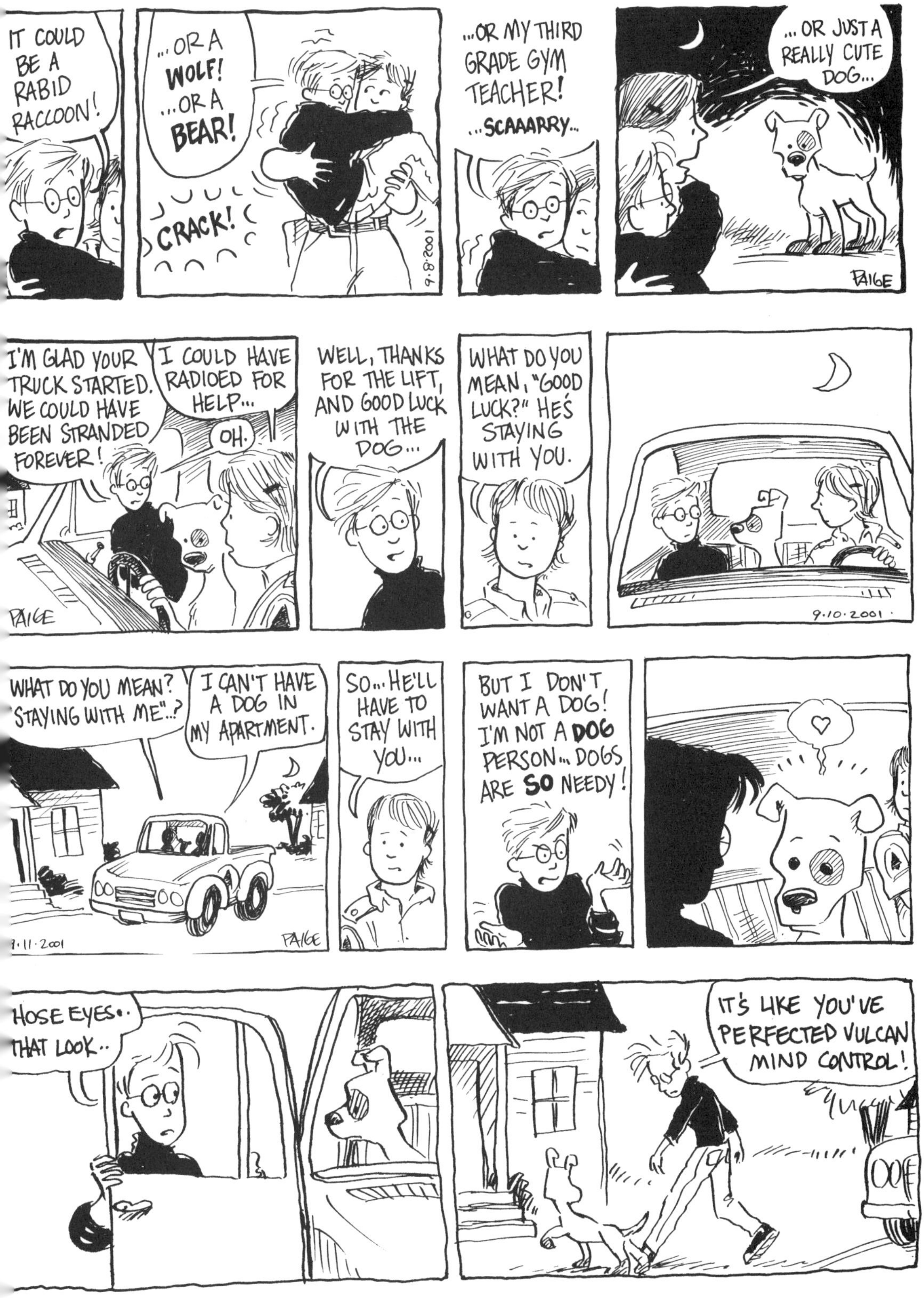
IT COULD BE A RABID RACCOON!
...OR A WOLF! ...OR A BEAR!
CRACK!
9·8·2001
...OR MY THIRD GRADE GYM TEACHER! ...SCAAARRY...
...OR JUST A REALLY CUTE DOG...
PAIGE
I'M GLAD YOUR TRUCK STARTED. WE COULD HAVE BEEN STRANDED FOREVER!
I COULD HAVE RADIOED FOR HELP...
OH.
PAIGE
WELL, THANKS FOR THE LIFT, AND GOOD LUCK WITH THE DOG...
WHAT DO YOU MEAN, "GOOD LUCK?" HE'S STAYING WITH YOU.
9·10·2001
WHAT DO YOU MEAN? "STAYING WITH ME"..?
I CAN'T HAVE A DOG IN MY APARTMENT.
9·11·2001
PAIGE
SO... HE'LL HAVE TO STAY WITH YOU...
BUT I DON'T WANT A DOG! I'M NOT A DOG PERSON... DOGS ARE SO NEEDY!
HOSE EYES.. THAT LOOK..
IT'S LIKE YOU'VE PERFECTED VULCAN MIND CONTROL!

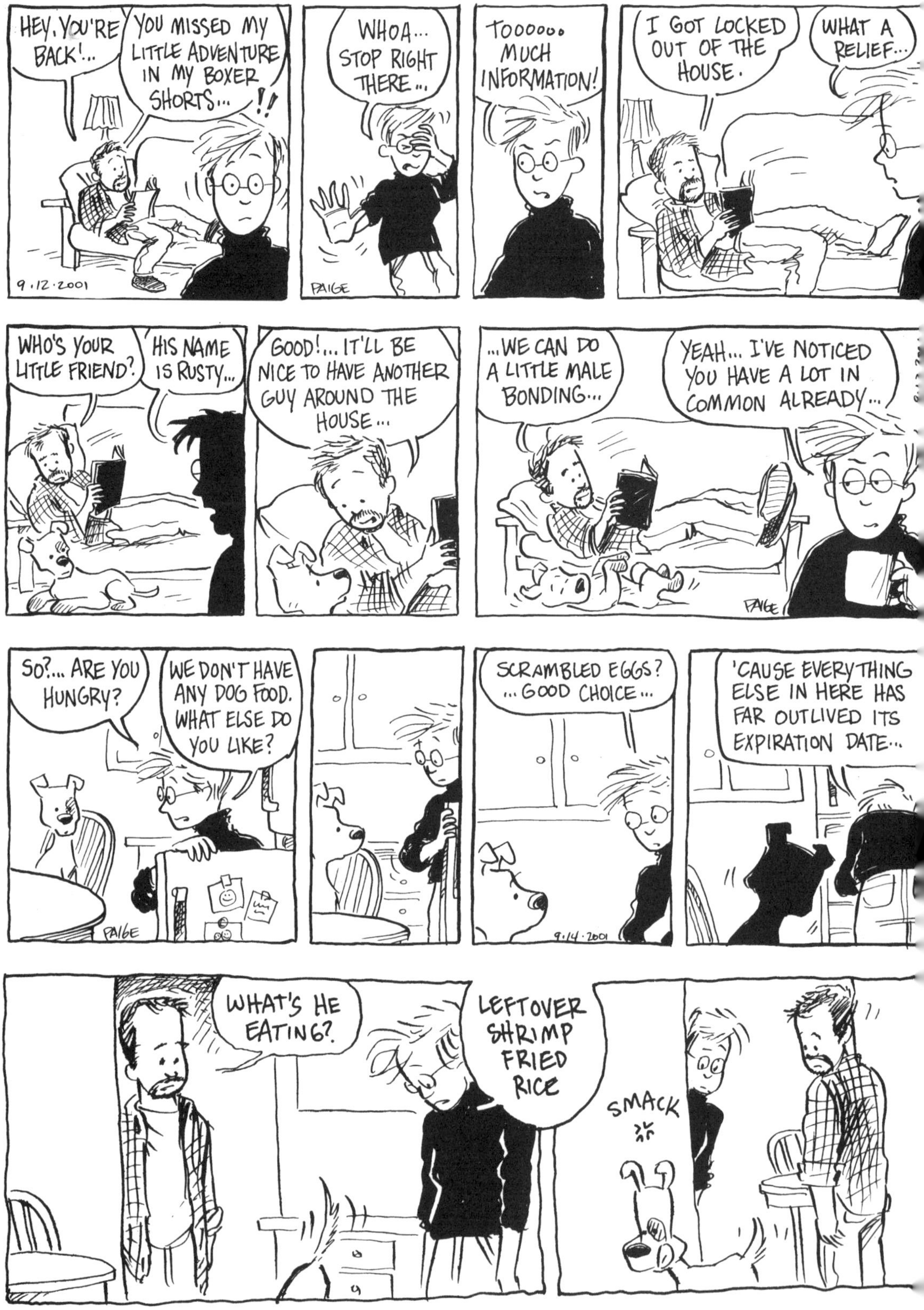
HEY, YOU'RE BACK!...
YOU MISSED MY LITTLE ADVENTURE IN MY BOXER SHORTS...
!!
9.12.2001
WHOA... STOP RIGHT THERE...
PAIGE
TOOOOOO MUCH INFORMATION!
I GOT LOCKED OUT OF THE HOUSE.
WHAT A RELIEF...
WHO'S YOUR LITTLE FRIEND?
HIS NAME IS RUSTY...
GOOD!... IT'LL BE NICE TO HAVE ANOTHER GUY AROUND THE HOUSE...
...WE CAN DO A LITTLE MALE BONDING...
YEAH... I'VE NOTICED YOU HAVE A LOT IN COMMON ALREADY...
PAIGE
SO?... ARE YOU HUNGRY?
WE DON'T HAVE ANY DOG FOOD. WHAT ELSE DO YOU LIKE?
PAIGE
SCRAMBLED EGGS? ...GOOD CHOICE...
9.14.2001
'CAUSE EVERYTHING ELSE IN HERE HAS FAR OUTLIVED ITS EXPIRATION DATE...
WHAT'S HE EATING?
LEFTOVER SHRIMP FRIED RICE
SMACK

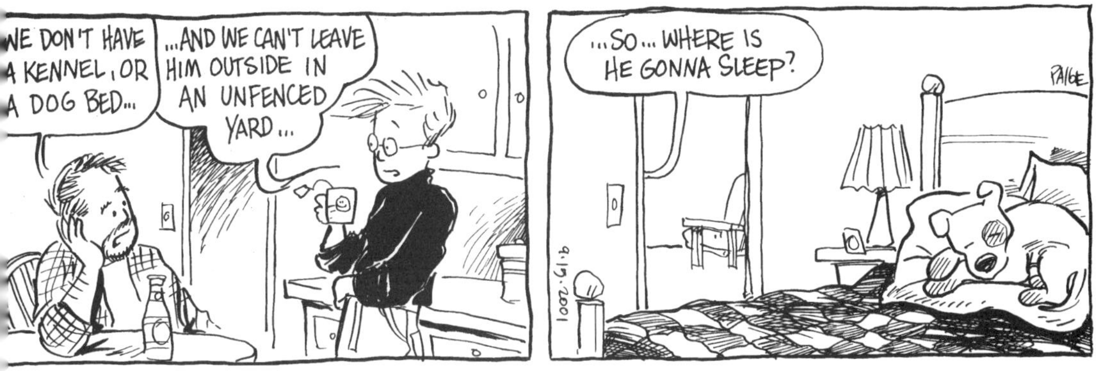
WE DON'T HAVE A KENNEL, OR A DOG BED...
...AND WE CAN'T LEAVE HIM OUTSIDE IN AN UNFENCED YARD...
...SO... WHERE IS HE GONNA SLEEP?
PAIGE
9.19.2001

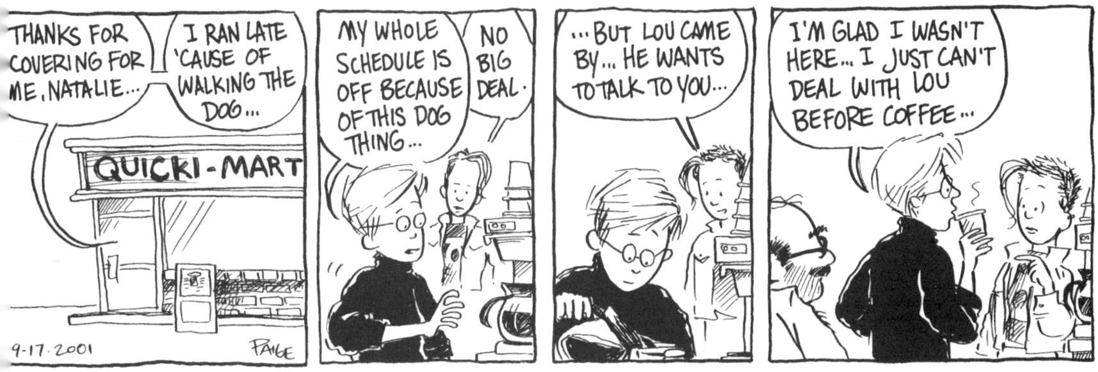
THANKS FOR COVERING FOR ME, NATALIE...
I RAN LATE 'CAUSE OF WALKING THE DOG...
QUICKI-MART
9-17-2001
PAIGE
MY WHOLE SCHEDULE IS OFF BECAUSE OF THIS DOG THING...
NO BIG DEAL.
...BUT LOU CAME BY... HE WANTS TO TALK TO YOU...
I'M GLAD I WASN'T HERE... I JUST CAN'T DEAL WITH LOU BEFORE COFFEE...

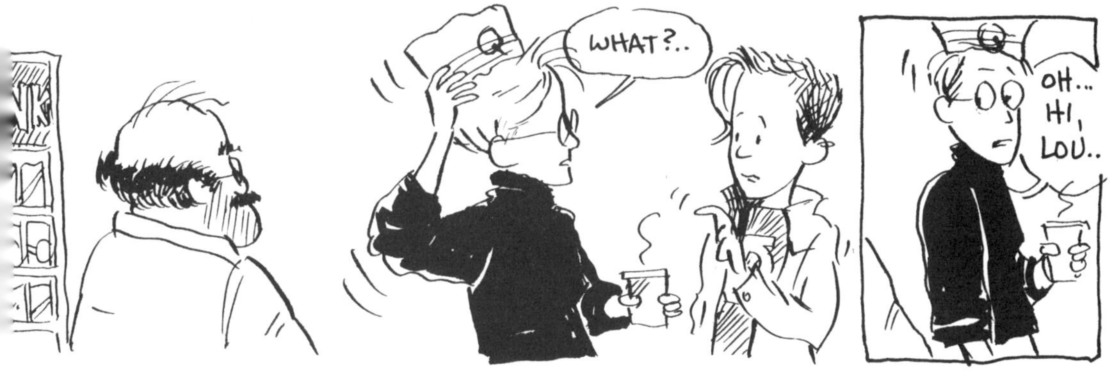
WHAT?..
OH... HI, LOU..

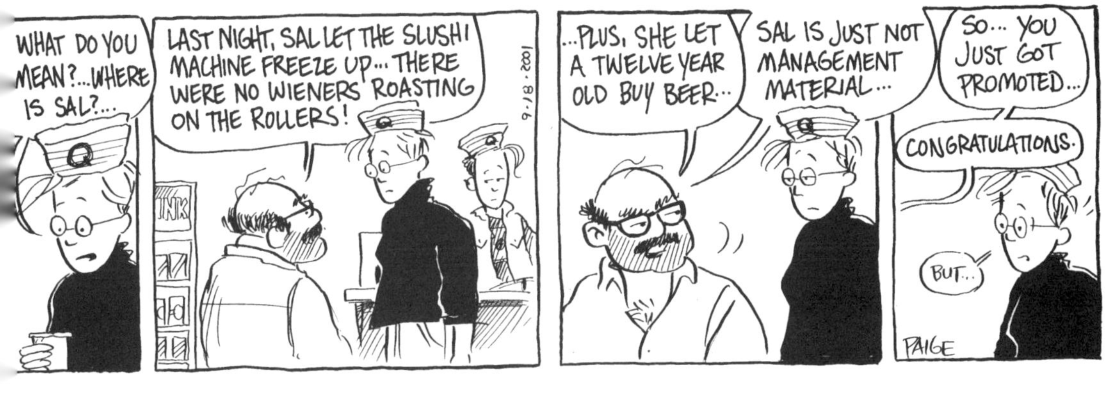
WHAT DO YOU MEAN?...WHERE IS SAL?...
LAST NIGHT, SAL LET THE SLUSHI MACHINE FREEZE UP... THERE WERE NO WIENERS ROASTING ON THE ROLLERS!
9.18.2001
...PLUS, SHE LET A TWELVE YEAR OLD BUY BEER...
SAL IS JUST NOT MANAGEMENT MATERIAL...
SO... YOU JUST GOT PROMOTED...
CONGRATULATIONS.
BUT...
PAIGE

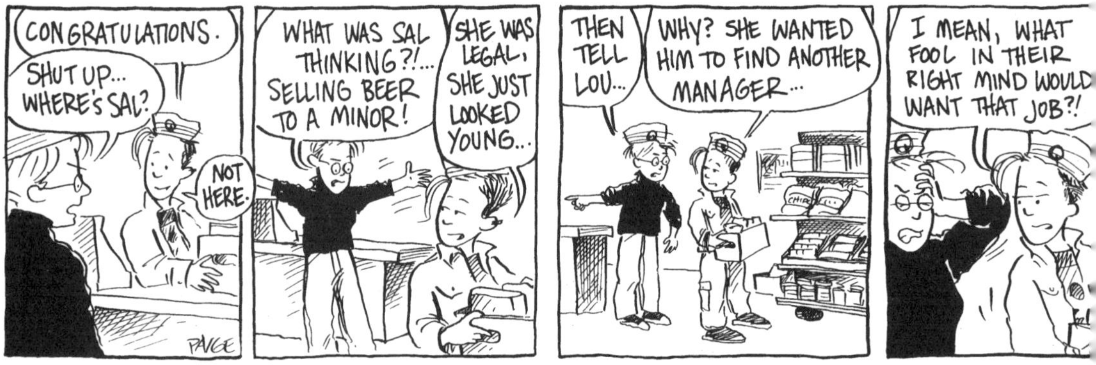
CONGRATULATIONS.
SHUT UP... WHERE'S SAL?
NOT HERE.
PAIGE
WHAT WAS SAL THINKING?!... SELLING BEER TO A MINOR!
SHE WAS LEGAL, SHE JUST LOOKED YOUNG...
THEN TELL LOU...
WHY? SHE WANTED HIM TO FIND ANOTHER MANAGER...
I MEAN, WHAT FOOL IN THEIR RIGHT MIND WOULD WANT THAT JOB?!

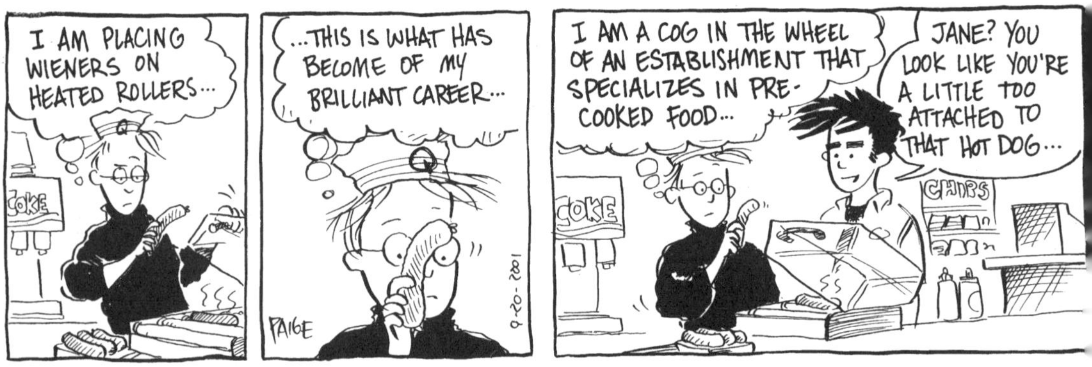
I AM PLACING WIENERS ON HEATED ROLLERS...
COKE
...THIS IS WHAT HAS BECOME OF MY BRILLIANT CAREER...
PAIGE
9-20-2001
I AM A COG IN THE WHEEL OF AN ESTABLISHMENT THAT SPECIALIZES IN PRE-COOKED FOOD...
JANE? YOU LOOK LIKE YOU'RE A LITTLE TOO ATTACHED TO THAT HOT DOG...
COKE
CHIPS

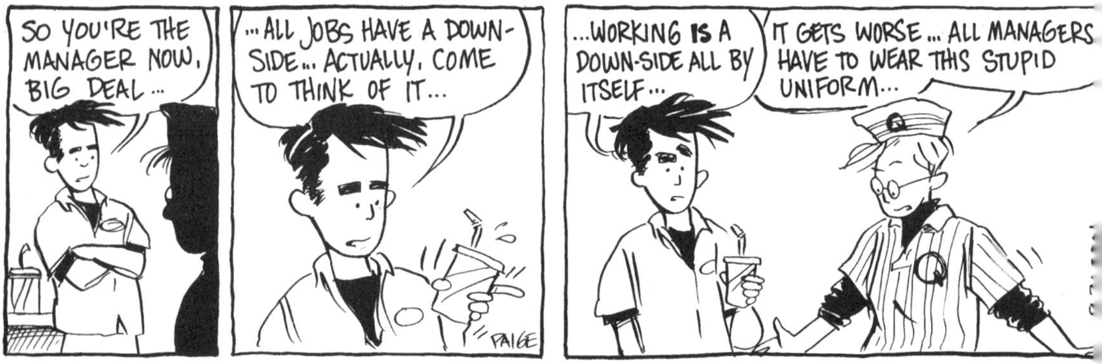
SO YOU'RE THE MANAGER NOW, BIG DEAL...
...ALL JOBS HAVE A DOWN-SIDE... ACTUALLY, COME TO THINK OF IT...
PAIGE
...WORKING IS A DOWN-SIDE ALL BY ITSELF...
IT GETS WORSE... ALL MANAGERS HAVE TO WEAR THIS STUPID UNIFORM...

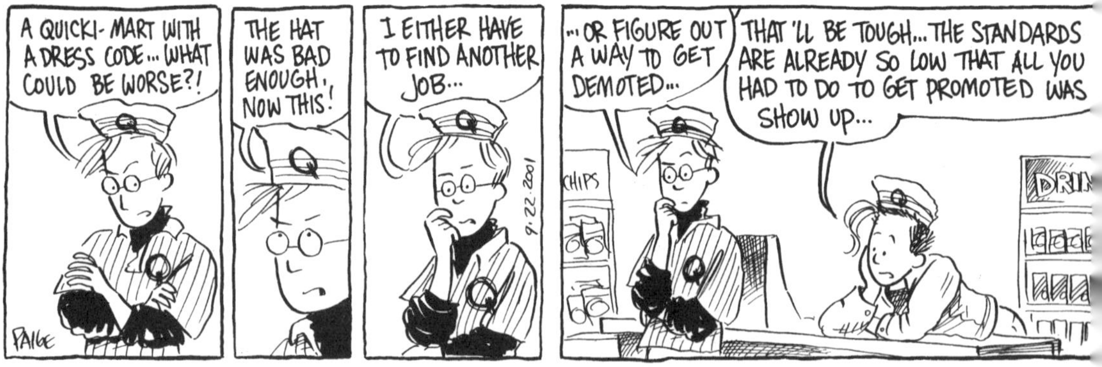
A QUICKI-MART WITH A DRESS CODE... WHAT COULD BE WORSE?!
PAIGE
THE HAT WAS BAD ENOUGH, NOW THIS!
I EITHER HAVE TO FIND ANOTHER JOB...
9-22-2001
...OR FIGURE OUT A WAY TO GET DEMOTED...
THAT'LL BE TOUGH... THE STANDARDS ARE ALREADY SO LOW THAT ALL YOU HAD TO DO TO GET PROMOTED WAS SHOW UP...
CHIPS

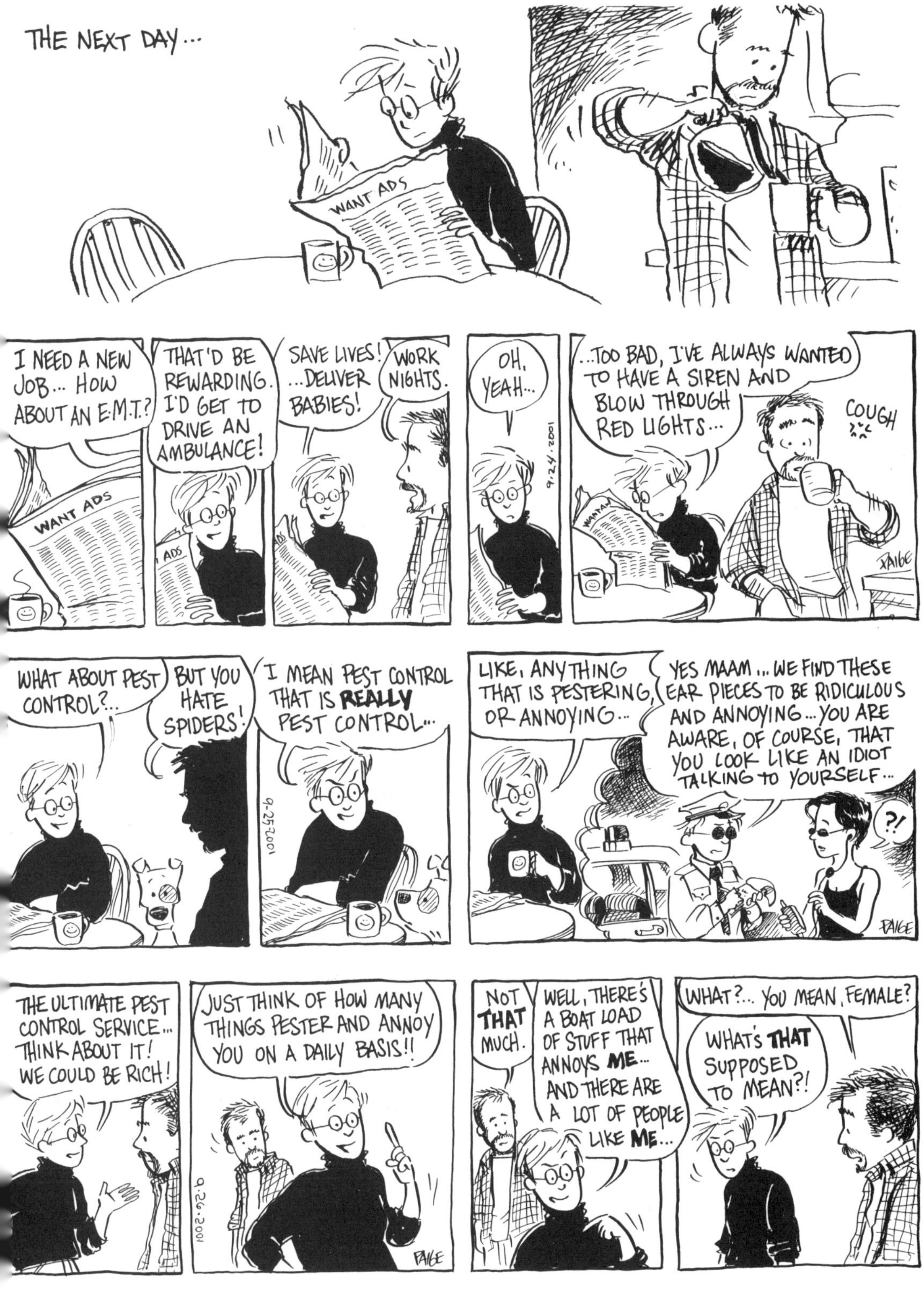
THE NEXT DAY...
WANT ADS
I NEED A NEW JOB... HOW ABOUT AN E.M.T.?
WANT ADS
THAT'D BE REWARDING. I'D GET TO DRIVE AN AMBULANCE!
SAVE LIVES! ...DELIVER BABIES!
WORK NIGHTS.
OH, YEAH...
9.24.2001
...TOO BAD, I'VE ALWAYS WANTED TO HAVE A SIREN AND BLOW THROUGH RED LIGHTS...
COUGH
PAIGE
WHAT ABOUT PEST CONTROL?...
BUT YOU HATE SPIDERS!
I MEAN PEST CONTROL THAT IS **REALLY** PEST CONTROL...
9-25-2001
LIKE, ANYTHING THAT IS PESTERING, OR ANNOYING...
YES MAAM... WE FIND THESE EAR PIECES TO BE RIDICULOUS AND ANNOYING... YOU ARE AWARE, OF COURSE, THAT YOU LOOK LIKE AN IDIOT TALKING TO YOURSELF...
?!
PAIGE
THE ULTIMATE PEST CONTROL SERVICE... THINK ABOUT IT! WE COULD BE RICH!
JUST THINK OF HOW MANY THINGS PESTER AND ANNOY YOU ON A DAILY BASIS!!
9.26.2001
PAIGE
NOT **THAT** MUCH.
WELL, THERE'S A BOAT LOAD OF STUFF THAT ANNOYS **ME**... AND THERE ARE A LOT OF PEOPLE LIKE **ME**...
WHAT?... YOU MEAN, FEMALE?
WHAT'S **THAT** SUPPOSED TO MEAN?!

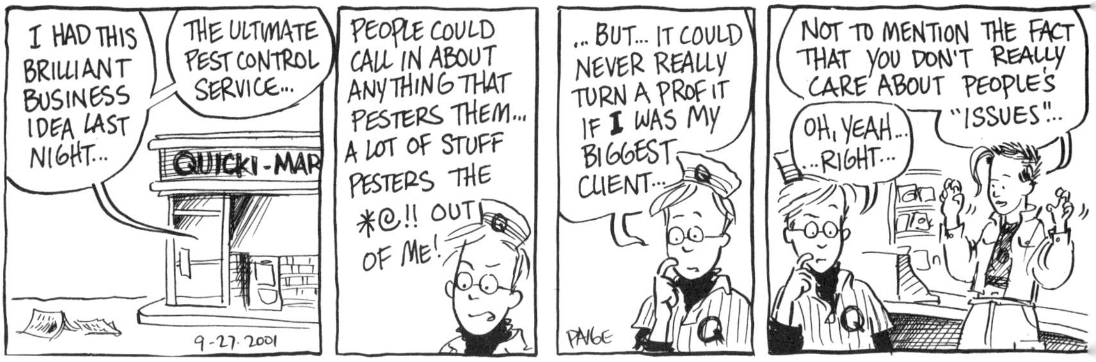
I HAD THIS BRILLIANT BUSINESS IDEA LAST NIGHT...
THE ULTIMATE PEST CONTROL SERVICE...
QUICKI-MAR
9-27-2001
PEOPLE COULD CALL IN ABOUT ANYTHING THAT PESTERS THEM... A LOT OF STUFF PESTERS THE *@!! OUT OF ME!
...BUT... IT COULD NEVER REALLY TURN A PROFIT IF I WAS MY BIGGEST CLIENT...
PAIGE
NOT TO MENTION THE FACT THAT YOU DON'T REALLY CARE ABOUT PEOPLE'S "ISSUES"...
OH, YEAH... ...RIGHT...

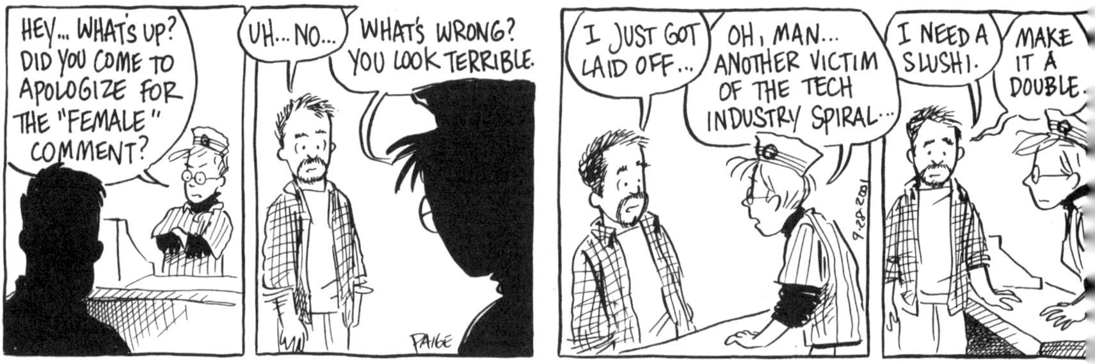
HEY... WHAT'S UP? DID YOU COME TO APOLOGIZE FOR THE "FEMALE" COMMENT?
UH... NO...
WHAT'S WRONG? YOU LOOK TERRIBLE.
PAIGE
I JUST GOT LAID OFF...
OH, MAN... ANOTHER VICTIM OF THE TECH INDUSTRY SPIRAL...
9-28-2001
I NEED A SLUSHI.
MAKE IT A DOUBLE.

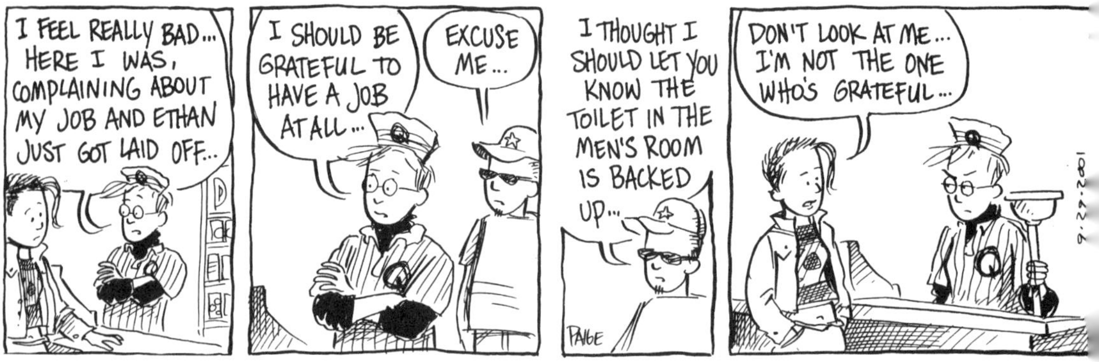
I FEEL REALLY BAD... HERE I WAS, COMPLAINING ABOUT MY JOB AND ETHAN JUST GOT LAID OFF...
I SHOULD BE GRATEFUL TO HAVE A JOB AT ALL...
EXCUSE ME...
I THOUGHT I SHOULD LET YOU KNOW THE TOILET IN THE MEN'S ROOM IS BACKED UP...
PAIGE
DON'T LOOK AT ME... I'M NOT THE ONE WHO'S GRATEFUL...
9-29-2001

THE NEXT MORNING...

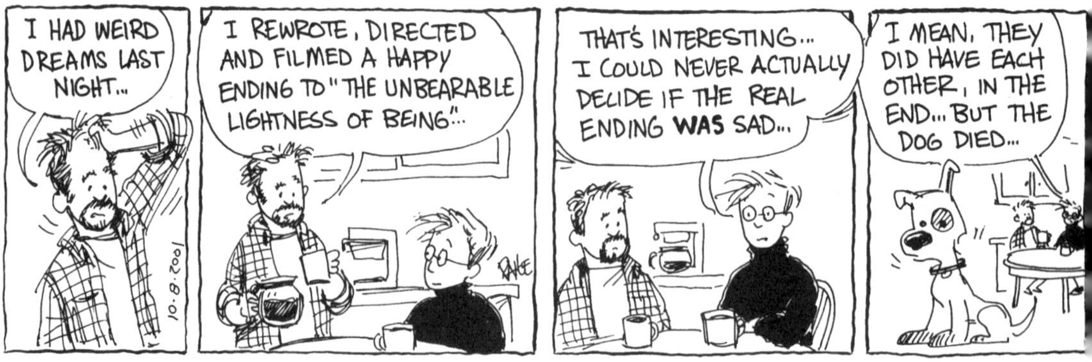
I HAD WEIRD DREAMS LAST NIGHT...
10-8-2001
I REWROTE, DIRECTED AND FILMED A HAPPY ENDING TO "THE UNBEARABLE LIGHTNESS OF BEING"...
PAIGE
THAT'S INTERESTING... I COULD NEVER ACTUALLY DECIDE IF THE REAL ENDING WAS SAD...
I MEAN, THEY DID HAVE EACH OTHER, IN THE END... BUT THE DOG DIED...

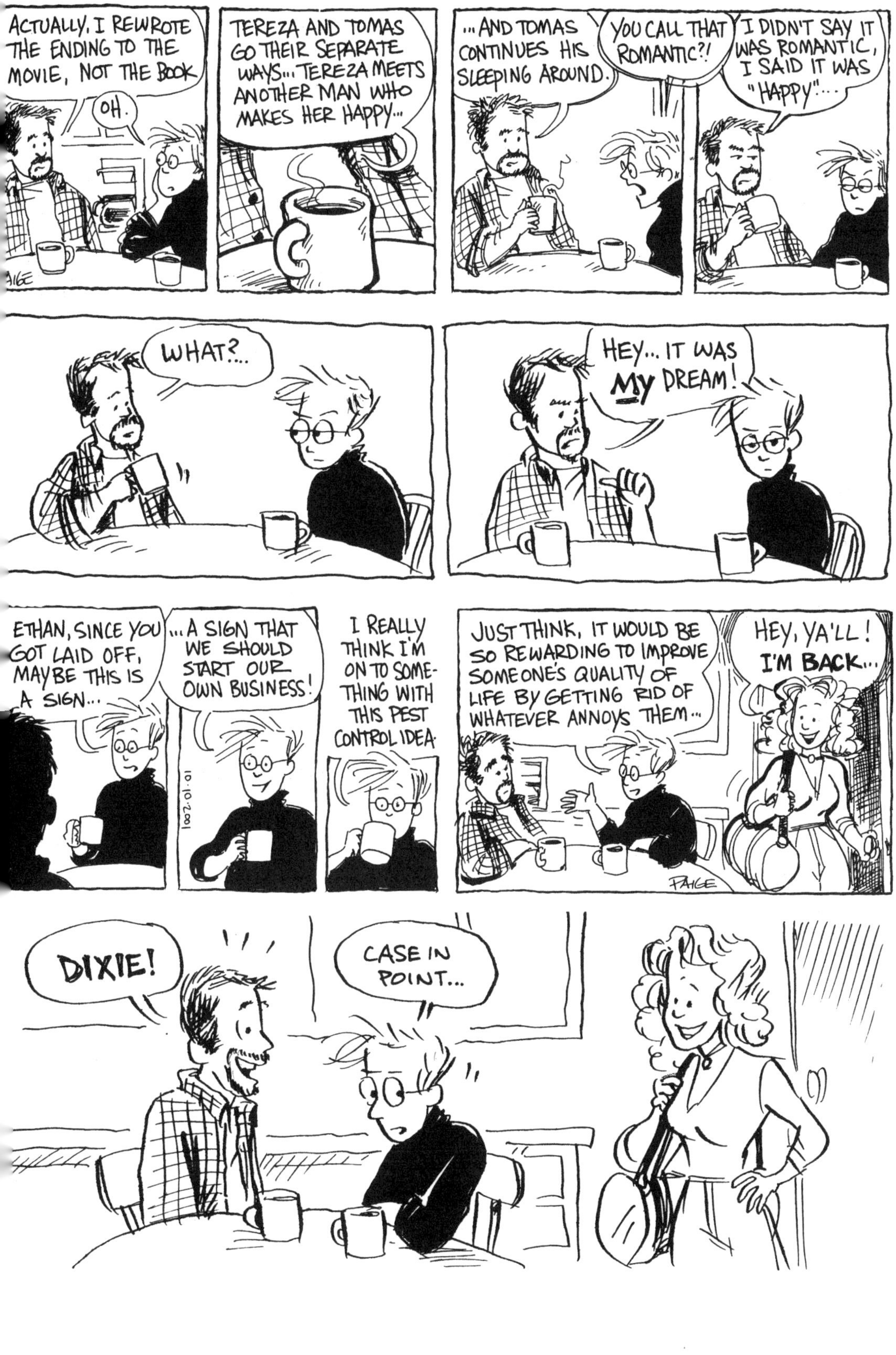
ACTUALLY, I REWROTE THE ENDING TO THE MOVIE, NOT THE BOOK
OH.
TEREZA AND TOMAS GO THEIR SEPARATE WAYS... TEREZA MEETS ANOTHER MAN WHO MAKES HER HAPPY...
...AND TOMAS CONTINUES HIS SLEEPING AROUND.
YOU CALL THAT ROMANTIC?!
I DIDN'T SAY IT WAS ROMANTIC, I SAID IT WAS "HAPPY"...
WHAT?...
HEY... IT WAS MY DREAM!
ETHAN, SINCE YOU GOT LAID OFF, MAYBE THIS IS A SIGN...
...A SIGN THAT WE SHOULD START OUR OWN BUSINESS!
I REALLY THINK I'M ON TO SOMETHING WITH THIS PEST CONTROL IDEA.
JUST THINK, IT WOULD BE SO REWARDING TO IMPROVE SOMEONE'S QUALITY OF LIFE BY GETTING RID OF WHATEVER ANNOYS THEM...
HEY, YA'LL! I'M BACK...
PAIGE
DIXIE!
CASE IN POINT...

LATER, AT THE QUICKI-MART....

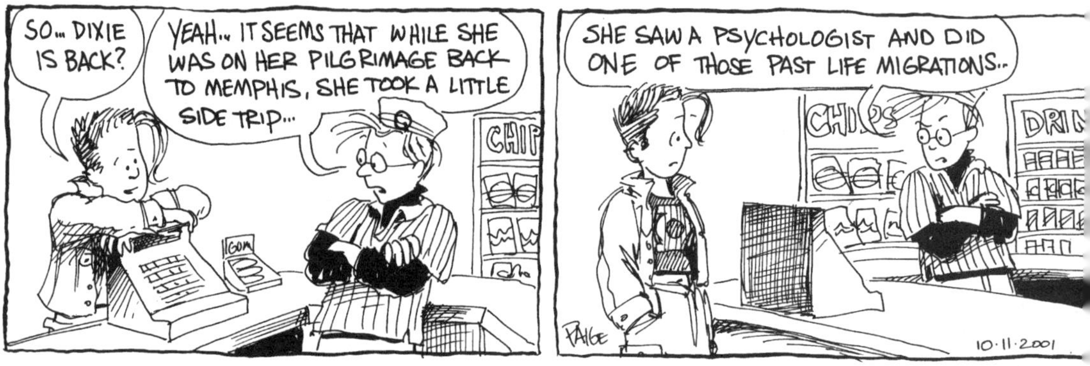

SO... DIXIE IS BACK?
YEAH.. IT SEEMS THAT WHILE SHE WAS ON HER PILGRIMAGE BACK TO MEMPHIS, SHE TOOK A LITTLE SIDE TRIP...
GUM
CHIP
SHE SAW A PSYCHOLOGIST AND DID ONE OF THOSE PAST LIFE MIGRATIONS..
CHIPS
DRIN
PAIGE
10·11·2001

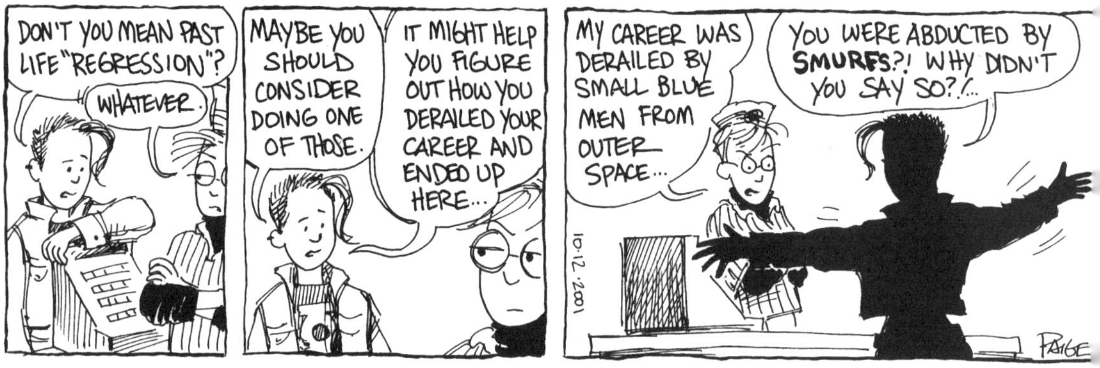

DON'T YOU MEAN PAST LIFE "REGRESSION"?
WHATEVER.
MAYBE YOU SHOULD CONSIDER DOING ONE OF THOSE.
IT MIGHT HELP YOU FIGURE OUT HOW YOU DERAILED YOUR CAREER AND ENDED UP HERE...
MY CAREER WAS DERAILED BY SMALL BLUE MEN FROM OUTER SPACE...
YOU WERE ABDUCTED BY **SMURFS**?! WHY DIDN'T YOU SAY SO?!..
10·12·2001
PAIGE

BACK AT JANE'S, LATER THAT DAY...

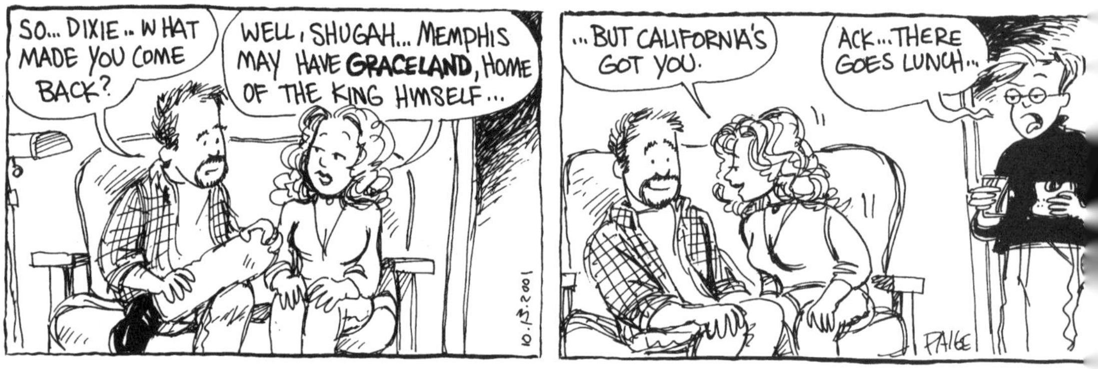

SO... DIXIE.. WHAT MADE YOU COME BACK?
WELL, SHUGAH... MEMPHIS MAY HAVE **GRACELAND**, HOME OF THE KING HIMSELF...
10·13·2001
...BUT CALIFORNIA'S GOT YOU.
ACK... THERE GOES LUNCH...
PAIGE

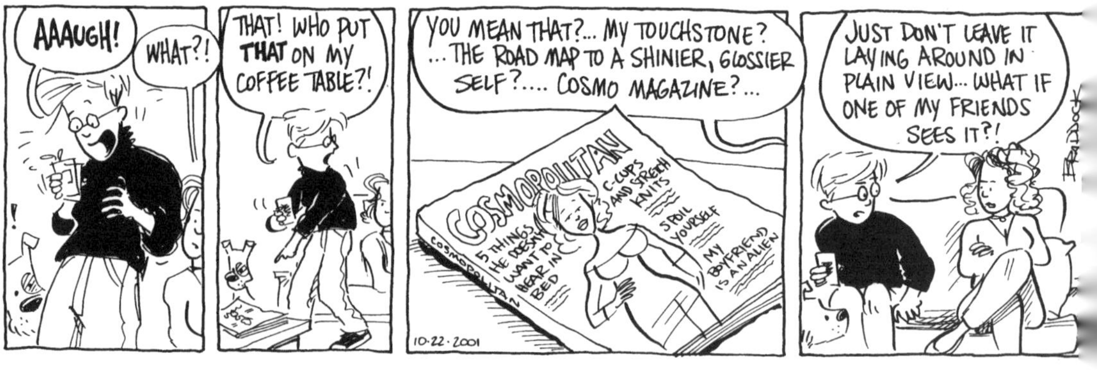

AAAUGH!
WHAT?!
THAT! WHO PUT **THAT** ON MY COFFEE TABLE?!
YOU MEAN THAT?... MY TOUCHSTONE? ... THE ROAD MAP TO A SHINIER, GLOSSIER SELF?.... COSMO MAGAZINE?...
COSMOPOLITAN
5 THINGS HE DOESN'T WANT TO HEAR IN BED
C-CUPS AND STRETCH KNITS
SPOIL YOURSELF
MY BOYFRIEND IS AN ALIEN
10·22·2001
JUST DON'T LEAVE IT LAYING AROUND IN PLAIN VIEW... WHAT IF ONE OF MY FRIENDS SEES IT?!
PADDOCK

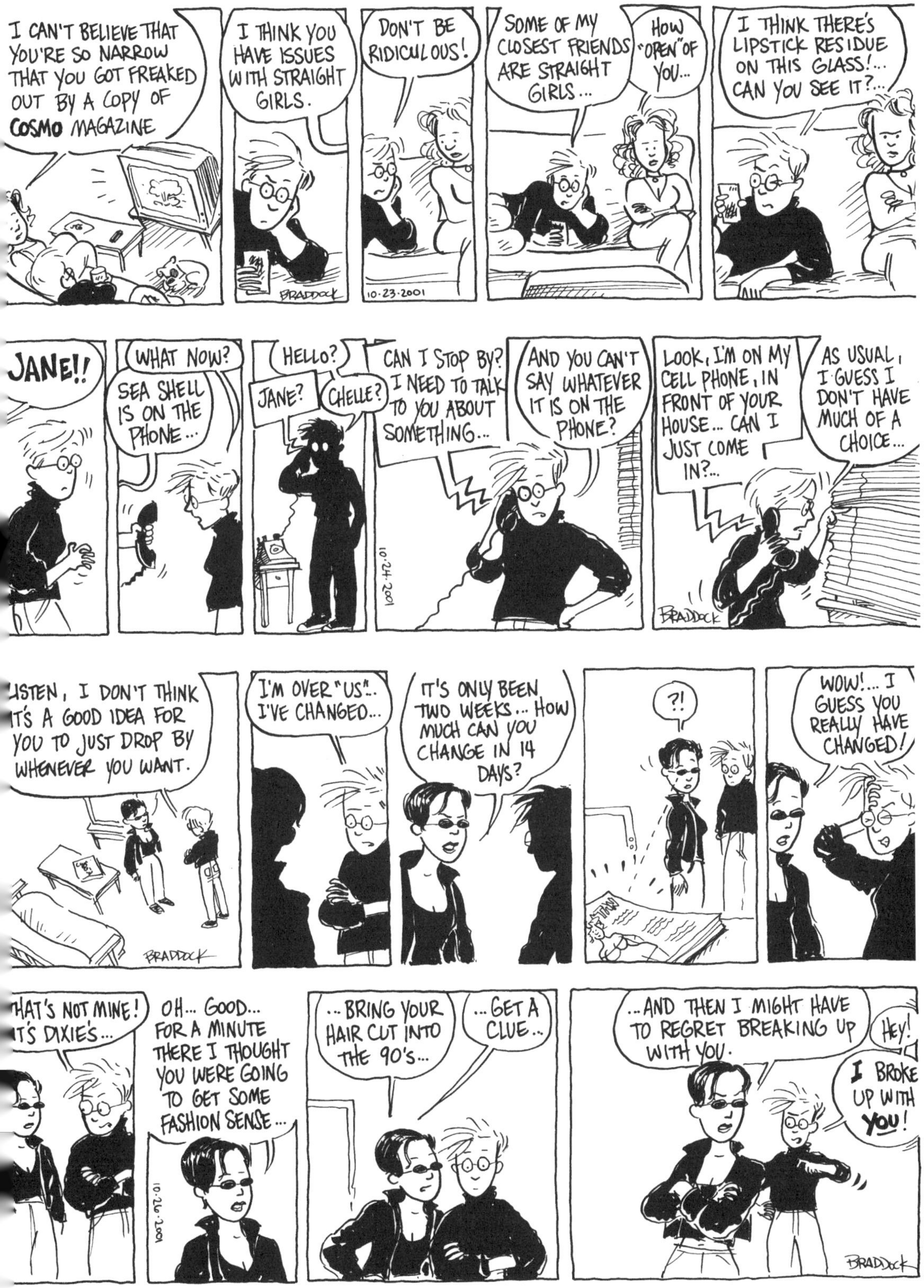
I CAN'T BELIEVE THAT YOU'RE SO NARROW THAT YOU GOT FREAKED OUT BY A COPY OF COSMO MAGAZINE
I THINK YOU HAVE ISSUES WITH STRAIGHT GIRLS.
BRADDOCK
DON'T BE RIDICULOUS!
10-23-2001
SOME OF MY CLOSEST FRIENDS ARE STRAIGHT GIRLS...
HOW "OPEN" OF YOU...
I THINK THERE'S LIPSTICK RESIDUE ON THIS GLASS!... CAN YOU SEE IT?...
JANE!!
WHAT NOW?
SEA SHELL IS ON THE PHONE...
HELLO?
JANE?
CHELLE?
10-24-2001
CAN I STOP BY? I NEED TO TALK TO YOU ABOUT SOMETHING...
AND YOU CAN'T SAY WHATEVER IT IS ON THE PHONE?
LOOK, I'M ON MY CELL PHONE, IN FRONT OF YOUR HOUSE... CAN I JUST COME IN?...
AS USUAL, I GUESS I DON'T HAVE MUCH OF A CHOICE...
BRADDOCK
LISTEN, I DON'T THINK IT'S A GOOD IDEA FOR YOU TO JUST DROP BY WHENEVER YOU WANT.
BRADDOCK
I'M OVER "US"... I'VE CHANGED...
IT'S ONLY BEEN TWO WEEKS... HOW MUCH CAN YOU CHANGE IN 14 DAYS?
?!
WOW!... I GUESS YOU REALLY HAVE CHANGED!
THAT'S NOT MINE! IT'S DIXIE'S...
OH... GOOD... FOR A MINUTE THERE I THOUGHT YOU WERE GOING TO GET SOME FASHION SENSE...
10-26-2001
...BRING YOUR HAIR CUT INTO THE 90's...
...GET A CLUE...
...AND THEN I MIGHT HAVE TO REGRET BREAKING UP WITH YOU.
HEY!
I BROKE UP WITH YOU!
BRADDOCK

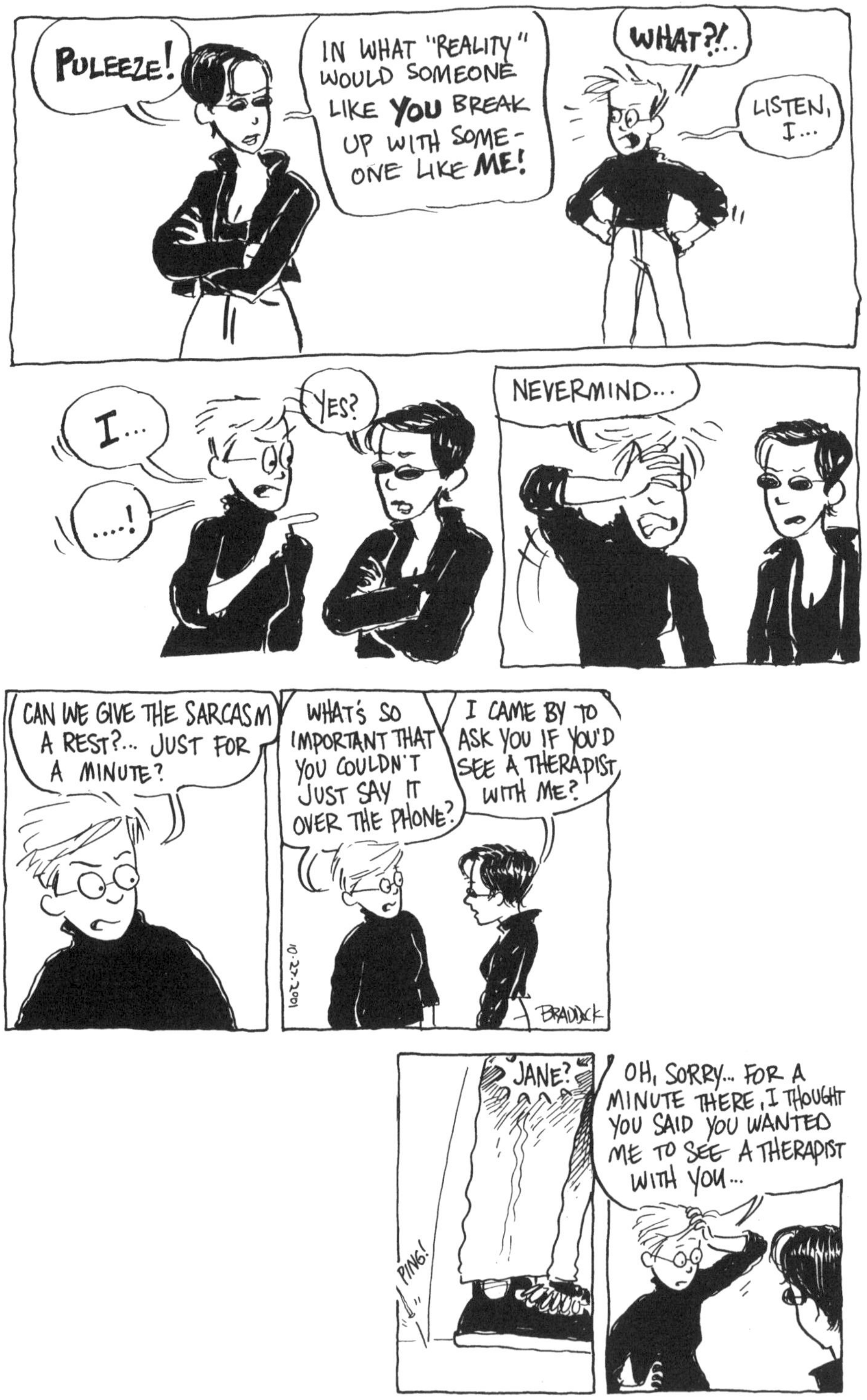
PULEEZE!
IN WHAT "REALITY" WOULD SOMEONE LIKE YOU BREAK UP WITH SOME-ONE LIKE ME!
WHAT?!..
LISTEN, I...
I...
....!
YES?
NEVERMIND...
CAN WE GIVE THE SARCASM A REST?... JUST FOR A MINUTE?
WHAT'S SO IMPORTANT THAT YOU COULDN'T JUST SAY IT OVER THE PHONE?
I CAME BY TO ASK YOU IF YOU'D SEE A THERAPIST WITH ME?
10-27-2001
BRADDOCK
JANE?
PING!
OH, SORRY... FOR A MINUTE THERE, I THOUGHT YOU SAID YOU WANTED ME TO SEE A THERAPIST WITH YOU...

Chapter three

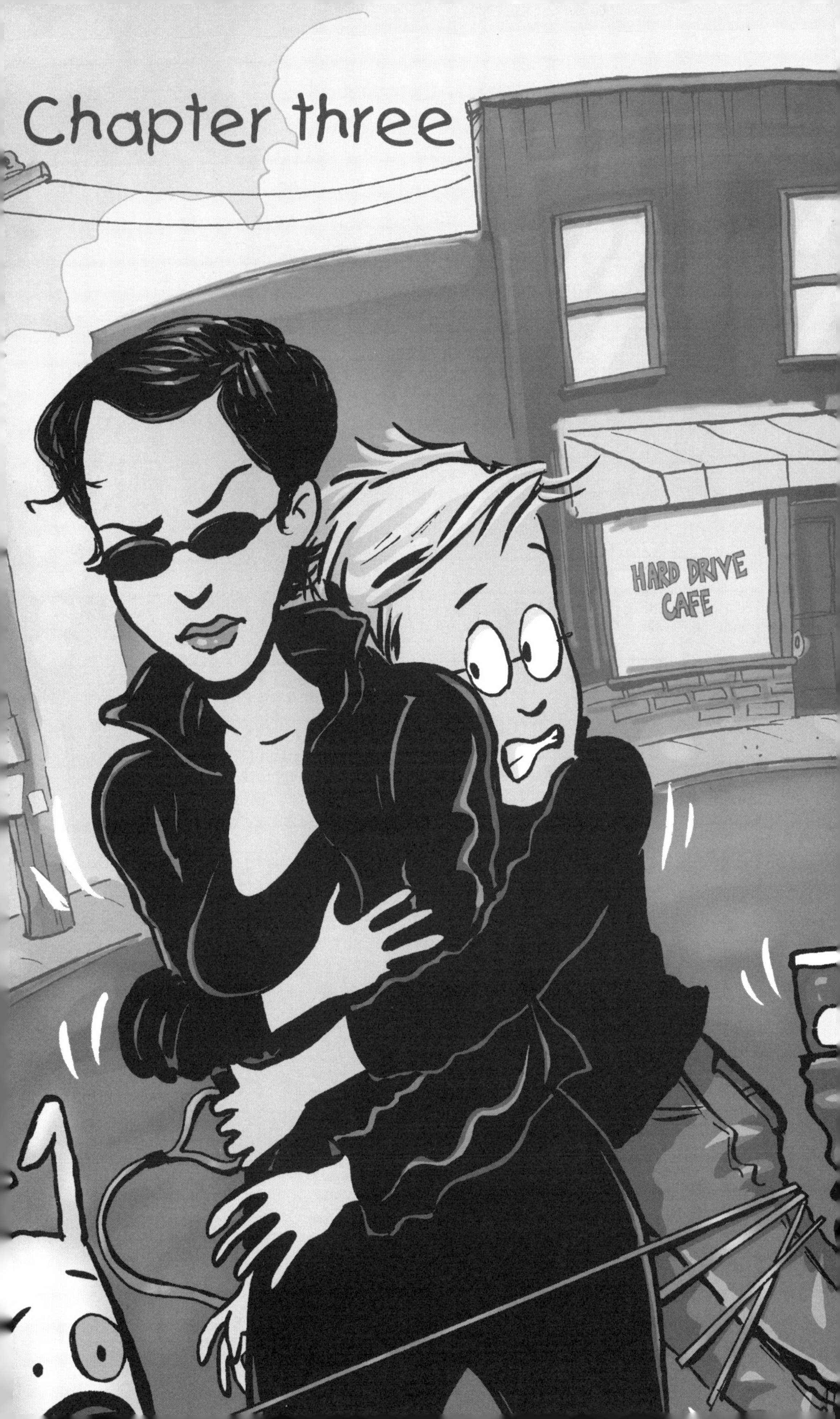
HARD DRIVE
CAFE

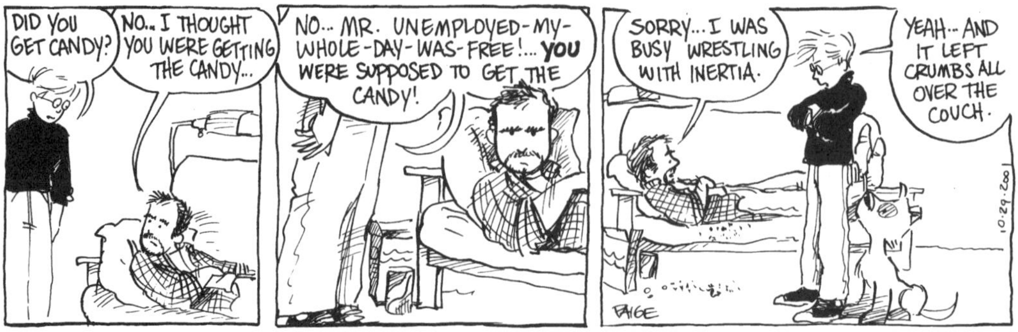
DID YOU GET CANDY?
NO.. I THOUGHT YOU WERE GETTING THE CANDY...
NO... MR. UNEMPLOYED-MY-WHOLE-DAY-WAS-FREE!... **YOU** WERE SUPPOSED TO GET THE CANDY!
SORRY... I WAS BUSY WRESTLING WITH INERTIA.
YEAH.. AND IT LEFT CRUMBS ALL OVER THE COUCH.
PAIGE
10.29.2001

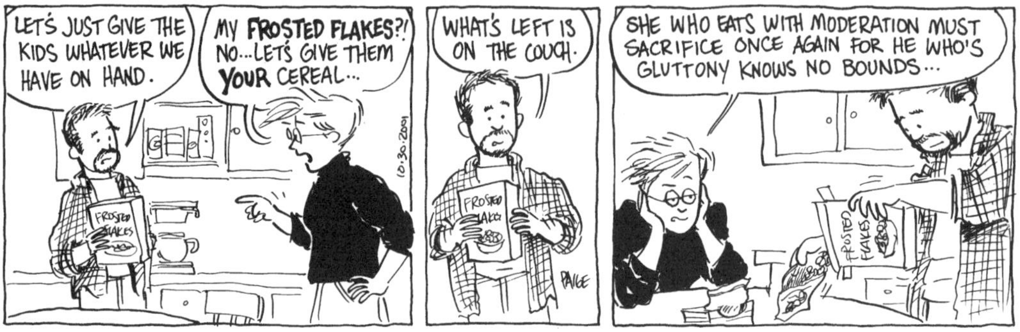
LET'S JUST GIVE THE KIDS WHATEVER WE HAVE ON HAND.
MY **FROSTED FLAKES**?! NO... LET'S GIVE THEM **YOUR** CEREAL...
10.30.2001
WHAT'S LEFT IS ON THE COUCH.
PAIGE
SHE WHO EATS WITH MODERATION MUST SACRIFICE ONCE AGAIN FOR HE WHO'S GLUTTONY KNOWS NO BOUNDS...

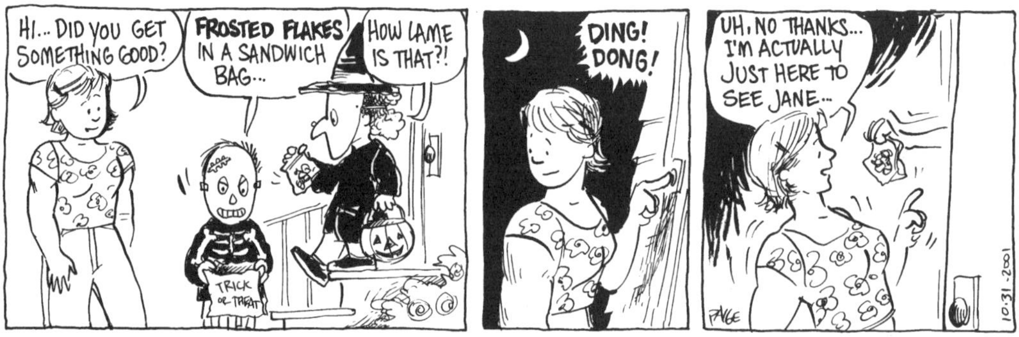
HI... DID YOU GET SOMETHING GOOD?
FROSTED FLAKES IN A SANDWICH BAG...
HOW LAME IS THAT?!
TRICK OR TREAT
DING! DONG!
UH, NO THANKS... I'M ACTUALLY JUST HERE TO SEE JANE...
PAIGE
10.31.2001

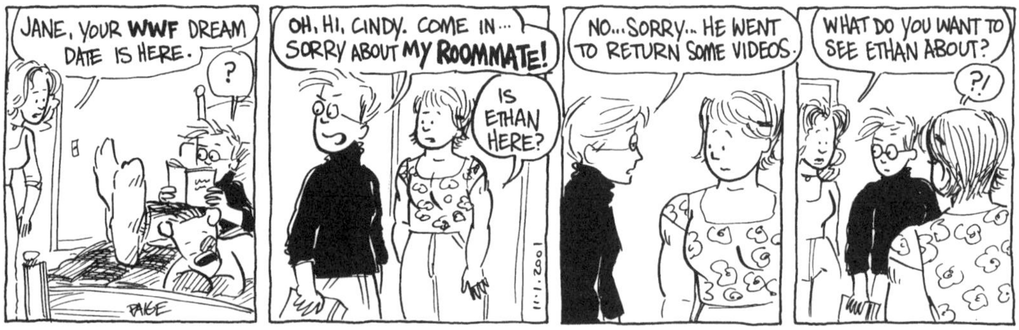
JANE, YOUR **WWF** DREAM DATE IS HERE.
?
PAIGE
OH, HI, CINDY. COME IN... SORRY ABOUT **MY ROOMMATE**!
IS ETHAN HERE?
11.1.2001
NO... SORRY... HE WENT TO RETURN SOME VIDEOS.
WHAT DO YOU WANT TO SEE ETHAN ABOUT?
?!

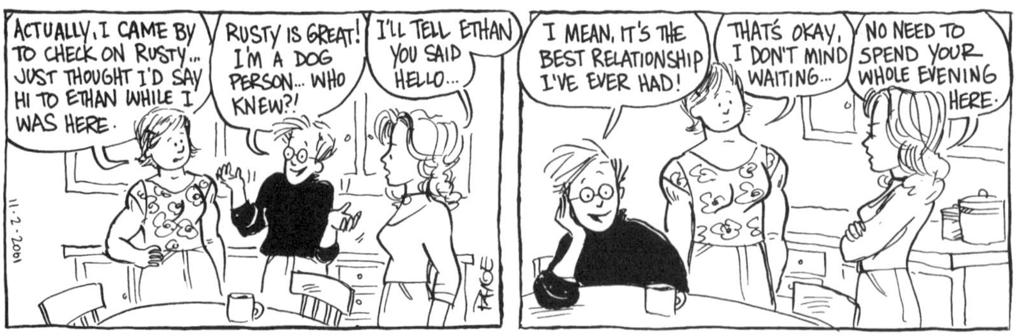
ACTUALLY, I CAME BY TO CHECK ON RUSTY... JUST THOUGHT I'D SAY HI TO ETHAN WHILE I WAS HERE.
RUSTY IS GREAT! I'M A DOG PERSON... WHO KNEW?!
I'LL TELL ETHAN YOU SAID HELLO...
11.2.2001
PAIGE
I MEAN, IT'S THE BEST RELATIONSHIP I'VE EVER HAD!
THAT'S OKAY, I DON'T MIND WAITING...
NO NEED TO SPEND YOUR WHOLE EVENING HERE.

A few minutes later...

SHE'S GOT SOME **BIG** NERVE COMING HERE...

...TRYING TO HIT ON ETHAN, RIGHT UNDER MY NOSE!

SHE JUST WANTED TO SAY HI!... I THINK YOU'RE MAKING A BIG DEAL OUT OF NOTHING.

I JUST ASSUMED SHE WAS HERE TO SEE YOU. ETHAN IS ANOTHER STORY.

WHAT DOES THAT MEAN?

IT MEANS **SHE-HULK** BETTER FIND ANOTHER BOY TOY OR I'M GONNA HAVE TO INVITE HER TO A LITTLE FEMME-BUTCH SMACK DOWN...

Then, the next day...

I DON'T KNOW WHY YOU FELT LIKE YOU HAD TO STOP BY AGAIN... I SAID I'D THINK ABOUT IT!

I DON'T KNOW WHY YOU'RE SO THREATENED BY THE SUGGESTION OF THERAPY...

YOU KNOW, MOST OF THE TIME, PEOPLE DO THERAPY TO FIGURE OUT WHAT THE PROBLEM IS...

...WE KNOW WHAT THE PROBLEM IS!... BASIC, FUNDAMENTAL, INCOMPATIBILITY...

MY THERAPIST THINKS I HAVE UNRESOLVED ISSUES WITH YOU...AND THAT'S WHY I CAN'T MOVE FORWARD WITH A NEW RELATIONSHIP.

IT'S ONLY BEEN A FEW WEEKS!

MAYBE YOUR THERAPIST SHOULD BE SAYING THAT IT'S NORMAL TO TAKE A WEEK OR TWO OFF BETWEEN RELATIONSHIPS!

ARE YOU FINISHED?

I WAS FINISHED BEFORE I STARTED...

JUST THINK ABOUT IT, OKAY?... BY THE WAY, I'M IMPRESSED WITH THE COMPLETE LACK OF FOLIAGE YOU'VE GOT GOING ON BACK HERE...

HEY! I LIKE THIS LOOK! I CALL IT "MUDSLIDE!"

I'VE GOT ONE WORD FOR YOU... "CONDO"...

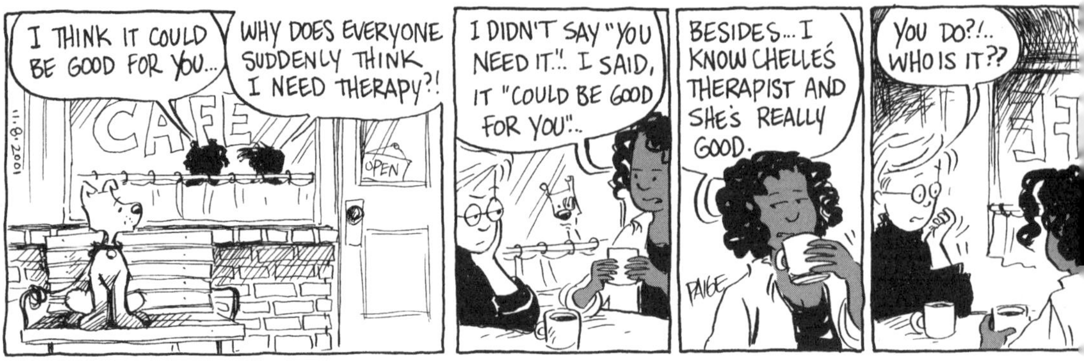
I THINK IT COULD BE GOOD FOR YOU...
WHY DOES EVERYONE SUDDENLY THINK I NEED THERAPY?!
CAFE
OPEN
11·8·2001
I DIDN'T SAY "YOU NEED IT"! I SAID, IT "COULD BE GOOD FOR YOU"...
BESIDES... I KNOW CHELLE'S THERAPIST AND SHE'S REALLY GOOD.
PAIGE
YOU DO?!.. WHO IS IT??

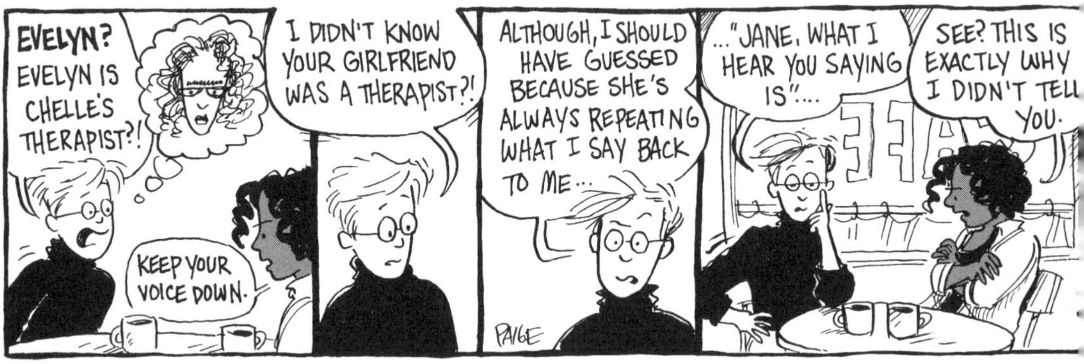
EVELYN? EVELYN IS CHELLE'S THERAPIST?!
KEEP YOUR VOICE DOWN.
I DIDN'T KNOW YOUR GIRLFRIEND WAS A THERAPIST?!
ALTHOUGH, I SHOULD HAVE GUESSED BECAUSE SHE'S ALWAYS REPEATING WHAT I SAY BACK TO ME...
PAIGE
..."JANE, WHAT I HEAR YOU SAYING IS"...
SEE? THIS IS EXACTLY WHY I DIDN'T TELL YOU.

Later, back at Jane's...

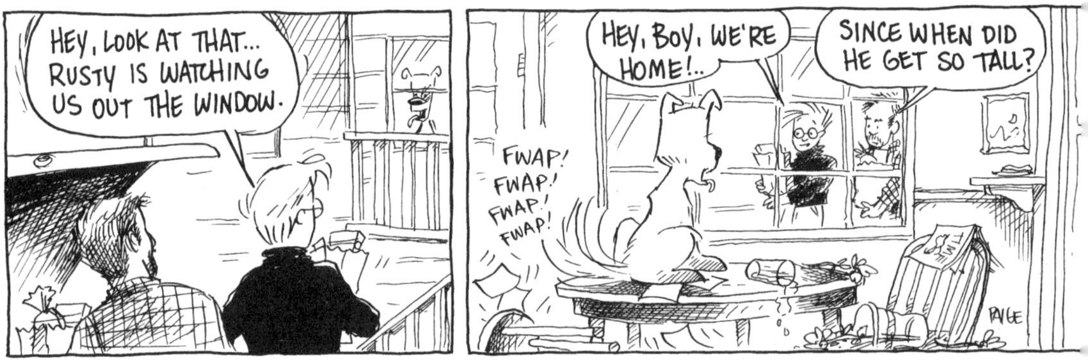
HEY, LOOK AT THAT... RUSTY IS WATCHING US OUT THE WINDOW.
HEY, BOY, WE'RE HOME!..
SINCE WHEN DID HE GET SO TALL?
FWAP! FWAP! FWAP! FWAP!
PAIGE

...and the next day, more drama on the home front...

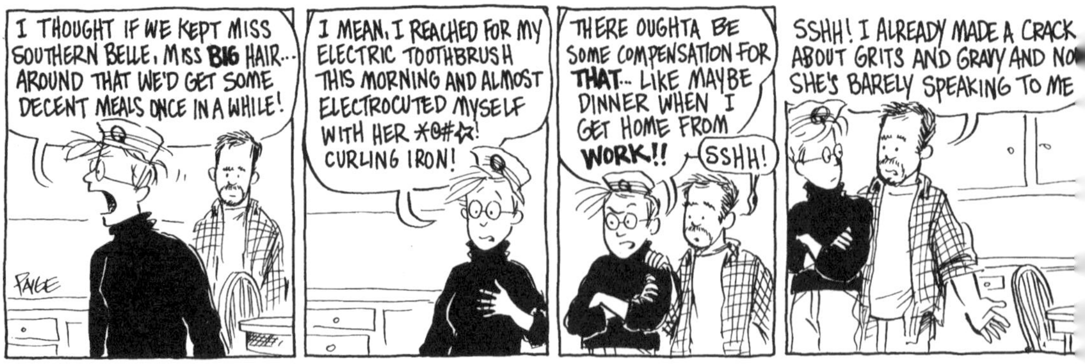
I THOUGHT IF WE KEPT MISS SOUTHERN BELLE, MISS BIG HAIR... AROUND THAT WE'D GET SOME DECENT MEALS ONCE IN A WHILE!
PAIGE
I MEAN, I REACHED FOR MY ELECTRIC TOOTHBRUSH THIS MORNING AND ALMOST ELECTROCUTED MYSELF WITH HER *@#☆! CURLING IRON!
THERE OUGHTA BE SOME COMPENSATION FOR THAT... LIKE MAYBE DINNER WHEN I GET HOME FROM WORK!!
SSHH!
SSHH! I ALREADY MADE A CRACK ABOUT GRITS AND GRAVY AND NO SHE'S BARELY SPEAKING TO ME

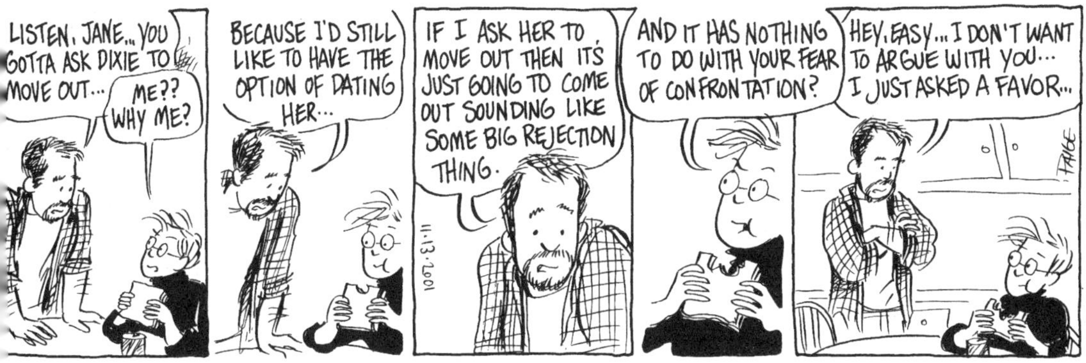
LISTEN, JANE... YOU GOTTA ASK DIXIE TO MOVE OUT...
ME?? WHY ME?
BECAUSE I'D STILL LIKE TO HAVE THE OPTION OF DATING HER...
IF I ASK HER TO MOVE OUT THEN IT'S JUST GOING TO COME OUT SOUNDING LIKE SOME BIG REJECTION THING.
11·13·2001
AND IT HAS NOTHING TO DO WITH YOUR FEAR OF CONFRONTATION?
HEY, EASY... I DON'T WANT TO ARGUE WITH YOU... I JUST ASKED A FAVOR...
PAIGE

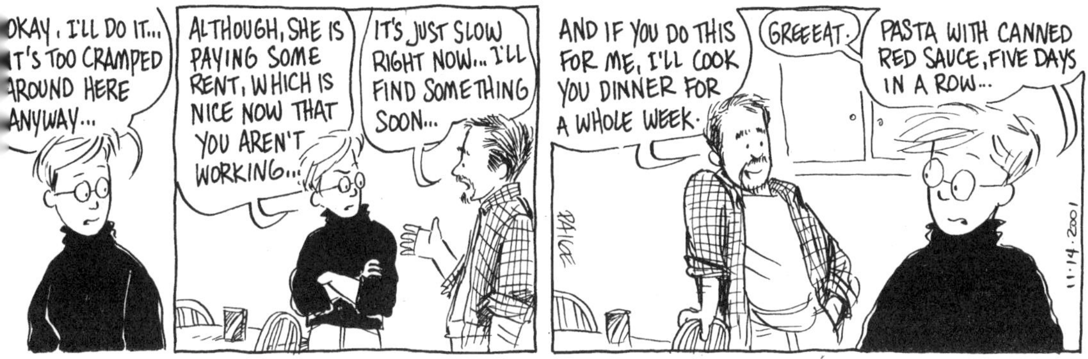
OKAY, I'LL DO IT... IT'S TOO CRAMPED AROUND HERE ANYWAY...
ALTHOUGH, SHE IS PAYING SOME RENT, WHICH IS NICE NOW THAT YOU AREN'T WORKING...
IT'S JUST SLOW RIGHT NOW... I'LL FIND SOMETHING SOON...
PAIGE
AND IF YOU DO THIS FOR ME, I'LL COOK YOU DINNER FOR A WHOLE WEEK.
GREEEAT.
PASTA WITH CANNED RED SAUCE, FIVE DAYS IN A ROW...
11·14·2001

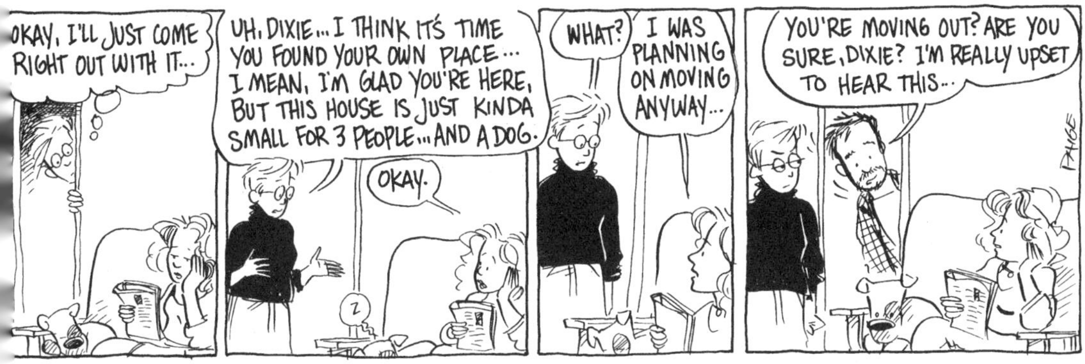
OKAY, I'LL JUST COME RIGHT OUT WITH IT...
UH, DIXIE... I THINK IT'S TIME YOU FOUND YOUR OWN PLACE... I MEAN, I'M GLAD YOU'RE HERE, BUT THIS HOUSE IS JUST KINDA SMALL FOR 3 PEOPLE... AND A DOG.
OKAY.
WHAT?
I WAS PLANNING ON MOVING ANYWAY...
YOU'RE MOVING OUT? ARE YOU SURE, DIXIE? I'M REALLY UPSET TO HEAR THIS...
PAIGE

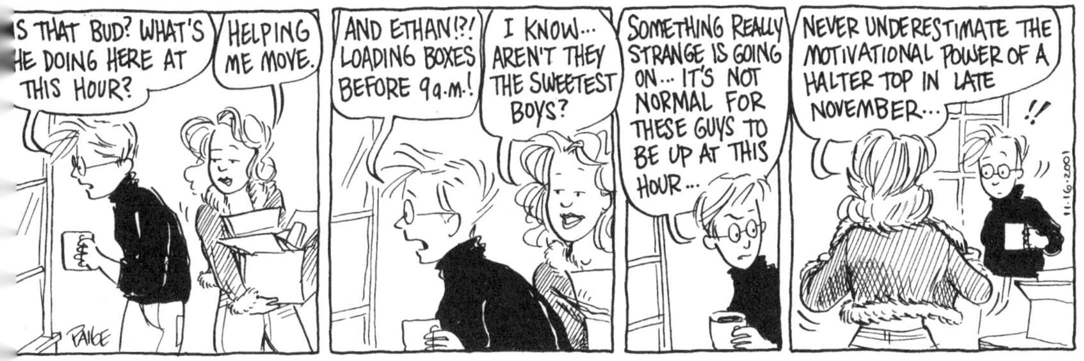
IS THAT BUD? WHAT'S HE DOING HERE AT THIS HOUR?
HELPING ME MOVE.
PAIGE
AND ETHAN!?! LOADING BOXES BEFORE 9 a.m.!
I KNOW... AREN'T THEY THE SWEETEST BOYS?
SOMETHING REALLY STRANGE IS GOING ON... IT'S NOT NORMAL FOR THESE GUYS TO BE UP AT THIS HOUR...
NEVER UNDERESTIMATE THE MOTIVATIONAL POWER OF A HALTER TOP IN LATE NOVEMBER...
!!
11·16·2001

After the move, at Bud's place....

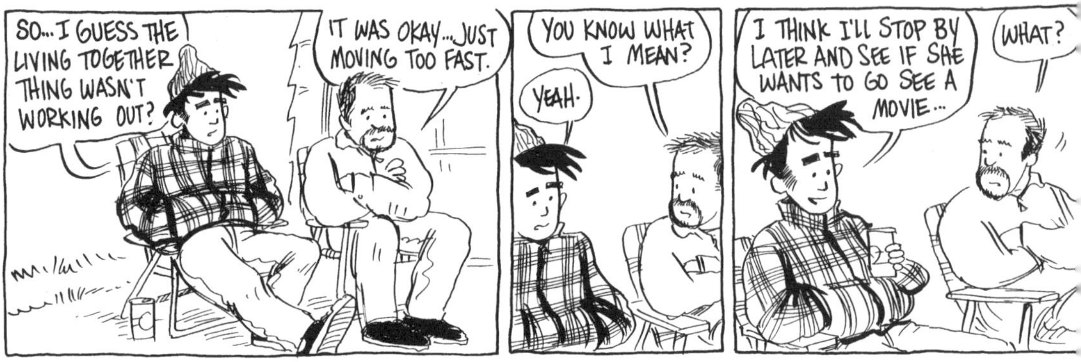
SO... I GUESS THE LIVING TOGETHER THING WASN'T WORKING OUT?
IT WAS OKAY... JUST MOVING TOO FAST.
YOU KNOW WHAT I MEAN?
YEAH.
I THINK I'LL STOP BY LATER AND SEE IF SHE WANTS TO GO SEE A MOVIE...
WHAT?

...and then later, at the cafe...

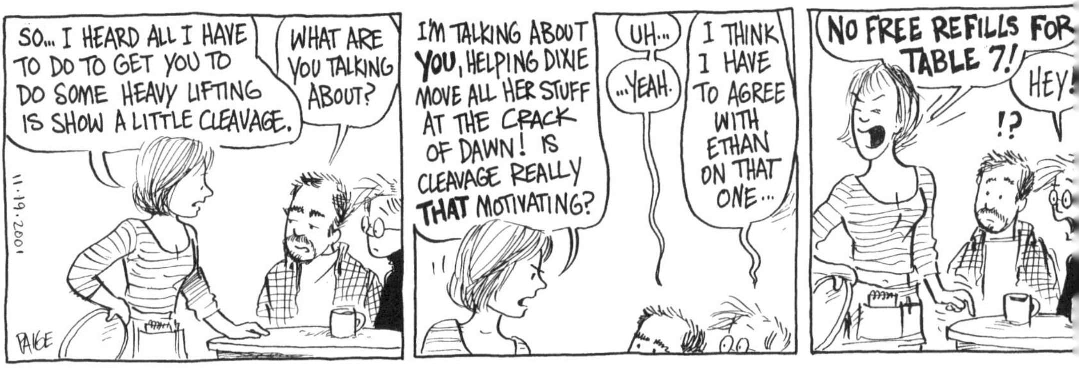
SO... I HEARD ALL I HAVE TO DO TO GET YOU TO DO SOME HEAVY LIFTING IS SHOW A LITTLE CLEAVAGE.
WHAT ARE YOU TALKING ABOUT?
11·19·2001
PAIGE
I'M TALKING ABOUT YOU, HELPING DIXIE MOVE ALL HER STUFF AT THE CRACK OF DAWN! IS CLEAVAGE REALLY THAT MOTIVATING?
UH...
...YEAH.
I THINK I HAVE TO AGREE WITH ETHAN ON THAT ONE...
NO FREE REFILLS FOR TABLE 7!
HEY!
!?

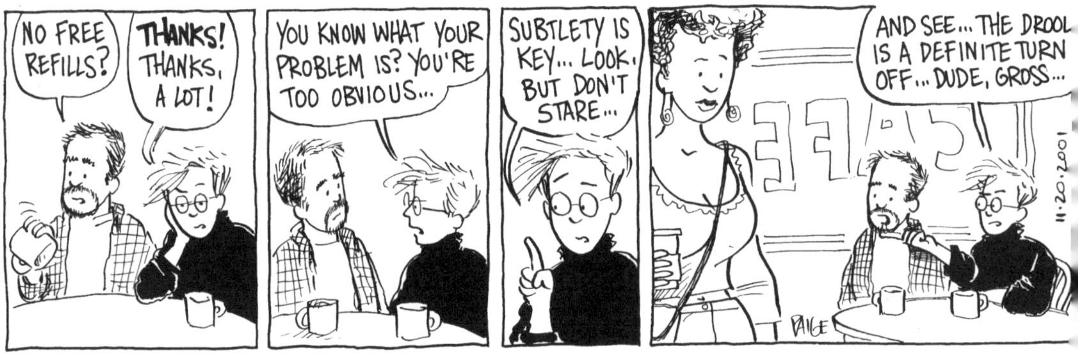
NO FREE REFILLS?
THANKS! THANKS, A LOT!
YOU KNOW WHAT YOUR PROBLEM IS? YOU'RE TOO OBVIOUS...
SUBTLETY IS KEY... LOOK, BUT DON'T STARE...
AND SEE... THE DROOL IS A DEFINITE TURN OFF... DUDE, GROSS...
11·20·2001
PAIGE

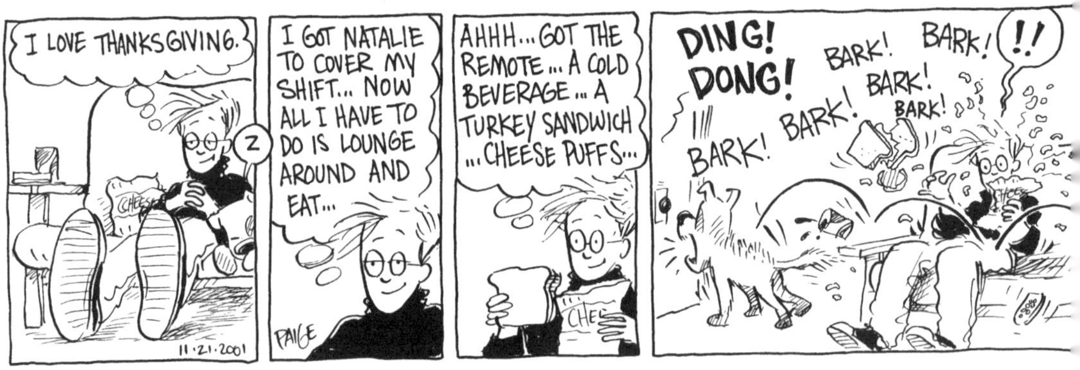
I LOVE THANKSGIVING.
Z
11·21·2001
I GOT NATALIE TO COVER MY SHIFT... NOW ALL I HAVE TO DO IS LOUNGE AROUND AND EAT...
PAIGE
AHHH... GOT THE REMOTE... A COLD BEVERAGE... A TURKEY SANDWICH ...CHEESE PUFFS...
DING! DONG!
BARK! BARK! BARK! BARK! BARK! BARK!
!!

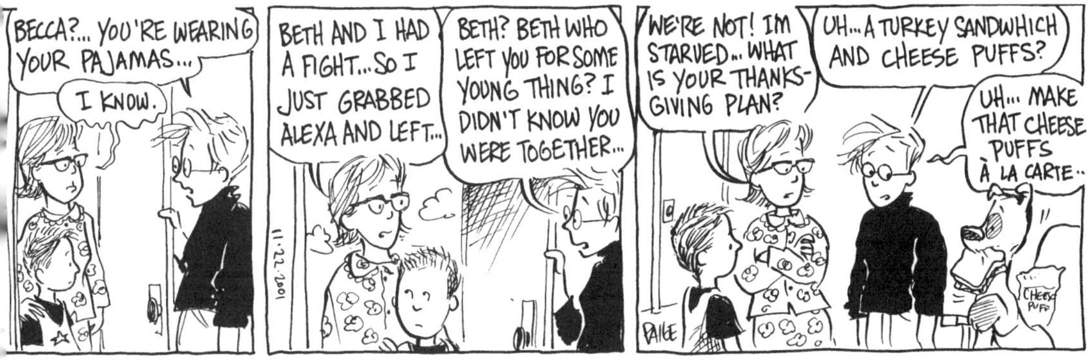
BECCA?... YOU'RE WEARING YOUR PAJAMAS...
I KNOW.
BETH AND I HAD A FIGHT... SO I JUST GRABBED ALEXA AND LEFT...
BETH? BETH WHO LEFT YOU FOR SOME YOUNG THING? I DIDN'T KNOW YOU WERE TOGETHER...
11·22·2001
WE'RE NOT! I'M STARVED... WHAT IS YOUR THANKSGIVING PLAN?
UH... A TURKEY SANDWHICH AND CHEESE PUFFS?
UH... MAKE THAT CHEESE PUFFS À LA CARTE..
CHEESE PUFFS
PAIGE

'he next day, the Thanksgiving-family-invasion continues...

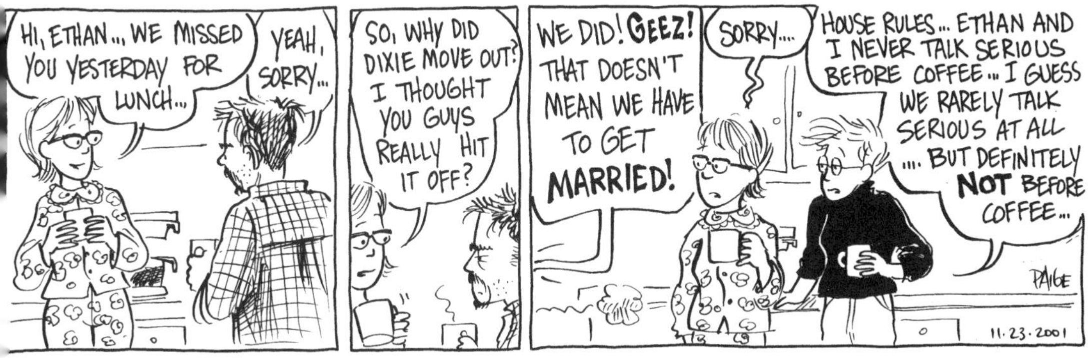
HI, ETHAN... WE MISSED YOU YESTERDAY FOR LUNCH...
YEAH, SORRY...
SO, WHY DID DIXIE MOVE OUT? I THOUGHT YOU GUYS REALLY HIT IT OFF?
WE DID! GEEZ! THAT DOESN'T MEAN WE HAVE TO GET MARRIED!
SORRY....
HOUSE RULES... ETHAN AND I NEVER TALK SERIOUS BEFORE COFFEE... I GUESS WE RARELY TALK SERIOUS AT ALL .... BUT DEFINITELY NOT BEFORE COFFEE...
PAIGE
11·23·2001

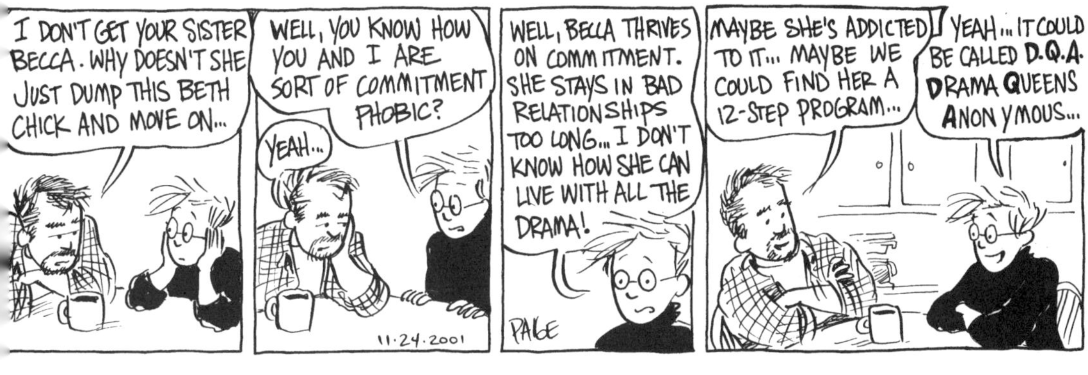
I DON'T GET YOUR SISTER BECCA. WHY DOESN'T SHE JUST DUMP THIS BETH CHICK AND MOVE ON...
WELL, YOU KNOW HOW YOU AND I ARE SORT OF COMMITMENT PHOBIC?
YEAH...
11·24·2001
WELL, BECCA THRIVES ON COMMITMENT. SHE STAYS IN BAD RELATIONSHIPS TOO LONG... I DON'T KNOW HOW SHE CAN LIVE WITH ALL THE DRAMA!
PAIGE
MAYBE SHE'S ADDICTED TO IT... MAYBE WE COULD FIND HER A 12-STEP PROGRAM...
YEAH... IT COULD BE CALLED D.Q.A. DRAMA QUEENS ANONYMOUS...

'ater that week, Jane takes the plunge...

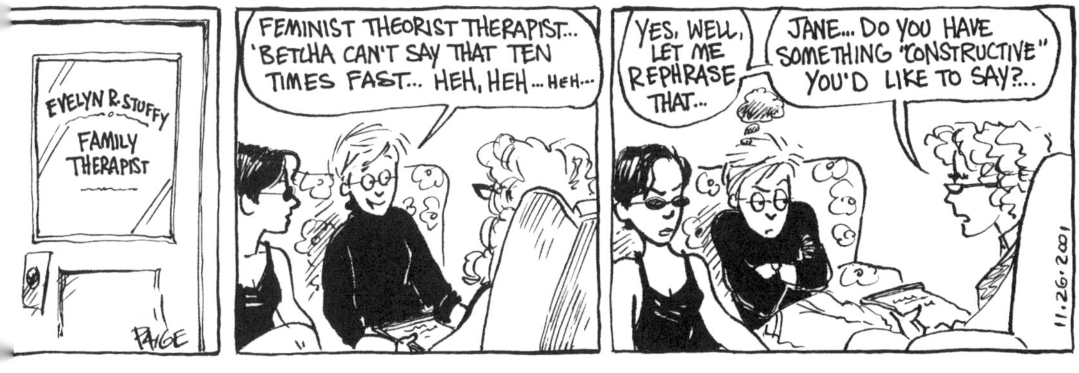
EVELYN R. STUFFY
FAMILY THERAPIST
PAIGE
FEMINIST THEORIST THERAPIST... 'BETCHA CAN'T SAY THAT TEN TIMES FAST... HEH, HEH... HEH...
YES, WELL, LET ME REPHRASE THAT...
JANE... DO YOU HAVE SOMETHING "CONSTRUCTIVE" YOU'D LIKE TO SAY?...
11·26·2001

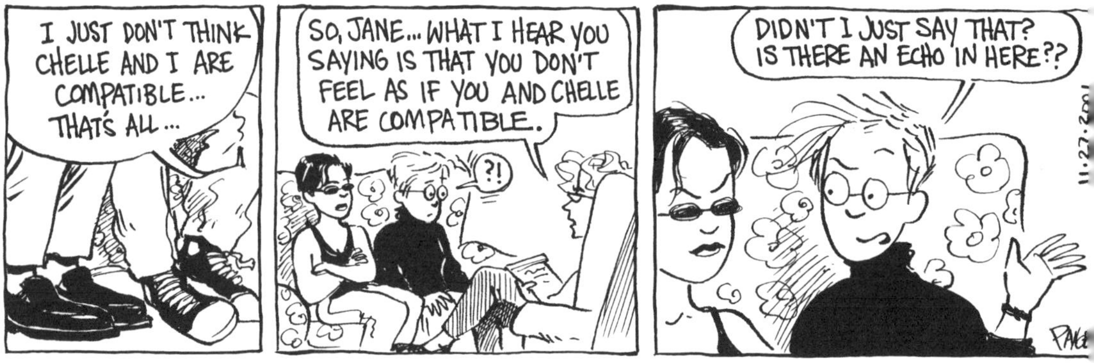
I JUST DON'T THINK CHELLE AND I ARE COMPATIBLE... THAT'S ALL...
SO, JANE... WHAT I HEAR YOU SAYING IS THAT YOU DON'T FEEL AS IF YOU AND CHELLE ARE COMPATIBLE.
?!
DIDN'T I JUST SAY THAT? IS THERE AN ECHO IN HERE??
11·27·2001

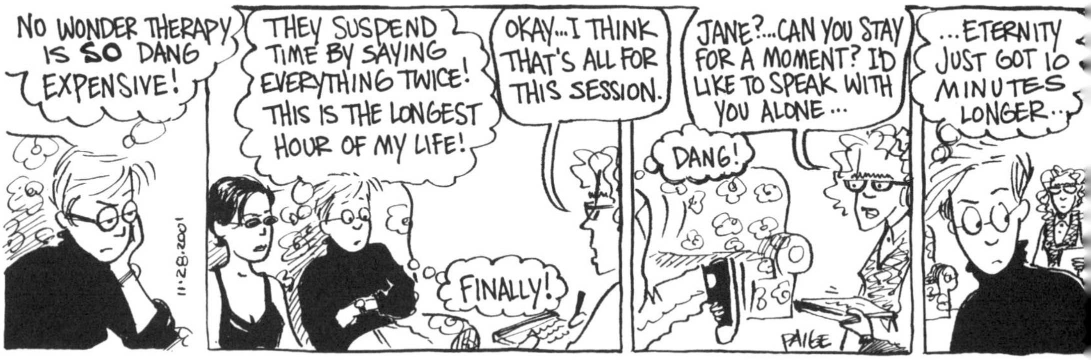
NO WONDER THERAPY IS SO DANG EXPENSIVE!
11·28·2001
THEY SUSPEND TIME BY SAYING EVERYTHING TWICE! THIS IS THE LONGEST HOUR OF MY LIFE!
OKAY... I THINK THAT'S ALL FOR THIS SESSION.
FINALLY!
JANE?... CAN YOU STAY FOR A MOMENT? I'D LIKE TO SPEAK WITH YOU ALONE...
DANG!
PAIGE
...ETERNITY JUST GOT 10 MINUTES LONGER...

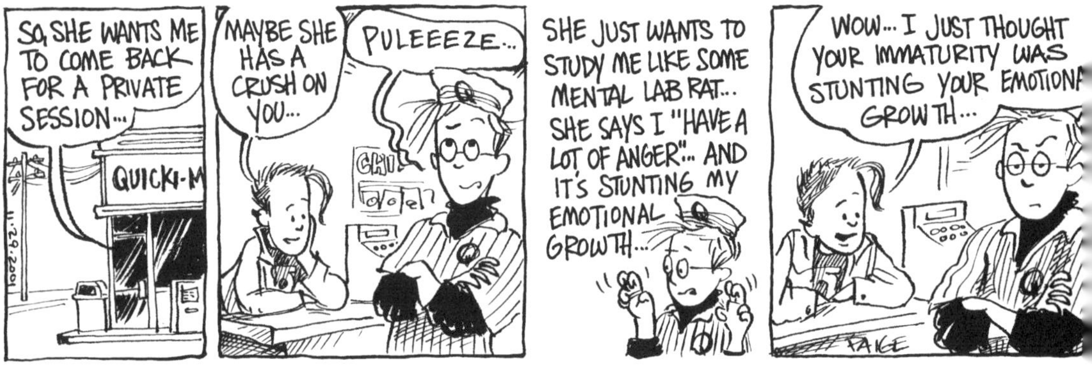
SO, SHE WANTS ME TO COME BACK FOR A PRIVATE SESSION...
QUICKI-M
11·29·2001
MAYBE SHE HAS A CRUSH ON YOU...
PULEEEEZE...
SHE JUST WANTS TO STUDY ME LIKE SOME MENTAL LAB RAT... SHE SAYS I "HAVE A LOT OF ANGER"... AND IT'S STUNTING MY EMOTIONAL GROWTH...
WOW... I JUST THOUGHT YOUR IMMATURITY WAS STUNTING YOUR EMOTIONA GROWTH...
PAIGE

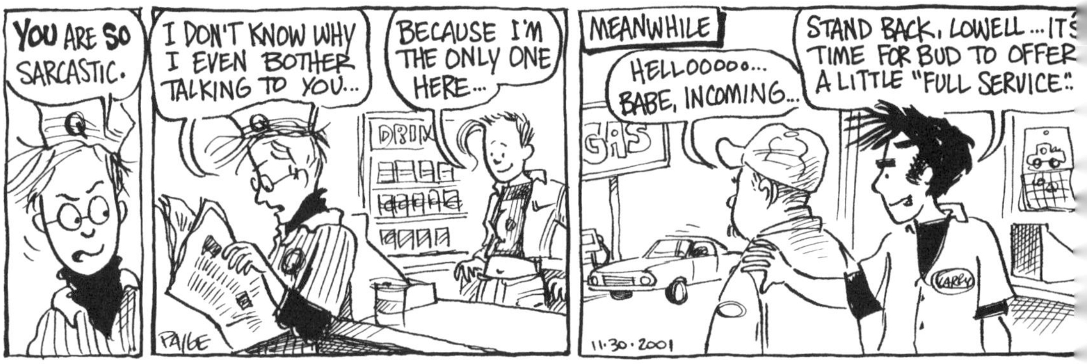
YOU ARE SO SARCASTIC.
I DON'T KNOW WHY I EVEN BOTHER TALKING TO YOU...
BECAUSE I'M THE ONLY ONE HERE...
PAIGE
MEANWHILE
HELLOOOOO... BABE, INCOMING...
STAND BACK, LOWELL... IT'S TIME FOR BUD TO OFFER A LITTLE "FULL SERVICE."
GAS
11·30·2001

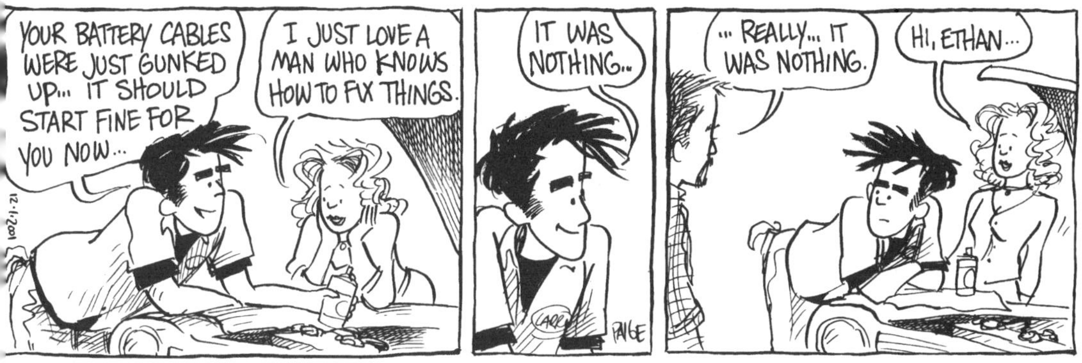
YOUR BATTERY CABLES WERE JUST GUNKED UP... IT SHOULD START FINE FOR YOU NOW...
I JUST LOVE A MAN WHO KNOWS HOW TO FIX THINGS.
12·1·2001
IT WAS NOTHING..
PAIGE
... REALLY... IT WAS NOTHING.
HI, ETHAN...

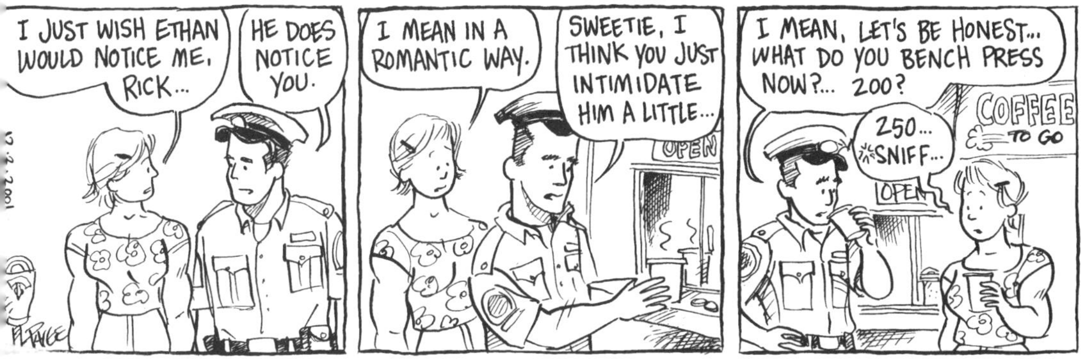
I JUST WISH ETHAN WOULD NOTICE ME, RICK...
HE DOES NOTICE YOU.
I MEAN IN A ROMANTIC WAY.
SWEETIE, I THINK YOU JUST INTIMIDATE HIM A LITTLE...
OPEN
I MEAN, LET'S BE HONEST... WHAT DO YOU BENCH PRESS NOW?... 200?
250... *SNIFF...
COFFEE TO GO
OPEN

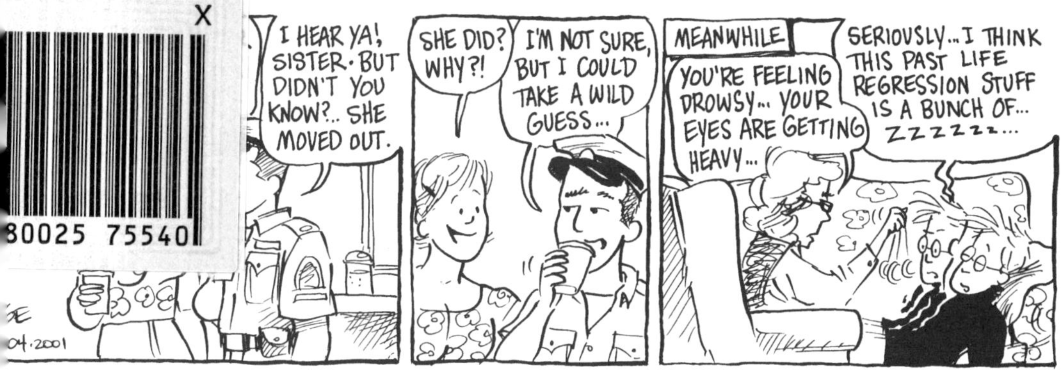
I HEAR YA! SISTER. BUT DIDN'T YOU KNOW?.. SHE MOVED OUT.
SHE DID? WHY?!
I'M NOT SURE, BUT I COULD TAKE A WILD GUESS...
MEANWHILE
YOU'RE FEELING DROWSY... YOUR EYES ARE GETTING HEAVY...
SERIOUSLY... I THINK THIS PAST LIFE REGRESSION STUFF IS A BUNCH OF... ZZZZZZ...

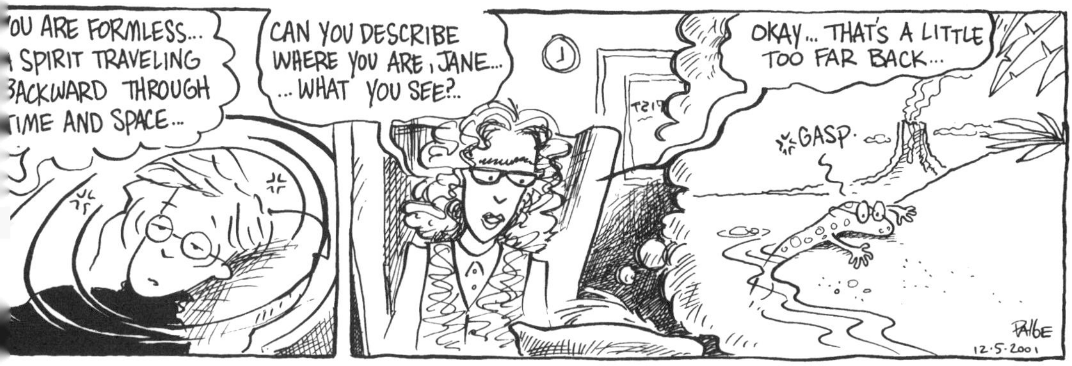
OU ARE FORMLESS... SPIRIT TRAVELING ACKWARD THROUGH IME AND SPACE...
CAN YOU DESCRIBE WHERE YOU ARE, JANE... ... WHAT YOU SEE?..
OKAY... THAT'S A LITTLE TOO FAR BACK...
GASP
PAIGE
12·5·2001

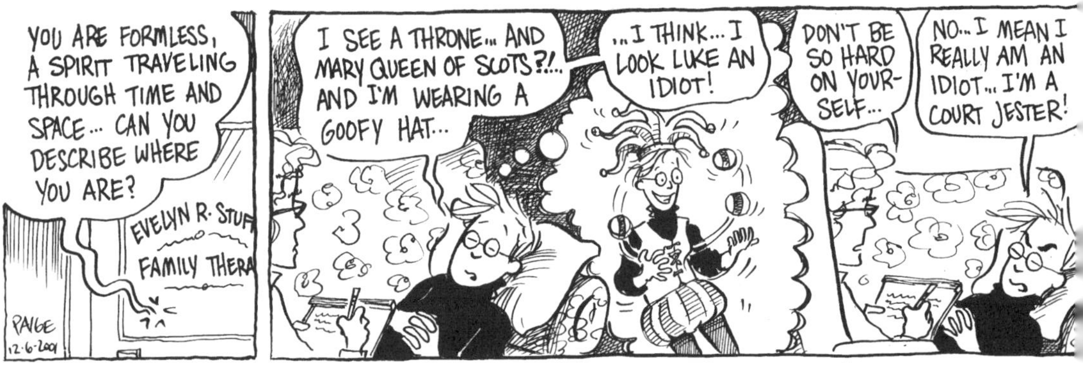
YOU ARE FORMLESS, A SPIRIT TRAVELING THROUGH TIME AND SPACE... CAN YOU DESCRIBE WHERE YOU ARE?
EVELYN R. STUF
FAMILY THERA
PAIGE
12·6·2001
I SEE A THRONE... AND MARY QUEEN OF SCOTS?!... AND I'M WEARING A GOOFY HAT...
...I THINK... I LOOK LIKE AN IDIOT!
DON'T BE SO HARD ON YOURSELF...
NO... I MEAN I REALLY AM AN IDIOT... I'M A COURT JESTER!

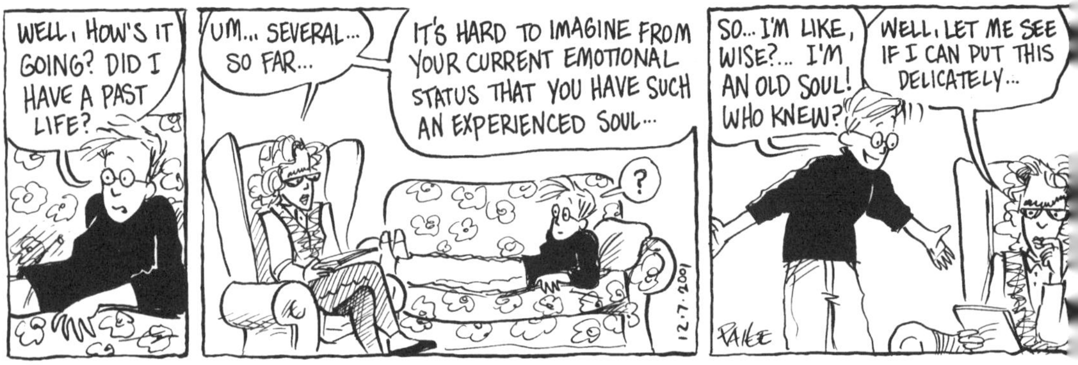
WELL, HOW'S IT GOING? DID I HAVE A PAST LIFE?
UM... SEVERAL... SO FAR...
IT'S HARD TO IMAGINE FROM YOUR CURRENT EMOTIONAL STATUS THAT YOU HAVE SUCH AN EXPERIENCED SOUL...
?
12·7·2001
SO... I'M LIKE, WISE?... I'M AN OLD SOUL! WHO KNEW?
WELL, LET ME SEE IF I CAN PUT THIS DELICATELY...
PAIGE

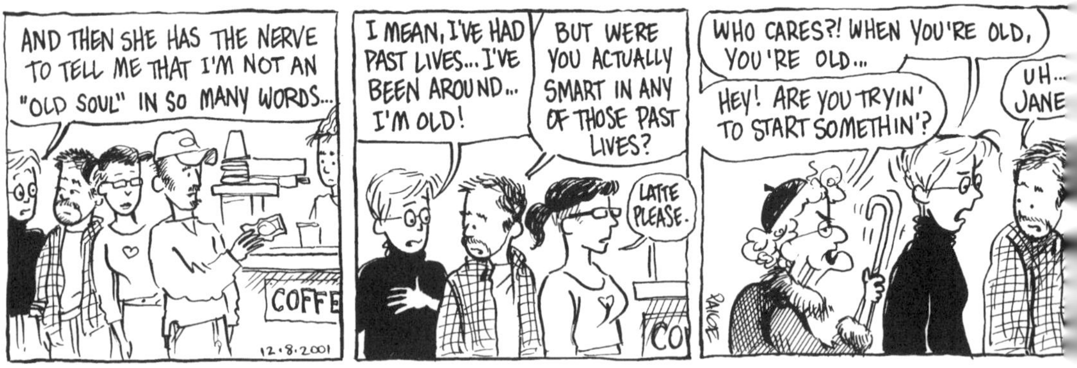
AND THEN SHE HAS THE NERVE TO TELL ME THAT I'M NOT AN "OLD SOUL" IN SO MANY WORDS...
COFFE
12·8·2001
I MEAN, I'VE HAD PAST LIVES... I'VE BEEN AROUND... I'M OLD!
BUT WERE YOU ACTUALLY SMART IN ANY OF THOSE PAST LIVES?
LATTE PLEASE.
CO
WHO CARES?! WHEN YOU'RE OLD, YOU'RE OLD...
HEY! ARE YOU TRYIN' TO START SOMETHIN'?
UH... JANE
PAIGE

Back in therapy, a few days later...

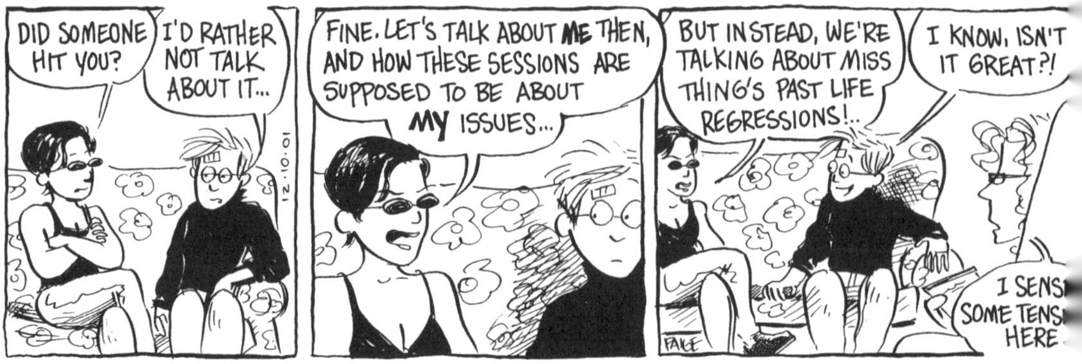
DID SOMEONE HIT YOU?
I'D RATHER NOT TALK ABOUT IT...
12·10·01
FINE. LET'S TALK ABOUT ME THEN, AND HOW THESE SESSIONS ARE SUPPOSED TO BE ABOUT MY ISSUES...
BUT INSTEAD, WE'RE TALKING ABOUT MISS THING'S PAST LIFE REGRESSIONS!..
I KNOW, ISN'T IT GREAT?!
I SENS SOME TENS HERE
PAIGE

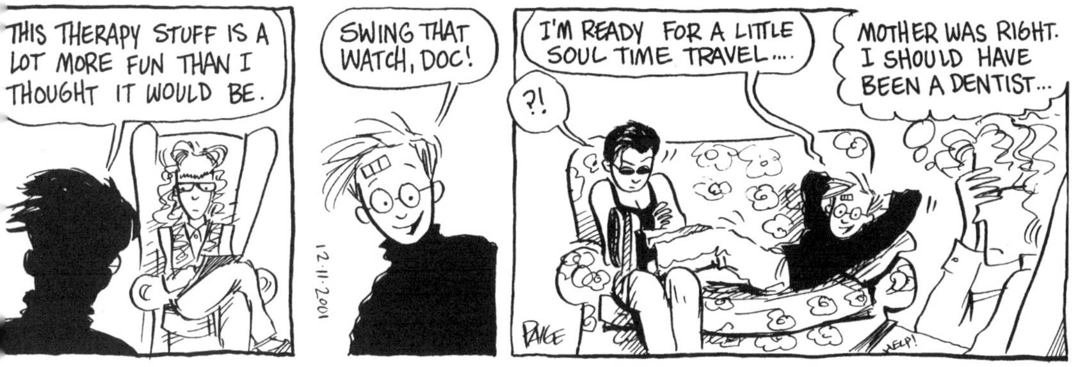
THIS THERAPY STUFF IS A LOT MORE FUN THAN I THOUGHT IT WOULD BE.
12·11·2001
SWING THAT WATCH, DOC!
I'M READY FOR A LITTLE SOUL TIME TRAVEL....
?!
MOTHER WAS RIGHT. I SHOULD HAVE BEEN A DENTIST...
PAIGE
HELP!

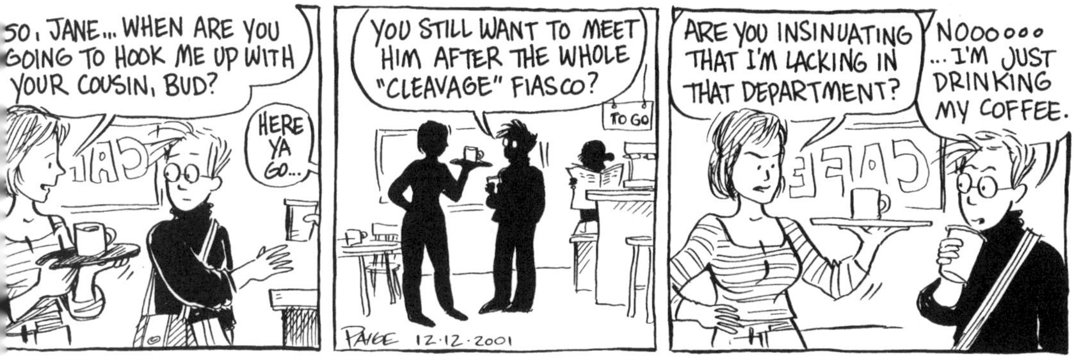
SO, JANE... WHEN ARE YOU GOING TO HOOK ME UP WITH YOUR COUSIN, BUD?
HERE YA GO...
YOU STILL WANT TO MEET HIM AFTER THE WHOLE "CLEAVAGE" FIASCO?
TO GO
PAIGE 12·12·2001
ARE YOU INSINUATING THAT I'M LACKING IN THAT DEPARTMENT?
NOOOooo ...I'M JUST DRINKING MY COFFEE.

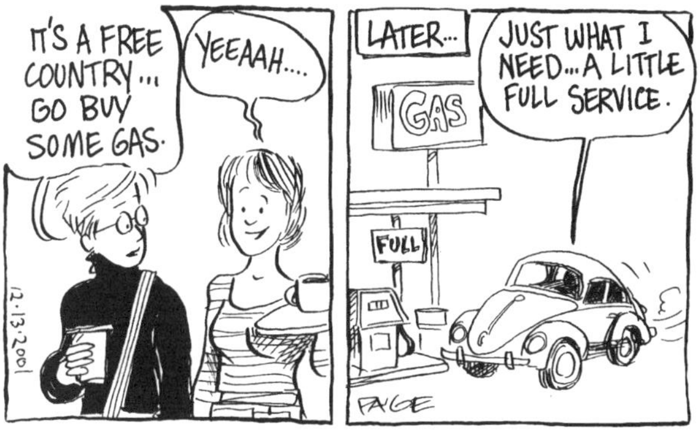
IT'S A FREE COUNTRY... GO BUY SOME GAS.
YEEAAH....
12·13·2001
LATER...
JUST WHAT I NEED...A LITTLE FULL SERVICE.
GAS
FULL
PAIGE

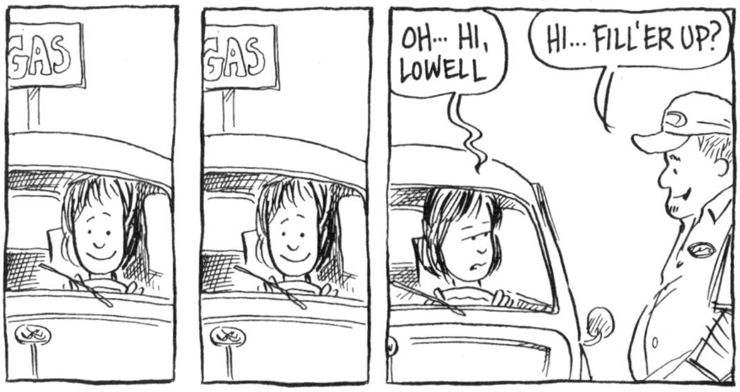
GAS
GAS
OH... HI, LOWELL
HI... FILL'ER UP?

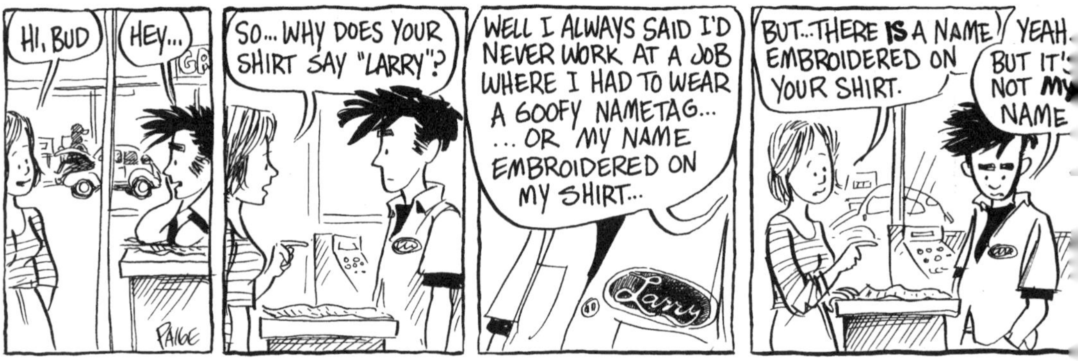
HI, BUD
HEY...
SO... WHY DOES YOUR SHIRT SAY "LARRY"?
WELL I ALWAYS SAID I'D NEVER WORK AT A JOB WHERE I HAD TO WEAR A GOOFY NAMETAG... ... OR MY NAME EMBROIDERED ON MY SHIRT...
Larry
BUT...THERE **IS** A NAME EMBROIDERED ON YOUR SHIRT.
YEAH... BUT IT'S NOT **MY** NAME
PAIGE

Meanwhile...

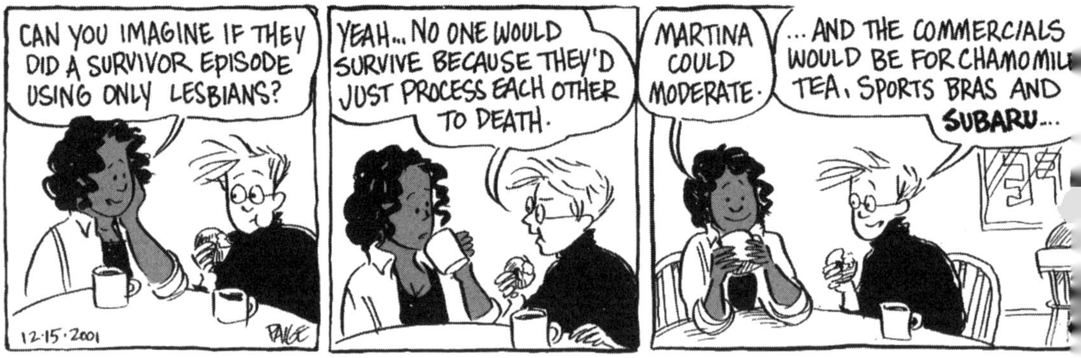
CAN YOU IMAGINE IF THEY DID A SURVIVOR EPISODE USING ONLY LESBIANS?
YEAH... NO ONE WOULD SURVIVE BECAUSE THEY'D JUST PROCESS EACH OTHER TO DEATH.
MARTINA COULD MODERATE.
... AND THE COMMERCIALS WOULD BE FOR CHAMOMILE TEA, SPORTS BRAS AND **SUBARU**...
12·15·2001
PAIGE

...and now, a little belated Christmas cheer, "Peanuts" style...

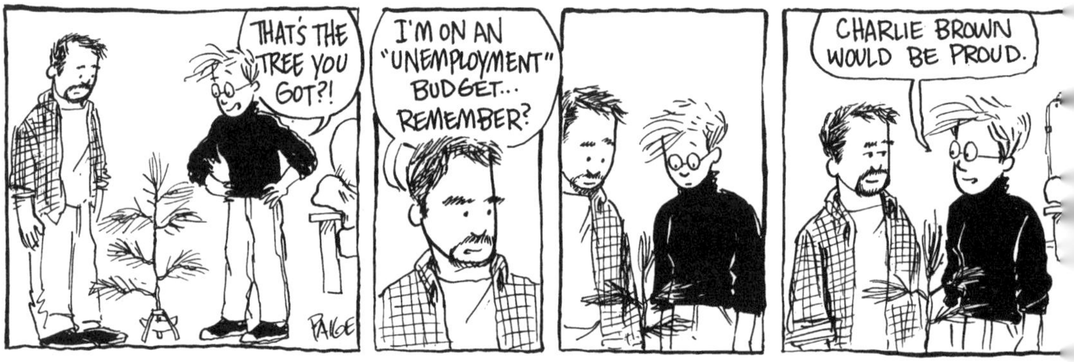
THAT'S THE TREE YOU GOT?!
I'M ON AN "UNEMPLOYMENT" BUDGET... REMEMBER?
CHARLIE BROWN WOULD BE PROUD.
PAIGE

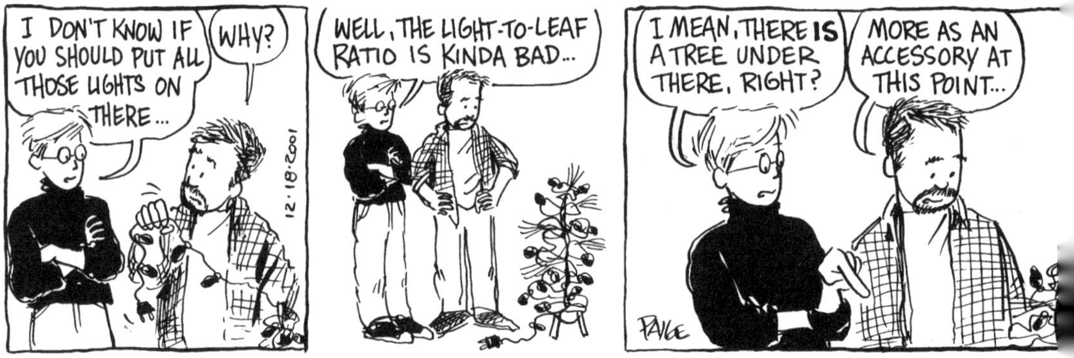
I DON'T KNOW IF YOU SHOULD PUT ALL THOSE LIGHTS ON THERE...
WHY?
12·18·2001
WELL, THE LIGHT-TO-LEAF RATIO IS KINDA BAD...
I MEAN, THERE **IS** A TREE UNDER THERE, RIGHT?
MORE AS AN ACCESSORY AT THIS POINT...
PAIGE

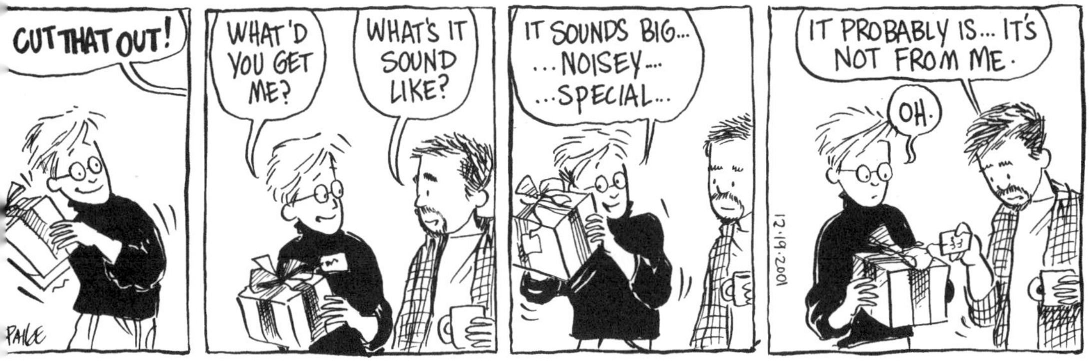
CUT THAT OUT!
PAIGE
WHAT'D YOU GET ME?
WHAT'S IT SOUND LIKE?
IT SOUNDS BIG... ...NOISEY... ...SPECIAL...
12·19·2001
IT PROBABLY IS... IT'S NOT FROM ME.
OH.

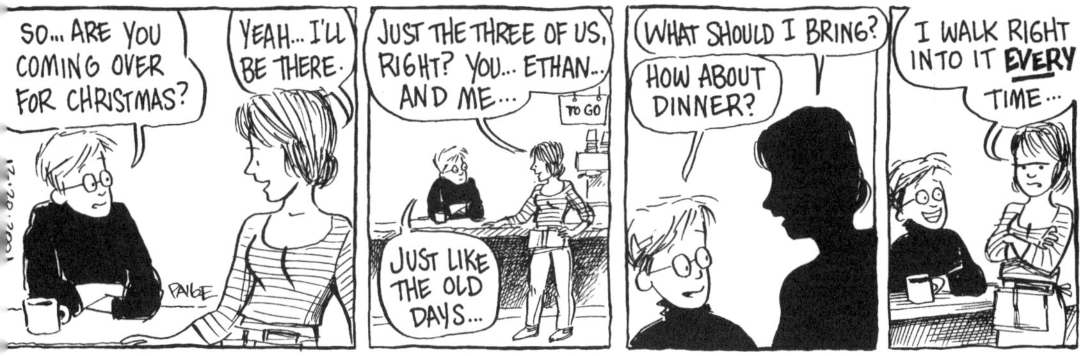
SO... ARE YOU COMING OVER FOR CHRISTMAS?
YEAH... I'LL BE THERE.
12·20·2001
PAIGE
JUST THE THREE OF US, RIGHT? YOU... ETHAN... AND ME...
TO GO
JUST LIKE THE OLD DAYS...
WHAT SHOULD I BRING?
HOW ABOUT DINNER?
I WALK RIGHT INTO IT **EVERY** TIME...

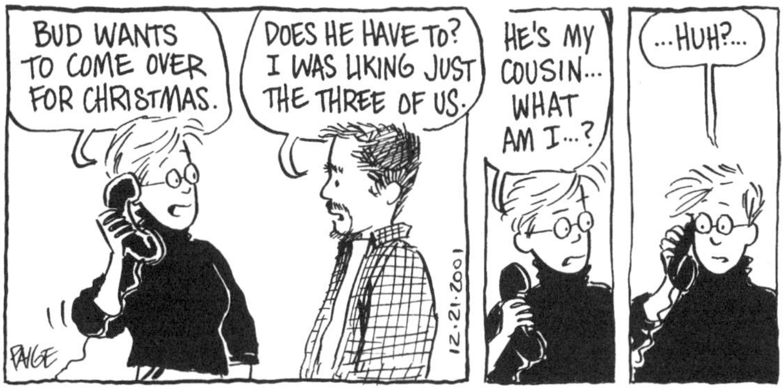
BUD WANTS TO COME OVER FOR CHRISTMAS.
DOES HE HAVE TO? I WAS LIKING JUST THE THREE OF US.
PAIGE
12·21·2001
HE'S MY COUSIN... WHAT AM I...?
...HUH?...

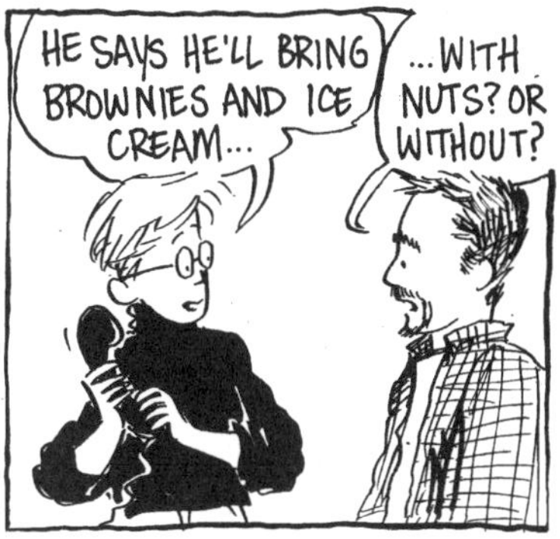
HE SAYS HE'LL BRING BROWNIES AND ICE CREAM...
...WITH NUTS? OR WITHOUT?

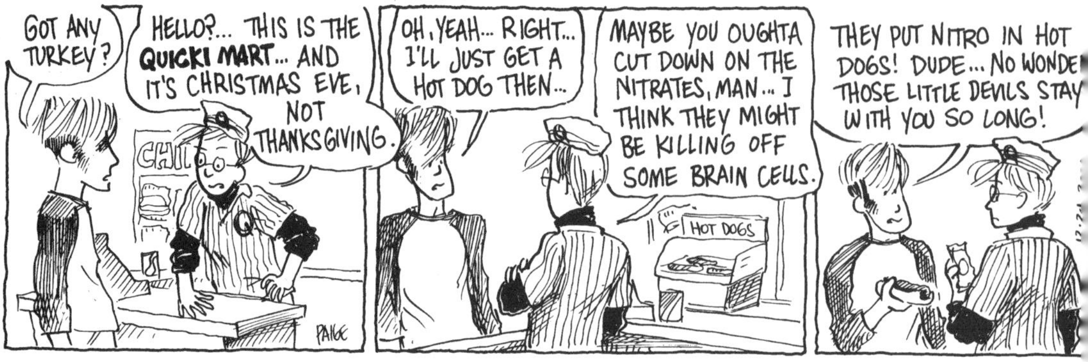
GOT ANY TURKEY?
HELLO?... THIS IS THE QUICKI MART... AND IT'S CHRISTMAS EVE, NOT THANKSGIVING.
OH, YEAH... RIGHT... I'LL JUST GET A HOT DOG THEN...
MAYBE YOU OUGHTA CUT DOWN ON THE NITRATES, MAN... I THINK THEY MIGHT BE KILLING OFF SOME BRAIN CELLS.
HOT DOGS
THEY PUT NITRO IN HOT DOGS! DUDE... NO WONDE
THOSE LITTLE DEVILS STAY WITH YOU SO LONG!
PAIGE

Later, back at Jane's...

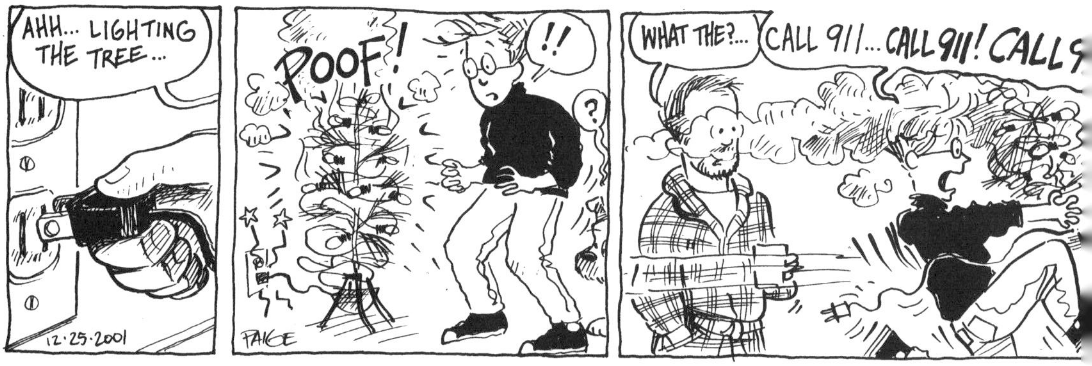
AHH... LIGHTING THE TREE...
12·25·2001
POOF!
!!
?
PAIGE
WHAT THE?...
CALL 911... CALL 911! CALL 9

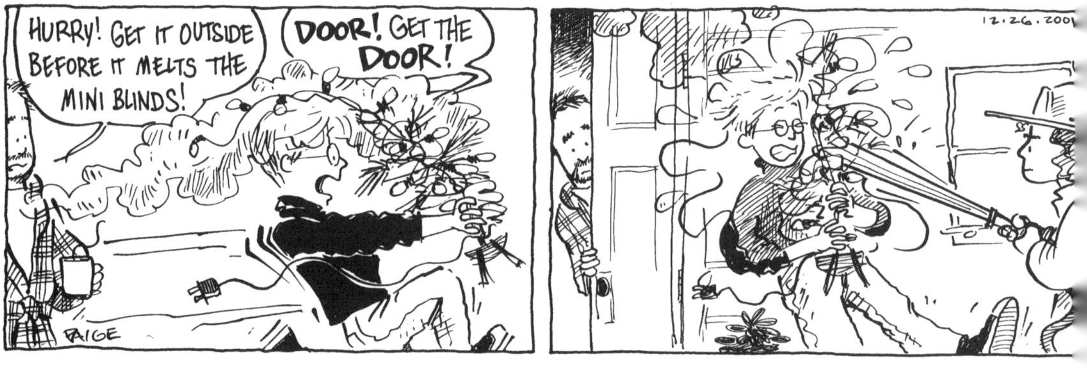
HURRY! GET IT OUTSIDE BEFORE IT MELTS THE MINI BLINDS!
DOOR! GET THE DOOR!
PAIGE
12·26·2001

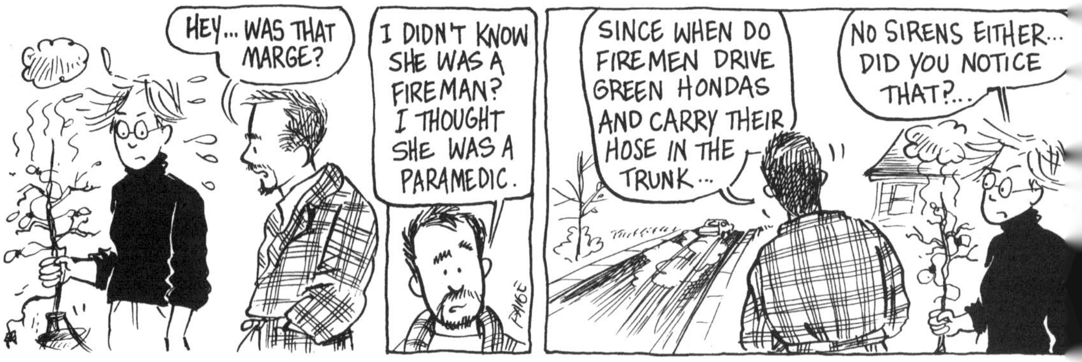
HEY... WAS THAT MARGE?
I DIDN'T KNOW SHE WAS A FIREMAN? I THOUGHT SHE WAS A PARAMEDIC.
PAIGE
SINCE WHEN DO FIREMEN DRIVE GREEN HONDAS AND CARRY THEIR HOSE IN THE TRUNK...
NO SIRENS EITHER... DID YOU NOTICE THAT?...

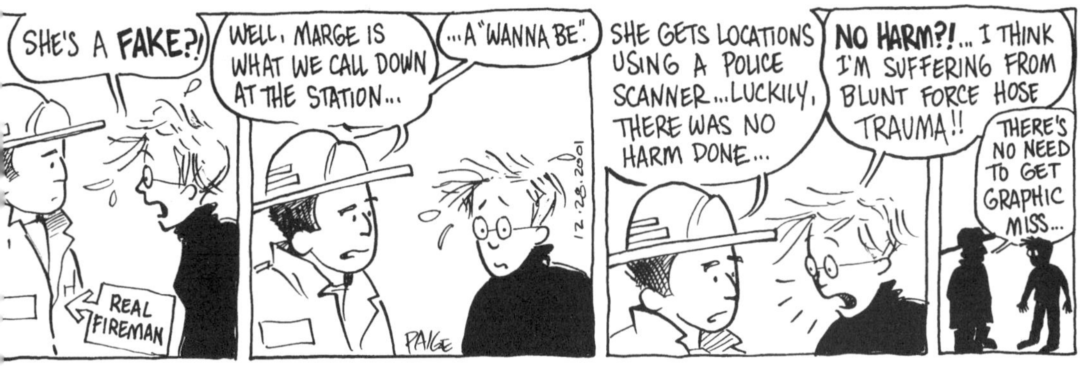
SHE'S A FAKE?!
WELL, MARGE IS WHAT WE CALL DOWN AT THE STATION...
...A "WANNA BE."
REAL FIREMAN
12.28.2001
PAIGE
SHE GETS LOCATIONS USING A POLICE SCANNER...LUCKILY, THERE WAS NO HARM DONE...
NO HARM?!... I THINK I'M SUFFERING FROM BLUNT FORCE HOSE TRAUMA!!
THERE'S NO NEED TO GET GRAPHIC MISS...

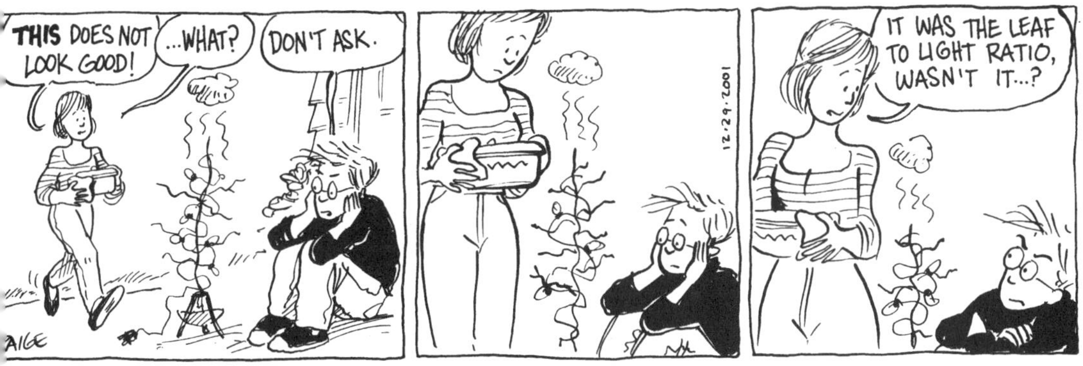
THIS DOES NOT LOOK GOOD!
...WHAT?
DON'T ASK.
PAIGE
12.29.2001
IT WAS THE LEAF TO LIGHT RATIO, WASN'T IT...?

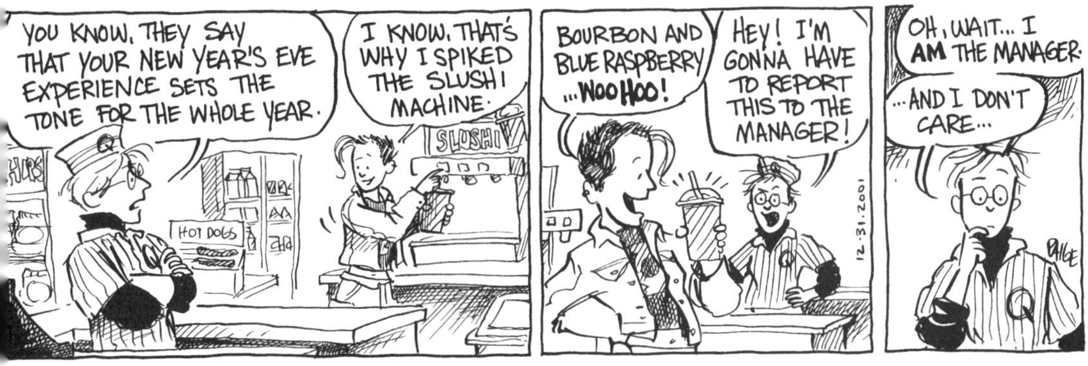
YOU KNOW, THEY SAY THAT YOUR NEW YEAR'S EVE EXPERIENCE SETS THE TONE FOR THE WHOLE YEAR.
I KNOW, THAT'S WHY I SPIKED THE SLUSHI MACHINE.
SLUSHI
HOT DOGS
BOURBON AND BLUE RASPBERRY ...WOO HOO!
HEY! I'M GONNA HAVE TO REPORT THIS TO THE MANAGER!
12.31.2001
OH, WAIT... I AM THE MANAGER.
...AND I DON'T CARE...
PAIGE

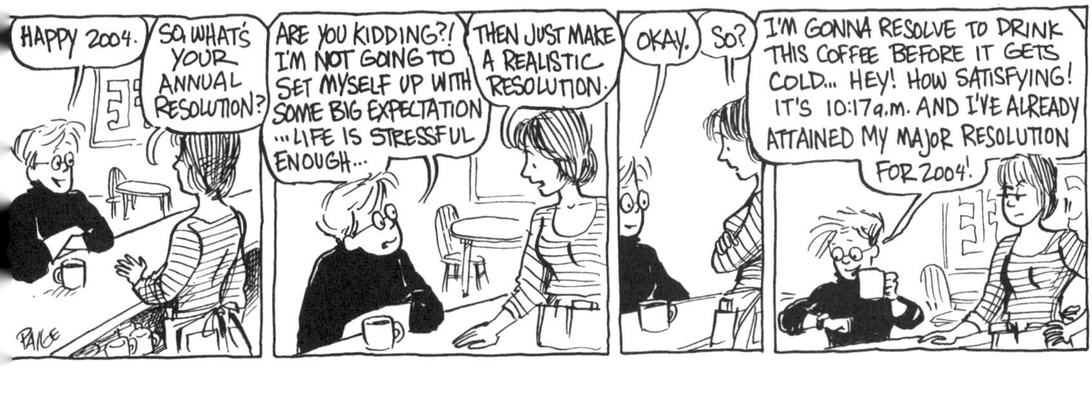
HAPPY 2004.
SO, WHAT'S YOUR ANNUAL RESOLUTION?
PAIGE
ARE YOU KIDDING?! I'M NOT GOING TO SET MYSELF UP WITH SOME BIG EXPECTATION ...LIFE IS STRESSFUL ENOUGH...
THEN JUST MAKE A REALISTIC RESOLUTION.
OKAY.
SO?
I'M GONNA RESOLVE TO DRINK THIS COFFEE BEFORE IT GETS COLD... HEY! HOW SATISFYING! IT'S 10:17a.m. AND I'VE ALREADY ATTAINED MY MAJOR RESOLUTION FOR 2004!

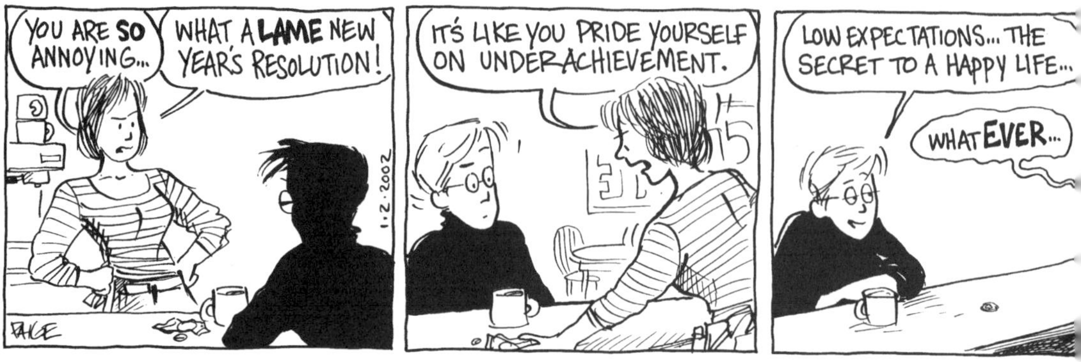
YOU ARE SO ANNOYING...
WHAT A LAME NEW YEAR'S RESOLUTION!
1·2·2002
IT'S LIKE YOU PRIDE YOURSELF ON UNDERACHIEVEMENT.
LOW EXPECTATIONS... THE SECRET TO A HAPPY LIFE...
WHATEVER...

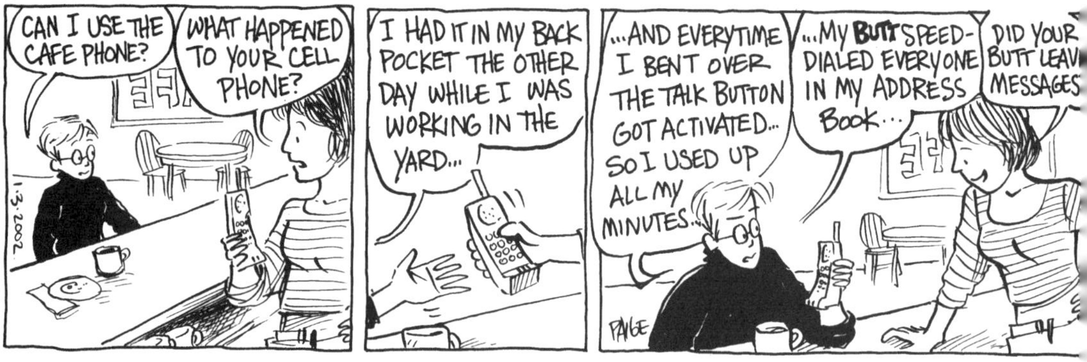
CAN I USE THE CAFE PHONE?
WHAT HAPPENED TO YOUR CELL PHONE?
1·3·2002
I HAD IT IN MY BACK POCKET THE OTHER DAY WHILE I WAS WORKING IN THE YARD...
...AND EVERYTIME I BENT OVER THE TALK BUTTON GOT ACTIVATED... SO I USED UP ALL MY MINUTES...
...MY BUTT SPEED-DIALED EVERYONE IN MY ADDRESS BOOK...
DID YOUR BUTT LEAV MESSAGES

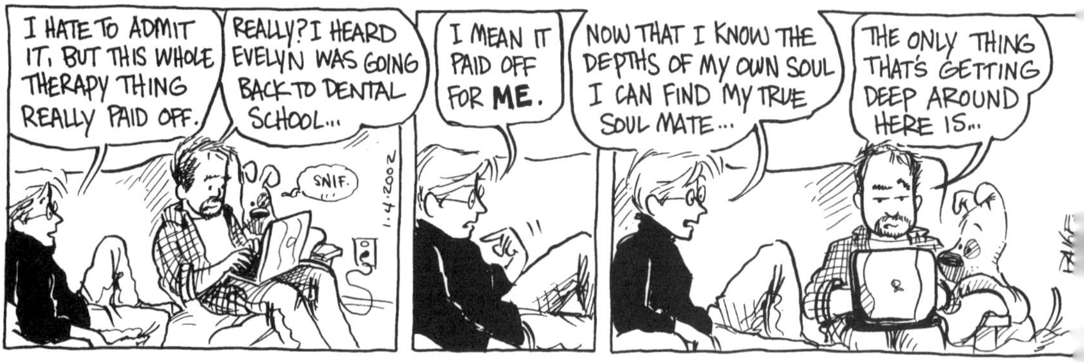
I HATE TO ADMIT IT, BUT THIS WHOLE THERAPY THING REALLY PAID OFF.
REALLY? I HEARD EVELYN WAS GOING BACK TO DENTAL SCHOOL...
SNIF.
1·4·2002
I MEAN IT PAID OFF FOR ME.
NOW THAT I KNOW THE DEPTHS OF MY OWN SOUL I CAN FIND MY TRUE SOUL MATE...
THE ONLY THING THAT'S GETTING DEEP AROUND HERE IS...

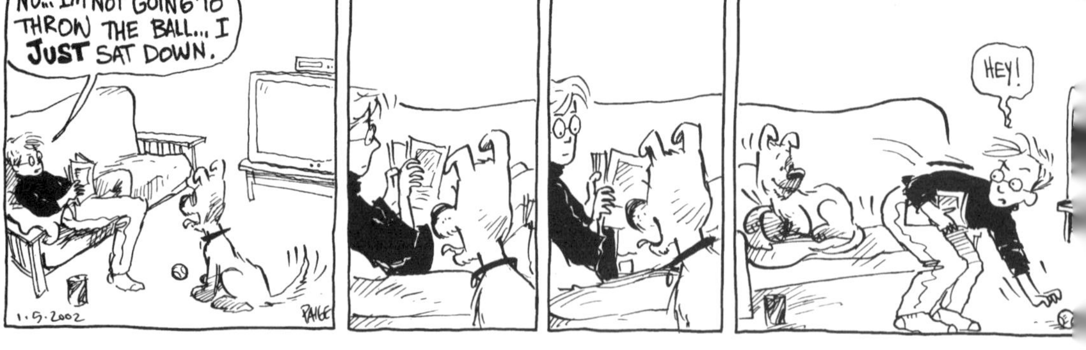
NO... I'M NOT GOING TO THROW THE BALL... I JUST SAT DOWN.
1·5·2002
HEY!

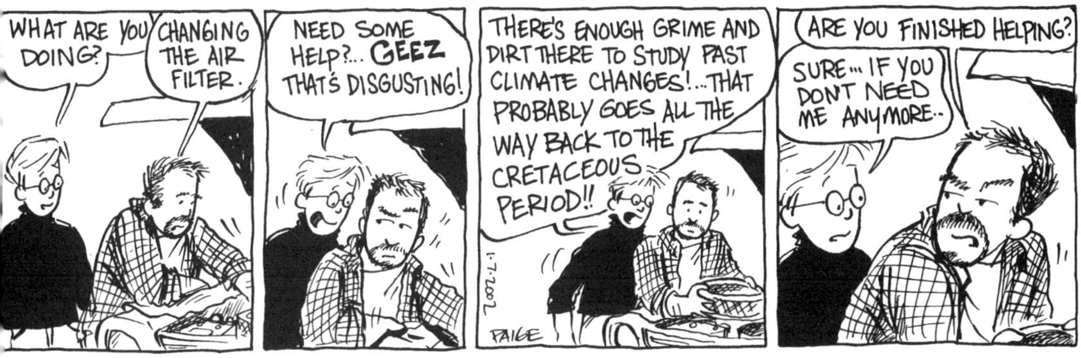
WHAT ARE YOU DOING?
CHANGING THE AIR FILTER.
NEED SOME HELP?... GEEZ THAT'S DISGUSTING!
THERE'S ENOUGH GRIME AND DIRT THERE TO STUDY PAST CLIMATE CHANGES!... THAT PROBABLY GOES ALL THE WAY BACK TO THE CRETACEOUS PERIOD!!
1·7·2002
PAIGE
ARE YOU FINISHED HELPING?
SURE... IF YOU DON'T NEED ME ANYMORE..

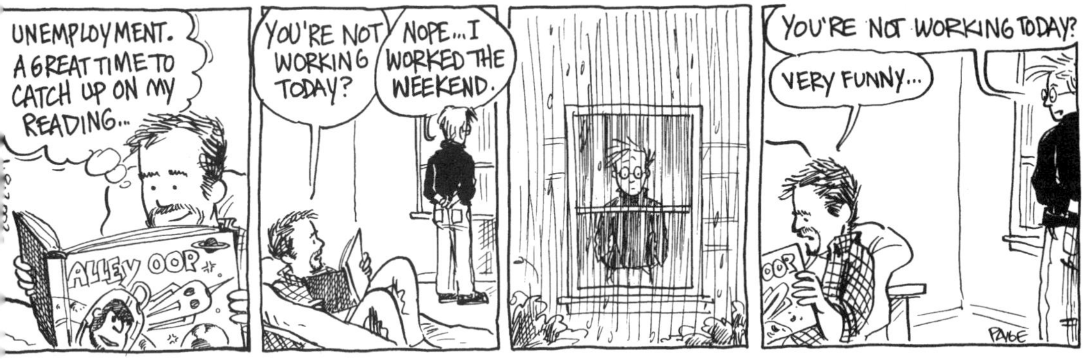
UNEMPLOYMENT. A GREAT TIME TO CATCH UP ON MY READING...
ALLEY OOP
YOU'RE NOT WORKING TODAY?
NOPE... I WORKED THE WEEKEND.
YOU'RE NOT WORKING TODAY?
VERY FUNNY...
OOP
PAIGE

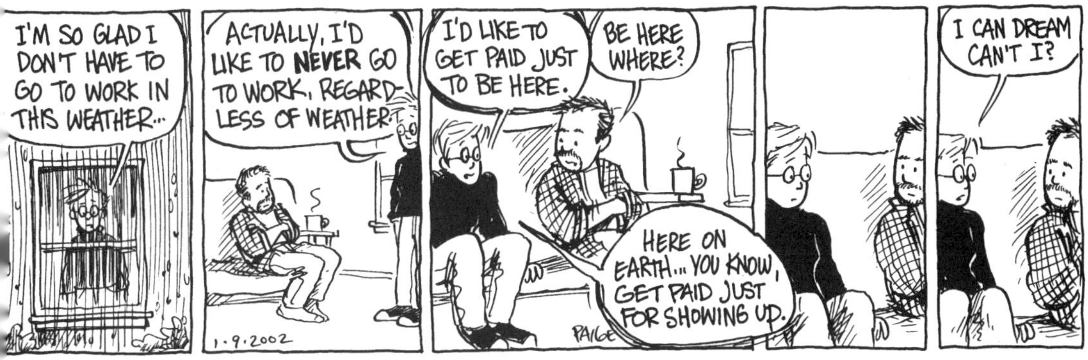
I'M SO GLAD I DON'T HAVE TO GO TO WORK IN THIS WEATHER...
ACTUALLY, I'D LIKE TO NEVER GO TO WORK, REGARDLESS OF WEATHER.
1·9·2002
I'D LIKE TO GET PAID JUST TO BE HERE.
BE HERE WHERE?
HERE ON EARTH... YOU KNOW, GET PAID JUST FOR SHOWING UP.
PAIGE
I CAN DREAM CAN'T I?

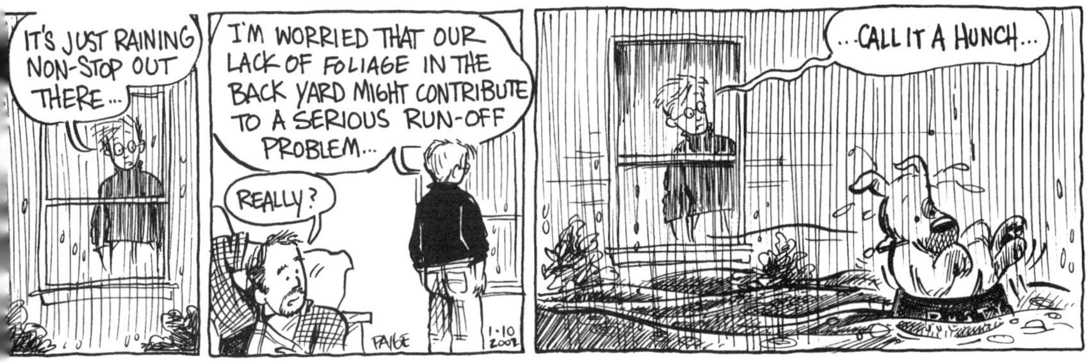
IT'S JUST RAINING NON-STOP OUT THERE...
I'M WORRIED THAT OUR LACK OF FOLIAGE IN THE BACK YARD MIGHT CONTRIBUTE TO A SERIOUS RUN-OFF PROBLEM...
REALLY?
PAIGE
1·10 2002
...CALL IT A HUNCH...

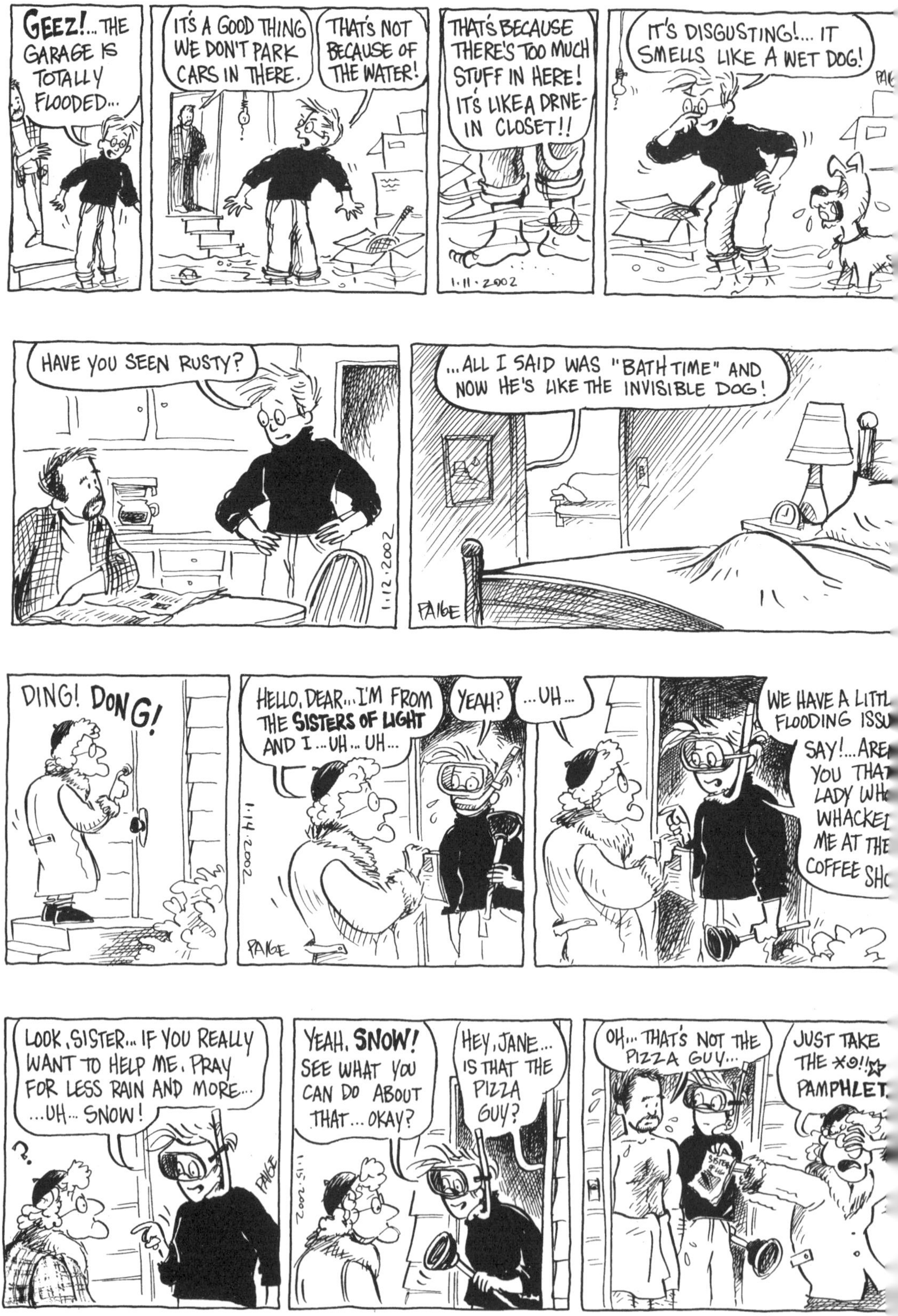
GEEZ!... THE GARAGE IS TOTALLY FLOODED...
IT'S A GOOD THING WE DON'T PARK CARS IN THERE.
THAT'S NOT BECAUSE OF THE WATER!
THAT'S BECAUSE THERE'S TOO MUCH STUFF IN HERE! IT'S LIKE A DRIVE-IN CLOSET!!
1.11.2002
IT'S DISGUSTING!... IT SMELLS LIKE A WET DOG!
HAVE YOU SEEN RUSTY?
1.12.2002
...ALL I SAID WAS "BATH TIME" AND NOW HE'S LIKE THE INVISIBLE DOG!
PAIGE
DING! DONG!
HELLO, DEAR... I'M FROM THE **SISTERS OF LIGHT** AND I... UH... UH...
YEAH?
...UH...
1.14.2002
PAIGE
WE HAVE A LITTL FLOODING ISSU
SAY!... ARE YOU THAT LADY WH WHACKED ME AT THE COFFEE SH
LOOK, SISTER... IF YOU REALLY WANT TO HELP ME, PRAY FOR LESS RAIN AND MORE... ...UH... SNOW!
PAIGE
YEAH, **SNOW!** SEE WHAT YOU CAN DO ABOUT THAT... OKAY?
1.15.2002
HEY, JANE... IS THAT THE PIZZA GUY?
OH... THAT'S NOT THE PIZZA GUY...
JUST TAKE THE *@!!☆ **PAMPHLET.**

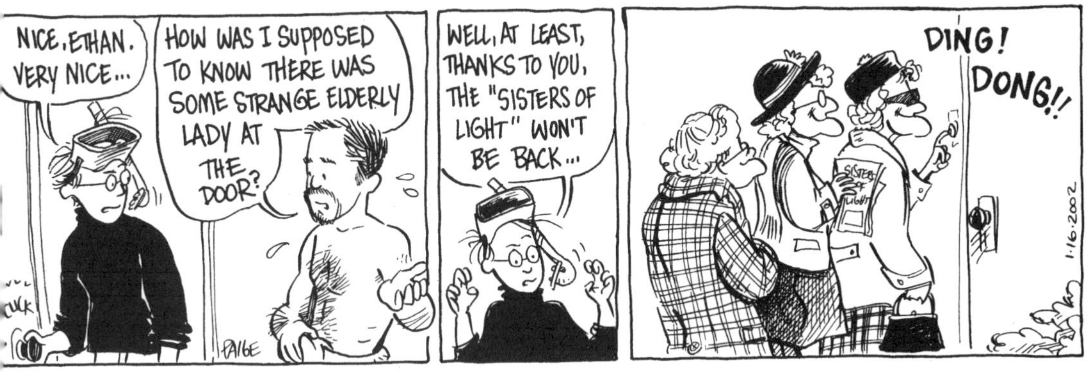
NICE, ETHAN. VERY NICE...
HOW WAS I SUPPOSED TO KNOW THERE WAS SOME STRANGE ELDERLY LADY AT THE DOOR?
PAIGE
WELL, AT LEAST, THANKS TO YOU, THE "SISTERS OF LIGHT" WON'T BE BACK...
DING! DONG!!
SISTERS OF LIGHT
1·16·2002

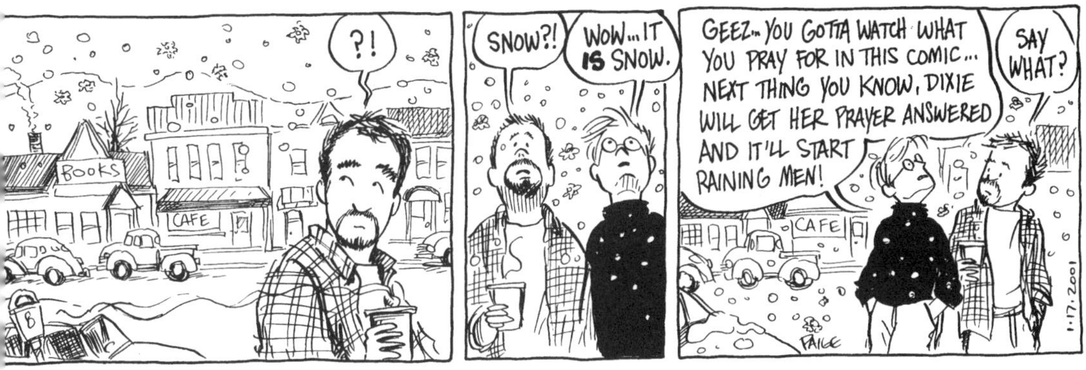
BOOKS
CAFE
?!
SNOW?!
WOW... IT **IS** SNOW.
GEEZ... YOU GOTTA WATCH WHAT YOU PRAY FOR IN THIS COMIC... NEXT THING YOU KNOW, DIXIE WILL GET HER PRAYER ANSWERED AND IT'LL START RAINING MEN!
SAY WHAT?
CAFE
PAIGE
1·17·2001

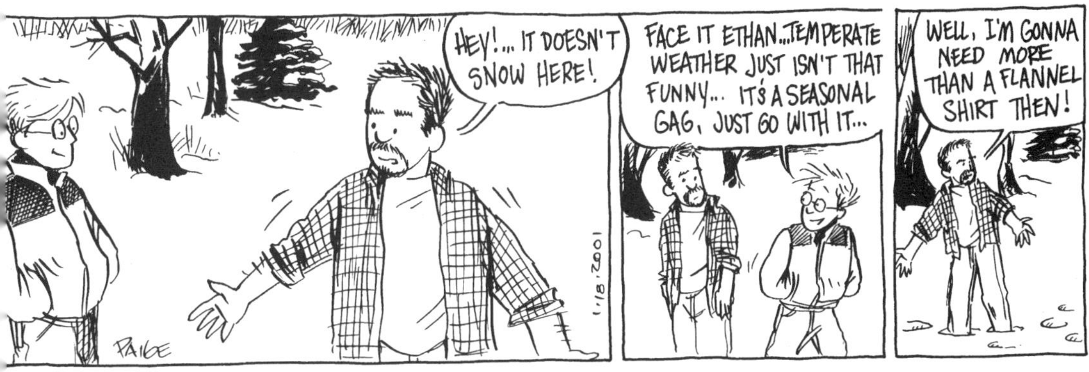
HEY!... IT DOESN'T SNOW HERE!
PAIGE
1·18·2001
FACE IT ETHAN... TEMPERATE WEATHER JUST ISN'T THAT FUNNY... IT'S A SEASONAL GAG, JUST GO WITH IT...
WELL, I'M GONNA NEED MORE THAN A FLANNEL SHIRT THEN!

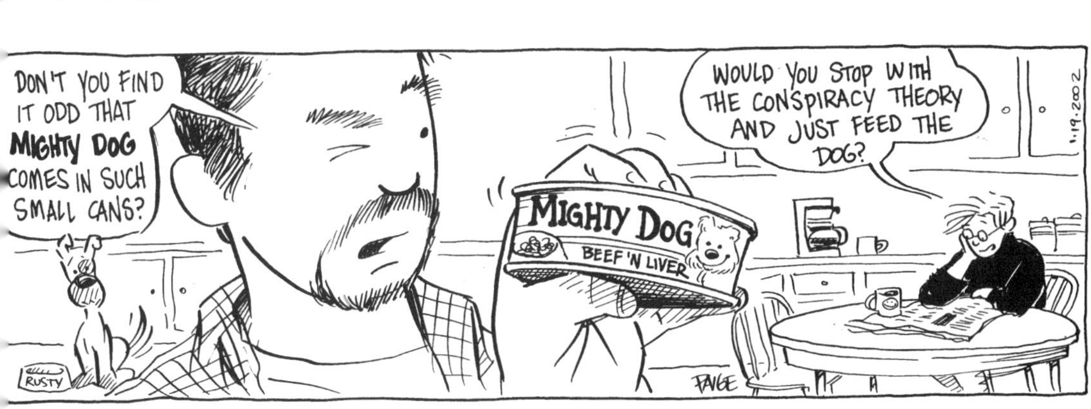
DON'T YOU FIND IT ODD THAT **MIGHTY DOG** COMES IN SUCH SMALL CANS?
RUSTY
MIGHTY DOG
BEEF 'N LIVER
WOULD YOU STOP WITH THE CONSPIRACY THEORY AND JUST FEED THE DOG?
PAIGE
1·19·2002

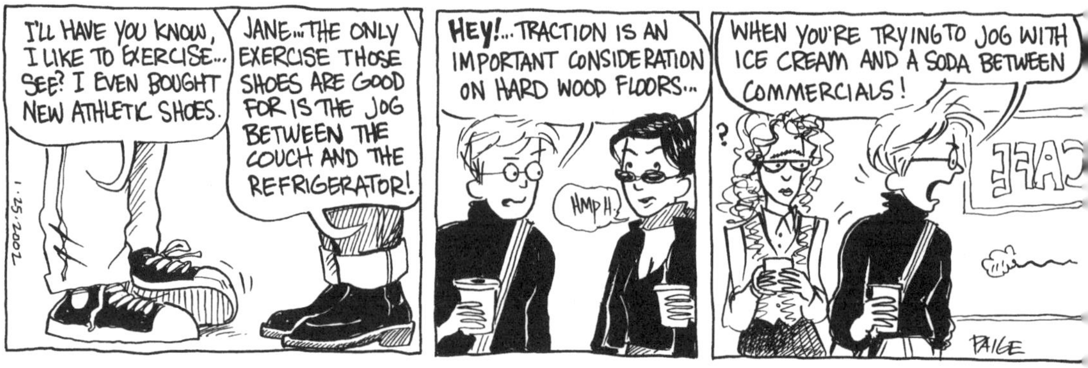
I'LL HAVE YOU KNOW, I LIKE TO EXERCISE... SEE? I EVEN BOUGHT NEW ATHLETIC SHOES.
1.25.2002
JANE... THE ONLY EXERCISE THOSE SHOES ARE GOOD FOR IS THE JOG BETWEEN THE COUCH AND THE REFRIGERATOR!
HEY!... TRACTION IS AN IMPORTANT CONSIDERATION ON HARD WOOD FLOORS...
HMPH.
WHEN YOU'RE TRYING TO JOG WITH ICE CREAM AND A SODA BETWEEN COMMERCIALS!
?
CAFE
PAIGE

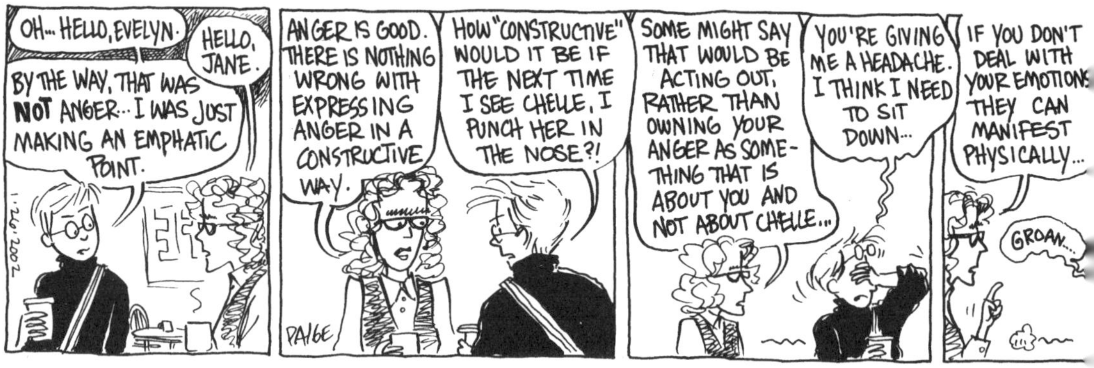
OH... HELLO, EVELYN.
HELLO, JANE.
BY THE WAY, THAT WAS NOT ANGER... I WAS JUST MAKING AN EMPHATIC POINT.
1.26.2002
ANGER IS GOOD. THERE IS NOTHING WRONG WITH EXPRESSING ANGER IN A CONSTRUCTIVE WAY.
HOW "CONSTRUCTIVE" WOULD IT BE IF THE NEXT TIME I SEE CHELLE, I PUNCH HER IN THE NOSE?!
PAIGE
SOME MIGHT SAY THAT WOULD BE ACTING OUT, RATHER THAN OWNING YOUR ANGER AS SOMETHING THAT IS ABOUT YOU AND NOT ABOUT CHELLE...
YOU'RE GIVING ME A HEADACHE. I THINK I NEED TO SIT DOWN...
IF YOU DON'T DEAL WITH YOUR EMOTIONS THEY CAN MANIFEST PHYSICALLY...
GROAN...

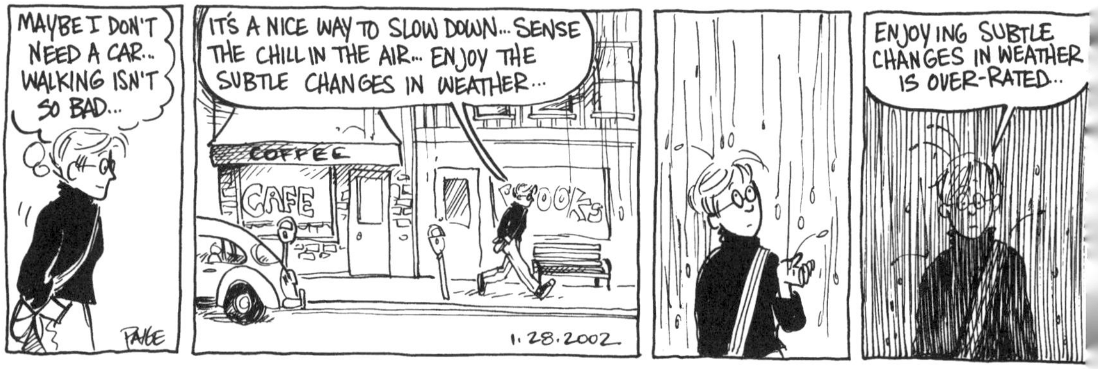
MAYBE I DON'T NEED A CAR... WALKING ISN'T SO BAD...
PAIGE
IT'S A NICE WAY TO SLOW DOWN... SENSE THE CHILL IN THE AIR... ENJOY THE SUBTLE CHANGES IN WEATHER...
COFFEE
CAFE
BOOKS
1.28.2002
ENJOYING SUBTLE CHANGES IN WEATHER IS OVER-RATED...

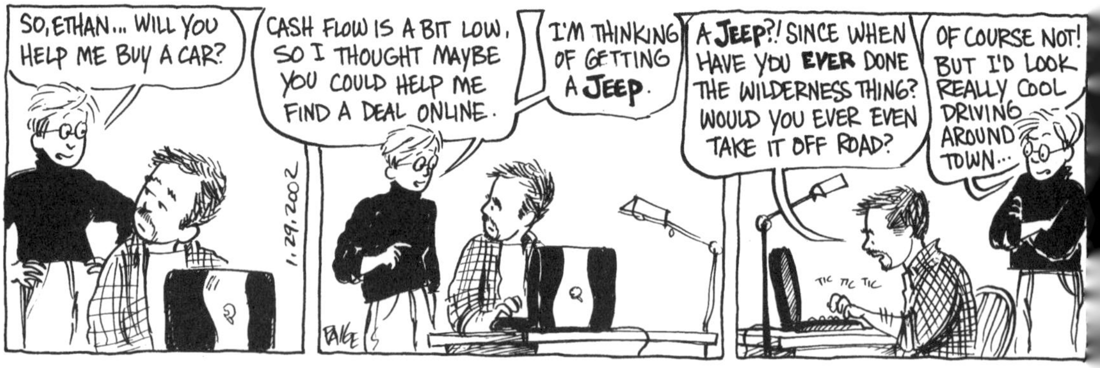
SO, ETHAN... WILL YOU HELP ME BUY A CAR?
1.29.2002
CASH FLOW IS A BIT LOW, SO I THOUGHT MAYBE YOU COULD HELP ME FIND A DEAL ONLINE.
I'M THINKING OF GETTING A JEEP.
PAIGE
A JEEP?! SINCE WHEN HAVE YOU EVER DONE THE WILDERNESS THING? WOULD YOU EVER EVEN TAKE IT OFF ROAD?
TIC TIC TIC
OF COURSE NOT! BUT I'D LOOK REALLY COOL DRIVING AROUND TOWN...

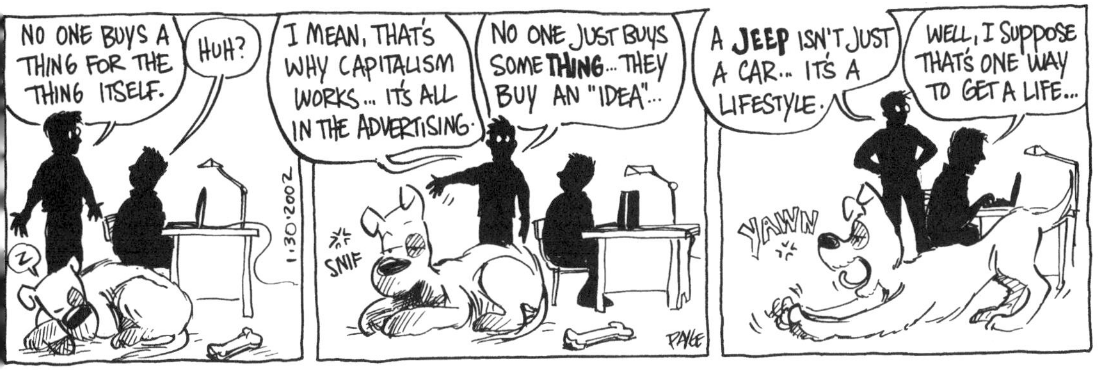
NO ONE BUYS A THING FOR THE THING ITSELF.
HUH?
Z
1.30.2002
I MEAN, THAT'S WHY CAPITALISM WORKS... IT'S ALL IN THE ADVERTISING.
NO ONE JUST BUYS SOME **THING**... THEY BUY AN "IDEA"...
SNIF
A **JEEP** ISN'T JUST A CAR... IT'S A LIFESTYLE.
WELL, I SUPPOSE THAT'S ONE WAY TO GET A LIFE...
YAWN
PAIGE

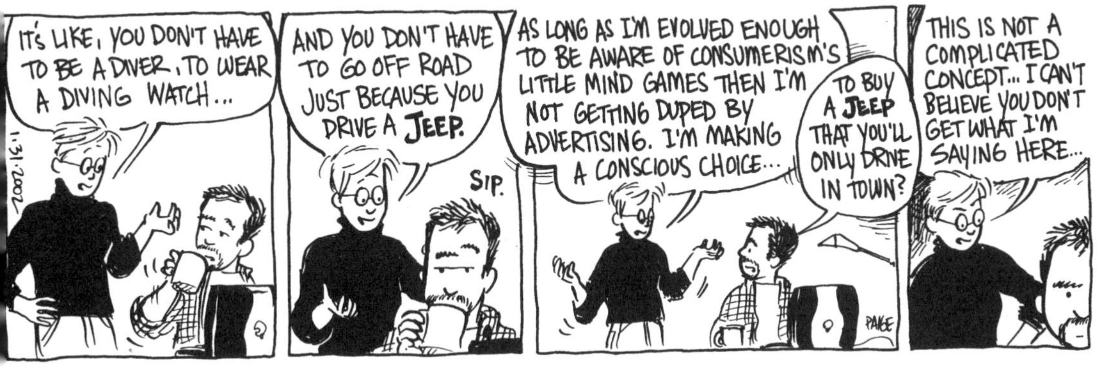
IT'S LIKE, YOU DON'T HAVE TO BE A DIVER, TO WEAR A DIVING WATCH...
1.31.2002
AND YOU DON'T HAVE TO GO OFF ROAD JUST BECAUSE YOU DRIVE A **JEEP**.
SIP.
AS LONG AS I'M EVOLVED ENOUGH TO BE AWARE OF CONSUMERISM'S LITTLE MIND GAMES THEN I'M NOT GETTING DUPED BY ADVERTISING. I'M MAKING A CONSCIOUS CHOICE...
TO BUY A **JEEP** THAT YOU'LL ONLY DRIVE IN TOWN?
PAIGE
THIS IS NOT A COMPLICATED CONCEPT... I CAN'T BELIEVE YOU DON'T GET WHAT I'M SAYING HERE...

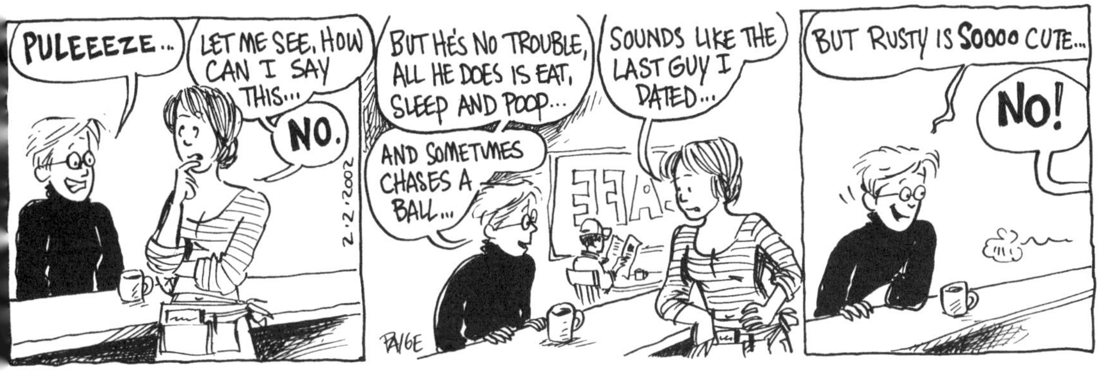
PULEEEZE...
LET ME SEE, HOW CAN I SAY THIS...
NO.
2.2.2002
BUT HE'S NO TROUBLE, ALL HE DOES IS EAT, SLEEP AND POOP...
AND SOMETIMES CHASES A BALL...
SOUNDS LIKE THE LAST GUY I DATED...
PAIGE
BUT RUSTY IS **SOOOO** CUTE...
NO!

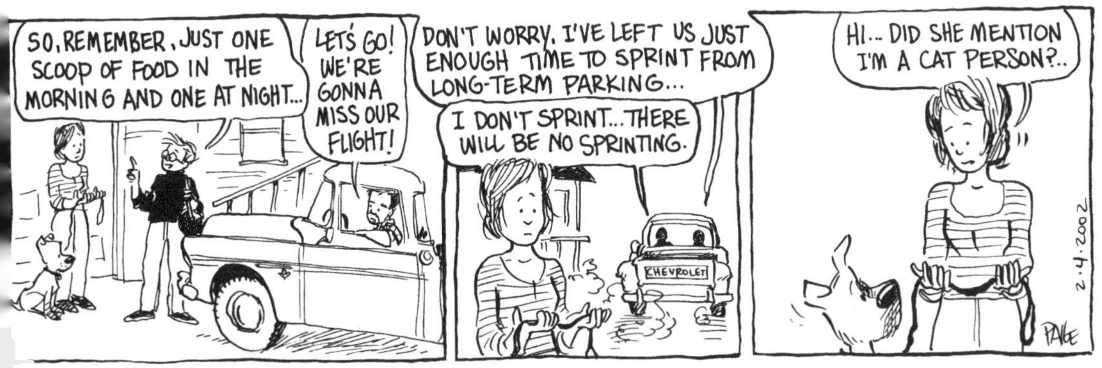
SO, REMEMBER, JUST ONE SCOOP OF FOOD IN THE MORNING AND ONE AT NIGHT...
LET'S GO! WE'RE GONNA MISS OUR FLIGHT!
DON'T WORRY. I'VE LEFT US JUST ENOUGH TIME TO SPRINT FROM LONG-TERM PARKING...
I DON'T SPRINT... THERE WILL BE NO SPRINTING.
CHEVROLET
HI... DID SHE MENTION I'M A CAT PERSON?..
2.4.2002
PAIGE

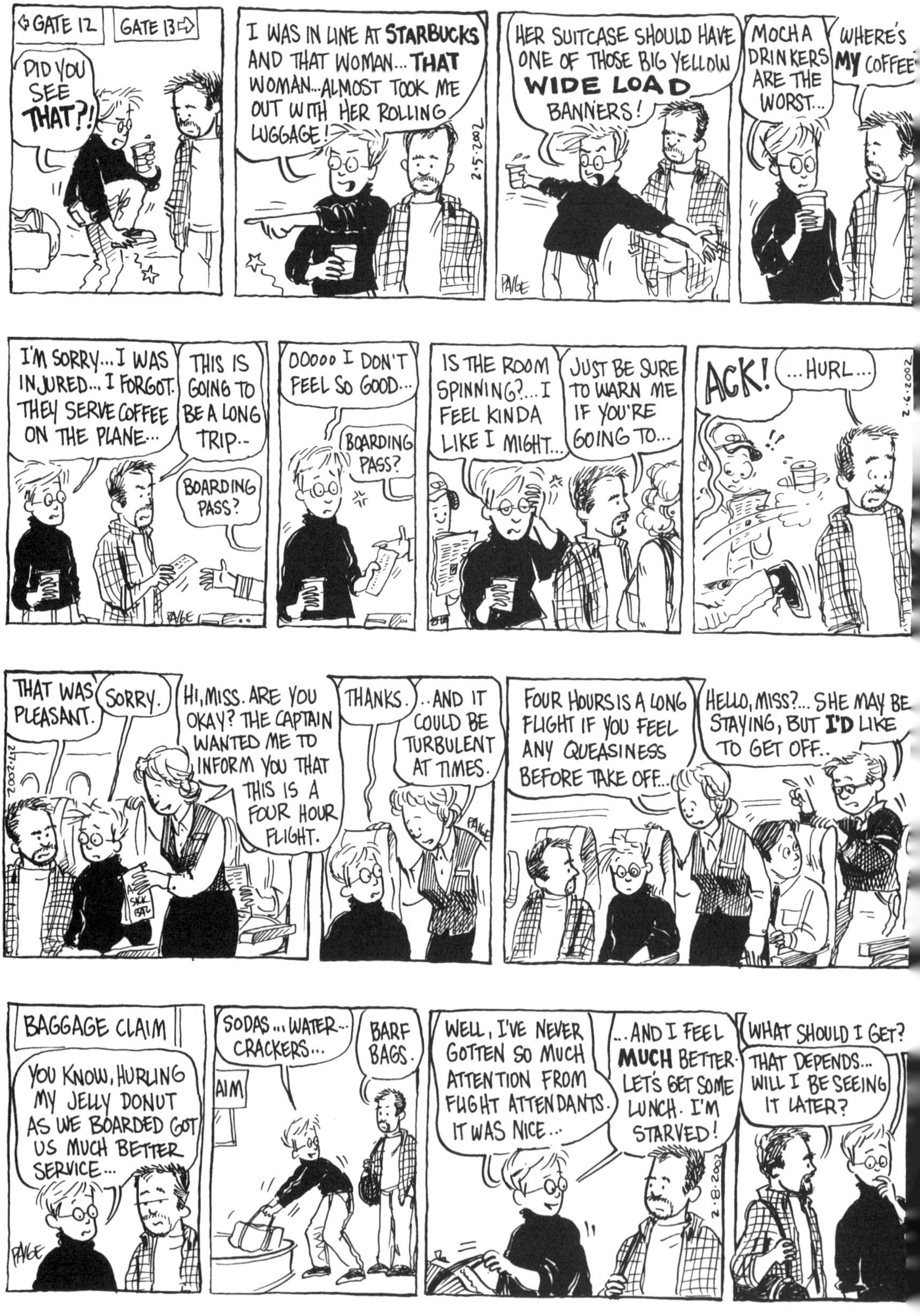
GATE 12
GATE 13
DID YOU SEE THAT?!
I WAS IN LINE AT STARBUCKS AND THAT WOMAN... THAT WOMAN...ALMOST TOOK ME OUT WITH HER ROLLING LUGGAGE!
2·5·2002
HER SUITCASE SHOULD HAVE ONE OF THOSE BIG YELLOW WIDE LOAD BANNERS!
PAIGE
MOCHA DRINKERS ARE THE WORST...
WHERE'S MY COFFEE
I'M SORRY... I WAS INJURED... I FORGOT. THEY SERVE COFFEE ON THE PLANE...
THIS IS GOING TO BE A LONG TRIP..
BOARDING PASS?
PAIGE
OOOOO I DON'T FEEL SO GOOD...
BOARDING PASS?
IS THE ROOM SPINNING?... I FEEL KINDA LIKE I MIGHT...
JUST BE SURE TO WARN ME IF YOU'RE GOING TO...
ACK!
...HURL...
2·6·2002
THAT WAS PLEASANT.
SORRY.
2·7·2002
HI, MISS. ARE YOU OKAY? THE CAPTAIN WANTED ME TO INFORM YOU THAT THIS IS A FOUR HOUR FLIGHT.
A SICK BAG
THANKS.
..AND IT COULD BE TURBULENT AT TIMES.
PAIGE
FOUR HOURS IS A LONG FLIGHT IF YOU FEEL ANY QUEASINESS BEFORE TAKE OFF...
HELLO, MISS?... SHE MAY BE STAYING, BUT I'D LIKE TO GET OFF..
BAGGAGE CLAIM
YOU KNOW, HURLING MY JELLY DONUT AS WE BOARDED GOT US MUCH BETTER SERVICE...
PAIGE
AIM
SODAS... WATER... CRACKERS...
BARF BAGS.
WELL, I'VE NEVER GOTTEN SO MUCH ATTENTION FROM FLIGHT ATTENDANTS. IT WAS NICE...
...AND I FEEL MUCH BETTER. LET'S GET SOME LUNCH. I'M STARVED!
2·8·2002
WHAT SHOULD I GET?
THAT DEPENDS... WILL I BE SEEING IT LATER?

Chapter four

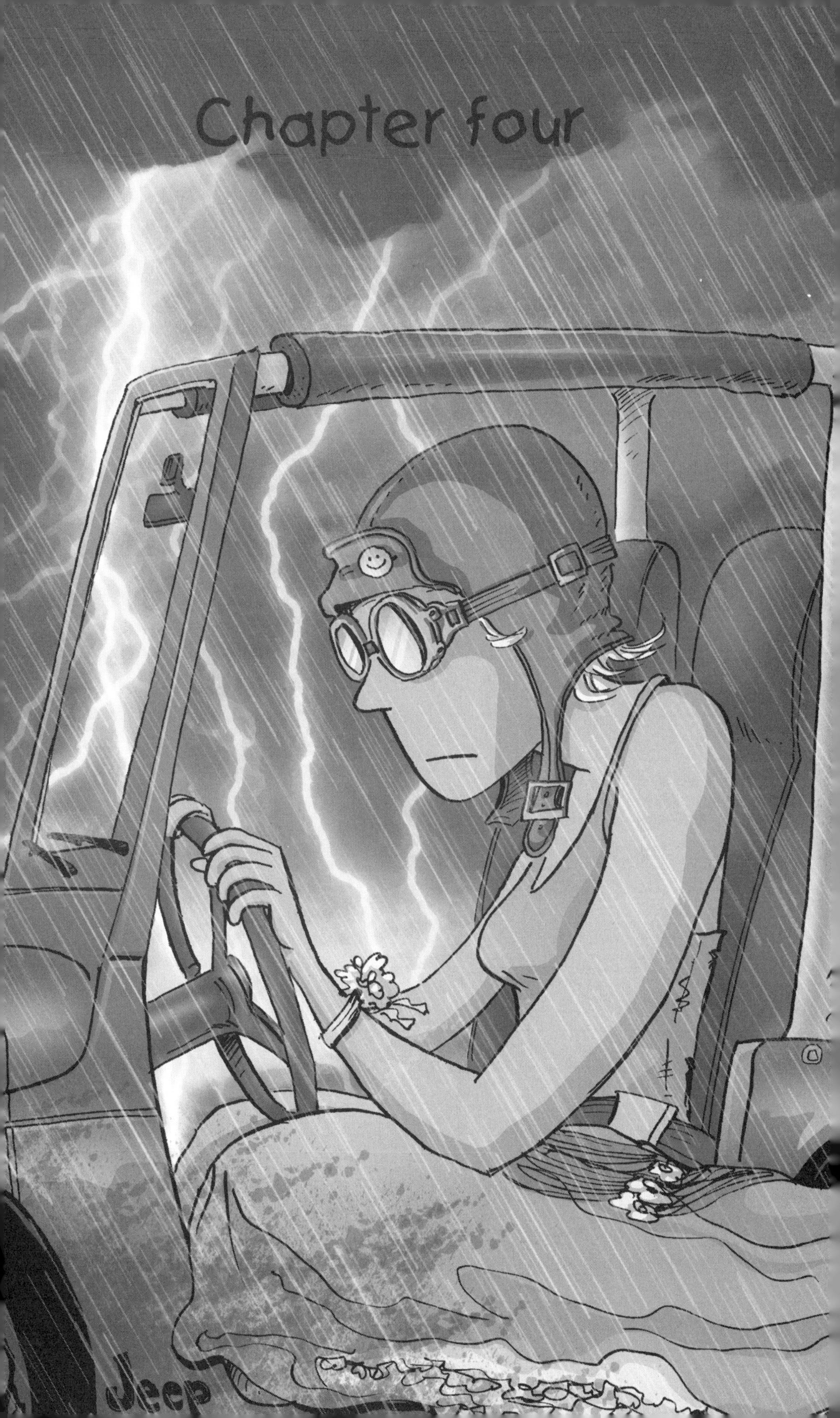
Jeep

It doesn't take long for a cat lover to be thrown off balance by a dog...

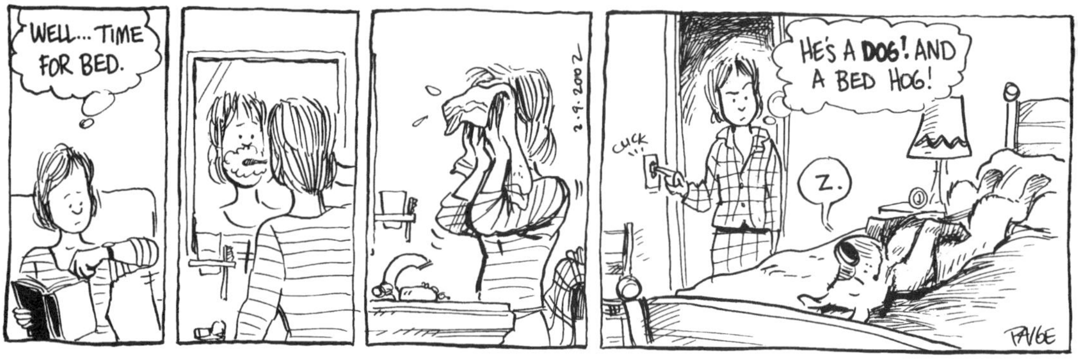
WELL... TIME FOR BED.
2.9.2002
CLICK
HE'S A **DOG**! AND A BED HOG!
Z.
PAIGE

A day later...

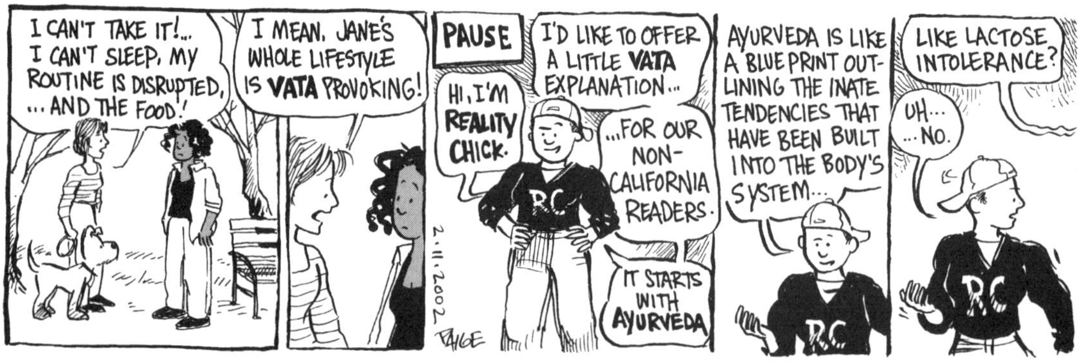
I CAN'T TAKE IT!... I CAN'T SLEEP, MY ROUTINE IS DISRUPTED, ... AND THE FOOD!
I MEAN, JANE'S WHOLE LIFESTYLE IS **VATA** PROVOKING!
PAUSE
HI, I'M **REALITY CHICK**.
I'D LIKE TO OFFER A LITTLE **VATA** EXPLANATION...
...FOR OUR NON-CALIFORNIA READERS.
IT STARTS WITH **AYURVEDA**
2.11.2002
PAIGE
AYURVEDA IS LIKE A BLUE PRINT OUT-LINING THE INATE TENDENCIES THAT HAVE BEEN BUILT INTO THE BODY'S SYSTEM...
LIKE LACTOSE INTOLERANCE?
UH... ...NO.

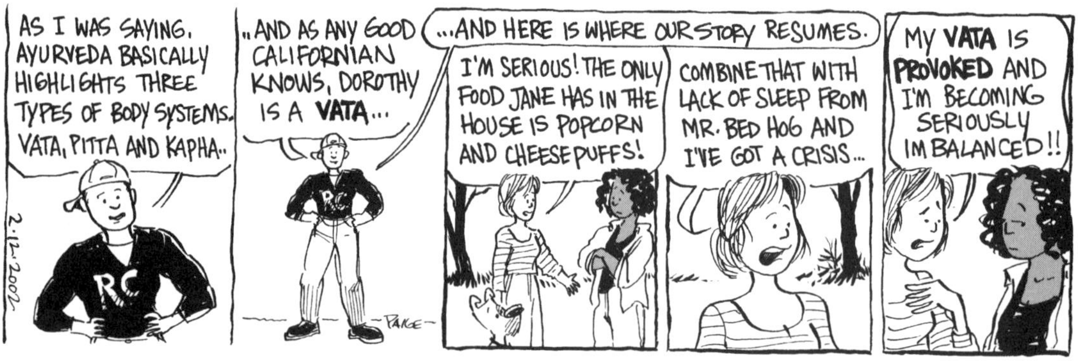
AS I WAS SAYING, AYURVEDA BASICALLY HIGHLIGHTS THREE TYPES OF BODY SYSTEMS. VATA, PITTA AND KAPHA..
2.12.2002
..AND AS ANY GOOD CALIFORNIAN KNOWS, DOROTHY IS A **VATA**...
PAIGE
...AND HERE IS WHERE OUR STORY RESUMES.
I'M SERIOUS! THE ONLY FOOD JANE HAS IN THE HOUSE IS POPCORN AND CHEESE PUFFS!
COMBINE THAT WITH LACK OF SLEEP FROM MR. BED HOG AND I'VE GOT A CRISIS...
MY **VATA** IS **PROVOKED** AND I'M BECOMING SERIOUSLY IMBALANCED!!

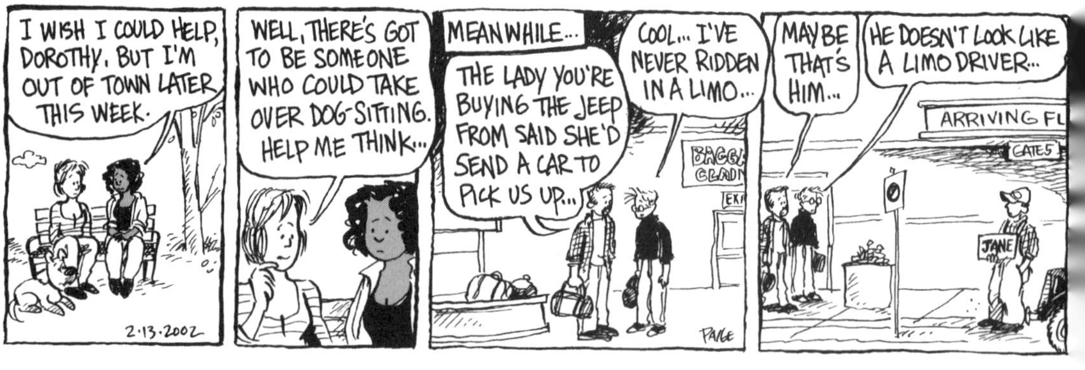
I WISH I COULD HELP, DOROTHY, BUT I'M OUT OF TOWN LATER THIS WEEK.
2.13.2002
WELL, THERE'S GOT TO BE SOMEONE WHO COULD TAKE OVER DOG-SITTING. HELP ME THINK...
MEANWHILE...
THE LADY YOU'RE BUYING THE JEEP FROM SAID SHE'D SEND A CAR TO PICK US UP...
COOL... I'VE NEVER RIDDEN IN A LIMO...
PAIGE
MAYBE THAT'S HIM...
HE DOESN'T LOOK LIKE A LIMO DRIVER...
ARRIVING FL
GATE 5
JANE

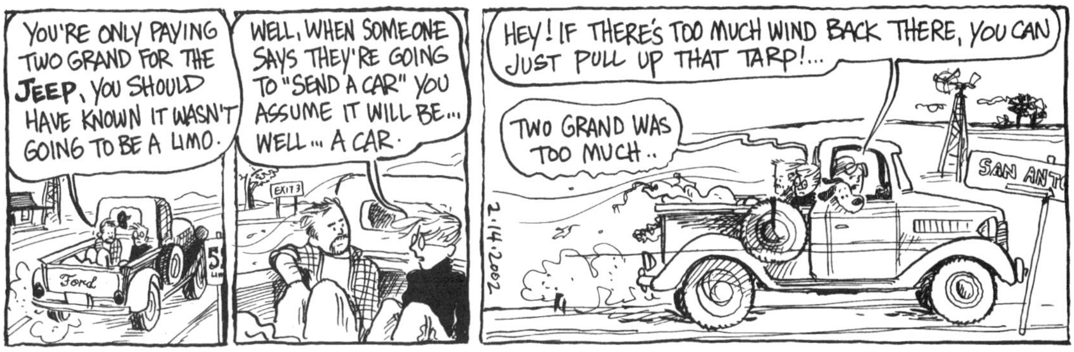
YOU'RE ONLY PAYING TWO GRAND FOR THE JEEP, YOU SHOULD HAVE KNOWN IT WASN'T GOING TO BE A LIMO.
Ford
WELL, WHEN SOMEONE SAYS THEY'RE GOING TO "SEND A CAR" YOU ASSUME IT WILL BE... WELL... A CAR.
EXIT 3
HEY! IF THERE'S TOO MUCH WIND BACK THERE, YOU CAN JUST PULL UP THAT TARP!...
TWO GRAND WAS TOO MUCH..
SAN ANT
2.14.2002

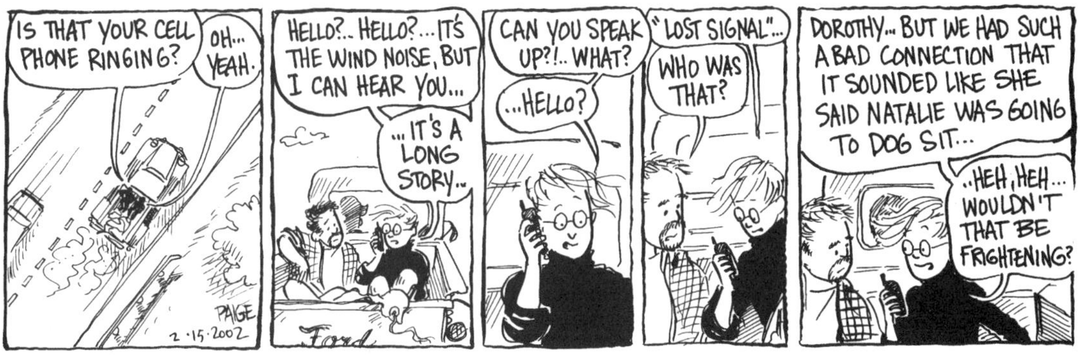
IS THAT YOUR CELL PHONE RINGING?
OH... YEAH.
PAIGE
2.15.2002
HELLO?.. HELLO?... IT'S THE WIND NOISE, BUT I CAN HEAR YOU...
... IT'S A LONG STORY...
Ford
CAN YOU SPEAK UP?!.. WHAT?
...HELLO?
"LOST SIGNAL"...
WHO WAS THAT?
DOROTHY... BUT WE HAD SUCH A BAD CONNECTION THAT IT SOUNDED LIKE SHE SAID NATALIE WAS GOING TO DOG SIT...
..HEH, HEH... WOULDN'T THAT BE FRIGHTENING?

Meanwhile, back at Jane's...

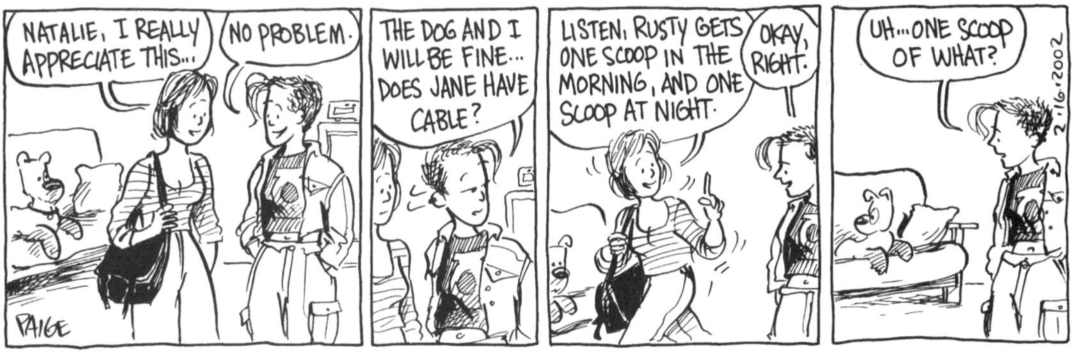
NATALIE, I REALLY APPRECIATE THIS...
NO PROBLEM.
PAIGE
THE DOG AND I WILL BE FINE... DOES JANE HAVE CABLE?
LISTEN, RUSTY GETS ONE SCOOP IN THE MORNING, AND ONE SCOOP AT NIGHT.
OKAY, RIGHT.
UH... ONE SCOOP OF WHAT?
2.16.2002

... while in Texas....

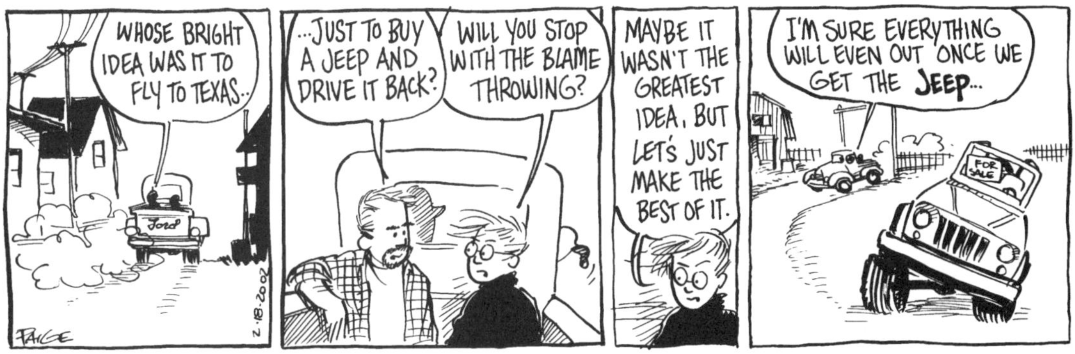
WHOSE BRIGHT IDEA WAS IT TO FLY TO TEXAS..
Ford
PAIGE
2.18.2002
...JUST TO BUY A JEEP AND DRIVE IT BACK?
WILL YOU STOP WITH THE BLAME THROWING?
MAYBE IT WASN'T THE GREATEST IDEA, BUT LET'S JUST MAKE THE BEST OF IT.
I'M SURE EVERYTHING WILL EVEN OUT ONCE WE GET THE JEEP...
FOR SALE

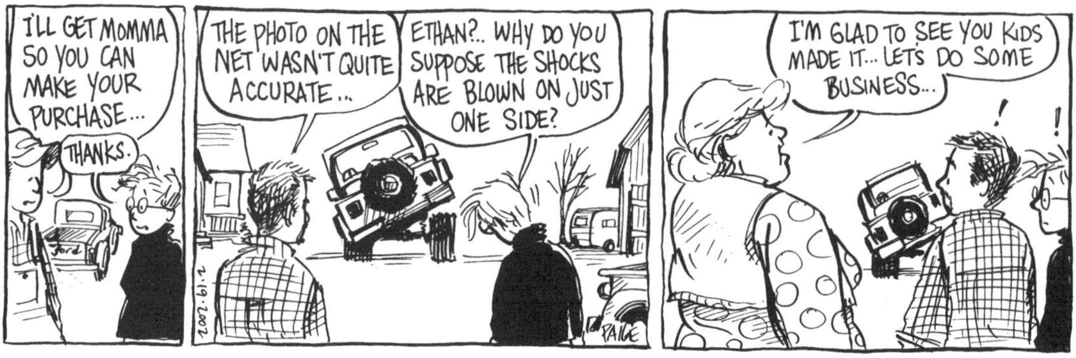
I'LL GET MOMMA SO YOU CAN MAKE YOUR PURCHASE...
THANKS.
Ford
THE PHOTO ON THE NET WASN'T QUITE ACCURATE...
2.19.2002
ETHAN?.. WHY DO YOU SUPPOSE THE SHOCKS ARE BLOWN ON JUST ONE SIDE?
PAIGE
I'M GLAD TO SEE YOU KIDS MADE IT... LET'S DO SOME BUSINESS...
!
!

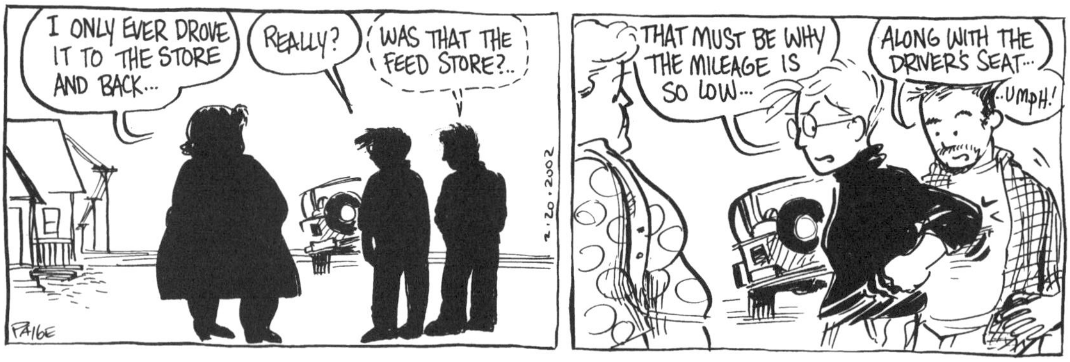
I ONLY EVER DROVE IT TO THE STORE AND BACK...
REALLY?
WAS THAT THE FEED STORE?..
2.20.2002
PAIGE
THAT MUST BE WHY THE MILEAGE IS SO LOW...
ALONG WITH THE DRIVER'S SEAT...
..UMPH!

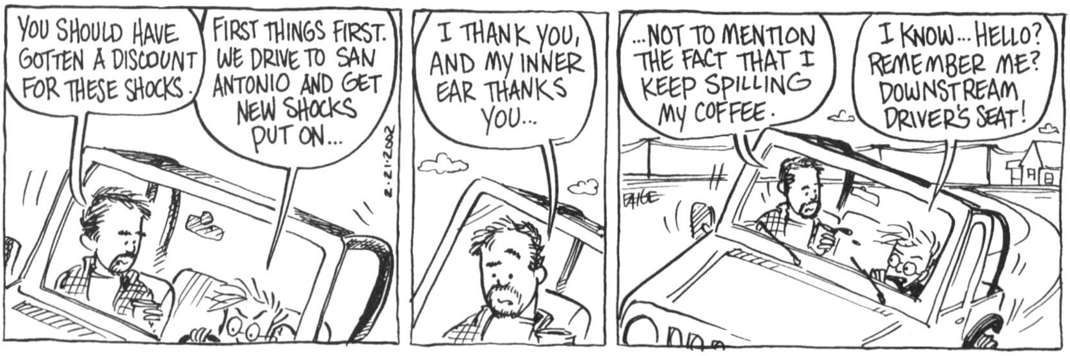
YOU SHOULD HAVE GOTTEN A DISCOUNT FOR THESE SHOCKS.
FIRST THINGS FIRST. WE DRIVE TO SAN ANTONIO AND GET NEW SHOCKS PUT ON...
2.21.2002
I THANK YOU, AND MY INNER EAR THANKS YOU...
...NOT TO MENTION THE FACT THAT I KEEP SPILLING MY COFFEE.
I KNOW... HELLO? REMEMBER ME? DOWNSTREAM DRIVER'S SEAT!
PAIGE

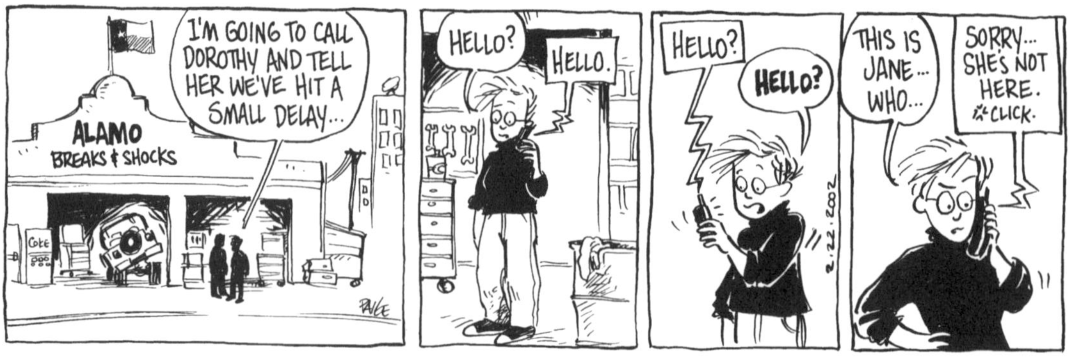
I'M GOING TO CALL DOROTHY AND TELL HER WE'VE HIT A SMALL DELAY...
ALAMO
BREAKS & SHOCKS
COKE
PAIGE
HELLO?
HELLO.
HELLO?
HELLO?
2.22.2002
THIS IS JANE... WHO...
SORRY... SHE'S NOT HERE.
CLICK.

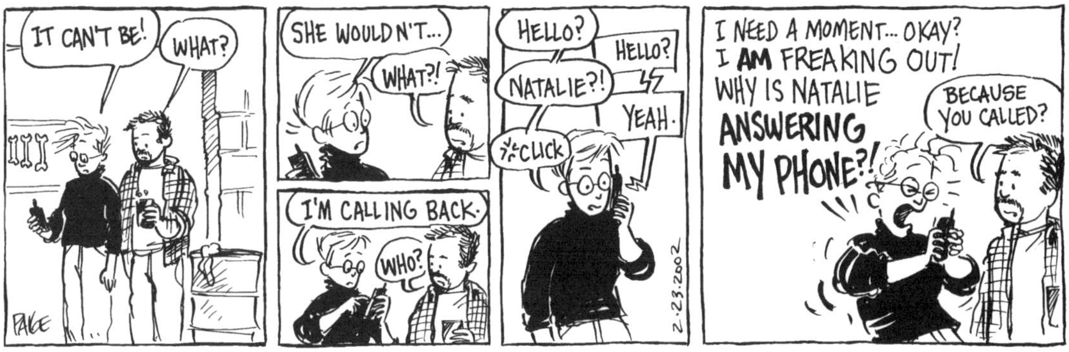
IT CAN'T BE!
WHAT?
PAIGE
SHE WOULDN'T...
WHAT?!
I'M CALLING BACK.
WHO?
HELLO?
HELLO?
NATALIE?!
YEAH.
CLICK
2·23·2002
I NEED A MOMENT... OKAY? I **AM** FREAKING OUT! WHY IS NATALIE **ANSWERING MY PHONE?!**
BECAUSE YOU CALLED?

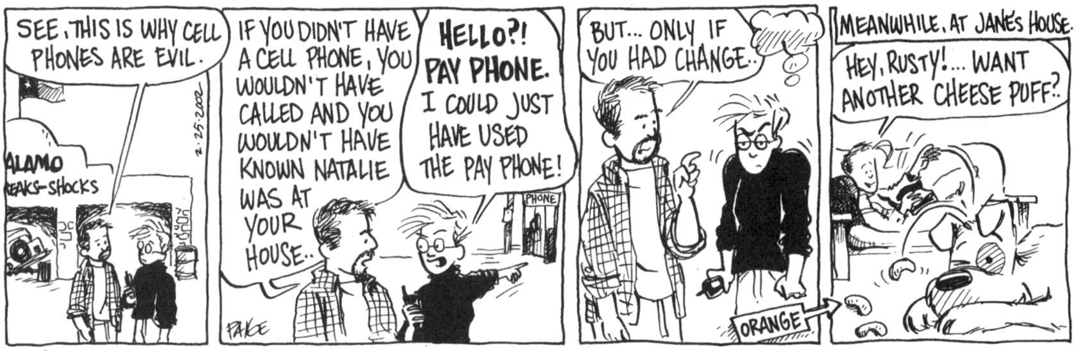
SEE, THIS IS WHY CELL PHONES ARE EVIL.
2·25·2002
ALAMO
BREAKS-SHOCKS
IF YOU DIDN'T HAVE A CELL PHONE, YOU WOULDN'T HAVE CALLED AND YOU WOULDN'T HAVE KNOWN NATALIE WAS AT YOUR HOUSE..
HELLO?! PAY PHONE. I COULD JUST HAVE USED THE PAY PHONE!
PHONE
PAIGE
BUT... ONLY IF YOU HAD CHANGE..
ORANGE
MEANWHILE, AT JANE'S HOUSE.
HEY, RUSTY!... WANT ANOTHER CHEESE PUFF?

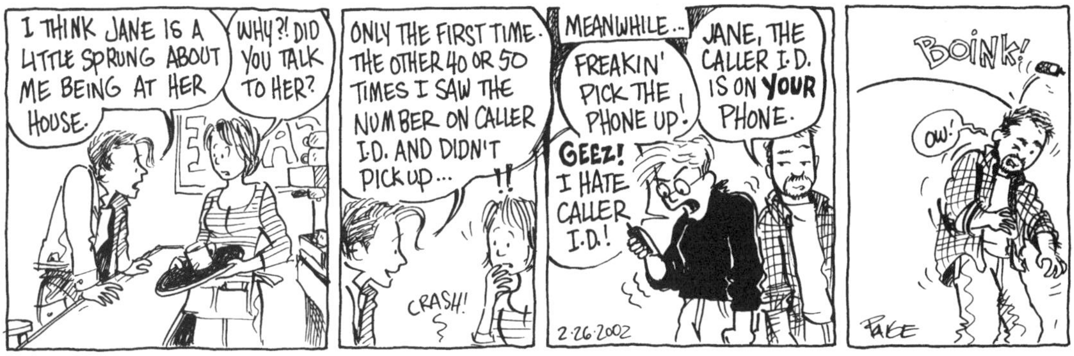
I THINK JANE IS A LITTLE SPRUNG ABOUT ME BEING AT HER HOUSE.
WHY?! DID YOU TALK TO HER?
ONLY THE FIRST TIME. THE OTHER 40 OR 50 TIMES I SAW THE NUMBER ON CALLER I.D. AND DIDN'T PICK UP...
!!
CRASH!
MEANWHILE...
FREAKIN' PICK THE PHONE UP!
JANE, THE CALLER I.D. IS ON **YOUR** PHONE.
GEEZ! I HATE CALLER I.D.!
2·26·2002
BOINK!
OW!
PAIGE

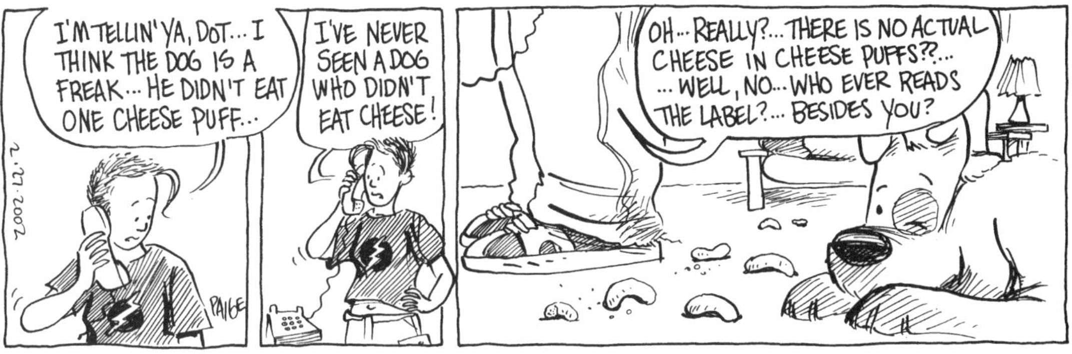
I'M TELLIN' YA, DOT... I THINK THE DOG IS A FREAK... HE DIDN'T EAT ONE CHEESE PUFF...
2·27·2002
PAIGE
I'VE NEVER SEEN A DOG WHO DIDN'T EAT CHEESE!
OH... REALLY?... THERE IS NO ACTUAL CHEESE IN CHEESE PUFFS??... ...WELL, NO... WHO EVER READS THE LABEL?... BESIDES YOU?

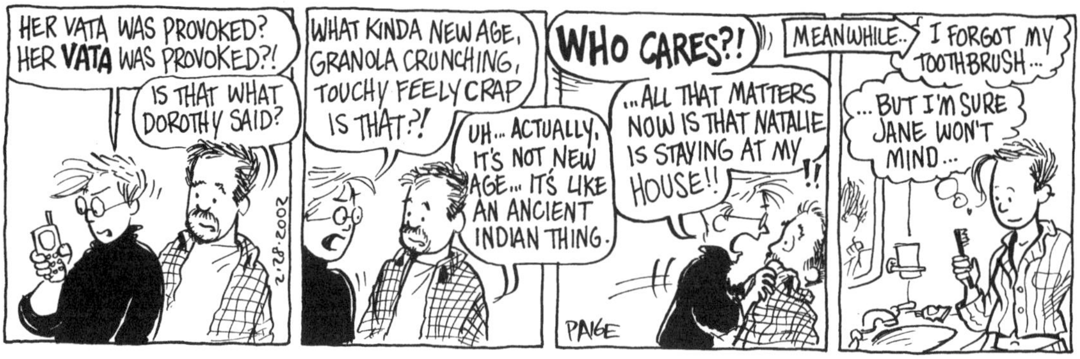
HER VATA WAS PROVOKED? HER **VATA** WAS PROVOKED?!
IS THAT WHAT DOROTHY SAID?
2·28·2002
WHAT KINDA NEW AGE, GRANOLA CRUNCHING, TOUCHY FEELY CRAP IS THAT?!
UH... ACTUALLY, IT'S NOT NEW AGE... IT'S LIKE AN ANCIENT INDIAN THING.
WHO CARES?!
...ALL THAT MATTERS NOW IS THAT NATALIE IS STAYING AT MY HOUSE!!
!!
PAIGE
MEANWHILE..
I FORGOT MY TOOTHBRUSH...
...BUT I'M SURE JANE WON'T MIND...

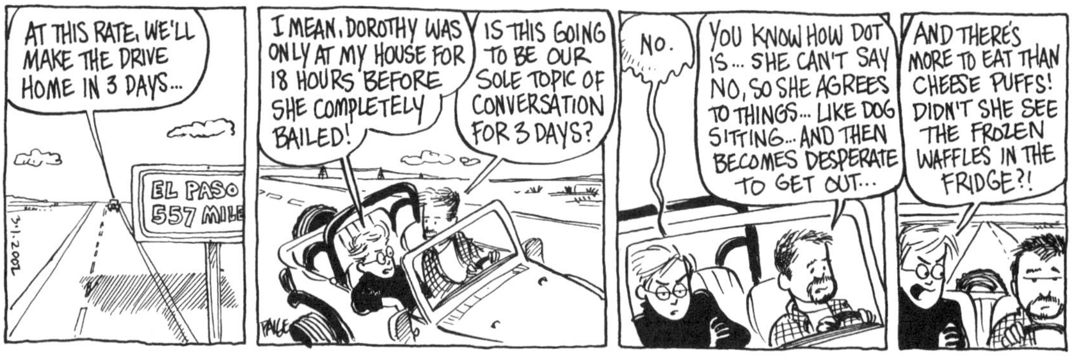
AT THIS RATE, WE'LL MAKE THE DRIVE HOME IN 3 DAYS...
EL PASO 557 MILE
3·1·2002
I MEAN, DOROTHY WAS ONLY AT MY HOUSE FOR 18 HOURS BEFORE SHE COMPLETELY BAILED!
IS THIS GOING TO BE OUR SOLE TOPIC OF CONVERSATION FOR 3 DAYS?
PAIGE
NO.
YOU KNOW HOW DOT IS... SHE CAN'T SAY NO, SO SHE AGREES TO THINGS... LIKE DOG SITTING... AND THEN BECOMES DESPERATE TO GET OUT...
AND THERE'S MORE TO EAT THAN CHEESE PUFFS! DIDN'T SHE SEE THE FROZEN WAFFLES IN THE FRIDGE?!

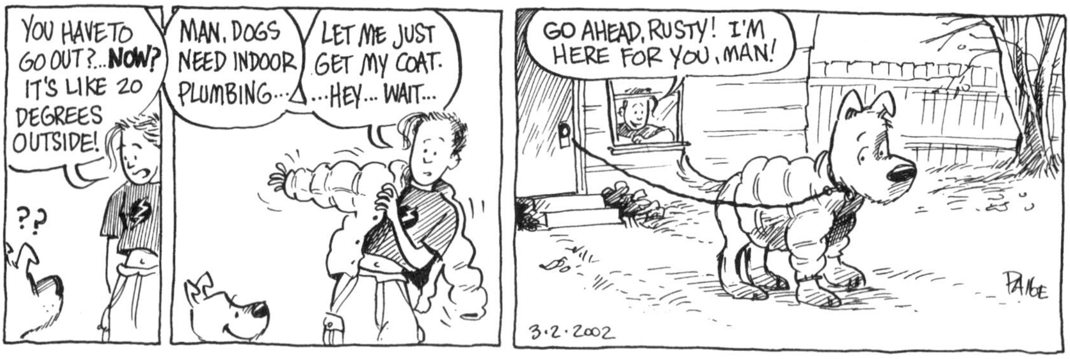
YOU HAVE TO GO OUT?...**NOW?** IT'S LIKE 20 DEGREES OUTSIDE!
??
MAN, DOGS NEED INDOOR PLUMBING...
LET ME JUST GET MY COAT. ...HEY... WAIT...
GO AHEAD, RUSTY! I'M HERE FOR YOU, MAN!
PAIGE
3·2·2002

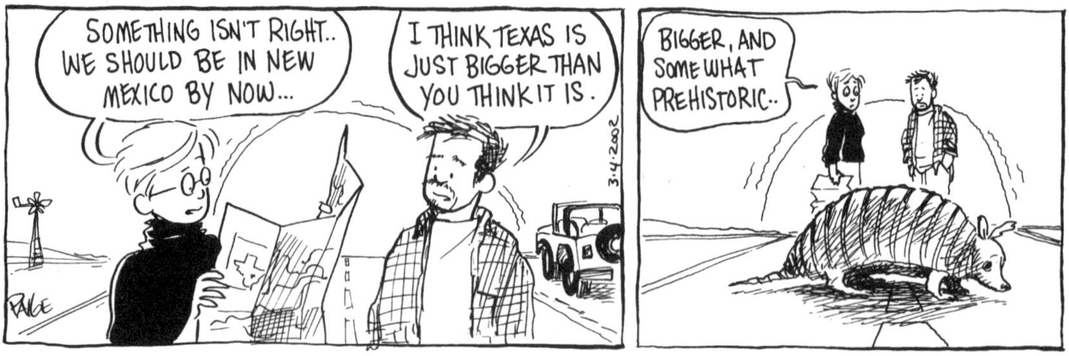
SOMETHING ISN'T RIGHT.. WE SHOULD BE IN NEW MEXICO BY NOW...
I THINK TEXAS IS JUST BIGGER THAN YOU THINK IT IS.
3·4·2002
PAIGE
BIGGER, AND SOMEWHAT PREHISTORIC..

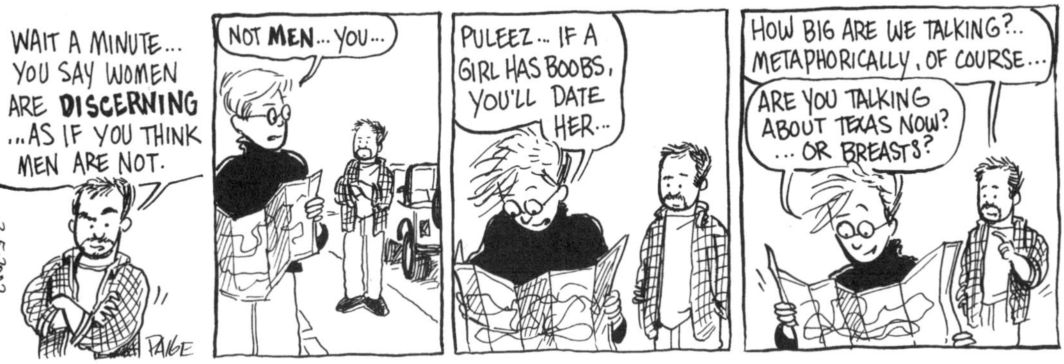
WAIT A MINUTE... YOU SAY WOMEN ARE **DISCERNING** ...AS IF YOU THINK MEN ARE NOT.
NOT **MEN**... YOU...
PULEEZ... IF A GIRL HAS BOOBS, YOU'LL DATE HER...
HOW BIG ARE WE TALKING?.. METAPHORICALLY, OF COURSE...
ARE YOU TALKING ABOUT TEXAS NOW? ... OR BREASTS?
PAIGE

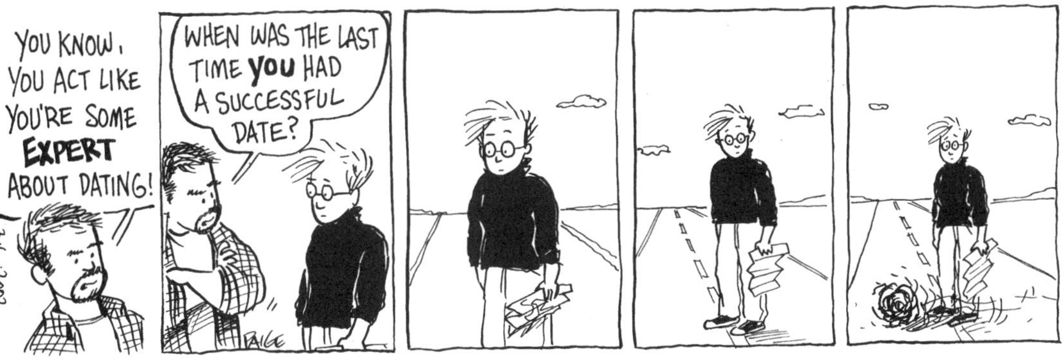
YOU KNOW, YOU ACT LIKE YOU'RE SOME **EXPERT** ABOUT DATING!
WHEN WAS THE LAST TIME **YOU** HAD A SUCCESSFUL DATE?
PAIGE

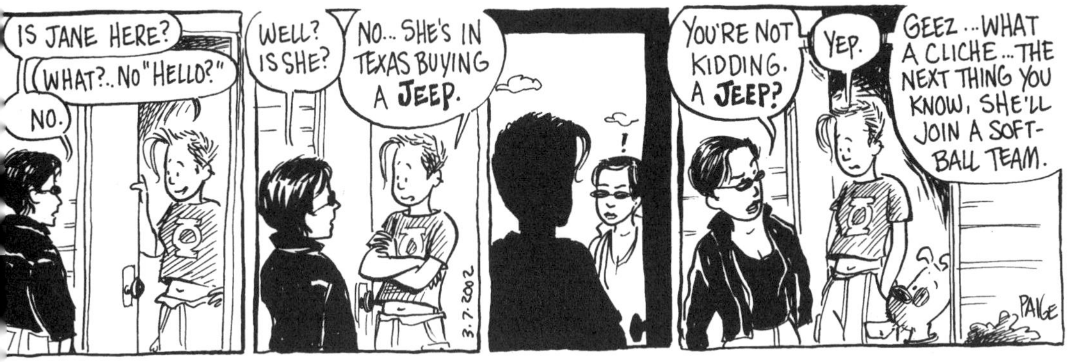
IS JANE HERE?
WHAT?.. NO "HELLO?"
NO.
WELL? IS SHE?
NO... SHE'S IN TEXAS BUYING A **JEEP**.
3.7.2002
!
YOU'RE NOT KIDDING. A **JEEP**?
YEP.
GEEZ ...WHAT A CLICHE... THE NEXT THING YOU KNOW, SHE'LL JOIN A SOFT-BALL TEAM.
PAIGE

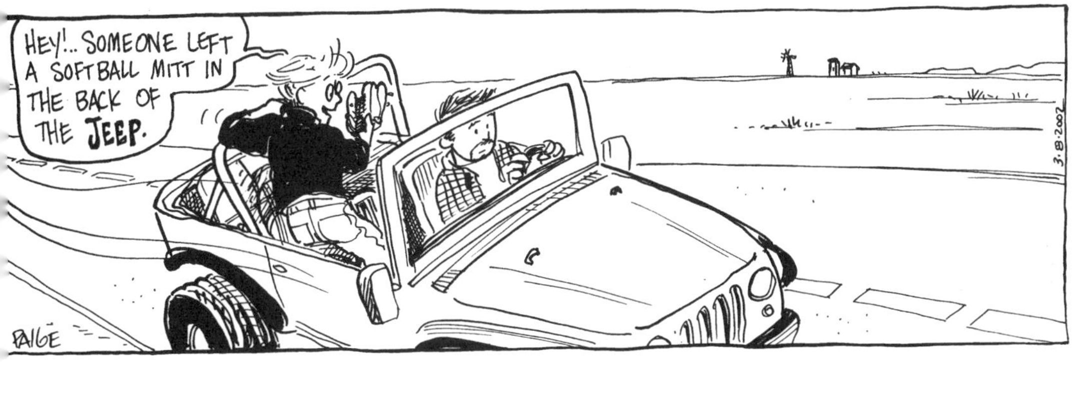
HEY!.. SOMEONE LEFT A SOFTBALL MITT IN THE BACK OF THE **JEEP**.
3.8.2002
PAIGE

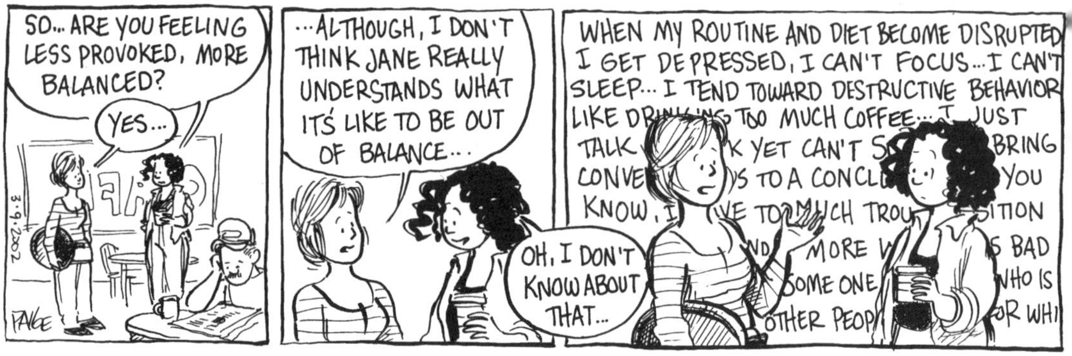
SO... ARE YOU FEELING LESS PROVOKED, MORE BALANCED?
YES...
3·9·2002
PAIGE
...ALTHOUGH, I DON'T THINK JANE REALLY UNDERSTANDS WHAT IT'S LIKE TO BE OUT OF BALANCE...
OH, I DON'T KNOW ABOUT THAT...
WHEN MY ROUTINE AND DIET BECOME DISRUPTED I GET DEPRESSED, I CAN'T FOCUS... I CAN'T SLEEP... I TEND TOWARD DESTRUCTIVE BEHAVIOR

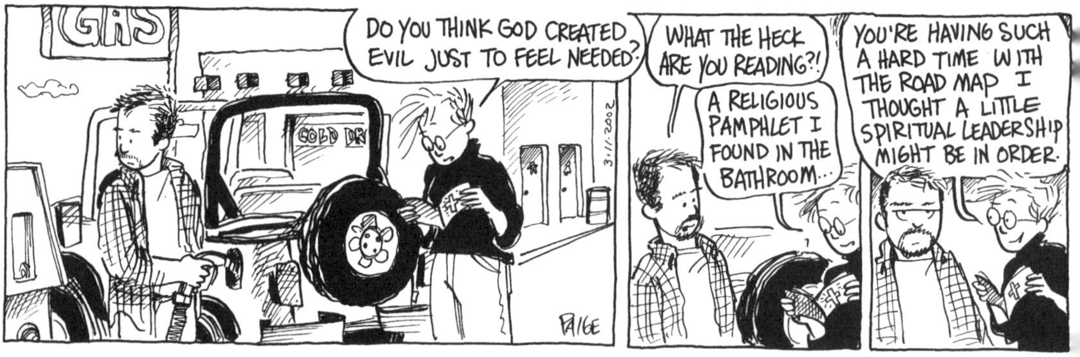
GAS
COLD DR
DO YOU THINK GOD CREATED EVIL JUST TO FEEL NEEDED?
3·11·2002
PAIGE
WHAT THE HECK ARE YOU READING?!
A RELIGIOUS PAMPHLET I FOUND IN THE BATHROOM...
YOU'RE HAVING SUCH A HARD TIME WITH THE ROAD MAP I THOUGHT A LITTLE SPIRITUAL LEADERSHIP MIGHT BE IN ORDER.

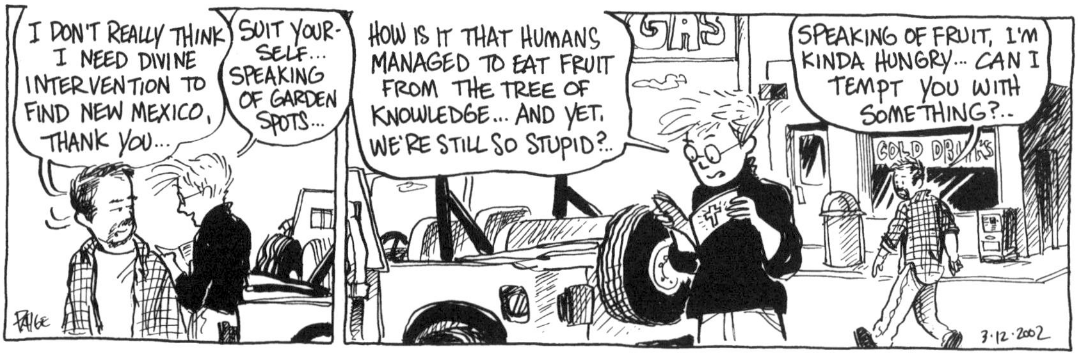
I DON'T REALLY THINK I NEED DIVINE INTERVENTION TO FIND NEW MEXICO, THANK YOU...
SUIT YOURSELF... SPEAKING OF GARDEN SPOTS...
PAIGE
HOW IS IT THAT HUMANS MANAGED TO EAT FRUIT FROM THE TREE OF KNOWLEDGE... AND YET, WE'RE STILL SO STUPID?..
GAS
SPEAKING OF FRUIT, I'M KINDA HUNGRY... CAN I TEMPT YOU WITH SOMETHING?..
3·12·2002

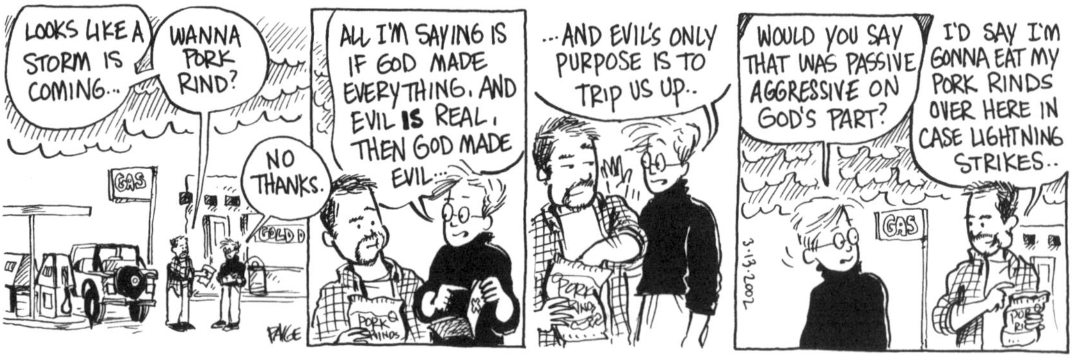
LOOKS LIKE A STORM IS COMING...
WANNA PORK RIND?
NO THANKS.
GAS
PAIGE
ALL I'M SAYING IS IF GOD MADE EVERYTHING, AND EVIL IS REAL, THEN GOD MADE EVIL...
PORK RINDS
...AND EVIL'S ONLY PURPOSE IS TO TRIP US UP..
WOULD YOU SAY THAT WAS PASSIVE AGGRESSIVE ON GOD'S PART?
I'D SAY I'M GONNA EAT MY PORK RINDS OVER HERE IN CASE LIGHTNING STRIKES..
3·13·2002
GAS

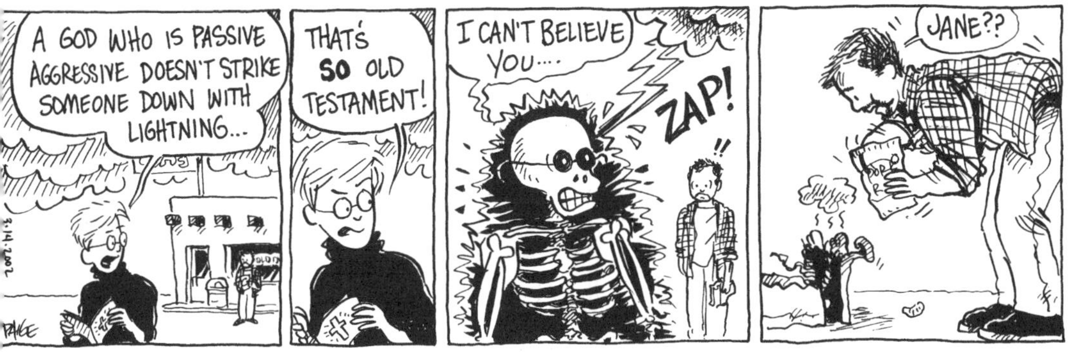
A GOD WHO IS PASSIVE AGGRESSIVE DOESN'T STRIKE SOMEONE DOWN WITH LIGHTNING...
3.14.2002
PAIGE
THAT'S SO OLD TESTAMENT!
I CAN'T BELIEVE YOU....
ZAP!
!!
JANE??

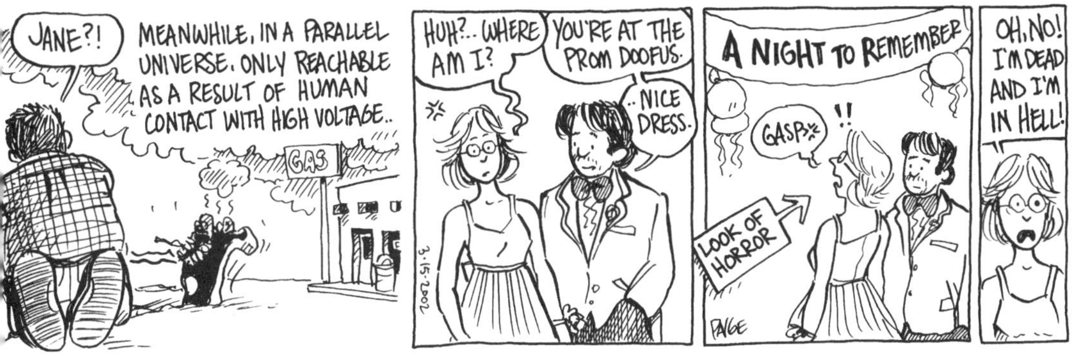
JANE?!
MEANWHILE, IN A PARALLEL UNIVERSE, ONLY REACHABLE AS A RESULT OF HUMAN CONTACT WITH HIGH VOLTAGE..
GAS
HUH?.. WHERE AM I?
YOU'RE AT THE PROM DOOFUS.
..NICE DRESS.
3.15.2002
A NIGHT TO REMEMBER
GASP
!!
LOOK OF HORROR
PAIGE
OH, NO! I'M DEAD AND I'M IN HELL!

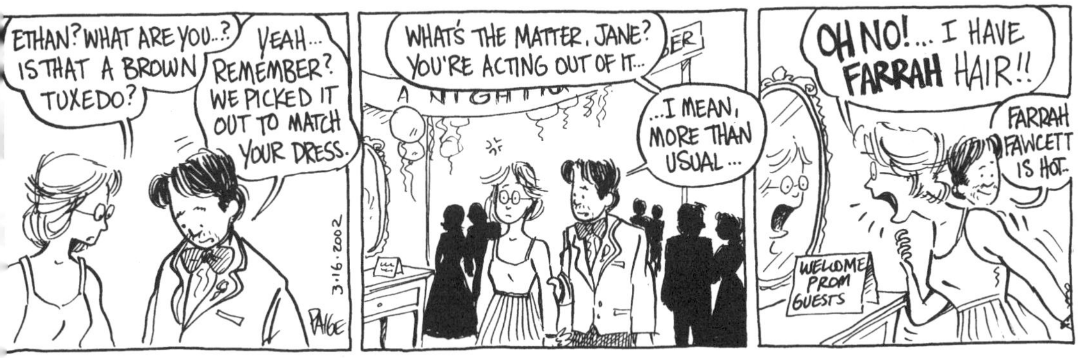
ETHAN? WHAT ARE YOU..? IS THAT A BROWN TUXEDO?
YEAH... REMEMBER? WE PICKED IT OUT TO MATCH YOUR DRESS.
3.16.2002
PAIGE
WHAT'S THE MATTER, JANE? YOU'RE ACTING OUT OF IT...
...I MEAN, MORE THAN USUAL...
OH NO!... I HAVE FARRAH HAIR!!
FARRAH FAWCETT IS HOT.
WELCOME PROM GUESTS

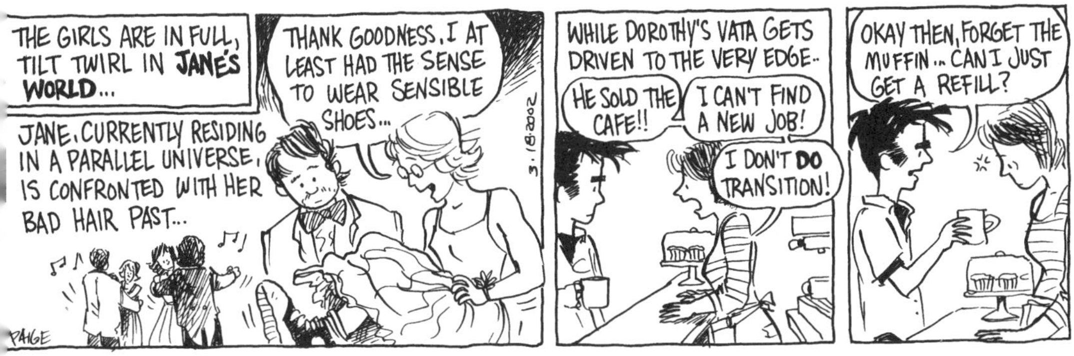
THE GIRLS ARE IN FULL, TILT TWIRL IN JANE'S WORLD...
JANE, CURRENTLY RESIDING IN A PARALLEL UNIVERSE, IS CONFRONTED WITH HER BAD HAIR PAST...
THANK GOODNESS, I AT LEAST HAD THE SENSE TO WEAR SENSIBLE SHOES...
3.18.2002
PAIGE
WHILE DOROTHY'S VATA GETS DRIVEN TO THE VERY EDGE..
HE SOLD THE CAFE!!
I CAN'T FIND A NEW JOB!
I DON'T DO TRANSITION!
OKAY THEN, FORGET THE MUFFIN.. CAN I JUST GET A REFILL?

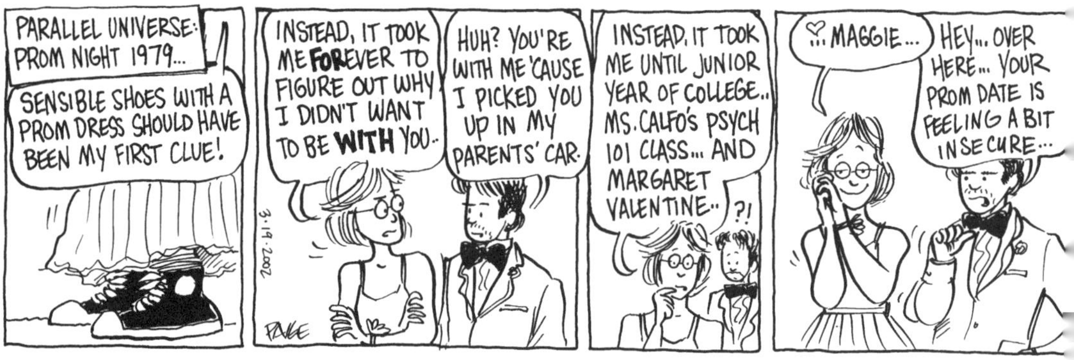
PARALLEL UNIVERSE: PROM NIGHT 1979...
SENSIBLE SHOES WITH A PROM DRESS SHOULD HAVE BEEN MY FIRST CLUE!
INSTEAD, IT TOOK ME **FOR**EVER TO FIGURE OUT WHY I DIDN'T WANT TO BE **WITH** YOU..
HUH? YOU'RE WITH ME 'CAUSE I PICKED YOU UP IN MY PARENTS' CAR.
3·19·2002
PAIGE
INSTEAD, IT TOOK ME UNTIL JUNIOR YEAR OF COLLEGE.. MS. CALFO'S PSYCH 101 CLASS... AND MARGARET VALENTINE..
?!
♡... MAGGIE...
HEY... OVER HERE... YOUR PROM DATE IS FEELING A BIT INSECURE...

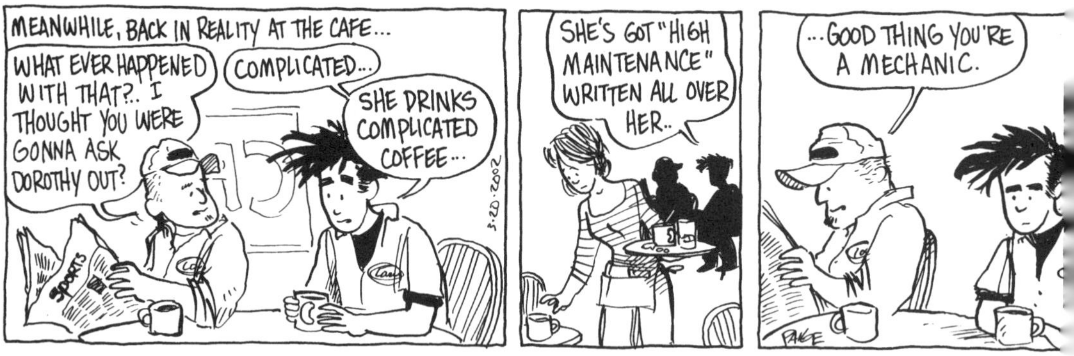
MEANWHILE, BACK IN REALITY AT THE CAFE...
WHAT EVER HAPPENED WITH THAT?.. I THOUGHT YOU WERE GONNA ASK DOROTHY OUT?
COMPLICATED...
SHE DRINKS COMPLICATED COFFEE...
SPORTS
3·20·2002
SHE'S GOT "HIGH MAINTENANCE" WRITTEN ALL OVER HER..
...GOOD THING YOU'RE A MECHANIC.
PAIGE

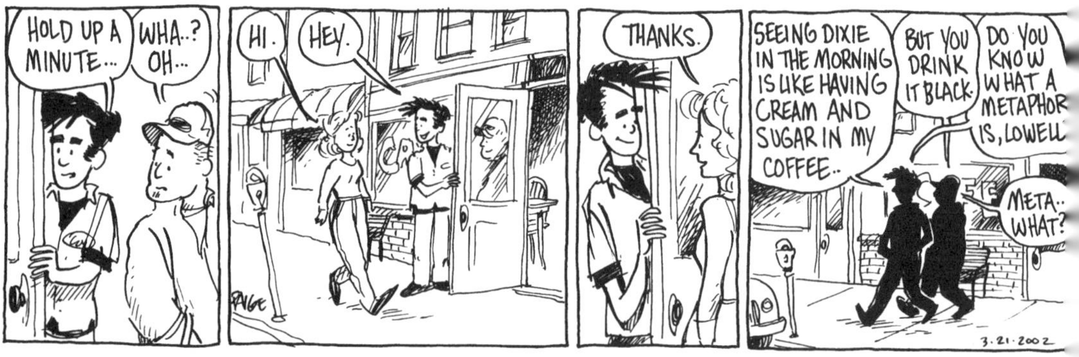
HOLD UP A MINUTE...
WHA..? OH...
HI.
HEY.
PAIGE
THANKS.
SEEING DIXIE IN THE MORNING IS LIKE HAVING CREAM AND SUGAR IN MY COFFEE..
BUT YOU DRINK IT BLACK.
DO YOU KNOW WHAT A METAPHOR IS, LOWELL
META.. WHAT?
3·21·2002

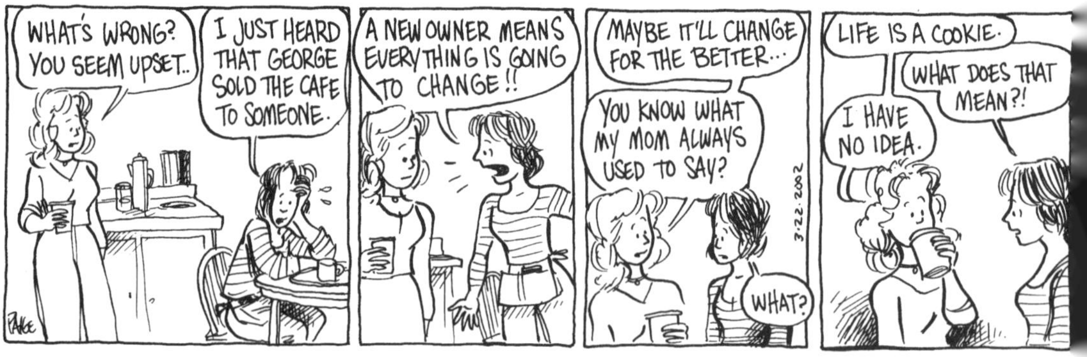
WHAT'S WRONG? YOU SEEM UPSET..
I JUST HEARD THAT GEORGE SOLD THE CAFE TO SOMEONE.
PAIGE
A NEW OWNER MEANS EVERYTHING IS GOING TO CHANGE!!
MAYBE IT'LL CHANGE FOR THE BETTER...
YOU KNOW WHAT MY MOM ALWAYS USED TO SAY?
WHAT?
3·22·2002
LIFE IS A COOKIE.
WHAT DOES THAT MEAN?!
I HAVE NO IDEA.

Meanwhile, somewhere in Texas...

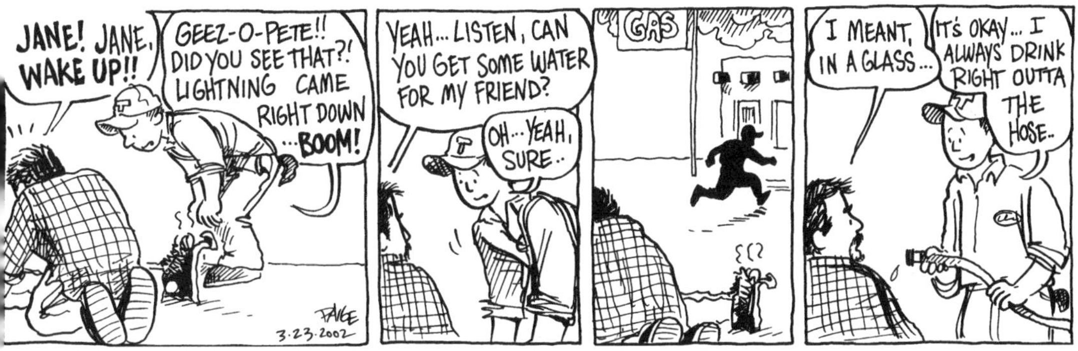
JANE! JANE, WAKE UP!!
GEEZ-O-PETE!! DID YOU SEE THAT?! LIGHTNING CAME RIGHT DOWN ...BOOM!
PAIGE 3·23·2002
YEAH... LISTEN, CAN YOU GET SOME WATER FOR MY FRIEND?
OH... YEAH, SURE..
GAS
I MEANT, IN A GLASS...
IT'S OKAY... I ALWAYS DRINK RIGHT OUTTA THE HOSE..

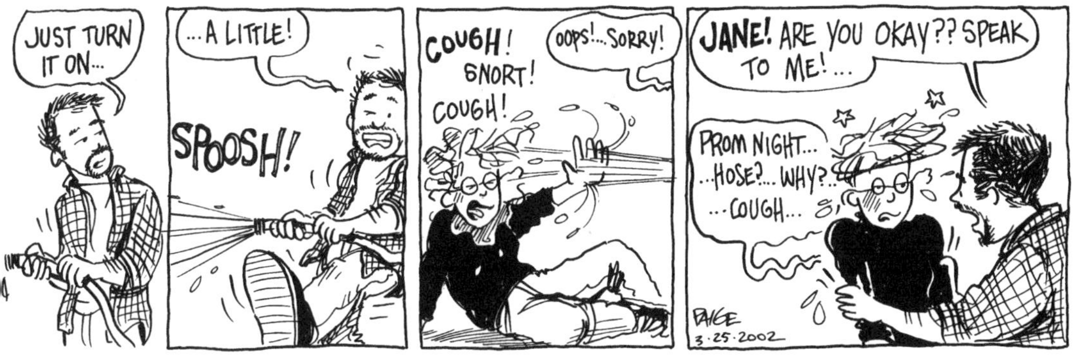
JUST TURN IT ON...
...A LITTLE!
SPOOSH!
COUGH! SNORT! COUGH!
OOPS!...SORRY!
JANE! ARE YOU OKAY?? SPEAK TO ME!...
PROM NIGHT... ...HOSE?... WHY?... ...COUGH...
PAIGE 3·25·2002

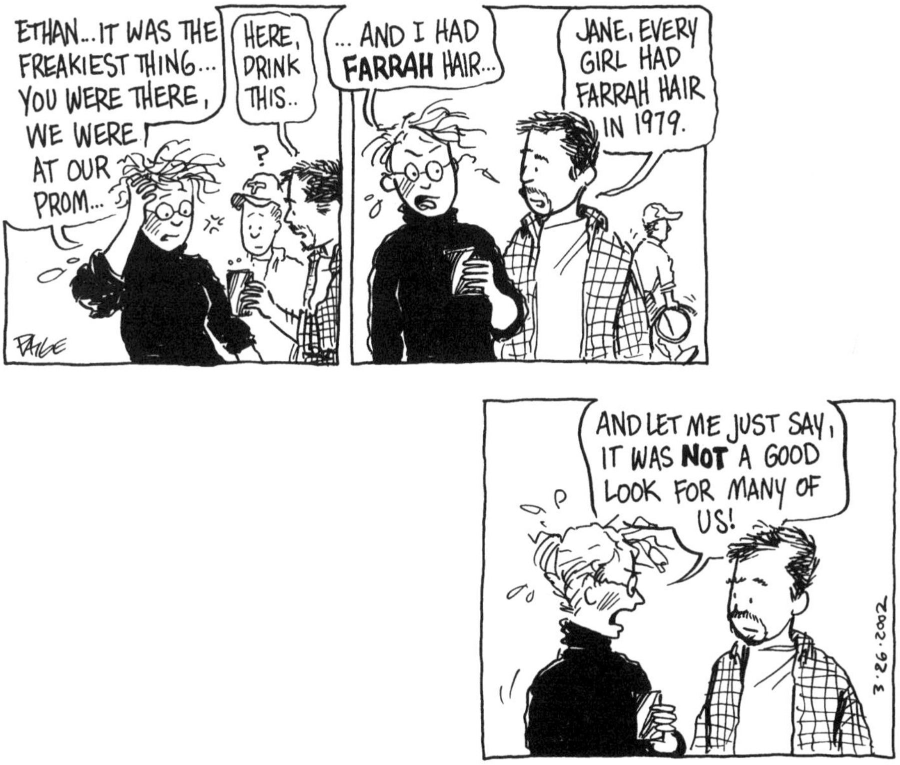
ETHAN... IT WAS THE FREAKIEST THING... YOU WERE THERE, WE WERE AT OUR PROM...
HERE, DRINK THIS..
?
PAIGE
... AND I HAD FARRAH HAIR...
JANE, EVERY GIRL HAD FARRAH HAIR IN 1979.
AND LET ME JUST SAY, IT WAS NOT A GOOD LOOK FOR MANY OF US!
3·26·2002

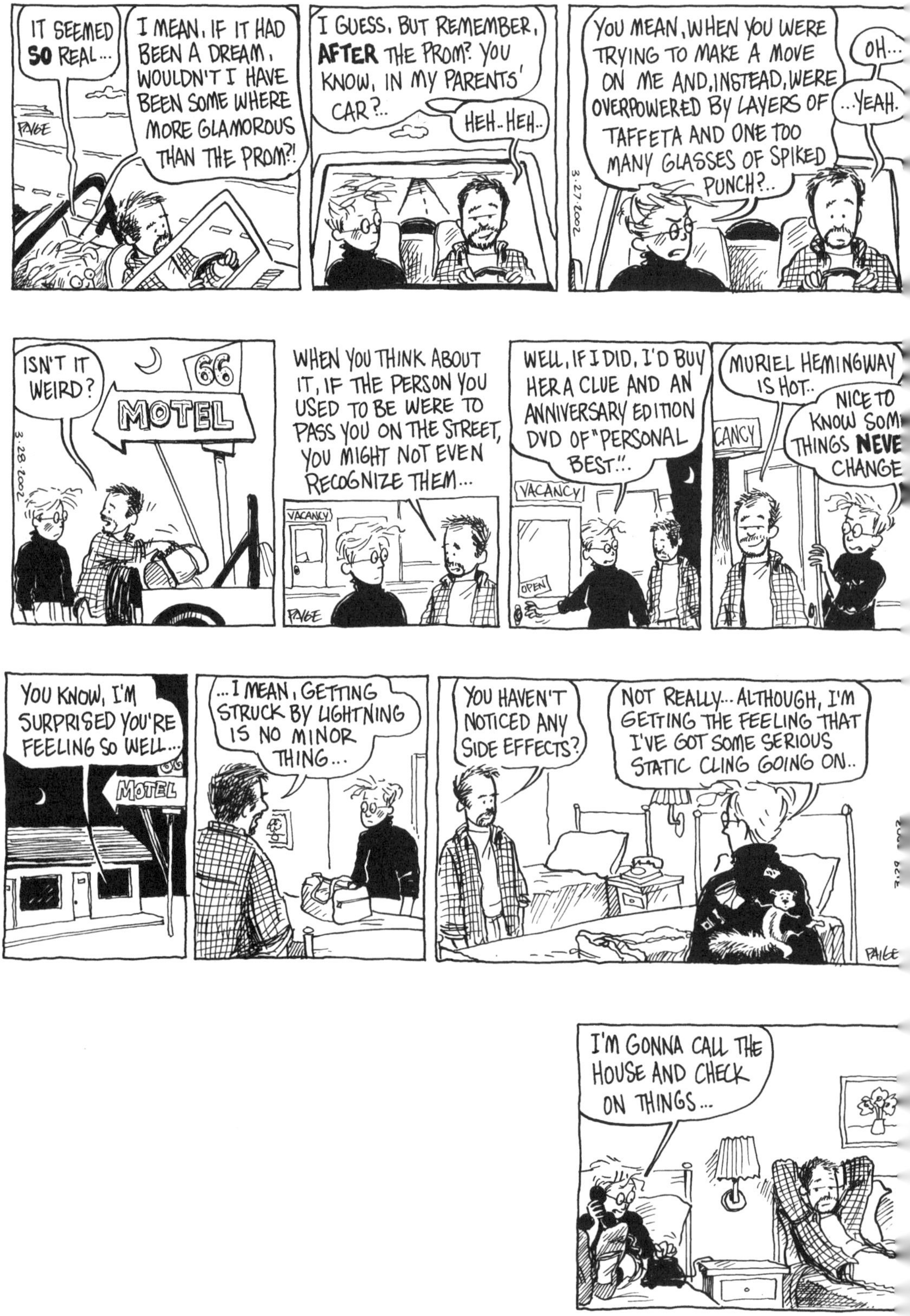
IT SEEMED **SO** REAL...
I MEAN, IF IT HAD BEEN A DREAM, WOULDN'T I HAVE BEEN SOME WHERE MORE GLAMOROUS THAN THE PROM?!
PAIGE
I GUESS, BUT REMEMBER, **AFTER** THE PROM? YOU KNOW, IN MY PARENTS' CAR?..
HEH.. HEH..
YOU MEAN, WHEN YOU WERE TRYING TO MAKE A MOVE ON ME AND, INSTEAD, WERE OVERPOWERED BY LAYERS OF TAFFETA AND ONE TOO MANY GLASSES OF SPIKED PUNCH?..
OH...
...YEAH.
3·27·2002
ISN'T IT WEIRD?
66
MOTEL
3·28·2002
WHEN YOU THINK ABOUT IT, IF THE PERSON YOU USED TO BE WERE TO PASS YOU ON THE STREET, YOU MIGHT NOT EVEN RECOGNIZE THEM...
VACANCY
PAIGE
WELL, IF I DID, I'D BUY HER A CLUE AND AN ANNIVERSARY EDITION DVD OF "PERSONAL BEST"!..
VACANCY
OPEN
MURIEL HEMINGWAY IS HOT..
NICE TO KNOW SOM THINGS **NEVE** CHANGE
CANCY
YOU KNOW, I'M SURPRISED YOU'RE FEELING SO WELL...
MOTEL
...I MEAN, GETTING STRUCK BY LIGHTNING IS NO MINOR THING...
YOU HAVEN'T NOTICED ANY SIDE EFFECTS?
NOT REALLY... ALTHOUGH, I'M GETTING THE FEELING THAT I'VE GOT SOME SERIOUS STATIC CLING GOING ON..
PAIGE
I'M GONNA CALL THE HOUSE AND CHECK ON THINGS...

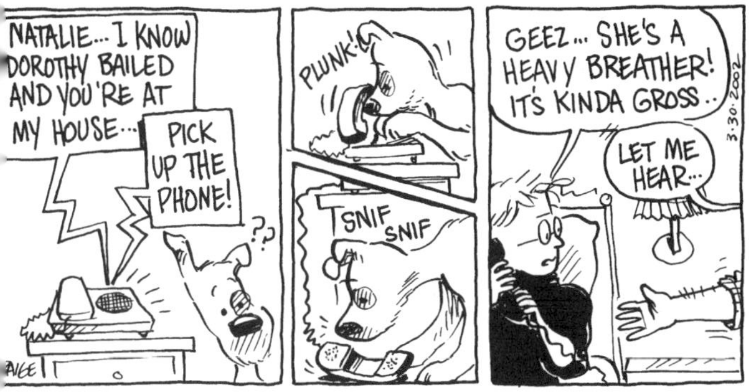
NATALIE... I KNOW DOROTHY BAILED AND YOU'RE AT MY HOUSE...
PICK UP THE PHONE!
PLINK!
SNIF SNIF
GEEZ... SHE'S A HEAVY BREATHER! IT'S KINDA GROSS..
LET ME HEAR...
3·30·2002
PAIGE

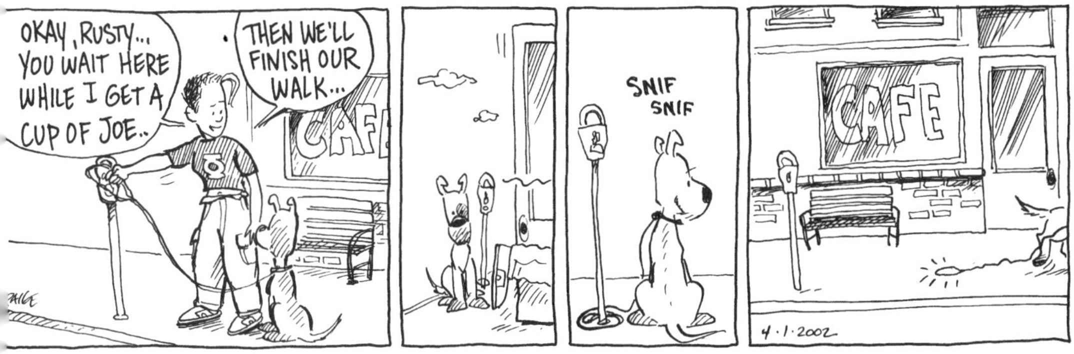
OKAY, RUSTY... YOU WAIT HERE WHILE I GET A CUP OF JOE..
THEN WE'LL FINISH OUR WALK...
CAFE
SNIF SNIF
CAFE
4·1·2002
PAIGE

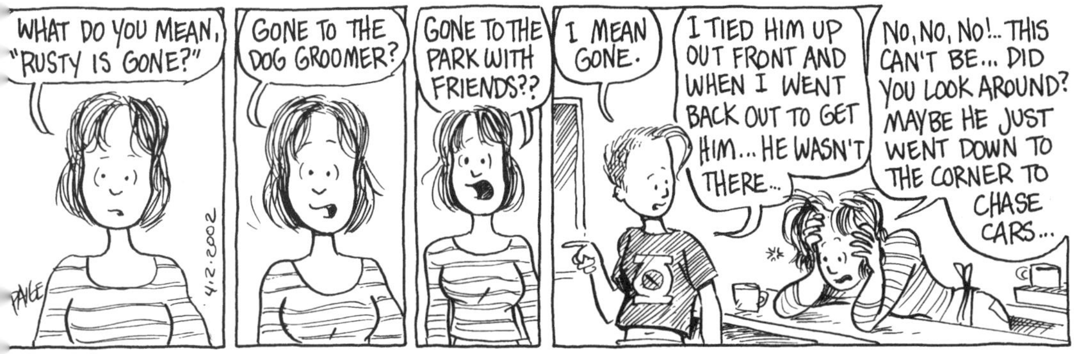
WHAT DO YOU MEAN, "RUSTY IS GONE?"
4·2·2002
GONE TO THE DOG GROOMER?
GONE TO THE PARK WITH FRIENDS??
I MEAN GONE.
I TIED HIM UP OUT FRONT AND WHEN I WENT BACK OUT TO GET HIM... HE WASN'T THERE...
NO, NO, NO!.. THIS CAN'T BE... DID YOU LOOK AROUND? MAYBE HE JUST WENT DOWN TO THE CORNER TO CHASE CARS...
PAIGE

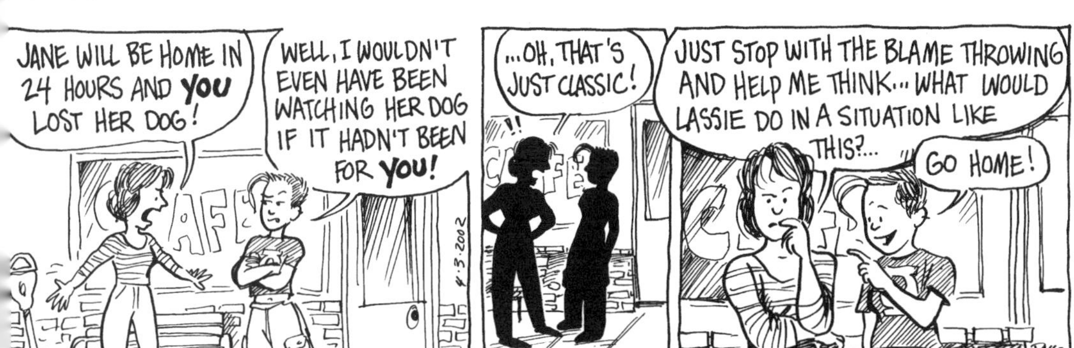
JANE WILL BE HOME IN 24 HOURS AND YOU LOST HER DOG!
WELL, I WOULDN'T EVEN HAVE BEEN WATCHING HER DOG IF IT HADN'T BEEN FOR YOU!
4·3·2002
...OH, THAT'S JUST CLASSIC!
JUST STOP WITH THE BLAME THROWING AND HELP ME THINK... WHAT WOULD LASSIE DO IN A SITUATION LIKE THIS?...
GO HOME!
PAIGE

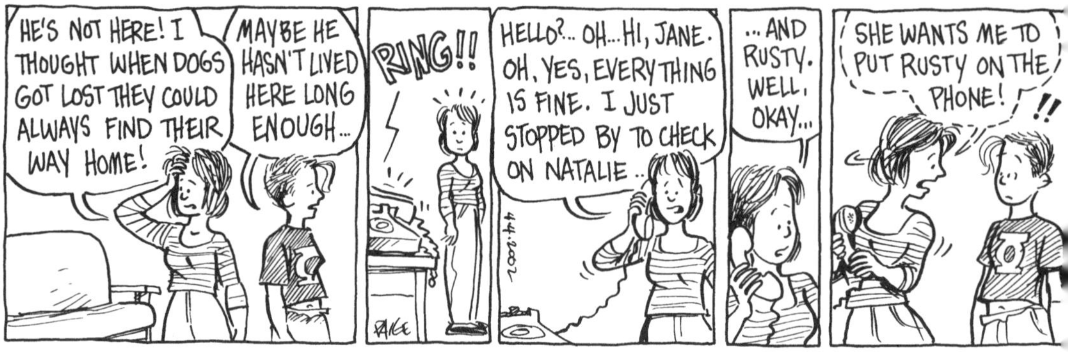
HE'S NOT HERE! I THOUGHT WHEN DOGS GOT LOST THEY COULD ALWAYS FIND THEIR WAY HOME!
MAYBE HE HASN'T LIVED HERE LONG ENOUGH...
PAGE
RING!!
4.4.2002
HELLO?... OH... HI, JANE. OH, YES, EVERYTHING IS FINE. I JUST STOPPED BY TO CHECK ON NATALIE...
...AND RUSTY. WELL, OKAY...
SHE WANTS ME TO PUT RUSTY ON THE PHONE!
!!

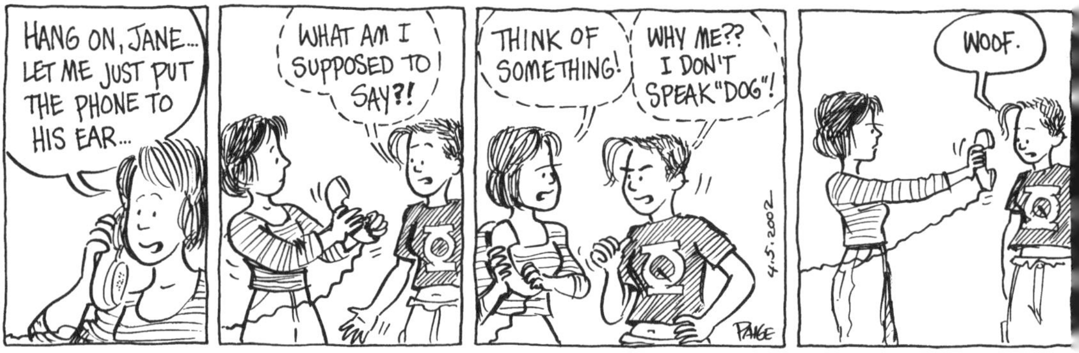
HANG ON, JANE... LET ME JUST PUT THE PHONE TO HIS EAR...
WHAT AM I SUPPOSED TO SAY?!
THINK OF SOMETHING!
WHY ME?? I DON'T SPEAK "DOG"!
4.5.2002
PAGE
WOOF.

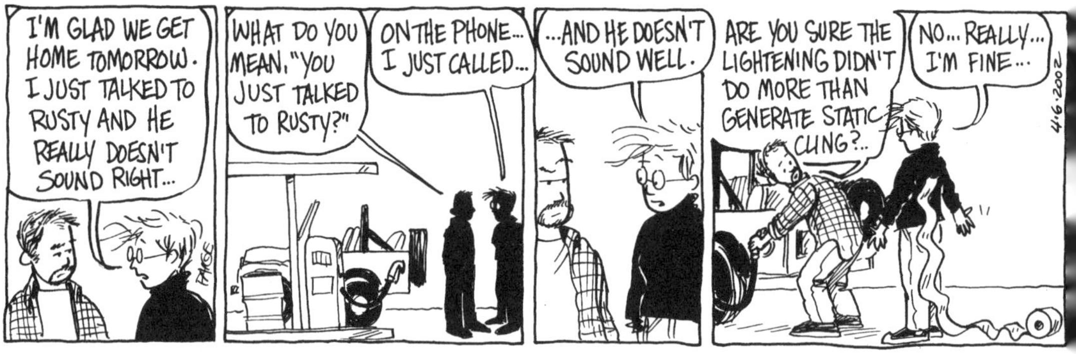
I'M GLAD WE GET HOME TOMORROW. I JUST TALKED TO RUSTY AND HE REALLY DOESN'T SOUND RIGHT...
PAGE
WHAT DO YOU MEAN, "YOU JUST TALKED TO RUSTY?"
ON THE PHONE... I JUST CALLED...
...AND HE DOESN'T SOUND WELL.
ARE YOU SURE THE LIGHTENING DIDN'T DO MORE THAN GENERATE STATIC CLING?...
NO... REALLY... I'M FINE...
4.6.2002

The next day...

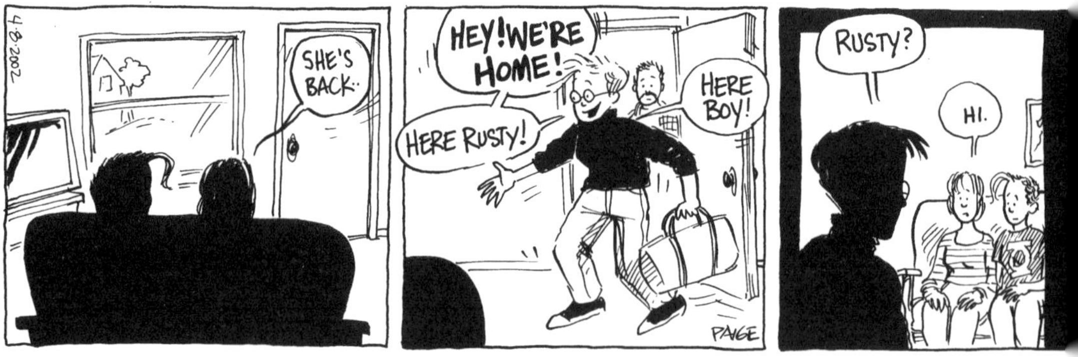
4.8.2002
SHE'S BACK.
HEY! WE'RE HOME!
HERE RUSTY!
HERE BOY!
PAGE
RUSTY?
HI.

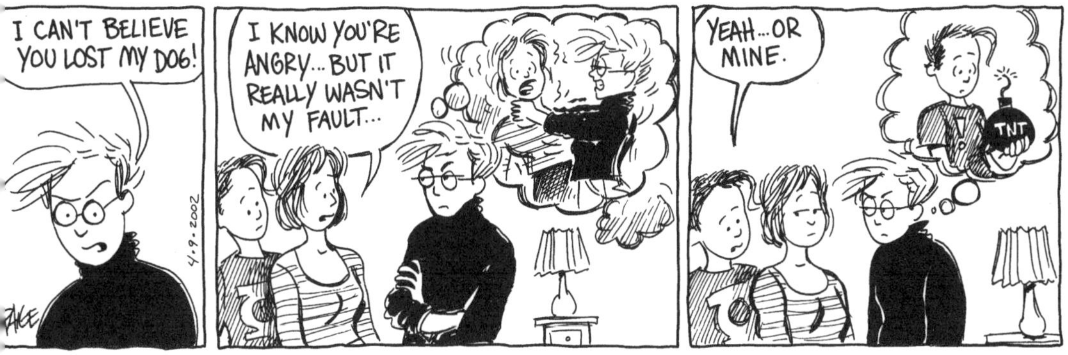
I CAN'T BELIEVE YOU LOST MY DOG!
4-9-2002
PAIGE
I KNOW YOU'RE ANGRY... BUT IT REALLY WASN'T MY FAULT...
YEAH... OR MINE.
TNT

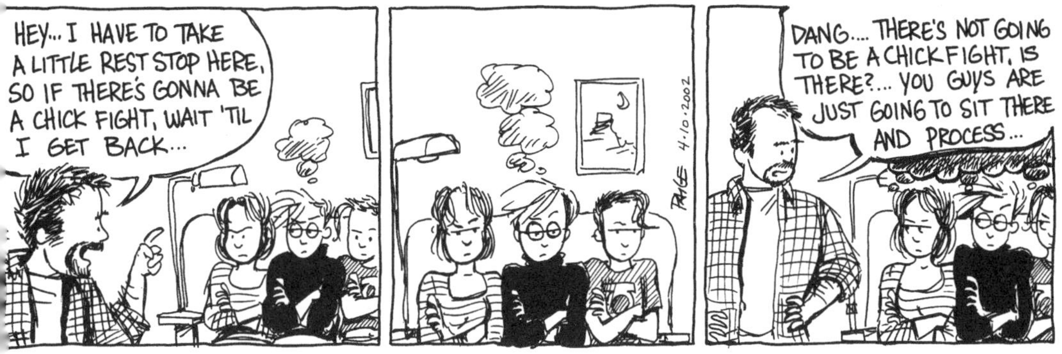
HEY... I HAVE TO TAKE A LITTLE REST STOP HERE, SO IF THERE'S GONNA BE A CHICK FIGHT, WAIT 'TIL I GET BACK...
PAIGE
4-10-2002
DANG.... THERE'S NOT GOING TO BE A CHICK FIGHT, IS THERE?... YOU GUYS ARE JUST GOING TO SIT THERE AND PROCESS...

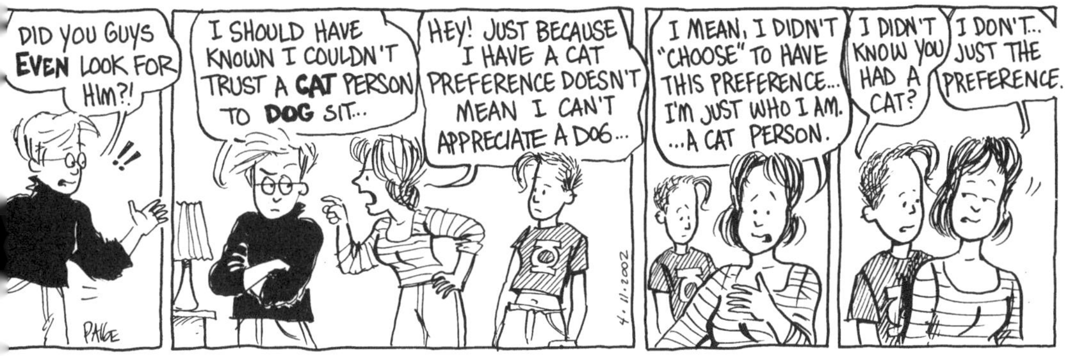
DID YOU GUYS EVEN LOOK FOR HIM?!
PAIGE
I SHOULD HAVE KNOWN I COULDN'T TRUST A CAT PERSON TO DOG SIT...
HEY! JUST BECAUSE I HAVE A CAT PREFERENCE DOESN'T MEAN I CAN'T APPRECIATE A DOG...
4-11-2002
I MEAN, I DIDN'T "CHOOSE" TO HAVE THIS PREFERENCE... I'M JUST WHO I AM. ...A CAT PERSON.
I DIDN'T KNOW YOU HAD A CAT?
I DON'T... JUST THE PREFERENCE.

ater that day...

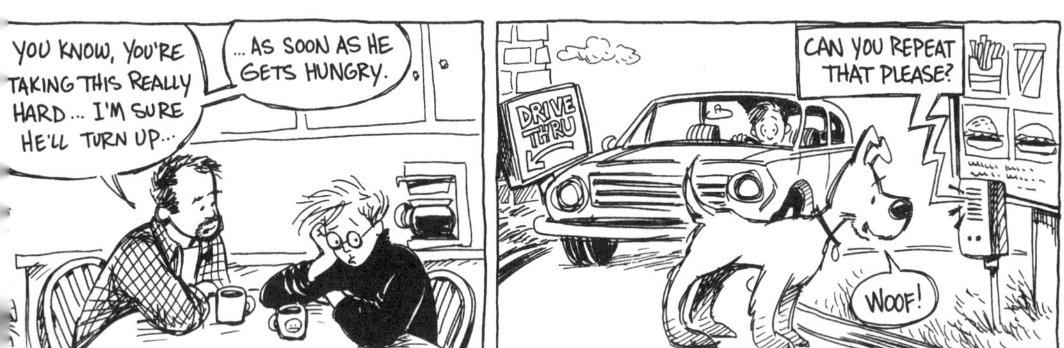
YOU KNOW, YOU'RE TAKING THIS REALLY HARD... I'M SURE HE'LL TURN UP...
...AS SOON AS HE GETS HUNGRY.
DRIVE THRU
CAN YOU REPEAT THAT PLEASE?
WOOF!

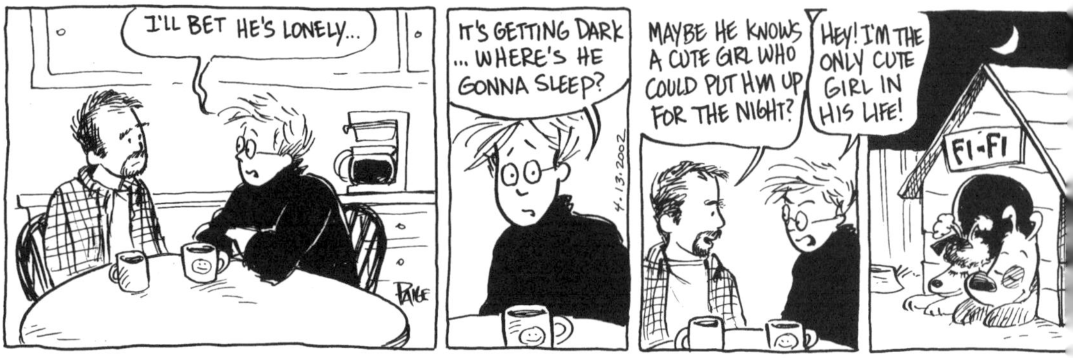
I'LL BET HE'S LONELY...
PAGE
IT'S GETTING DARK ... WHERE'S HE GONNA SLEEP?
4.13.2002
MAYBE HE KNOWS A CUTE GIRL WHO COULD PUT HIM UP FOR THE NIGHT?
HEY! I'M THE ONLY CUTE GIRL IN HIS LIFE!
FI-FI

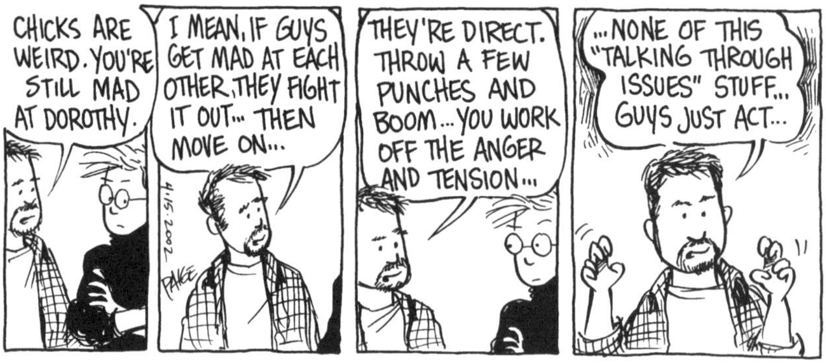
CHICKS ARE WEIRD. YOU'RE STILL MAD AT DOROTHY.
I MEAN, IF GUYS GET MAD AT EACH OTHER, THEY FIGHT IT OUT... THEN MOVE ON...
4.15.2002
PAGE
THEY'RE DIRECT. THROW A FEW PUNCHES AND BOOM... YOU WORK OFF THE ANGER AND TENSION...
...NONE OF THIS "TALKING THROUGH ISSUES" STUFF... GUYS JUST ACT...

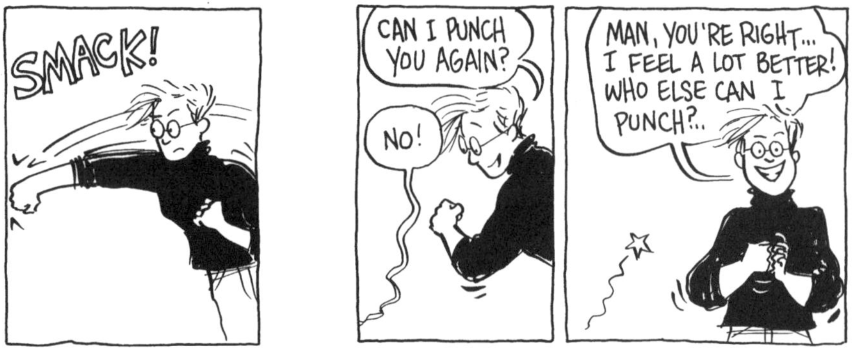
SMACK!
CAN I PUNCH YOU AGAIN?
NO!
MAN, YOU'RE RIGHT... I FEEL A LOT BETTER! WHO ELSE CAN I PUNCH?..

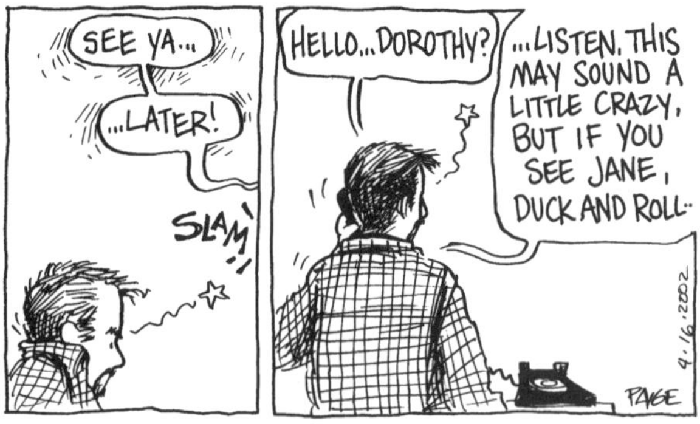
SEE YA...
...LATER!
SLAM!
HELLO... DOROTHY?
...LISTEN, THIS MAY SOUND A LITTLE CRAZY, BUT IF YOU SEE JANE, DUCK AND ROLL..
4.16.2002
PAGE

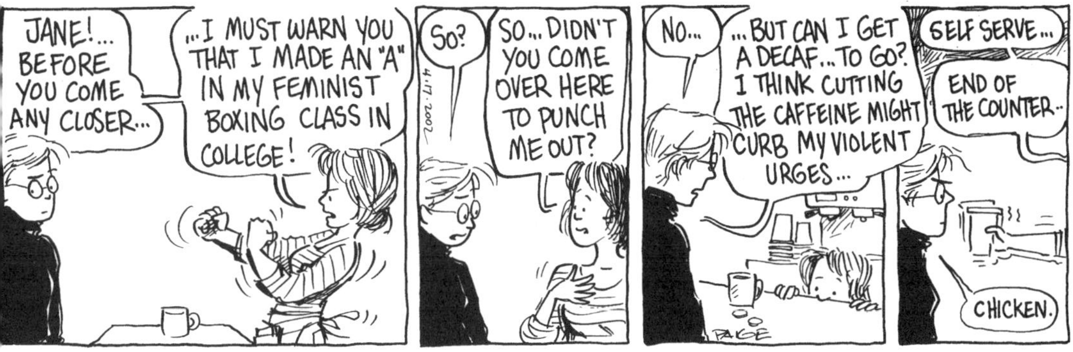
JANE!... BEFORE YOU COME ANY CLOSER...
...I MUST WARN YOU THAT I MADE AN "A" IN MY FEMINIST BOXING CLASS IN COLLEGE!
4.17.2002
SO?
SO... DIDN'T YOU COME OVER HERE TO PUNCH ME OUT?
NO...
...BUT CAN I GET A DECAF... TO GO? I THINK CUTTING THE CAFFEINE MIGHT CURB MY VIOLENT URGES...
PAIGE
SELF SERVE...
END OF THE COUNTER...
CHICKEN.

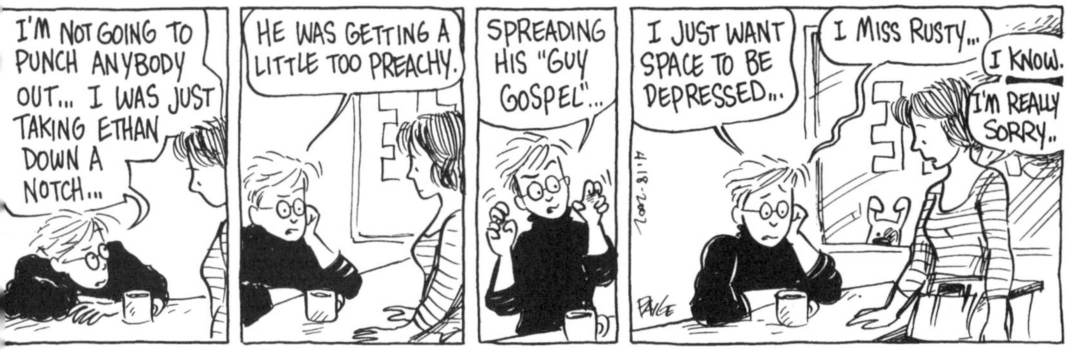
I'M NOT GOING TO PUNCH ANYBODY OUT... I WAS JUST TAKING ETHAN DOWN A NOTCH...
HE WAS GETTING A LITTLE TOO PREACHY.
SPREADING HIS "GUY GOSPEL"...
I JUST WANT SPACE TO BE DEPRESSED...
4.18.2002
PAIGE
I MISS RUSTY...
I KNOW.
I'M REALLY SORRY..

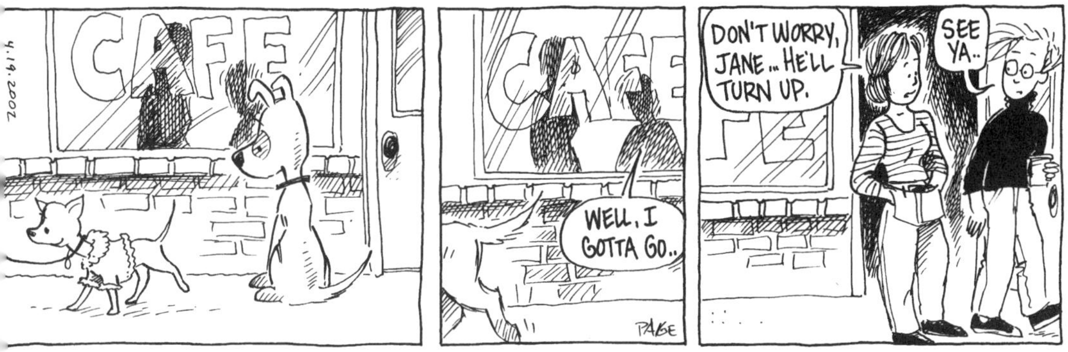
4.19.2002
CAFE
WELL, I GOTTA GO..
PAIGE
DON'T WORRY, JANE... HE'LL TURN UP.
SEE YA..

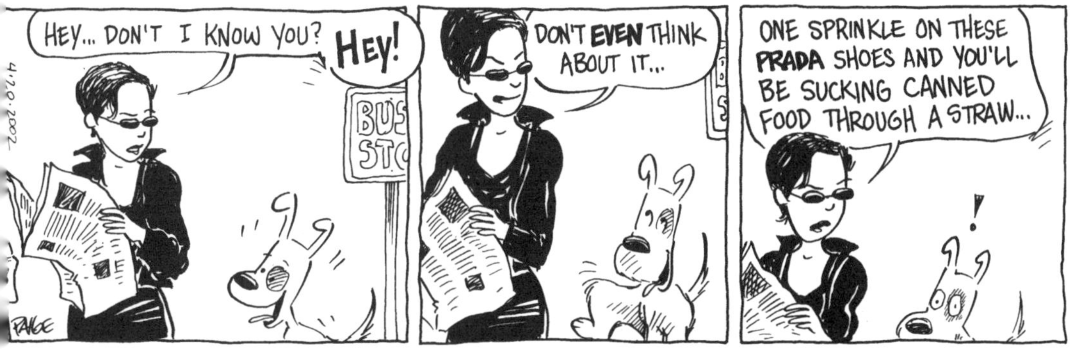
4.20.2002
HEY... DON'T I KNOW YOU?
HEY!
BUS STO
PAIGE
DON'T EVEN THINK ABOUT IT...
ONE SPRINKLE ON THESE PRADA SHOES AND YOU'LL BE SUCKING CANNED FOOD THROUGH A STRAW...
!

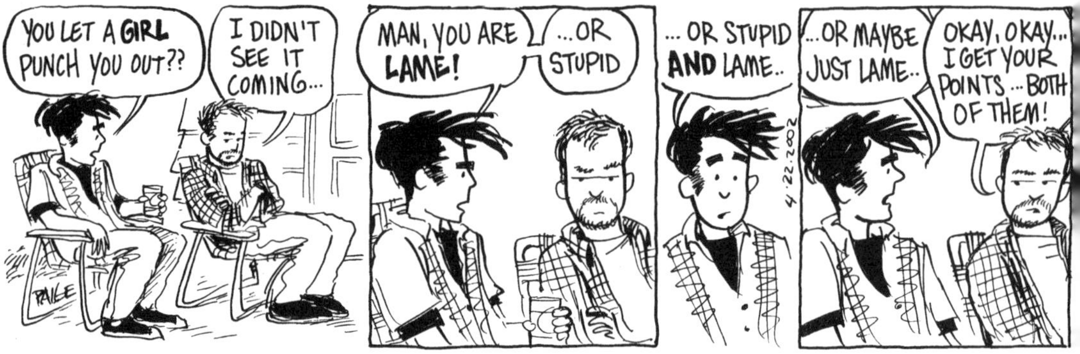
YOU LET A **GIRL** PUNCH YOU OUT??
I DIDN'T SEE IT COMING...
MAN, YOU ARE **LAME!**
...OR STUPID
... OR STUPID **AND** LAME..
...OR MAYBE JUST LAME..
OKAY, OKAY... I GET YOUR POINTS ... BOTH OF THEM!
PAIGE
4.22.2002

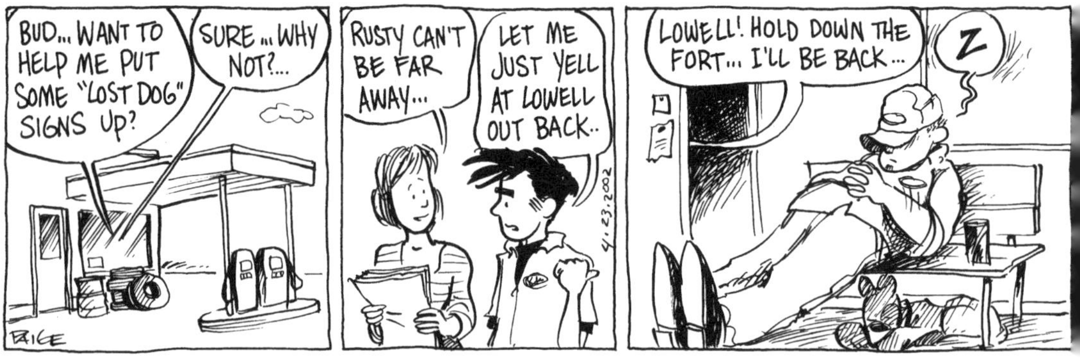
BUD... WANT TO HELP ME PUT SOME "LOST DOG" SIGNS UP?
SURE ... WHY NOT?...
RUSTY CAN'T BE FAR AWAY...
LET ME JUST YELL AT LOWELL OUT BACK..
LOWELL! HOLD DOWN THE FORT... I'LL BE BACK...
Z
PAIGE
4.23.2002

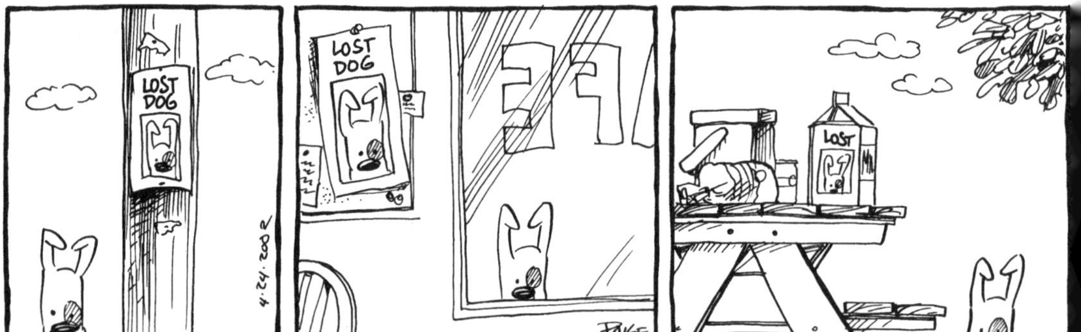
LOST DOG
LOST DOG
LOST
4.24.2002
PAIGE

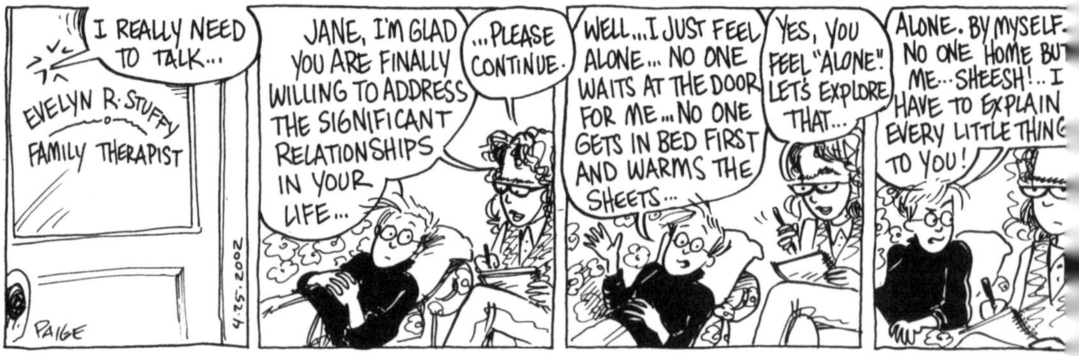
I REALLY NEED TO TALK...
EVELYN R. STUFFY
FAMILY THERAPIST
JANE, I'M GLAD YOU ARE FINALLY WILLING TO ADDRESS THE SIGNIFICANT RELATIONSHIPS IN YOUR LIFE...
...PLEASE CONTINUE.
WELL...I JUST FEEL ALONE... NO ONE WAITS AT THE DOOR FOR ME...NO ONE GETS IN BED FIRST AND WARMS THE SHEETS...
YES, YOU FEEL "ALONE." LET'S EXPLORE THAT...
ALONE. BY MYSELF. NO ONE HOME BUT ME...SHEESH!.. I HAVE TO EXPLAIN EVERY LITTLE THING TO YOU!
PAIGE
4.25.2002

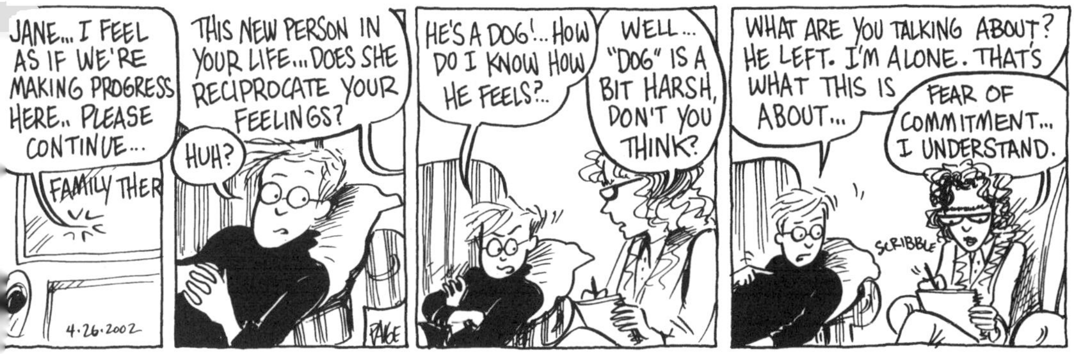
JANE... I FEEL AS IF WE'RE MAKING PROGRESS HERE.. PLEASE CONTINUE...
FAMILY THER
THIS NEW PERSON IN YOUR LIFE... DOES SHE RECIPROCATE YOUR FEELINGS?
HUH?
HE'S A DOG!... HOW DO I KNOW HOW HE FEELS?..
WELL... "DOG" IS A BIT HARSH, DON'T YOU THINK?
WHAT ARE YOU TALKING ABOUT? HE LEFT. I'M ALONE. THAT'S WHAT THIS IS ABOUT...
FEAR OF COMMITMENT... I UNDERSTAND.
SCRIBBLE
4·26·2002
PAIGE

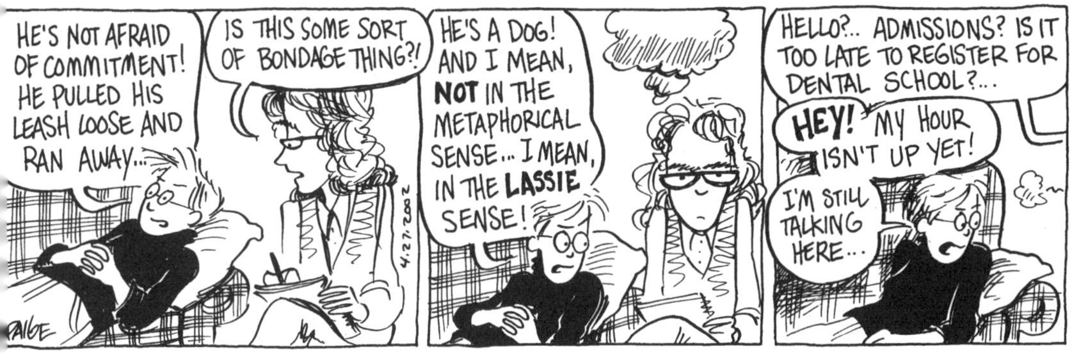
HE'S NOT AFRAID OF COMMITMENT! HE PULLED HIS LEASH LOOSE AND RAN AWAY...
IS THIS SOME SORT OF BONDAGE THING?!
HE'S A DOG! AND I MEAN, NOT IN THE METAPHORICAL SENSE... I MEAN, IN THE LASSIE SENSE!
HELLO?.. ADMISSIONS? IS IT TOO LATE TO REGISTER FOR DENTAL SCHOOL?...
HEY! MY HOUR ISN'T UP YET!
I'M STILL TALKING HERE...
4.27.2002
PAIGE

he next day...

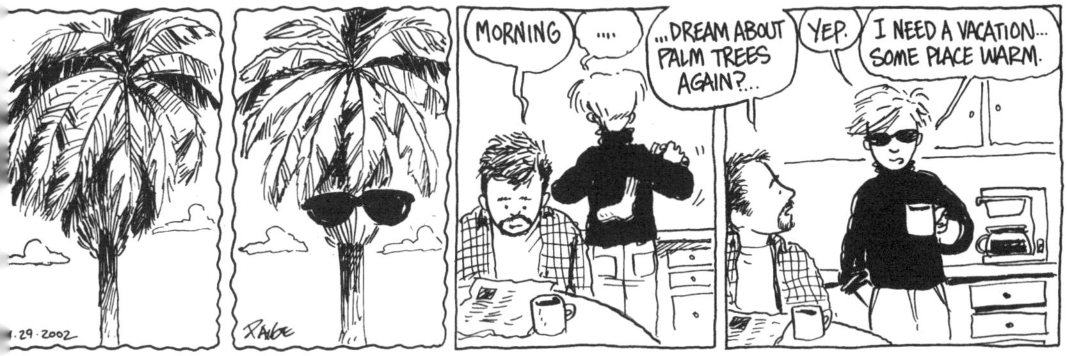
MORNING
....
...DREAM ABOUT PALM TREES AGAIN?...
YEP.
I NEED A VACATION... SOME PLACE WARM.
4.29.2002
PAIGE

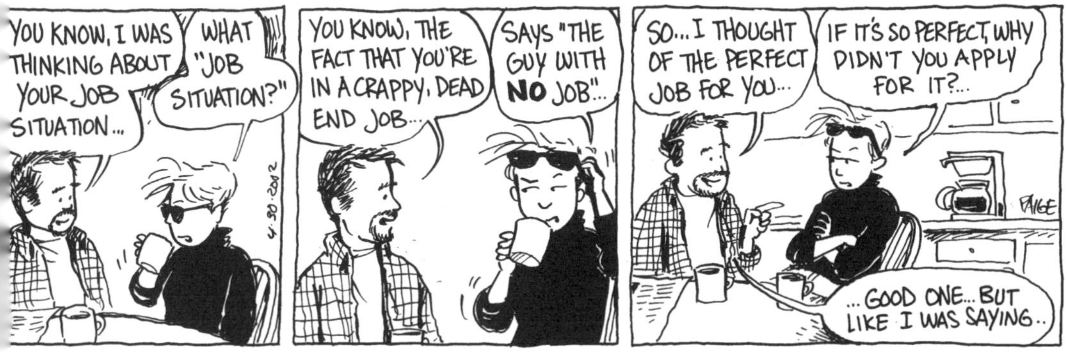
YOU KNOW, I WAS THINKING ABOUT YOUR JOB SITUATION...
WHAT "JOB SITUATION?"
YOU KNOW, THE FACT THAT YOU'RE IN A CRAPPY, DEAD END JOB...
SAYS "THE GUY WITH NO JOB"...
SO... I THOUGHT OF THE PERFECT JOB FOR YOU...
IF IT'S SO PERFECT, WHY DIDN'T YOU APPLY FOR IT?...
...GOOD ONE... BUT LIKE I WAS SAYING...
4.30.2002
PAIGE

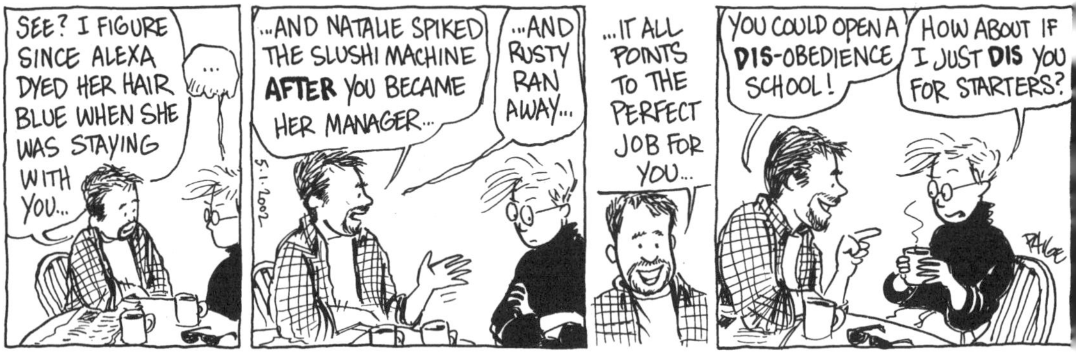
SEE? I FIGURE SINCE ALEXA DYED HER HAIR BLUE WHEN SHE WAS STAYING WITH YOU...
...
...AND NATALIE SPIKED THE SLUSHI MACHINE **AFTER** YOU BECAME HER MANAGER...
...AND RUSTY RAN AWAY...
5.1.2002
...IT ALL POINTS TO THE PERFECT JOB FOR YOU...
YOU COULD OPEN A **DIS**-OBEDIENCE SCHOOL!
HOW ABOUT IF I JUST **DIS** YOU FOR STARTERS?
PAIGE

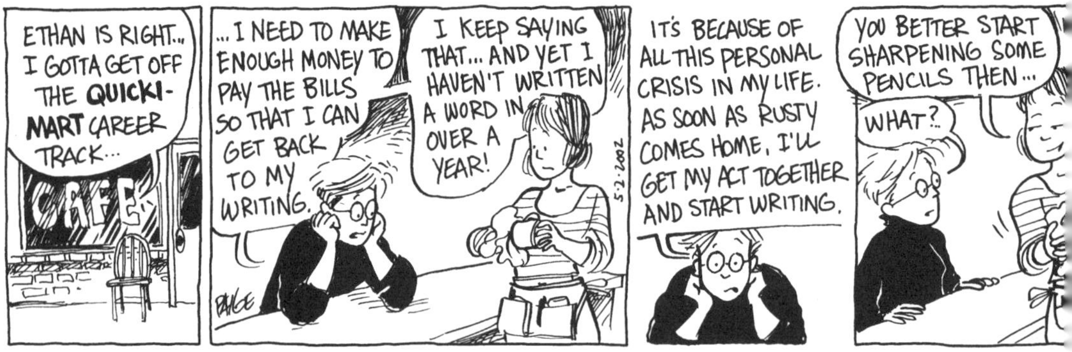
ETHAN IS RIGHT... I GOTTA GET OFF THE **QUICKI-MART** CAREER TRACK...
CAFE
...I NEED TO MAKE ENOUGH MONEY TO PAY THE BILLS SO THAT I CAN GET BACK TO MY WRITING.
I KEEP SAYING THAT... AND YET I HAVEN'T WRITTEN A WORD IN OVER A YEAR!
PAIGE
5.2.2002
IT'S BECAUSE OF ALL THIS PERSONAL CRISIS IN MY LIFE. AS SOON AS RUSTY COMES HOME, I'LL GET MY ACT TOGETHER AND START WRITING.
YOU BETTER START SHARPENING SOME PENCILS THEN...
WHAT?

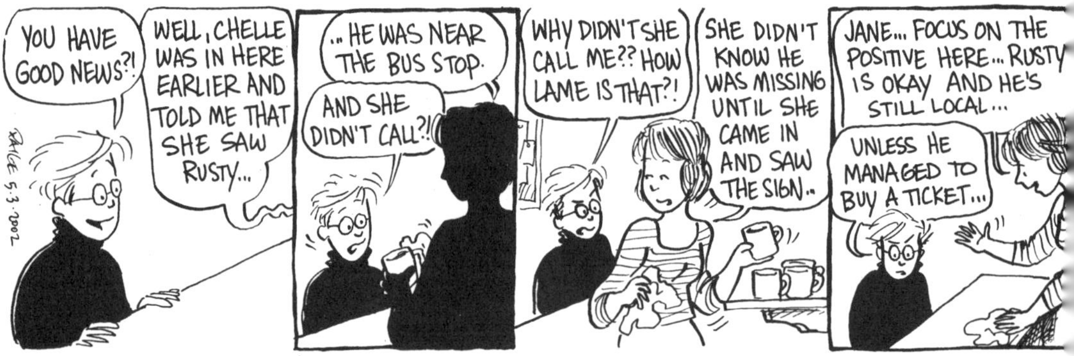
YOU HAVE GOOD NEWS?!
PAIGE 5.3.2002
WELL, CHELLE WAS IN HERE EARLIER AND TOLD ME THAT SHE SAW RUSTY...
...HE WAS NEAR THE BUS STOP.
AND SHE DIDN'T CALL?!
WHY DIDN'T SHE CALL ME?? HOW LAME IS THAT?!
SHE DIDN'T KNOW HE WAS MISSING UNTIL SHE CAME IN AND SAW THE SIGN..
JANE... FOCUS ON THE POSITIVE HERE... RUSTY IS OKAY AND HE'S STILL LOCAL...
UNLESS HE MANAGED TO BUY A TICKET...

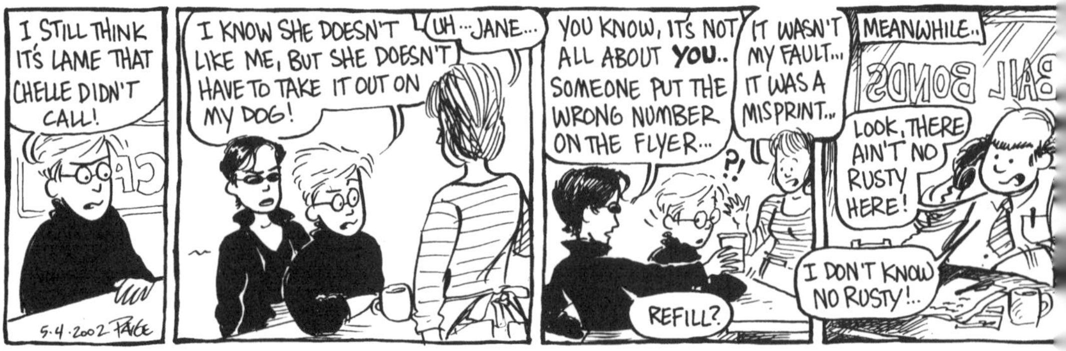
I STILL THINK IT'S LAME THAT CHELLE DIDN'T CALL!
5.4.2002 PAIGE
I KNOW SHE DOESN'T LIKE ME, BUT SHE DOESN'T HAVE TO TAKE IT OUT ON MY DOG!
UH...JANE...
YOU KNOW, IT'S NOT ALL ABOUT **YOU**.. SOMEONE PUT THE WRONG NUMBER ON THE FLYER...
IT WASN'T MY FAULT... IT WAS A MISPRINT...
?!
REFILL?
MEANWHILE..
BAIL BONDS
LOOK, THERE AIN'T NO RUSTY HERE!
I DON'T KNOW NO RUSTY!..

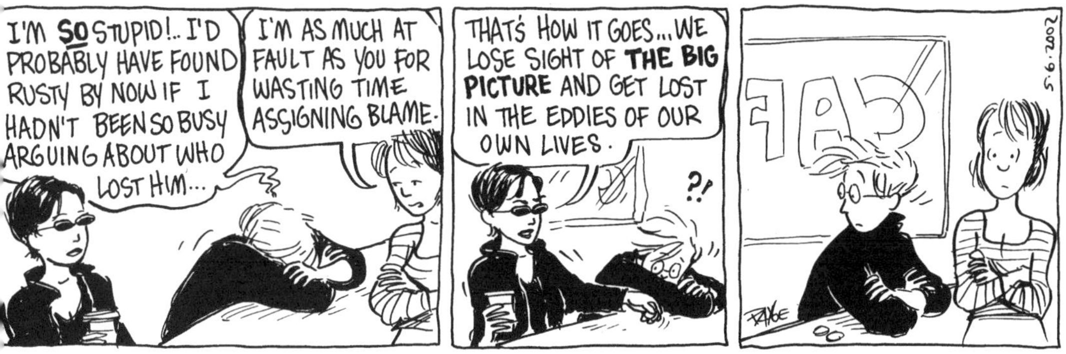
I'M **SO** STUPID!.. I'D PROBABLY HAVE FOUND RUSTY BY NOW IF I HADN'T BEEN SO BUSY ARGUING ABOUT WHO LOST HIM...
I'M AS MUCH AT FAULT AS YOU FOR WASTING TIME ASSIGNING BLAME.
THAT'S HOW IT GOES... WE LOSE SIGHT OF **THE BIG PICTURE** AND GET LOST IN THE EDDIES OF OUR OWN LIVES.
?!
5·6·2002
PAIGE

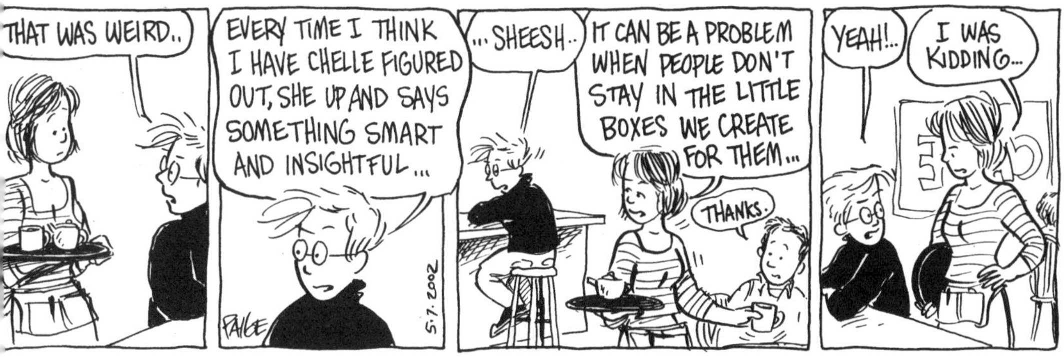
THAT WAS WEIRD..
EVERY TIME I THINK I HAVE CHELLE FIGURED OUT, SHE UP AND SAYS SOMETHING SMART AND INSIGHTFUL...
PAIGE
5·7·2002
...SHEESH..
IT CAN BE A PROBLEM WHEN PEOPLE DON'T STAY IN THE LITTLE BOXES WE CREATE FOR THEM...
THANKS.
YEAH!..
I WAS KIDDING...

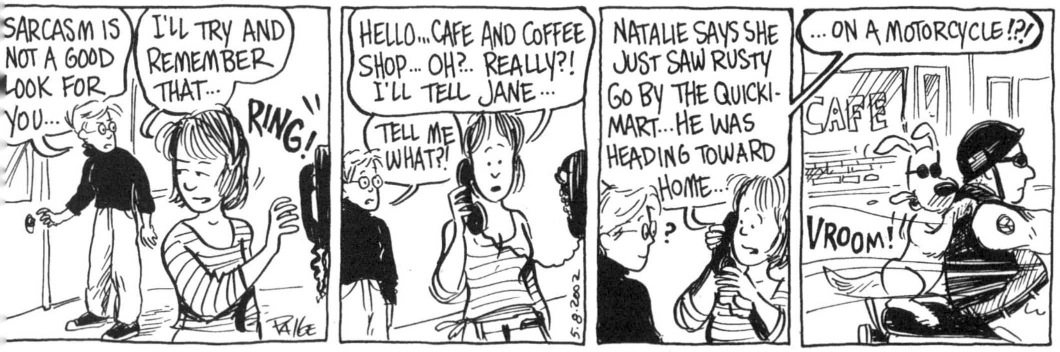
SARCASM IS NOT A GOOD LOOK FOR YOU...
I'LL TRY AND REMEMBER THAT...
RING!
PAIGE
HELLO... CAFE AND COFFEE SHOP... OH?.. REALLY?! I'LL TELL JANE...
TELL ME WHAT?!
5·8·2002
NATALIE SAYS SHE JUST SAW RUSTY GO BY THE QUICKI-MART... HE WAS HEADING TOWARD HOME...
?
...ON A MOTORCYCLE!?!
CAFE
VROOM!

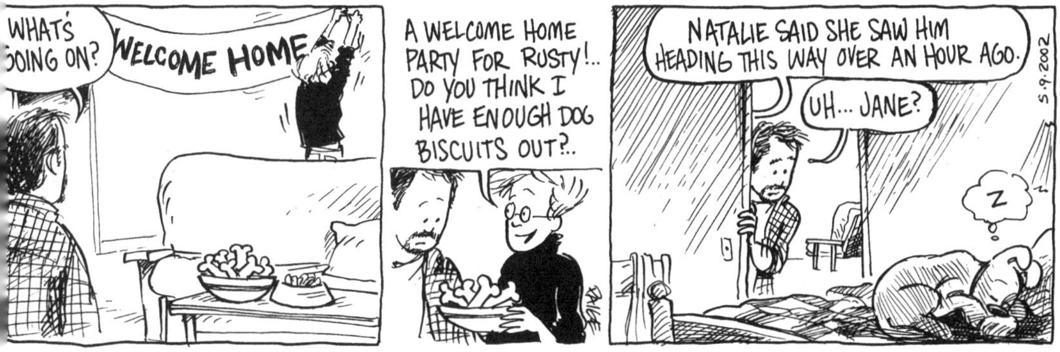
WHAT'S GOING ON?
WELCOME HOME
A WELCOME HOME PARTY FOR RUSTY!.. DO YOU THINK I HAVE ENOUGH DOG BISCUITS OUT?..
PAIGE
NATALIE SAID SHE SAW HIM HEADING THIS WAY OVER AN HOUR AGO.
UH... JANE?
Z
5·9·2002

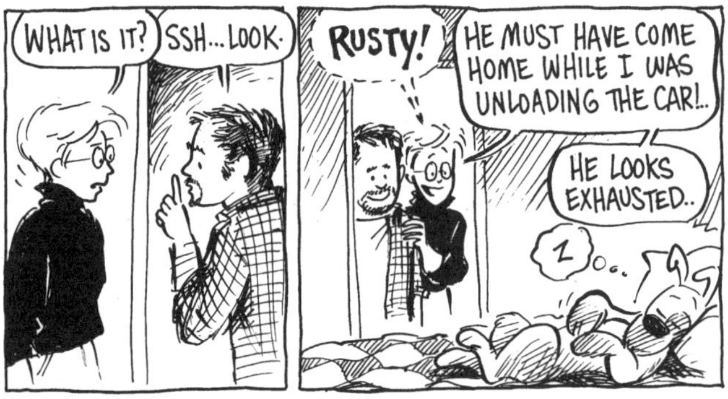
WHAT IS IT?
SSH... LOOK.
RUSTY!
HE MUST HAVE COME HOME WHILE I WAS UNLOADING THE CAR!..
HE LOOKS EXHAUSTED..
Z

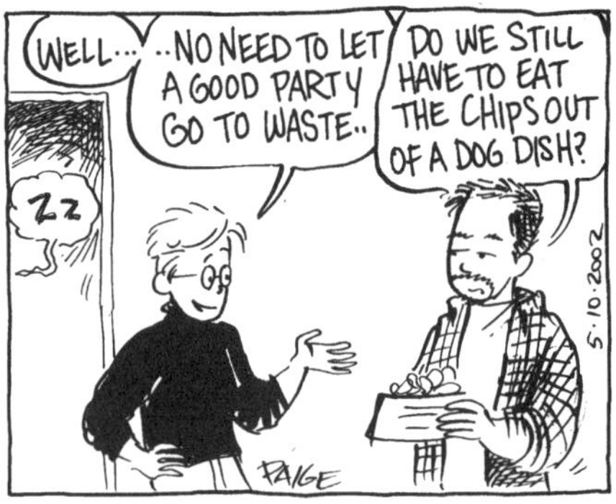
WELL...
..NO NEED TO LET A GOOD PARTY GO TO WASTE..
DO WE STILL HAVE TO EAT THE CHIPS OUT OF A DOG DISH?
ZZ
5·10·2002
PAIGE

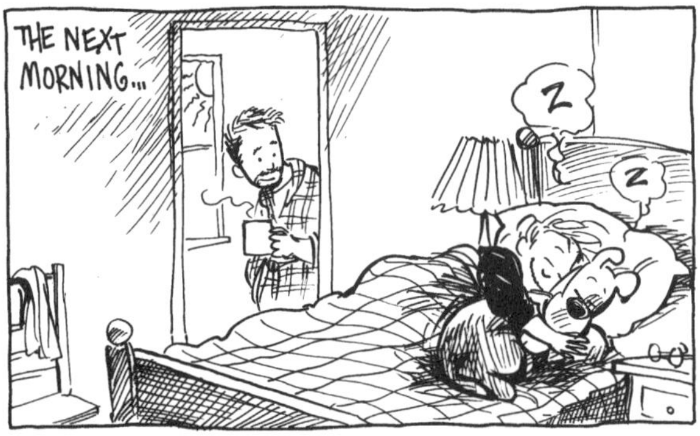
THE NEXT MORNING...
Z
Z

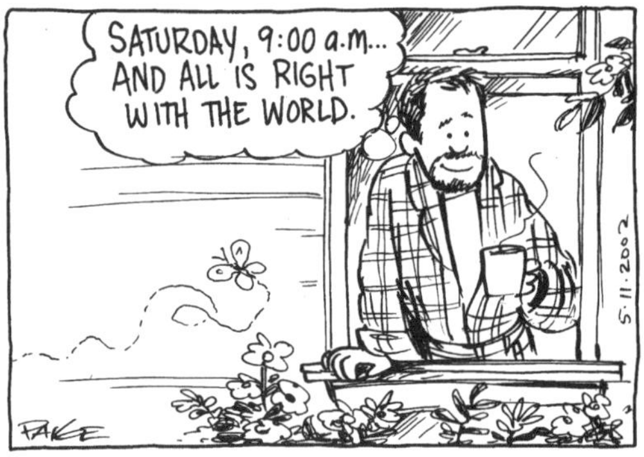
SATURDAY, 9:00 a.m... AND ALL IS RIGHT WITH THE WORLD.
5·11·2002
PAIGE

Chapter five

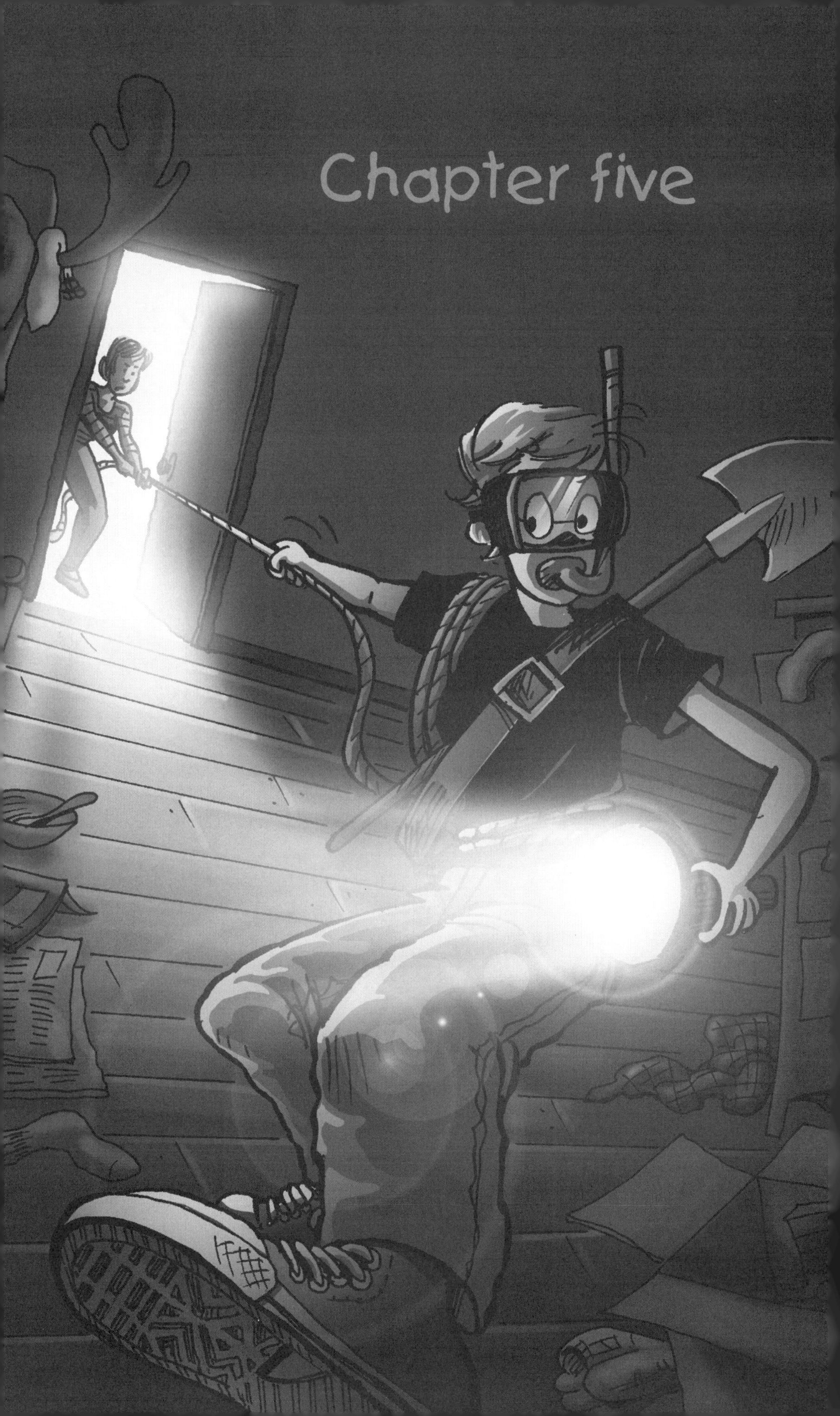

Rusty's first morning back...

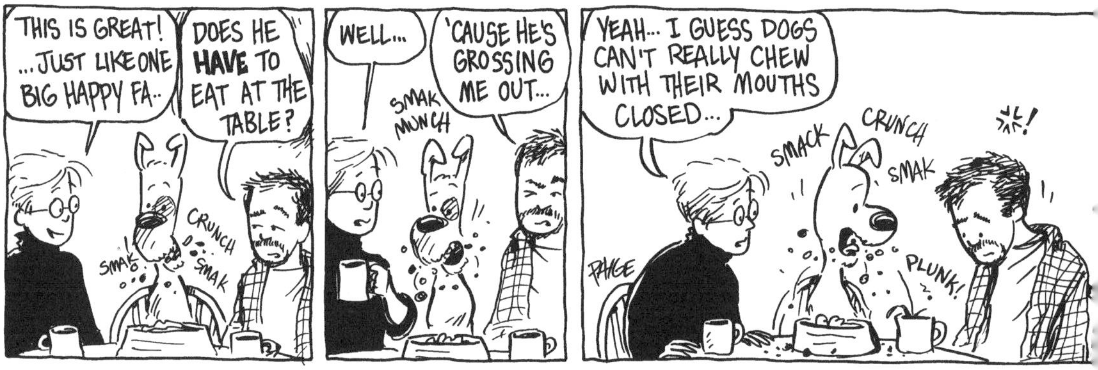
THIS IS GREAT! ...JUST LIKE ONE BIG HAPPY FA..
DOES HE **HAVE** TO EAT AT THE TABLE?
SMAK
CRUNCH
SMAK
WELL...
'CAUSE HE'S GROSSING ME OUT...
SMAK MUNCH
YEAH... I GUESS DOGS CAN'T REALLY CHEW WITH THEIR MOUTHS CLOSED...
SMACK
CRUNCH
SMAK
PLUNK!
PAIGE

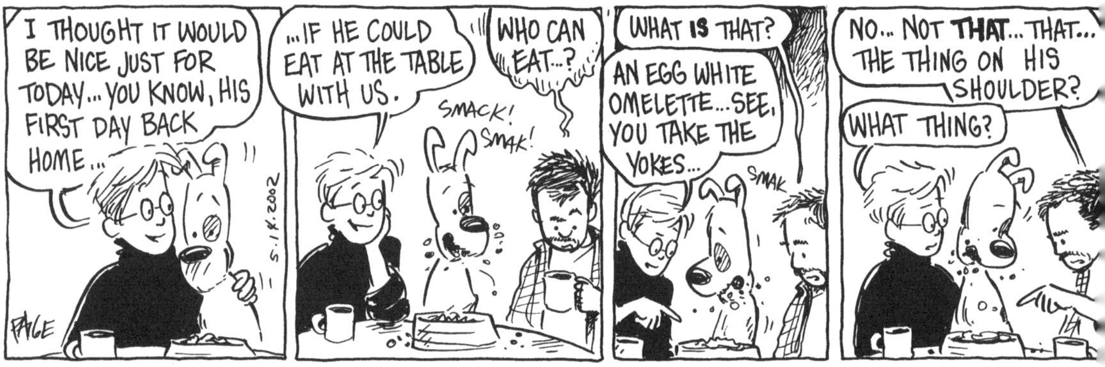
I THOUGHT IT WOULD BE NICE JUST FOR TODAY... YOU KNOW, HIS FIRST DAY BACK HOME...
PAIGE
5.14.2002
...IF HE COULD EAT AT THE TABLE WITH US.
WHO CAN EAT..?
SMACK!
SMAK!
WHAT **IS** THAT?
AN EGG WHITE OMELETTE... SEE, YOU TAKE THE YOKES...
SMAK
NO... NOT **THAT**... THAT... THE THING ON HIS SHOULDER?
WHAT THING?

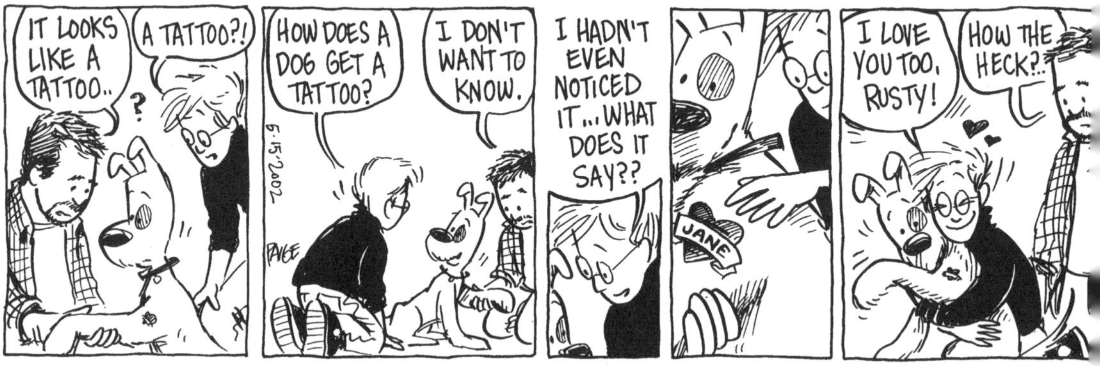
IT LOOKS LIKE A TATTOO..
A TATTOO?!
?
HOW DOES A DOG GET A TATTOO?
I DON'T WANT TO KNOW.
5.15.2002
PAIGE
I HADN'T EVEN NOTICED IT... WHAT DOES IT SAY??
JANE
I LOVE YOU TOO, RUSTY!
HOW THE HECK?..

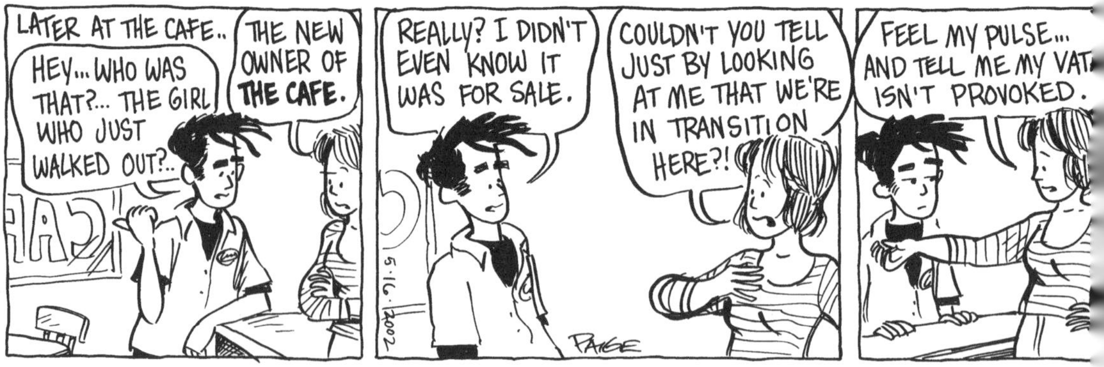
LATER AT THE CAFE..
HEY... WHO WAS THAT?... THE GIRL WHO JUST WALKED OUT?..
THE NEW OWNER OF **THE CAFE.**
REALLY? I DIDN'T EVEN KNOW IT WAS FOR SALE.
5.16.2002
PAIGE
COULDN'T YOU TELL JUST BY LOOKING AT ME THAT WE'RE IN TRANSITION HERE?!
FEEL MY PULSE... AND TELL ME MY VAT ISN'T PROVOKED.

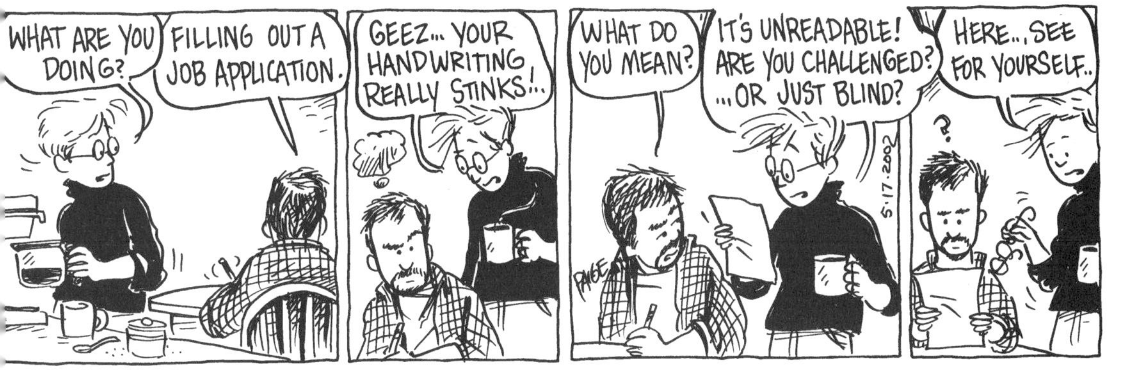
WHAT ARE YOU DOING?
FILLING OUT A JOB APPLICATION.
GEEZ... YOUR HANDWRITING REALLY STINKS!..
WHAT DO YOU MEAN?
IT'S UNREADABLE! ARE YOU CHALLENGED? ...OR JUST BLIND?
5.17.2002
PAIGE
HERE.., SEE FOR YOURSELF..
?

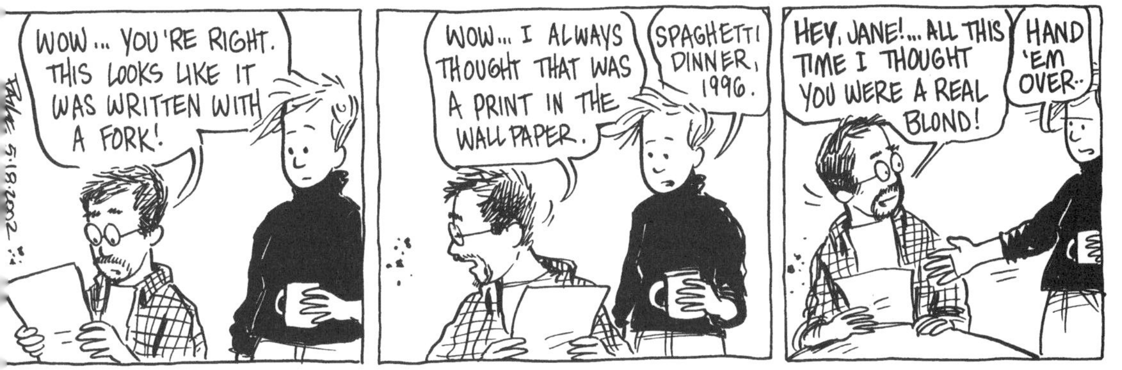
PAIGE 5.18.2002
WOW... YOU'RE RIGHT. THIS LOOKS LIKE IT WAS WRITTEN WITH A FORK!
WOW... I ALWAYS THOUGHT THAT WAS A PRINT IN THE WALLPAPER.
SPAGHETTI DINNER, 1996.
HEY, JANE!... ALL THIS TIME I THOUGHT YOU WERE A REAL BLOND!
HAND 'EM OVER..

The next morning...

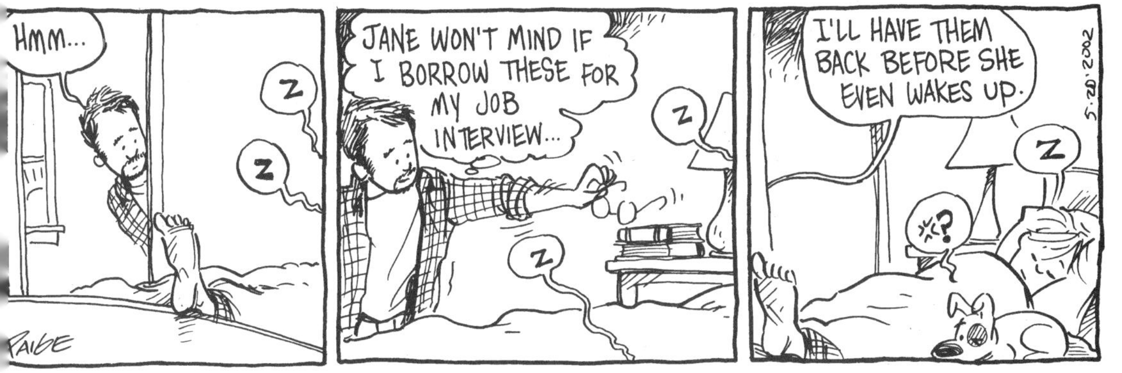
HMM...
Z
Z
PAIGE
JANE WON'T MIND IF I BORROW THESE FOR MY JOB INTERVIEW...
Z
Z
I'LL HAVE THEM BACK BEFORE SHE EVEN WAKES UP.
5.20.2002
Z

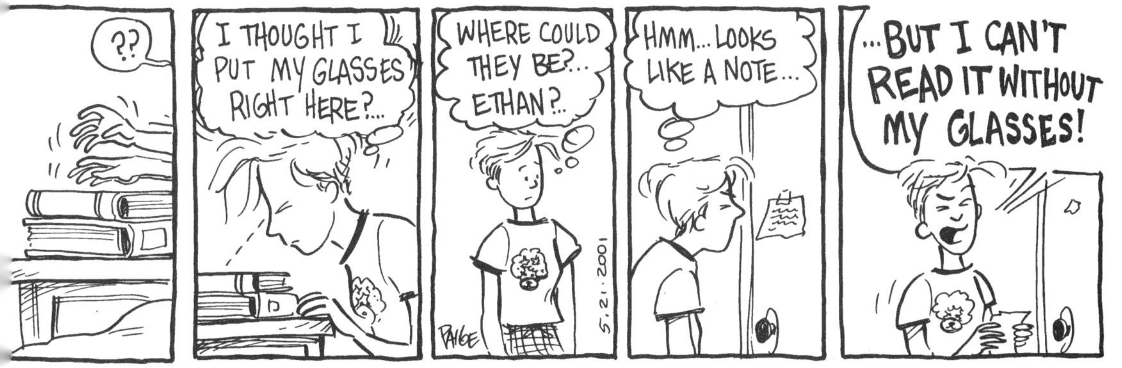
??
I THOUGHT I PUT MY GLASSES RIGHT HERE?...
WHERE COULD THEY BE?... ETHAN?...
5.21.2001
PAIGE
HMM... LOOKS LIKE A NOTE...
...BUT I CAN'T READ IT WITHOUT MY GLASSES!

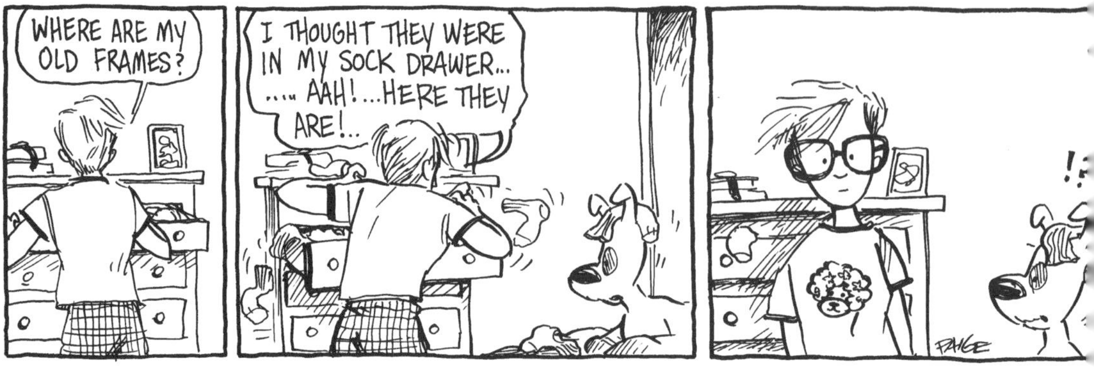
WHERE ARE MY OLD FRAMES?
I THOUGHT THEY WERE IN MY SOCK DRAWER... ..... AAH!...HERE THEY ARE!..
!?
PAIGE

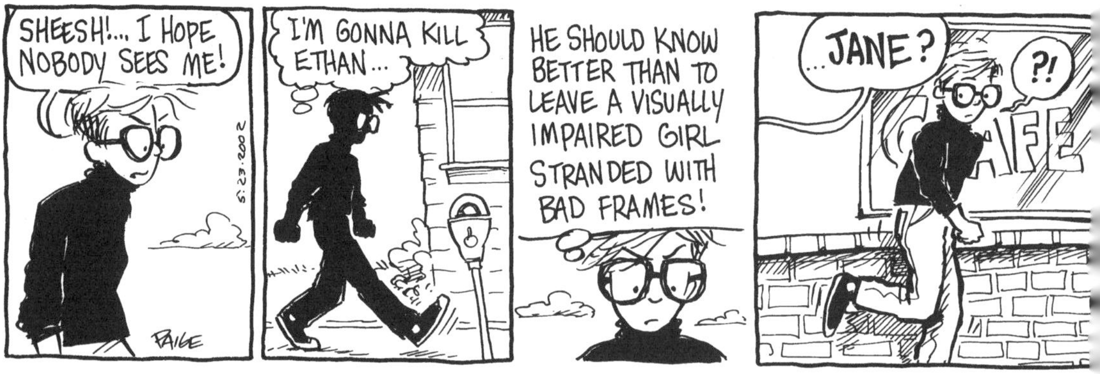
SHEESH!... I HOPE NOBODY SEES ME!
5.23.2002
PAIGE
I'M GONNA KILL ETHAN...
HE SHOULD KNOW BETTER THAN TO LEAVE A VISUALLY IMPAIRED GIRL STRANDED WITH BAD FRAMES!
...JANE?
?!

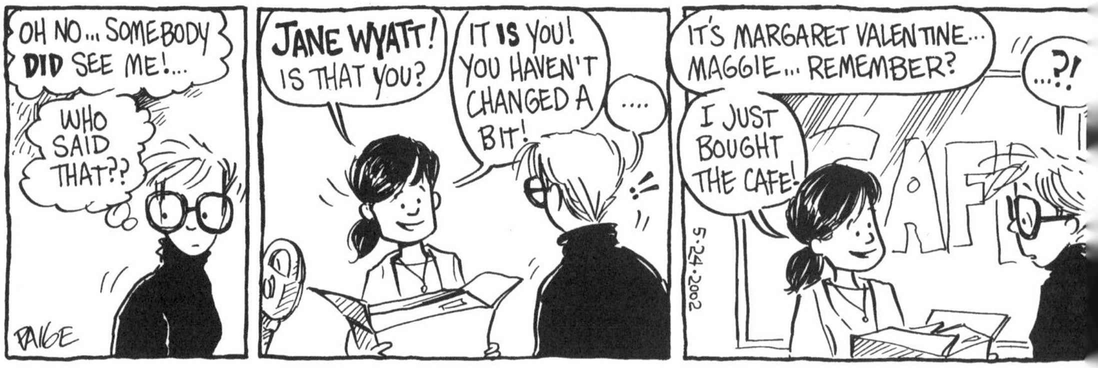
OH NO... SOMEBODY **DID** SEE ME!...
WHO SAID THAT??
PAIGE
JANE WYATT! IS THAT YOU?
IT **IS** YOU! YOU HAVEN'T CHANGED A BIT!
....
5.24.2002
IT'S MARGARET VALENTINE... MAGGIE... REMEMBER?
...?!
I JUST BOUGHT THE CAFE!

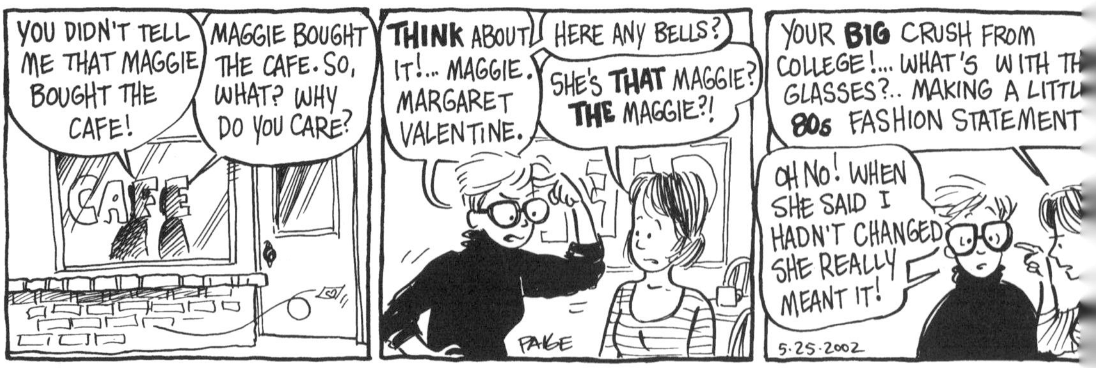
YOU DIDN'T TELL ME THAT MAGGIE BOUGHT THE CAFE!
MAGGIE BOUGHT THE CAFE. SO, WHAT? WHY DO YOU CARE?
CAFE
THINK ABOUT IT!... MAGGIE. MARGARET VALENTINE.
HERE ANY BELLS?
SHE'S **THAT** MAGGIE? **THE** MAGGIE?!
PAIGE
YOUR **BIG** CRUSH FROM COLLEGE!... WHAT'S WITH TH GLASSES?.. MAKING A LITTL **80s** FASHION STATEMENT
OH NO! WHEN SHE SAID I HADN'T CHANGED SHE REALLY MEANT IT!
5.25.2002

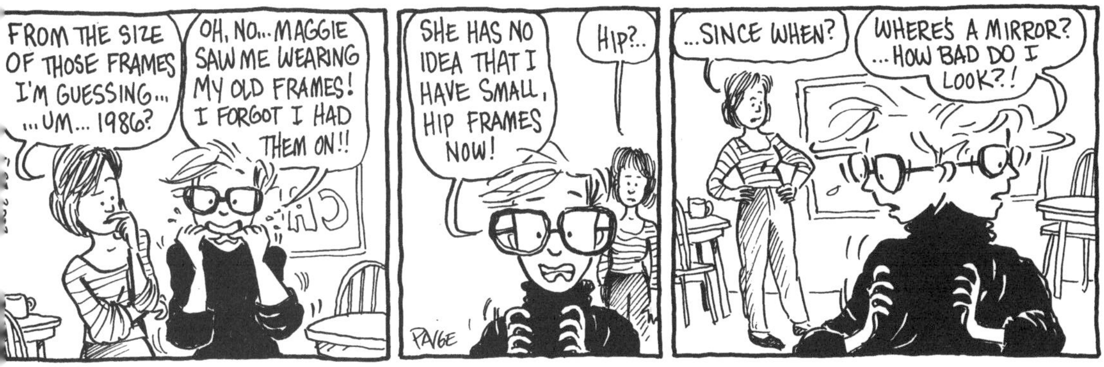
FROM THE SIZE OF THOSE FRAMES I'M GUESSING... ...UM... 1986?
OH, NO... MAGGIE SAW ME WEARING MY OLD FRAMES! I FORGOT I HAD THEM ON!!
SHE HAS NO IDEA THAT I HAVE SMALL, HIP FRAMES NOW!
HIP?..
...SINCE WHEN?
WHERE'S A MIRROR? ...HOW BAD DO I LOOK?!
PAIGE

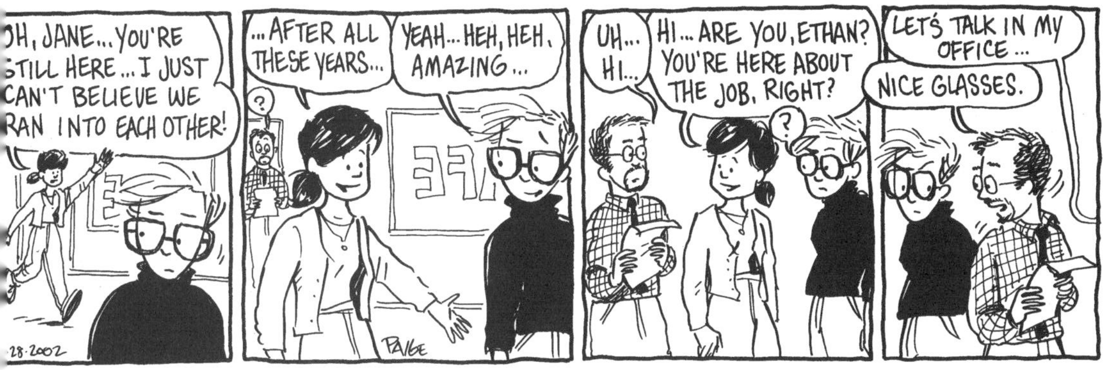
OH, JANE... YOU'RE STILL HERE... I JUST CAN'T BELIEVE WE RAN INTO EACH OTHER!
...AFTER ALL THESE YEARS...
YEAH... HEH, HEH, AMAZING...
UH... HI...
HI... ARE YOU, ETHAN? YOU'RE HERE ABOUT THE JOB, RIGHT?
LET'S TALK IN MY OFFICE...
NICE GLASSES.
28·2002
PAIGE

Shortly...

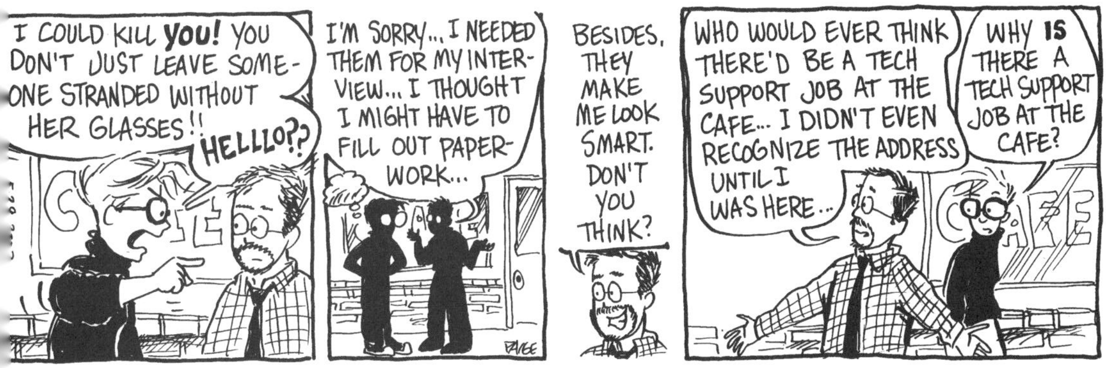
I COULD KILL YOU! YOU DON'T JUST LEAVE SOMEONE STRANDED WITHOUT HER GLASSES!!
HELLLO?!?
I'M SORRY... I NEEDED THEM FOR MY INTERVIEW... I THOUGHT I MIGHT HAVE TO FILL OUT PAPERWORK...
BESIDES, THEY MAKE ME LOOK SMART. DON'T YOU THINK?
WHO WOULD EVER THINK THERE'D BE A TECH SUPPORT JOB AT THE CAFE... I DIDN'T EVEN RECOGNIZE THE ADDRESS UNTIL I WAS HERE...
WHY IS THERE A TECH SUPPORT JOB AT THE CAFE?
PAIGE

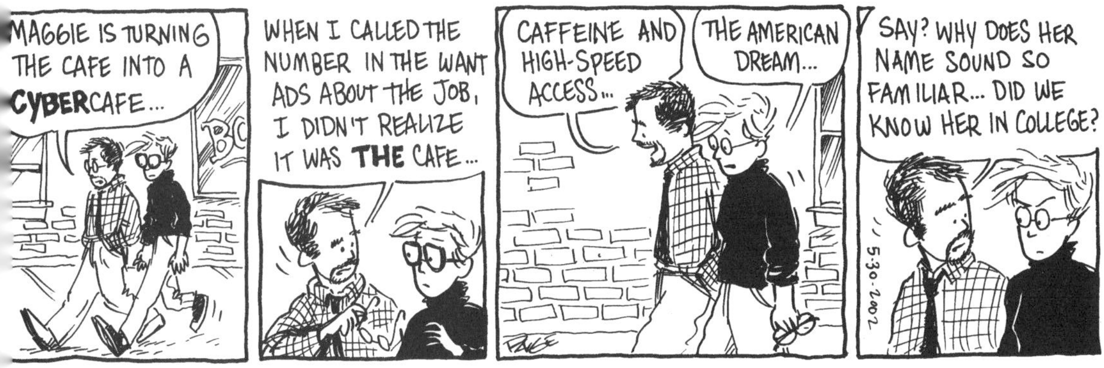
MAGGIE IS TURNING THE CAFE INTO A CYBERCAFE...
WHEN I CALLED THE NUMBER IN THE WANT ADS ABOUT THE JOB, I DIDN'T REALIZE IT WAS THE CAFE...
CAFFEINE AND HIGH-SPEED ACCESS...
THE AMERICAN DREAM...
SAY? WHY DOES HER NAME SOUND SO FAMILIAR... DID WE KNOW HER IN COLLEGE?
PAIGE
5·30·2002

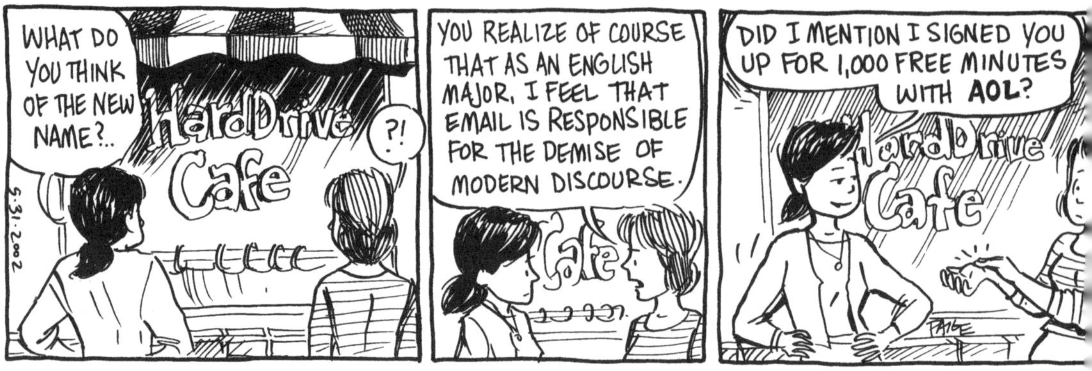
WHAT DO YOU THINK OF THE NEW NAME?..
HardDrive Cafe
?!
5.31.2002
YOU REALIZE OF COURSE THAT AS AN ENGLISH MAJOR, I FEEL THAT EMAIL IS RESPONSIBLE FOR THE DEMISE OF MODERN DISCOURSE.
DID I MENTION I SIGNED YOU UP FOR 1,000 FREE MINUTES WITH **AOL**?
PAIGE

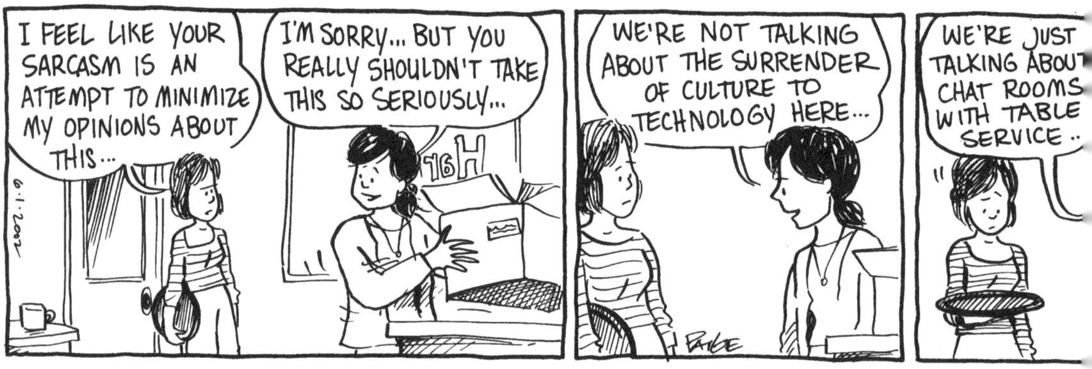
I FEEL LIKE YOUR SARCASM IS AN ATTEMPT TO MINIMIZE MY OPINIONS ABOUT THIS...
6.1.2002
I'M SORRY... BUT YOU REALLY SHOULDN'T TAKE THIS SO SERIOUSLY...
WE'RE NOT TALKING ABOUT THE SURRENDER OF CULTURE TO TECHNOLOGY HERE...
PAIGE
WE'RE JUST TALKING ABOUT CHAT ROOMS WITH TABLE SERVICE...

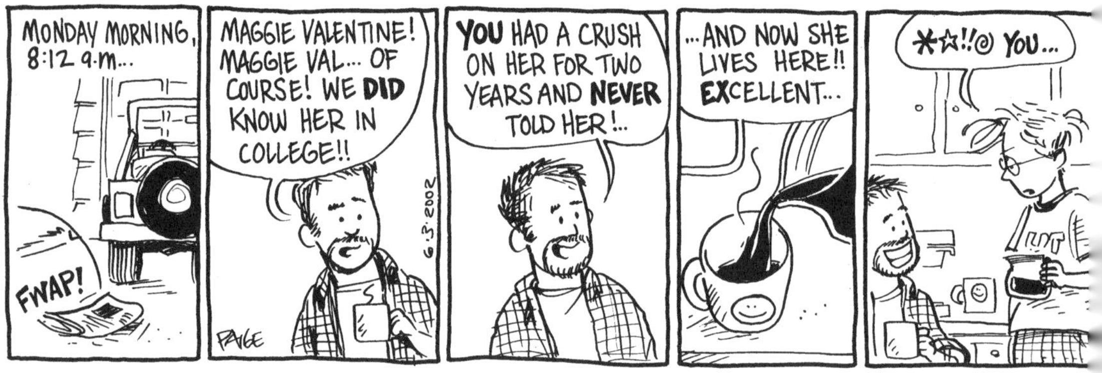
MONDAY MORNING, 8:12 a.m...
FWAP!
PAIGE
MAGGIE VALENTINE! MAGGIE VAL... OF COURSE! WE **DID** KNOW HER IN COLLEGE!!
6.3.2002
YOU HAD A CRUSH ON HER FOR TWO YEARS AND **NEVER** TOLD HER!..
...AND NOW SHE LIVES HERE!! **EX**CELLENT...
*☆!!@ YOU...

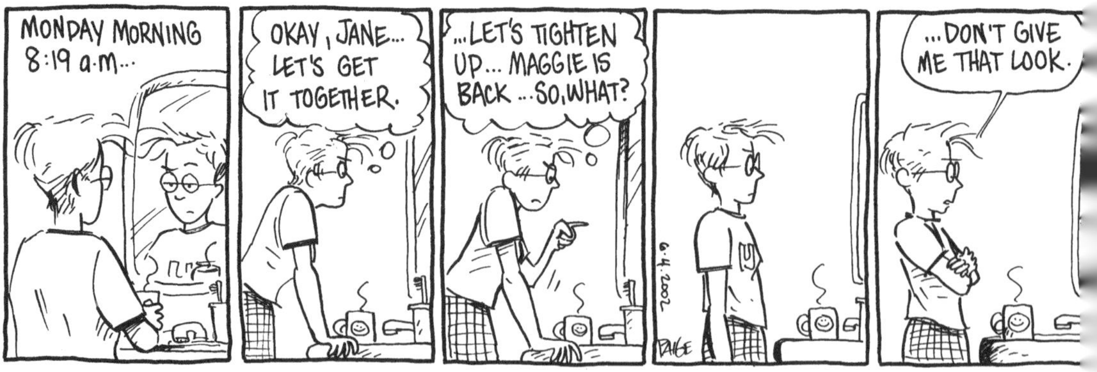
MONDAY MORNING 8:19 a.m...
OKAY, JANE... LET'S GET IT TOGETHER.
...LET'S TIGHTEN UP... MAGGIE IS BACK ...SO, WHAT?
6.4.2002
PAIGE
...DON'T GIVE ME THAT LOOK.

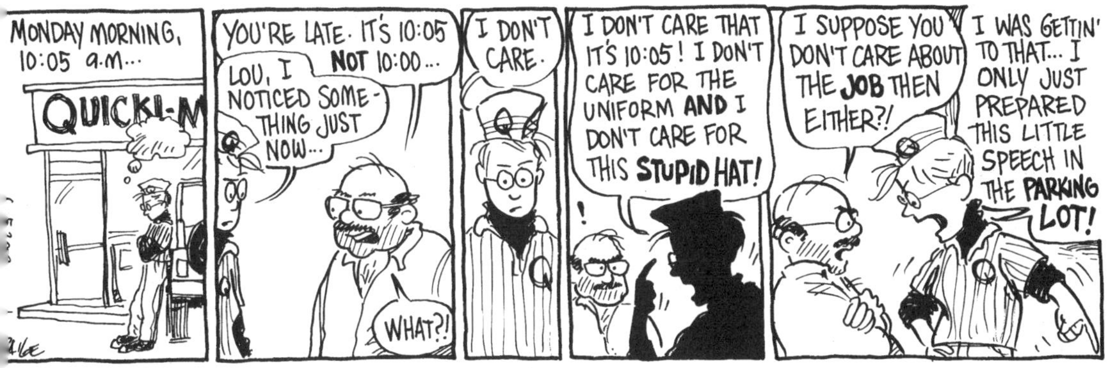
MONDAY MORNING, 10:05 a.m...
QUICKI-M
PAIGE
YOU'RE LATE. IT'S 10:05 **NOT** 10:00...
LOU, I NOTICED SOMETHING JUST NOW...
WHAT?!
I DON'T CARE.
I DON'T CARE THAT IT'S 10:05! I DON'T CARE FOR THE UNIFORM **AND** I DON'T CARE FOR THIS **STUPID HAT**!
!
I SUPPOSE YOU DON'T CARE ABOUT THE **JOB** THEN EITHER?!
I WAS GETTIN' TO THAT... I ONLY JUST PREPARED THIS LITTLE SPEECH IN THE **PARKING LOT**!

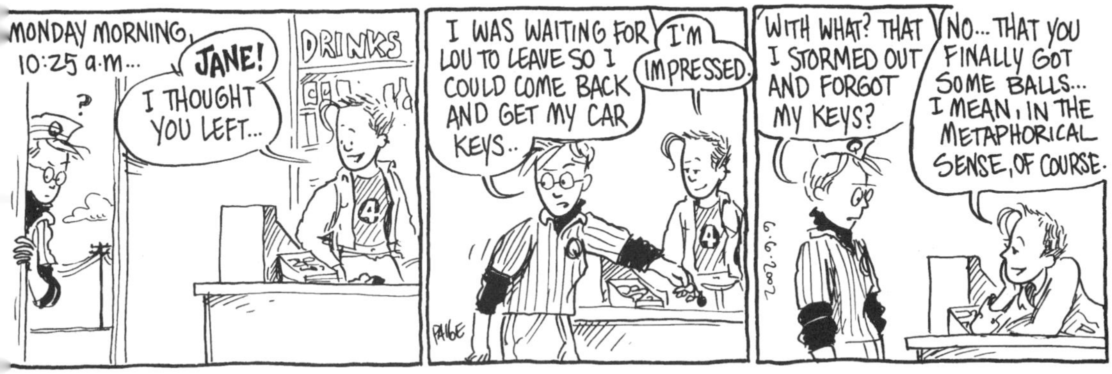
MONDAY MORNING, 10:25 a.m...
?
JANE!
I THOUGHT YOU LEFT...
DRINKS
I WAS WAITING FOR LOU TO LEAVE SO I COULD COME BACK AND GET MY CAR KEYS...
I'M IMPRESSED.
PAIGE
WITH WHAT? THAT I STORMED OUT AND FORGOT MY KEYS?
NO... THAT YOU FINALLY GOT SOME BALLS... I MEAN, IN THE METAPHORICAL SENSE, OF COURSE.
6·6·2002

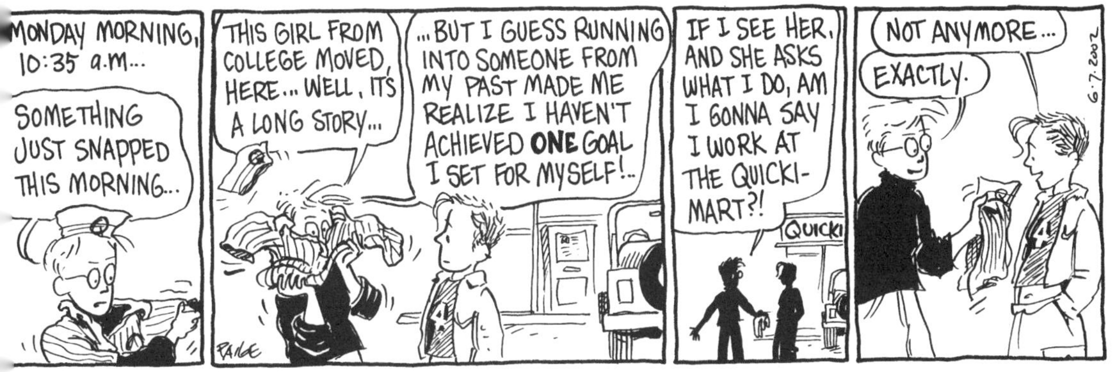
MONDAY MORNING, 10:35 a.m...
SOMETHING JUST SNAPPED THIS MORNING...
THIS GIRL FROM COLLEGE MOVED HERE... WELL, IT'S A LONG STORY...
PAIGE
...BUT I GUESS RUNNING INTO SOMEONE FROM MY PAST MADE ME REALIZE I HAVEN'T ACHIEVED **ONE** GOAL I SET FOR MYSELF!..
IF I SEE HER, AND SHE ASKS WHAT I DO, AM I GONNA SAY I WORK AT THE QUICKI-MART?!
QUICKI
NOT ANYMORE...
EXACTLY.
6·7·2002

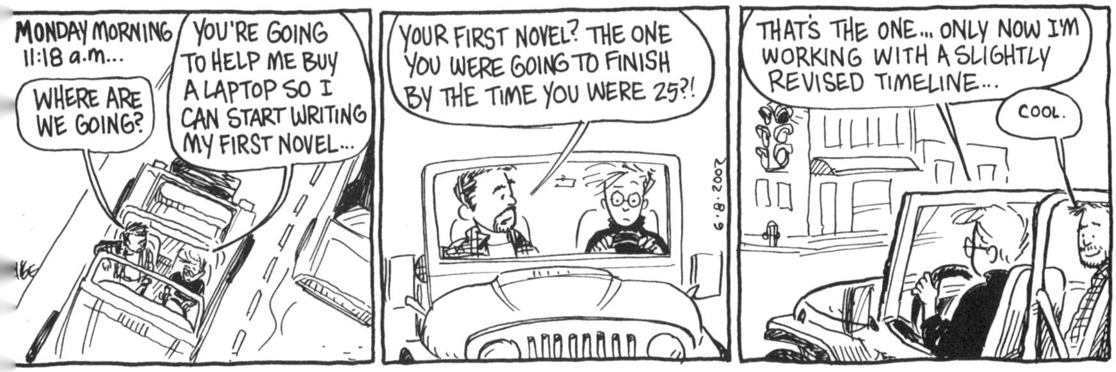
MONDAY MORNING 11:18 a.m...
WHERE ARE WE GOING?
YOU'RE GOING TO HELP ME BUY A LAPTOP SO I CAN START WRITING MY FIRST NOVEL...
YOUR FIRST NOVEL? THE ONE YOU WERE GOING TO FINISH BY THE TIME YOU WERE 25?!
6·8·2002
THAT'S THE ONE... ONLY NOW I'M WORKING WITH A SLIGHTLY REVISED TIMELINE...
COOL.

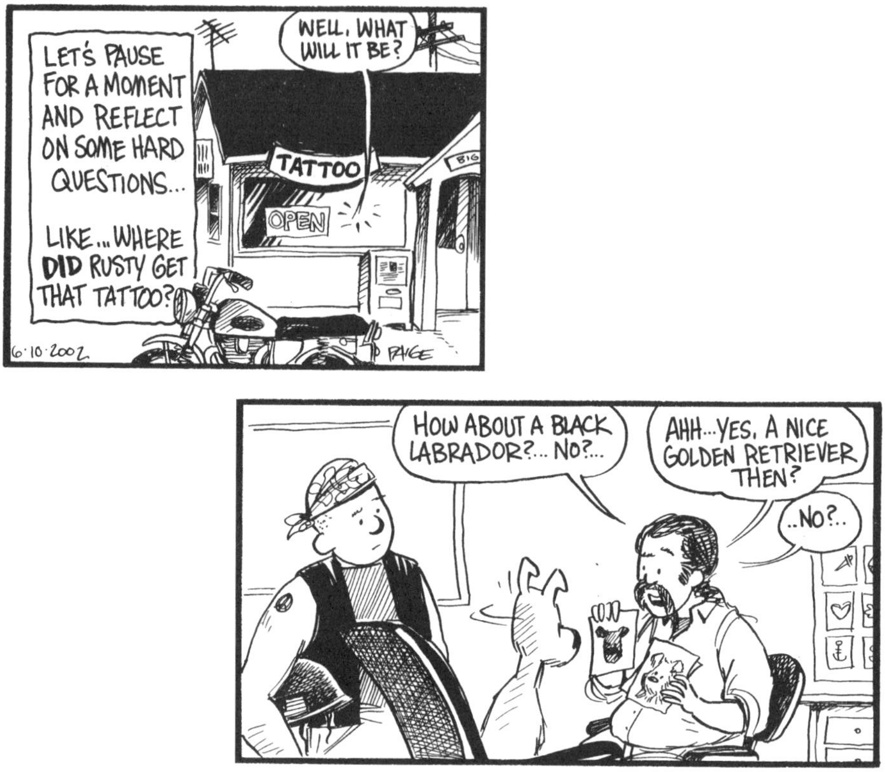
LET'S PAUSE FOR A MOMENT AND REFLECT ON SOME HARD QUESTIONS...
LIKE... WHERE **DID** RUSTY GET THAT TATTOO?
WELL, WHAT WILL IT BE?
TATTOO
OPEN
BIG
6·10·2002
PAGE
HOW ABOUT A BLACK LABRADOR?... NO?...
AHH...YES, A NICE GOLDEN RETRIEVER THEN?
..NO?..

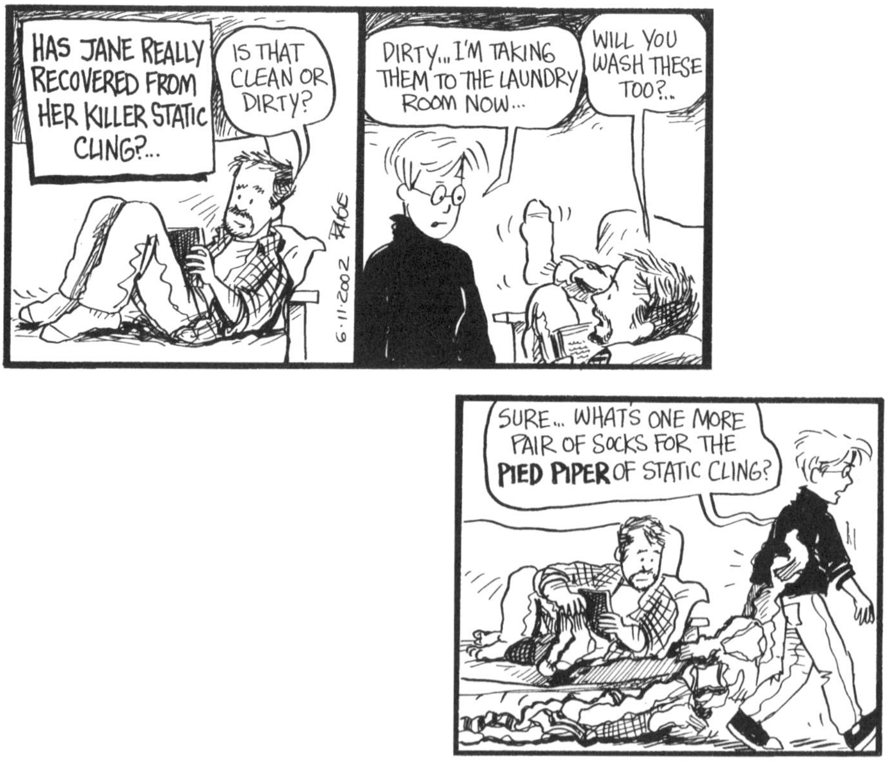
HAS JANE REALLY RECOVERED FROM HER KILLER STATIC CLING?...
IS THAT CLEAN OR DIRTY?
PAGE
6·11·2002
DIRTY... I'M TAKING THEM TO THE LAUNDRY ROOM NOW...
WILL YOU WASH THESE TOO?..
SURE... WHATS ONE MORE PAIR OF SOCKS FOR THE **PIED PIPER** OF STATIC CLING?

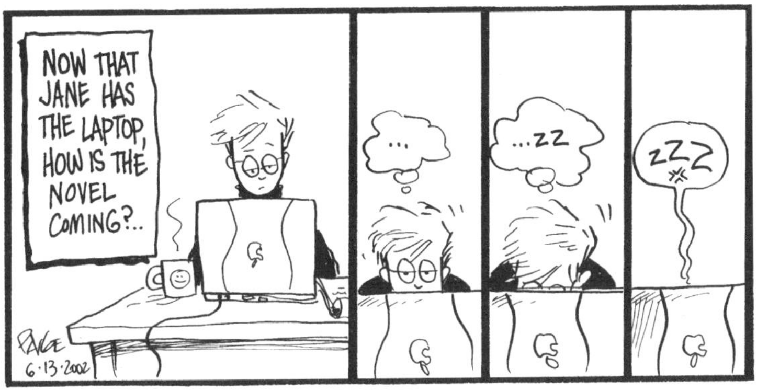
NOW THAT JANE HAS THE LAPTOP, HOW IS THE NOVEL COMING?..
...
...ZZ
ZZZ
6·13·2002

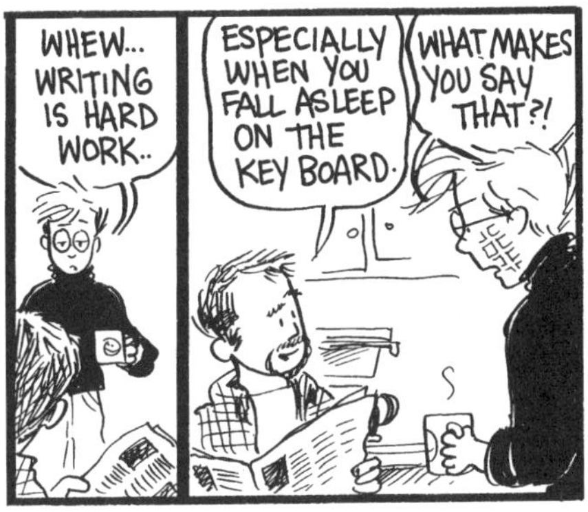
WHEW... WRITING IS HARD WORK..
ESPECIALLY WHEN YOU FALL ASLEEP ON THE KEY BOARD.
WHAT MAKES YOU SAY THAT?!

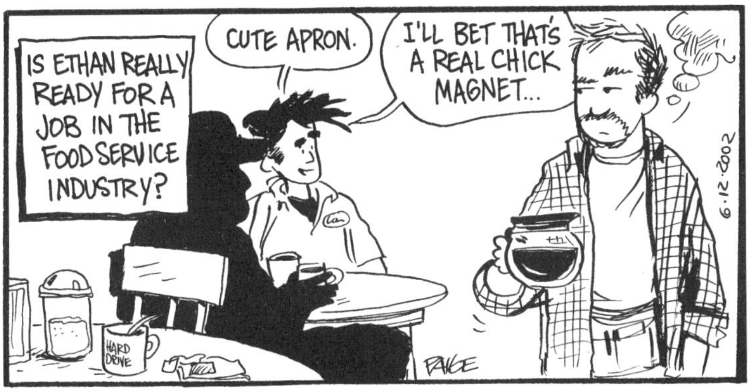
IS ETHAN REALLY READY FOR A JOB IN THE FOOD SERVICE INDUSTRY?
CUTE APRON.
I'LL BET THAT'S A REAL CHICK MAGNET...
HARD DRIVE
6·12·2002

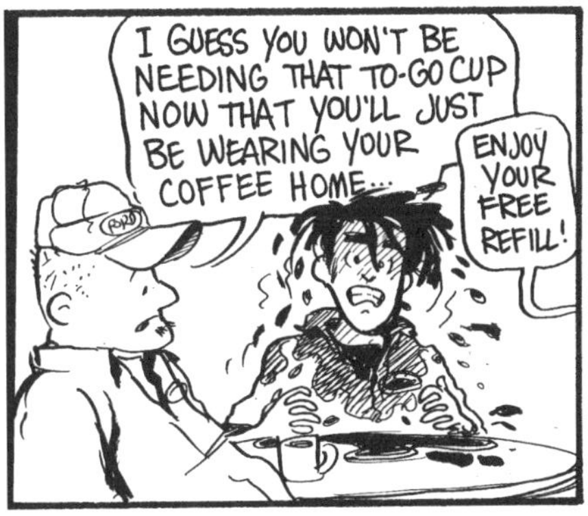
I GUESS YOU WON'T BE NEEDING THAT TO-GO CUP NOW THAT YOU'LL JUST BE WEARING YOUR COFFEE HOME...
ENJOY YOUR FREE REFILL!

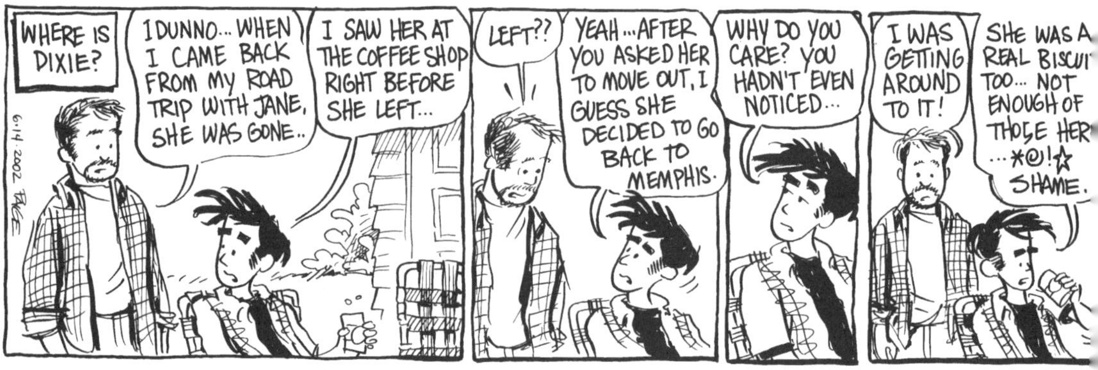
WHERE IS DIXIE?
I DUNNO... WHEN I CAME BACK FROM MY ROAD TRIP WITH JANE, SHE WAS GONE..
I SAW HER AT THE COFFEE SHOP RIGHT BEFORE SHE LEFT...
LEFT??
YEAH...AFTER YOU ASKED HER TO MOVE OUT, I GUESS SHE DECIDED TO GO BACK TO MEMPHIS.
WHY DO YOU CARE? YOU HADN'T EVEN NOTICED...
I WAS GETTING AROUND TO IT!
SHE WAS A REAL BISCU
TOO... NOT ENOUGH OF THOSE HER
...*@!☆ SHAME.
6·14·2002
PAIGE

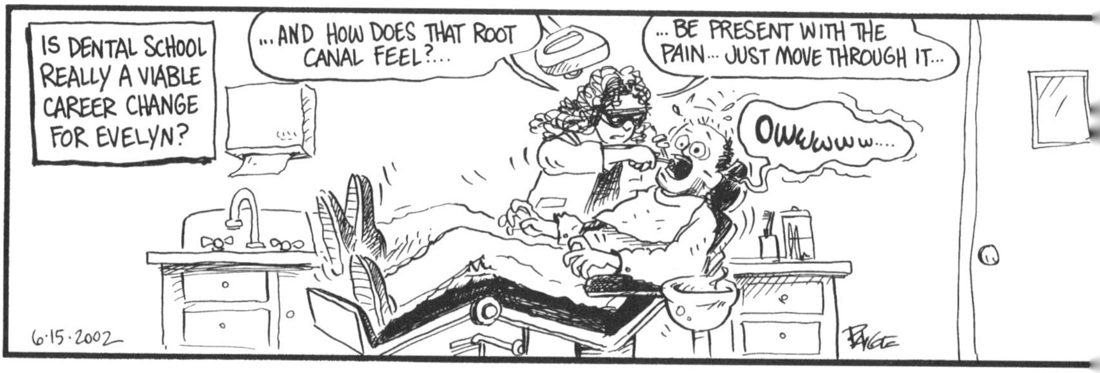
IS DENTAL SCHOOL REALLY A VIABLE CAREER CHANGE FOR EVELYN?
...AND HOW DOES THAT ROOT CANAL FEEL?...
...BE PRESENT WITH THE PAIN... JUST MOVE THROUGH IT...
OWWWWW....
6·15·2002
PAIGE

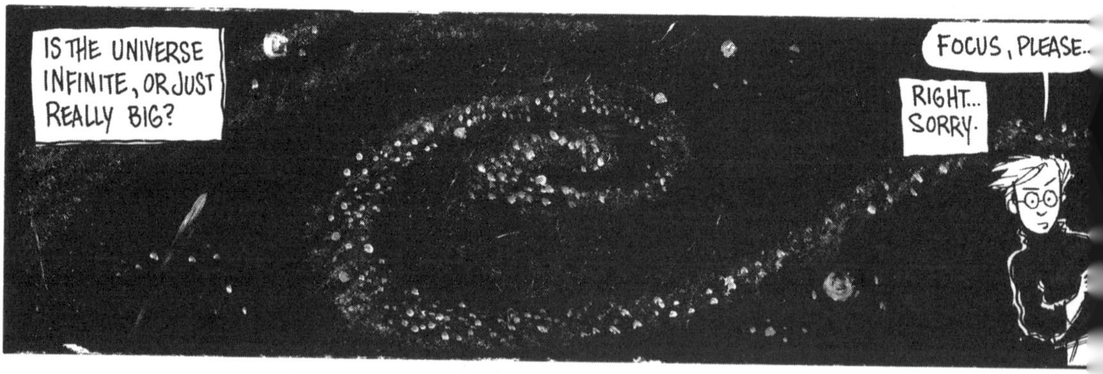
IS THE UNIVERSE INFINITE, OR JUST REALLY BIG?
FOCUS, PLEASE..
RIGHT... SORRY.

Okay, folks... we're back on track...

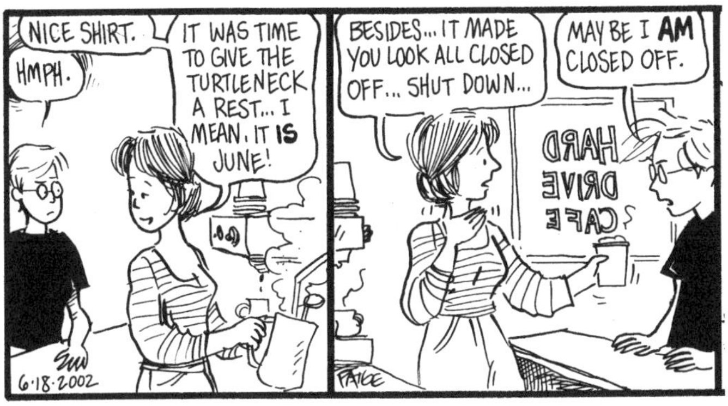
NICE SHIRT.
HMPH.
IT WAS TIME TO GIVE THE TURTLENECK A REST... I MEAN, IT **IS** JUNE!
BESIDES... IT MADE YOU LOOK ALL CLOSED OFF... SHUT DOWN...
MAYBE I **AM** CLOSED OFF.
6·18·2002
PAIGE

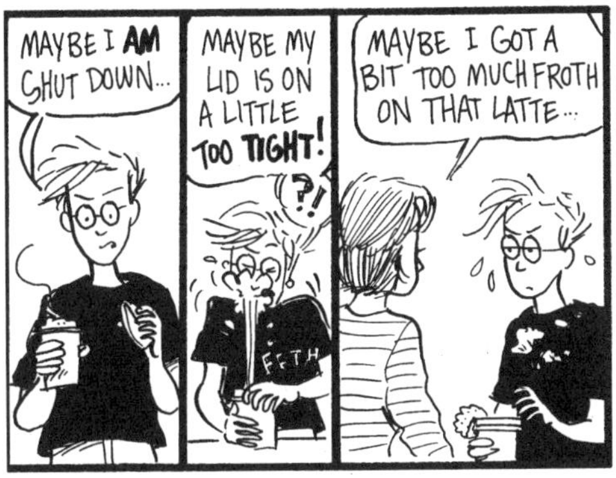
MAYBE I **AM** SHUT DOWN...
MAYBE MY LID IS ON A LITTLE **TOO TIGHT!**
?!
MAYBE I GOT A BIT TOO MUCH FROTH ON THAT LATTE...

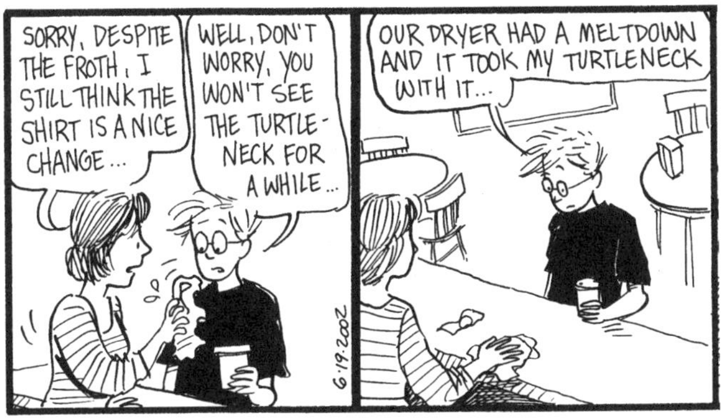
SORRY, DESPITE THE FROTH, I STILL THINK THE SHIRT IS A NICE CHANGE...
WELL, DON'T WORRY, YOU WON'T SEE THE TURTLE-NECK FOR A WHILE...
6·19·2002
OUR DRYER HAD A MELTDOWN AND IT TOOK MY TURTLENECK WITH IT...

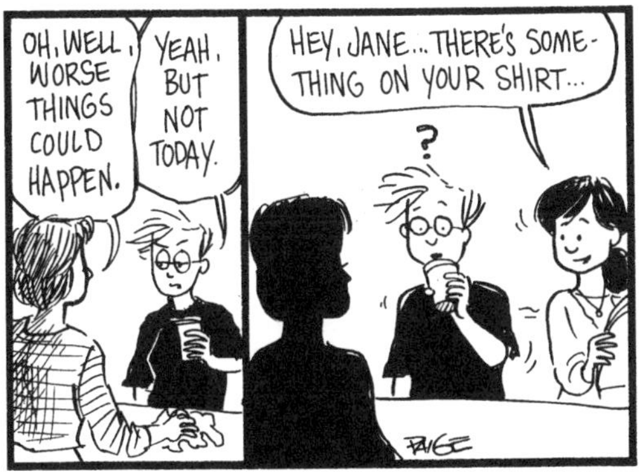
OH, WELL, WORSE THINGS COULD HAPPEN.
YEAH, BUT NOT TODAY.
HEY, JANE... THERE'S SOME-THING ON YOUR SHIRT...
?
PAIGE

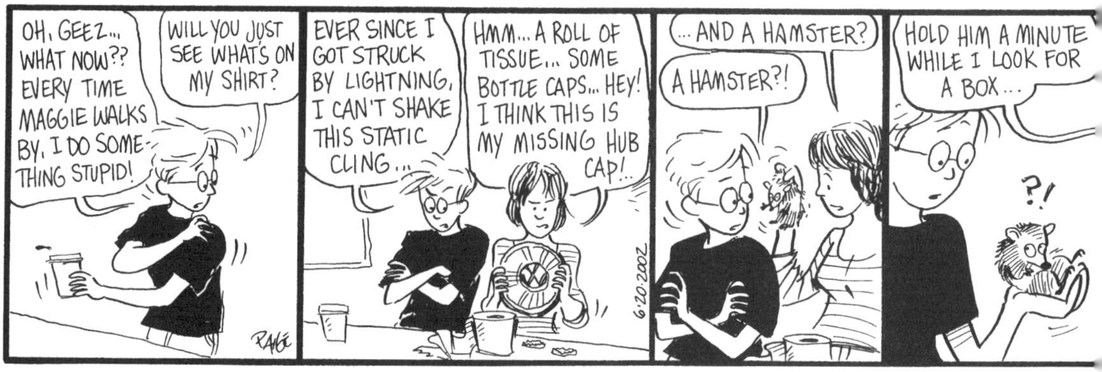
OH, GEEZ... WHAT NOW?? EVERY TIME MAGGIE WALKS BY, I DO SOMETHING STUPID!
WILL YOU JUST SEE WHAT'S ON MY SHIRT?
PAIGE
EVER SINCE I GOT STRUCK BY LIGHTNING, I CAN'T SHAKE THIS STATIC CLING...
HMM... A ROLL OF TISSUE... SOME BOTTLE CAPS... HEY! I THINK THIS IS MY MISSING HUB CAP!...
6·20·2002
...AND A HAMSTER?
A HAMSTER?!
HOLD HIM A MINUTE WHILE I LOOK FOR A BOX...
?!

Later, at Jane's...

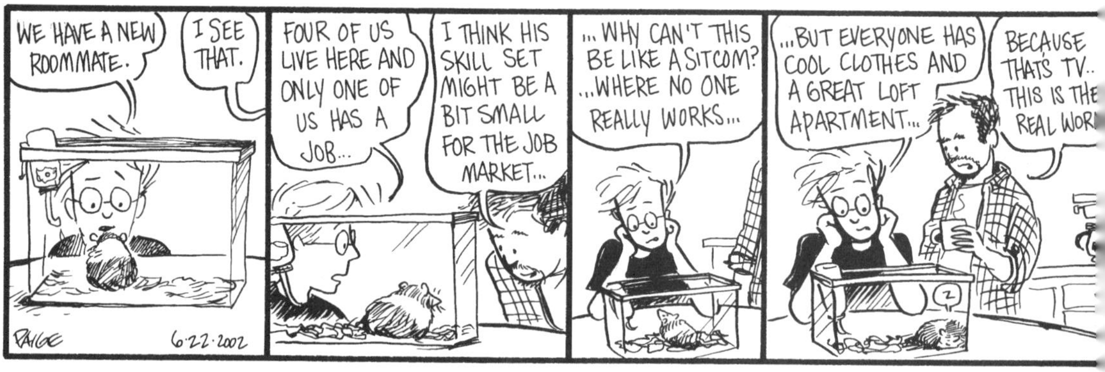
WE HAVE A NEW ROOMMATE.
I SEE THAT.
PAIGE
6·22·2002
FOUR OF US LIVE HERE AND ONLY ONE OF US HAS A JOB...
I THINK HIS SKILL SET MIGHT BE A BIT SMALL FOR THE JOB MARKET...
...WHY CAN'T THIS BE LIKE A SITCOM? ...WHERE NO ONE REALLY WORKS...
...BUT EVERYONE HAS COOL CLOTHES AND A GREAT LOFT APARTMENT...
BECAUSE THAT'S TV.. THIS IS THE REAL WOR

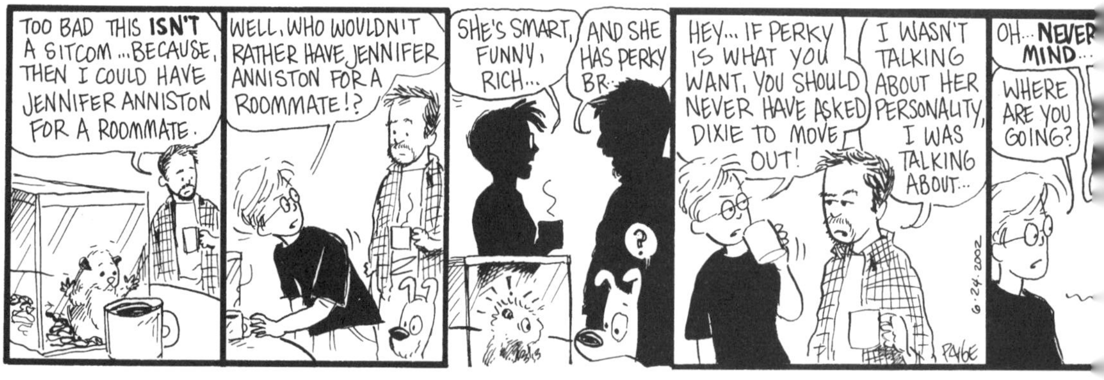
TOO BAD THIS **ISN'T** A SITCOM...BECAUSE, THEN I COULD HAVE JENNIFER ANNISTON FOR A ROOMMATE.
WELL, WHO WOULDN'T RATHER HAVE JENNIFER ANNISTON FOR A ROOMMATE!?
SHE'S SMART, FUNNY, RICH...
AND SHE HAS PERKY BR...
?
HEY... IF PERKY IS WHAT YOU WANT, YOU SHOULD NEVER HAVE ASKED DIXIE TO MOVE OUT!
I WASN'T TALKING ABOUT HER PERSONALITY, I WAS TALKING ABOUT...
6·24·2002
PAIGE
OH... **NEVER MIND**...
WHERE ARE YOU GOING?

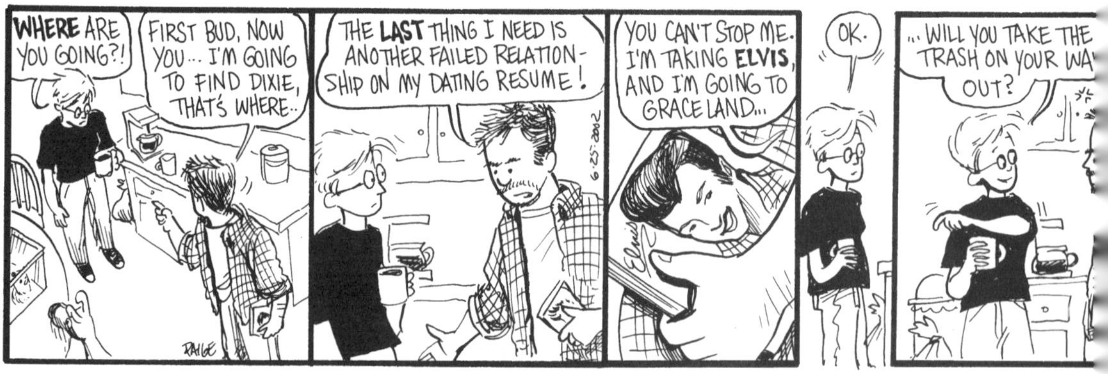
WHERE ARE YOU GOING?!
FIRST BUD, NOW YOU... I'M GOING TO FIND DIXIE, THAT'S WHERE..
PAIGE
THE **LAST** THING I NEED IS ANOTHER FAILED RELATIONSHIP ON MY DATING RESUME!
6·25·2002
YOU CAN'T STOP ME. I'M TAKING **ELVIS**, AND I'M GOING TO GRACELAND...
Elvis
OK.
...WILL YOU TAKE THE TRASH ON YOUR WA OUT?

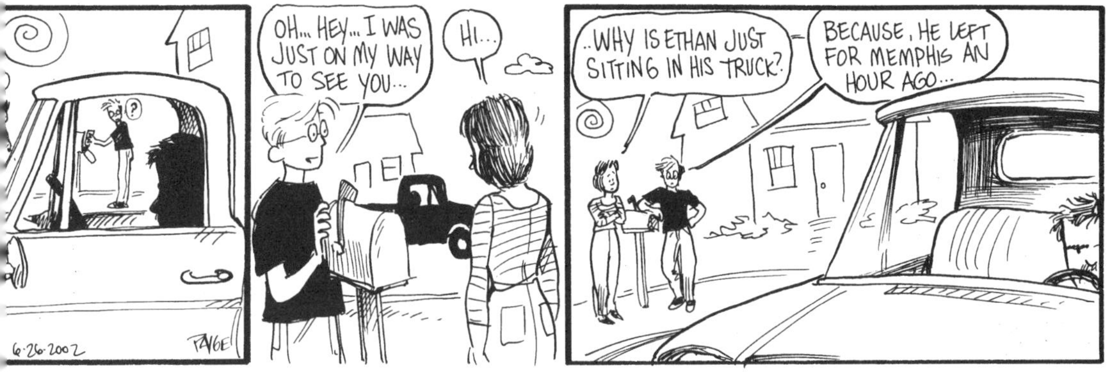
OH... HEY... I WAS JUST ON MY WAY TO SEE YOU...
HI...
..WHY IS ETHAN JUST SITTING IN HIS TRUCK?
BECAUSE, HE LEFT FOR MEMPHIS AN HOUR AGO...
6·26·2002
PAIGE

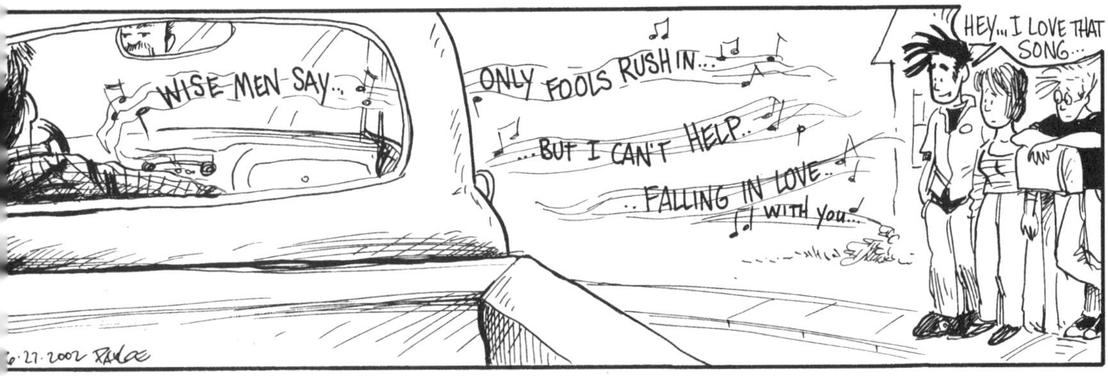
WISE MEN SAY...
ONLY FOOLS RUSH IN...
...BUT I CAN'T HELP...
...FALLING IN LOVE...
WITH YOU...
HEY... I LOVE THAT SONG...
6·27·2002 PAIGE

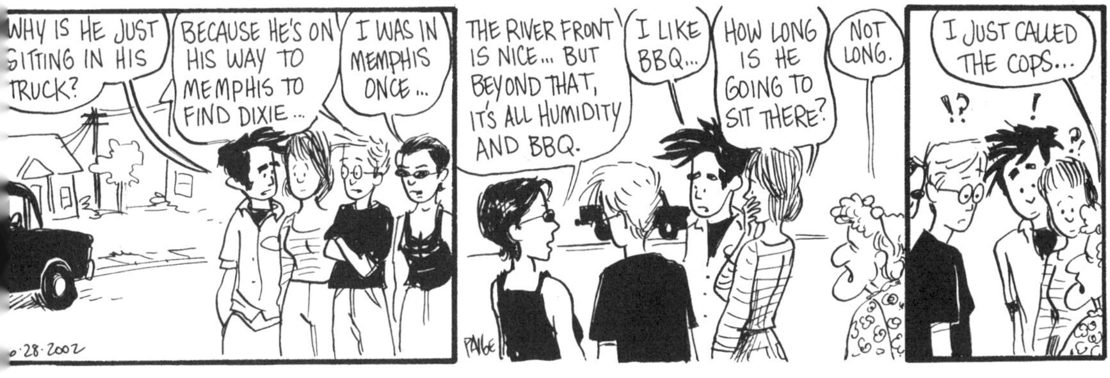
WHY IS HE JUST SITTING IN HIS TRUCK?
BECAUSE HE'S ON HIS WAY TO MEMPHIS TO FIND DIXIE...
I WAS IN MEMPHIS ONCE...
THE RIVER FRONT IS NICE... BUT BEYOND THAT, IT'S ALL HUMIDITY AND BBQ.
I LIKE BBQ...
HOW LONG IS HE GOING TO SIT THERE?
NOT LONG.
I JUST CALLED THE COPS...
!?
!
?!
6·28·2002
PAIGE

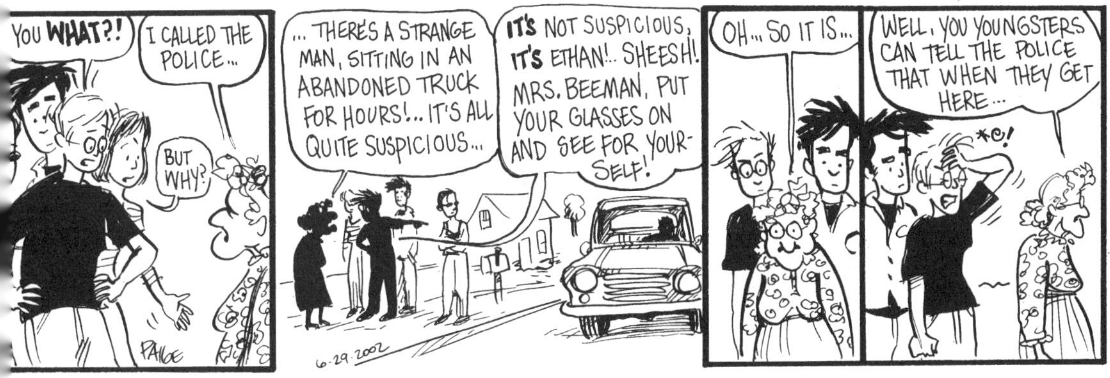
YOU WHAT?!
I CALLED THE POLICE...
BUT WHY?
PAIGE
... THERE'S A STRANGE MAN, SITTING IN AN ABANDONED TRUCK FOR HOURS!... IT'S ALL QUITE SUSPICIOUS...
IT'S NOT SUSPICIOUS, IT'S ETHAN!.. SHEESH! MRS. BEEMAN, PUT YOUR GLASSES ON AND SEE FOR YOURSELF!
6·29·2002
OH... SO IT IS...
WELL, YOU YOUNGSTERS CAN TELL THE POLICE THAT WHEN THEY GET HERE...
*@!

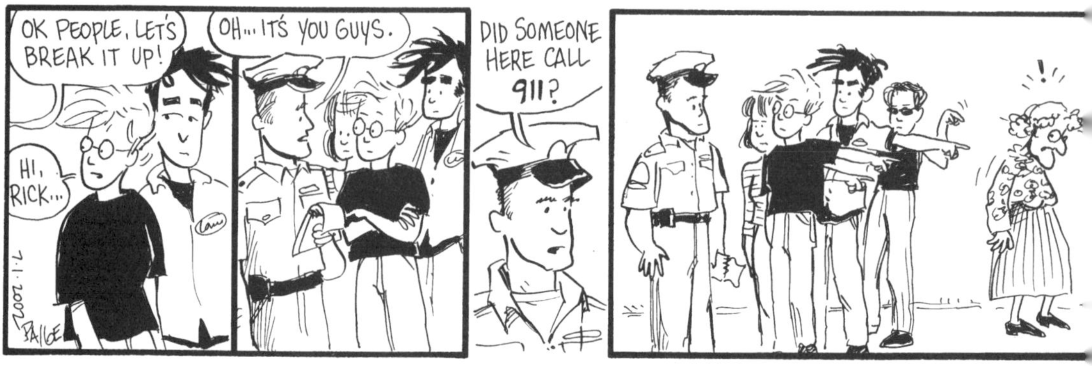
OK PEOPLE, LET'S BREAK IT UP!
HI, RICK...
OH... IT'S YOU GUYS.
DID SOMEONE HERE CALL 911?
!

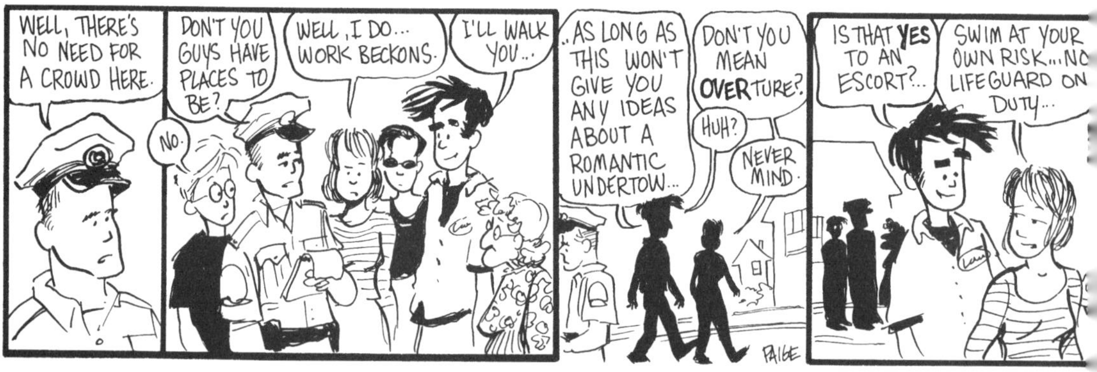
WELL, THERE'S NO NEED FOR A CROWD HERE.
DON'T YOU GUYS HAVE PLACES TO BE?
NO.
WELL, I DO... WORK BECKONS.
I'LL WALK YOU...
..AS LONG AS THIS WON'T GIVE YOU ANY IDEAS ABOUT A ROMANTIC UNDERTOW...
DON'T YOU MEAN **OVER**TURE?
HUH?
NEVER MIND.
IS THAT **YES** TO AN ESCORT?..
SWIM AT YOUR OWN RISK...NO LIFEGUARD ON DUTY...

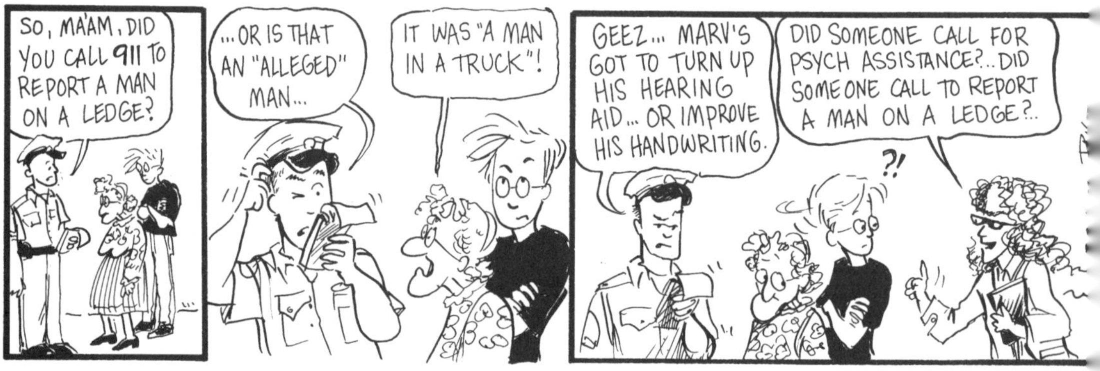
SO, MA'AM, DID YOU CALL **911** TO REPORT A MAN ON A LEDGE?
...OR IS THAT AN "ALLEGED" MAN...
IT WAS "A MAN IN A TRUCK"!
GEEZ... MARV'S GOT TO TURN UP HIS HEARING AID... OR IMPROVE HIS HANDWRITING.
DID SOMEONE CALL FOR PSYCH ASSISTANCE?..DID SOMEONE CALL TO REPORT A MAN ON A LEDGE?..
?!

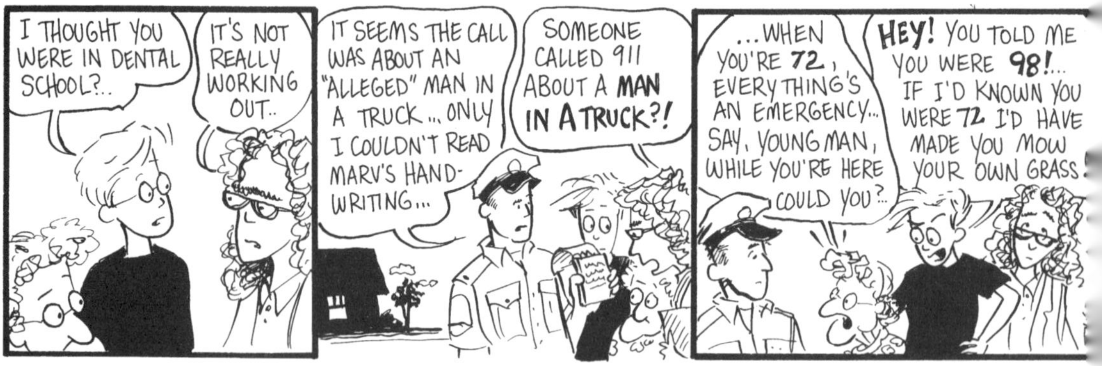
I THOUGHT YOU WERE IN DENTAL SCHOOL?..
IT'S NOT REALLY WORKING OUT..
IT SEEMS THE CALL WAS ABOUT AN "ALLEGED" MAN IN A TRUCK... ONLY I COULDN'T READ MARV'S HAND-WRITING...
SOMEONE CALLED 911 ABOUT A **MAN IN A TRUCK?!**
...WHEN YOU'RE **72**, EVERYTHING'S AN EMERGENCY... SAY, YOUNG MAN, WHILE YOU'RE HERE COULD YOU?..
HEY! YOU TOLD ME YOU WERE **98!**... IF I'D KNOWN YOU WERE **72** I'D HAVE MADE YOU MOW YOUR OWN GRASS.

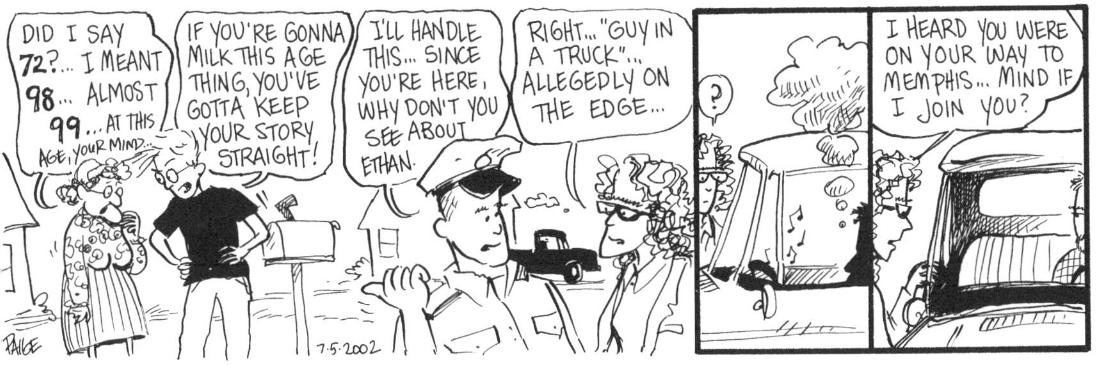
DID I SAY 72?... I MEANT 98... ALMOST 99... AT THIS AGE, YOUR MIND...
IF YOU'RE GONNA MILK THIS AGE THING, YOU'VE GOTTA KEEP YOUR STORY STRAIGHT!
I'LL HANDLE THIS... SINCE YOU'RE HERE, WHY DON'T YOU SEE ABOUT ETHAN.
RIGHT... "GUY IN A TRUCK"... ALLEGEDLY ON THE EDGE...
PAIGE
7·5·2002
?
I HEARD YOU WERE ON YOUR WAY TO MEMPHIS... MIND IF I JOIN YOU?

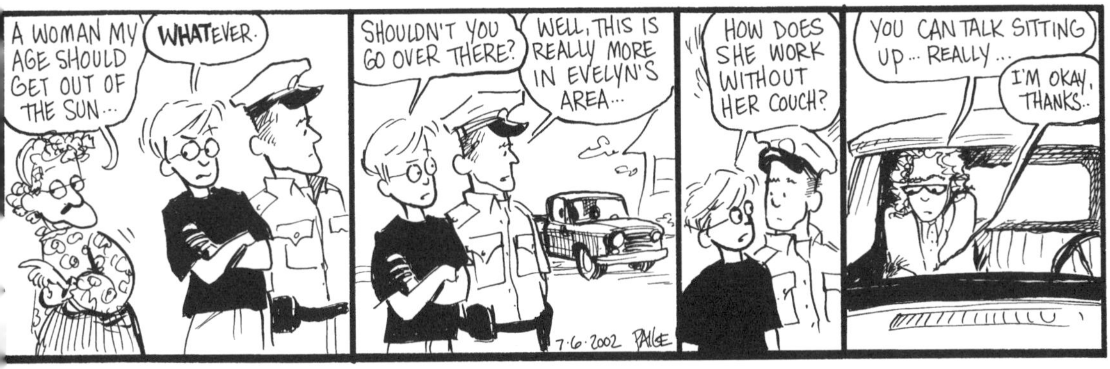
A WOMAN MY AGE SHOULD GET OUT OF THE SUN...
WHATEVER.
SHOULDN'T YOU GO OVER THERE?
WELL, THIS IS REALLY MORE IN EVELYN'S AREA...
7·6·2002 PAIGE
HOW DOES SHE WORK WITHOUT HER COUCH?
YOU CAN TALK SITTING UP... REALLY...
I'M OKAY, THANKS..

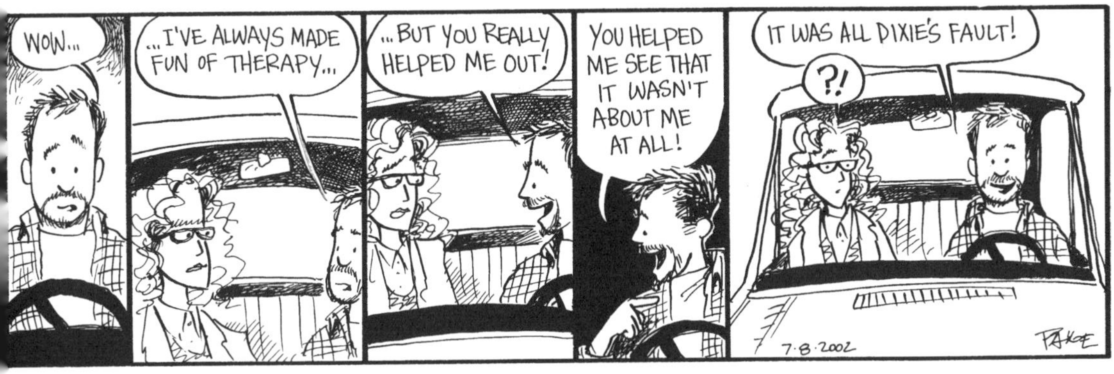
WOW...
...I'VE ALWAYS MADE FUN OF THERAPY...
...BUT YOU REALLY HELPED ME OUT!
YOU HELPED ME SEE THAT IT WASN'T ABOUT ME AT ALL!
IT WAS ALL DIXIE'S FAULT!
?!
7·8·2002
PAIGE

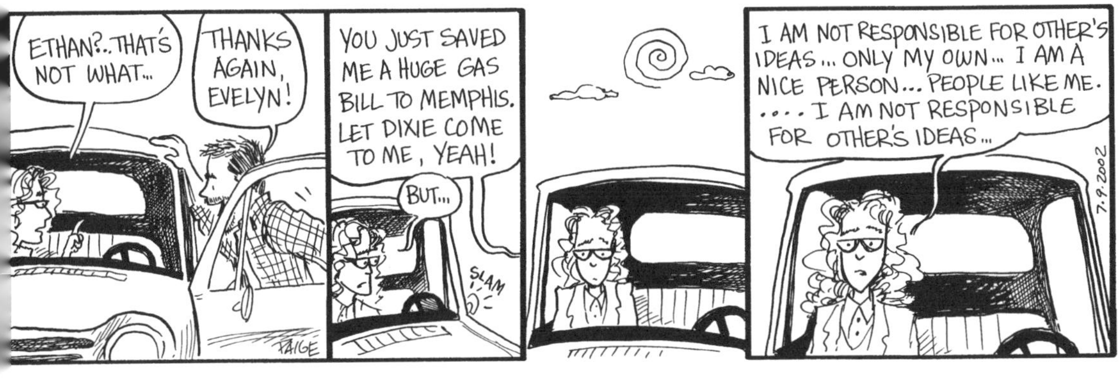
ETHAN?..THAT'S NOT WHAT...
THANKS AGAIN, EVELYN!
PAIGE
YOU JUST SAVED ME A HUGE GAS BILL TO MEMPHIS. LET DIXIE COME TO ME, YEAH!
BUT...
SLAM
I AM NOT RESPONSIBLE FOR OTHER'S IDEAS... ONLY MY OWN... I AM A NICE PERSON... PEOPLE LIKE ME. .... I AM NOT RESPONSIBLE FOR OTHER'S IDEAS...
7·9·2002

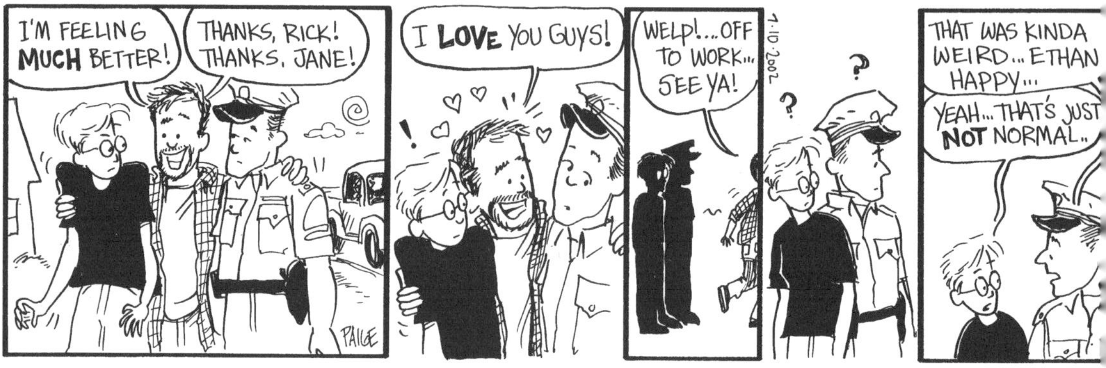
I'M FEELING MUCH BETTER!
THANKS, RICK! THANKS, JANE!
PAIGE
I LOVE YOU GUYS!
WELP!... OFF TO WORK... SEE YA!
7·10·2002
THAT WAS KINDA WEIRD... ETHAN HAPPY...
YEAH... THAT'S JUST NOT NORMAL...

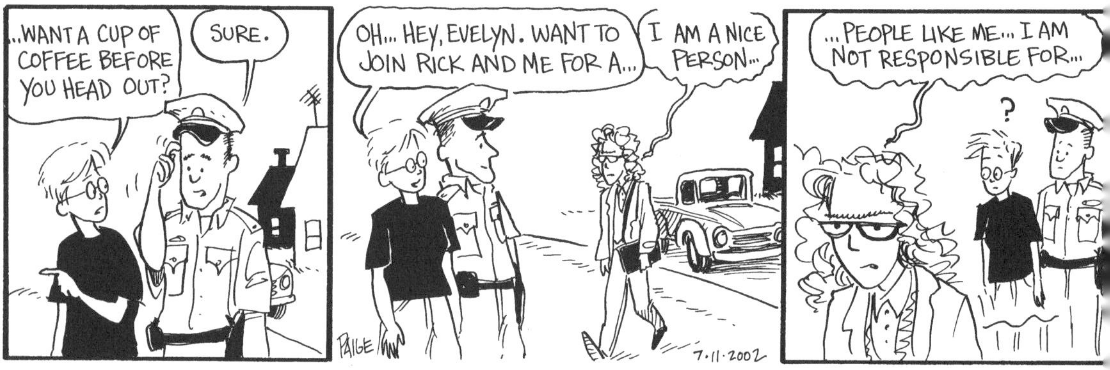
...WANT A CUP OF COFFEE BEFORE YOU HEAD OUT?
SURE.
OH... HEY, EVELYN. WANT TO JOIN RICK AND ME FOR A...
I AM A NICE PERSON...
PAIGE
7·11·2002
...PEOPLE LIKE ME... I AM NOT RESPONSIBLE FOR...

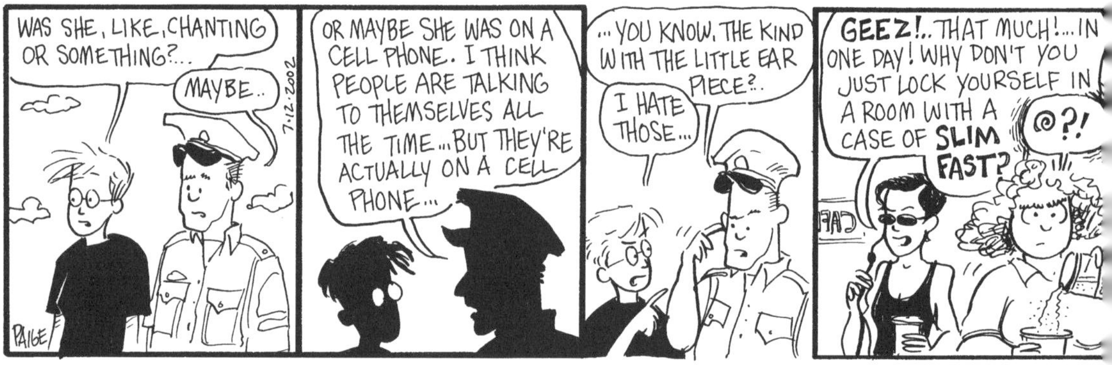
WAS SHE, LIKE, CHANTING OR SOMETHING?...
MAYBE..
7·12·2002
PAIGE
OR MAYBE SHE WAS ON A CELL PHONE. I THINK PEOPLE ARE TALKING TO THEMSELVES ALL THE TIME... BUT THEY'RE ACTUALLY ON A CELL PHONE...
...YOU KNOW, THE KIND WITH THE LITTLE EAR PIECE?..
I HATE THOSE...
GEEZ!.. THAT MUCH!... IN ONE DAY! WHY DON'T YOU JUST LOCK YOURSELF IN A ROOM WITH A CASE OF SLIM FAST?
@?!

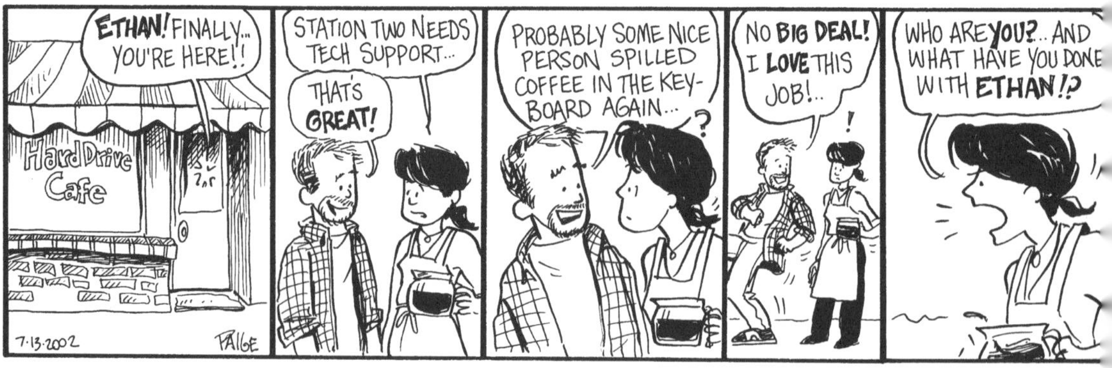
ETHAN! FINALLY... YOU'RE HERE!!
Hard Drive Cafe
7·13·2002
PAIGE
STATION TWO NEEDS TECH SUPPORT...
THAT'S GREAT!
PROBABLY SOME NICE PERSON SPILLED COFFEE IN THE KEY-BOARD AGAIN...
NO BIG DEAL! I LOVE THIS JOB!..
WHO ARE YOU?.. AND WHAT HAVE YOU DONE WITH ETHAN!?

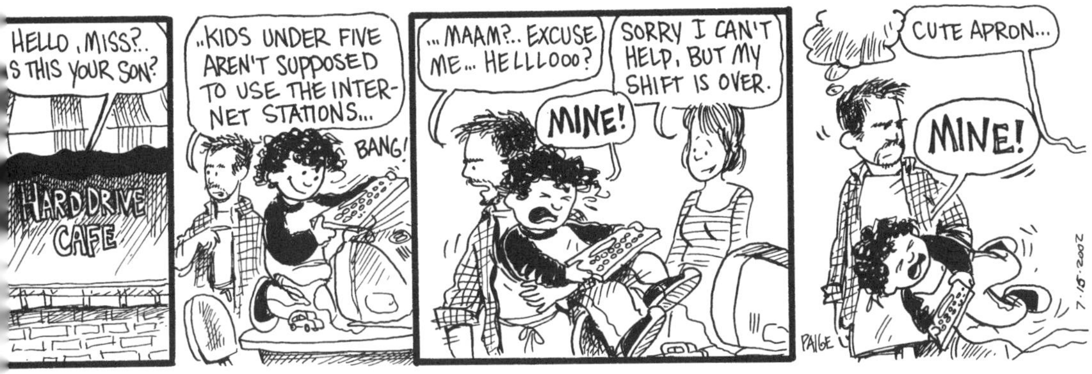
HELLO, MISS?.. S THIS YOUR SON?
HARD DRIVE CAFE
..KIDS UNDER FIVE AREN'T SUPPOSED TO USE THE INTER-NET STATIONS...
BANG!
...MAAM?.. EXCUSE ME... HELLLOoo?
MINE!
SORRY I CAN'T HELP, BUT MY SHIFT IS OVER.
CUTE APRON...
MINE!
PAIGE
7.15.2002

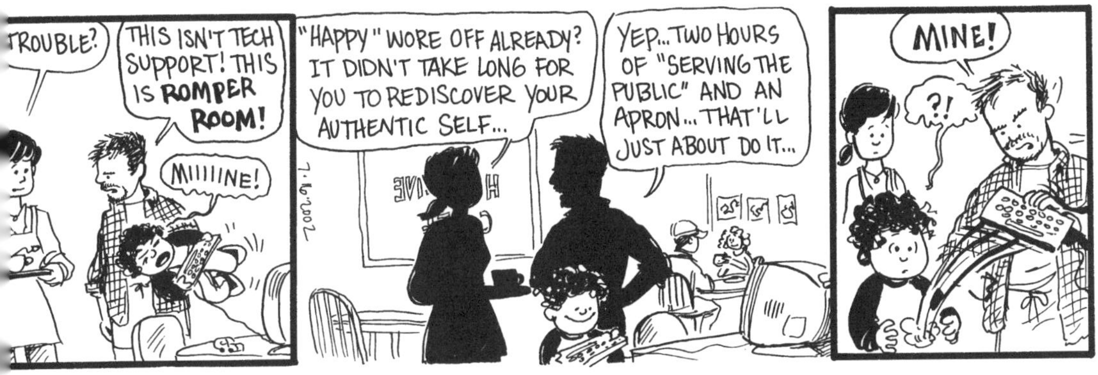
TROUBLE?
THIS ISN'T TECH SUPPORT! THIS IS ROMPER ROOM!
MIIIIINE!
7.16.2002
"HAPPY" WORE OFF ALREADY? IT DIDN'T TAKE LONG FOR YOU TO REDISCOVER YOUR AUTHENTIC SELF...
YEP... TWO HOURS OF "SERVING THE PUBLIC" AND AN APRON... THAT'LL JUST ABOUT DO IT...
MINE!
?!

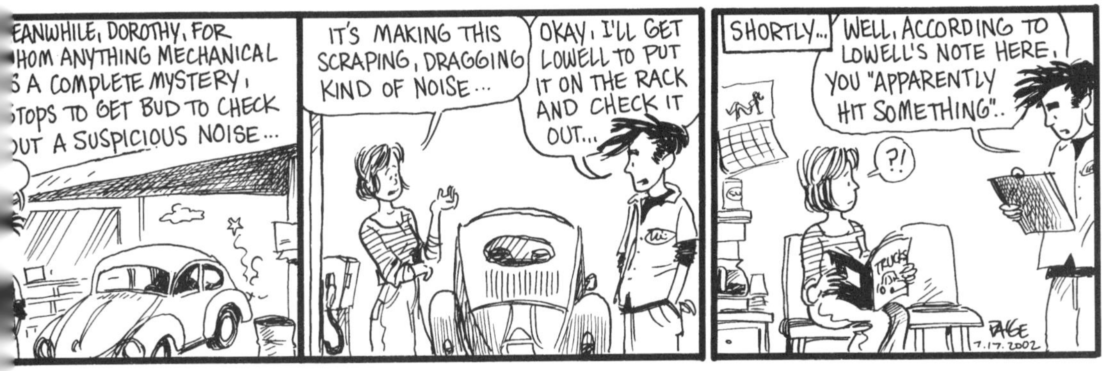
EANWHILE, DOROTHY, FOR HOM ANYTHING MECHANICAL S A COMPLETE MYSTERY, STOPS TO GET BUD TO CHECK OUT A SUSPICIOUS NOISE...
IT'S MAKING THIS SCRAPING, DRAGGING KIND OF NOISE...
OKAY, I'LL GET LOWELL TO PUT IT ON THE RACK AND CHECK IT OUT...
SHORTLY...
WELL, ACCORDING TO LOWELL'S NOTE HERE, YOU "APPARENTLY HIT SOMETHING"..
?!
TRUCKS
PAIGE
7.17.2002

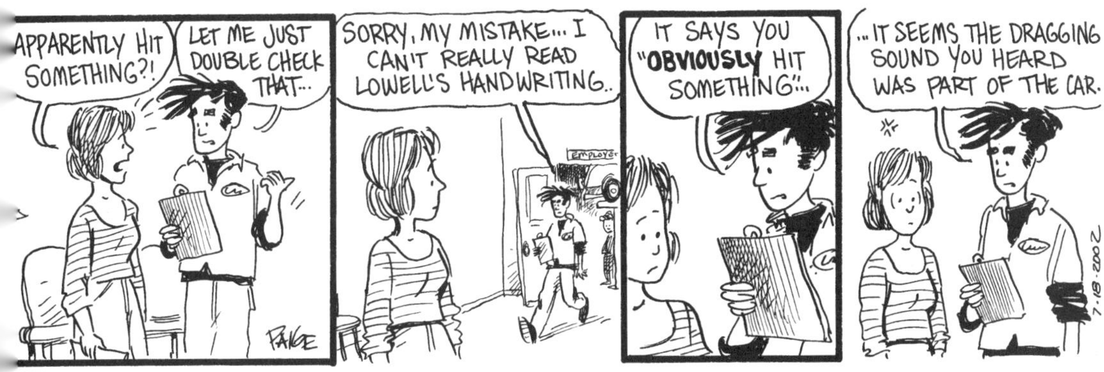
APPARENTLY HIT SOMETHING?!
LET ME JUST DOUBLE CHECK THAT...
PAIGE
SORRY, MY MISTAKE... I CAN'T REALLY READ LOWELL'S HANDWRITING..
EMPLOYEE
IT SAYS YOU "OBVIOUSLY HIT SOMETHING"...
...IT SEEMS THE DRAGGING SOUND YOU HEARD WAS PART OF THE CAR.
7.18.2002

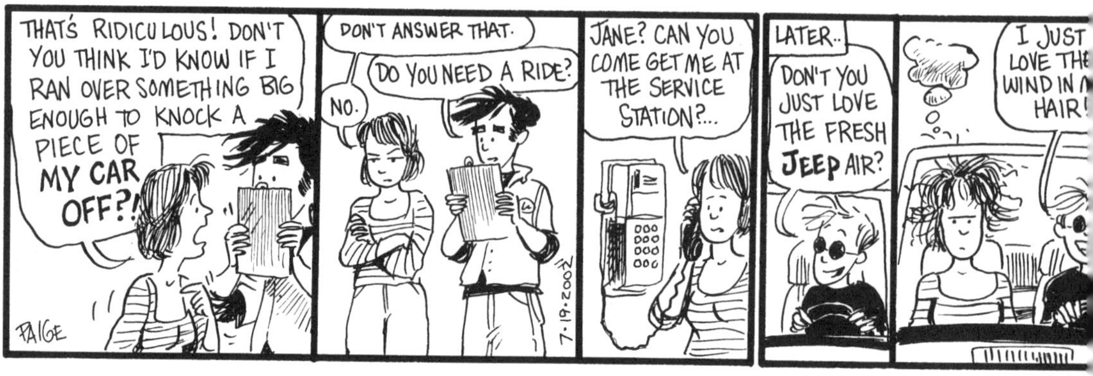
THAT'S RIDICULOUS! DON'T YOU THINK I'D KNOW IF I RAN OVER SOMETHING BIG ENOUGH TO KNOCK A PIECE OF **MY CAR OFF?!**
PAIGE
DON'T ANSWER THAT.
NO.
DO YOU NEED A RIDE?
7-19-2002
JANE? CAN YOU COME GET ME AT THE SERVICE STATION?...
LATER..
DON'T YOU JUST LOVE THE FRESH **JEEP** AIR?
I JUST LOVE THE WIND IN HAIR!

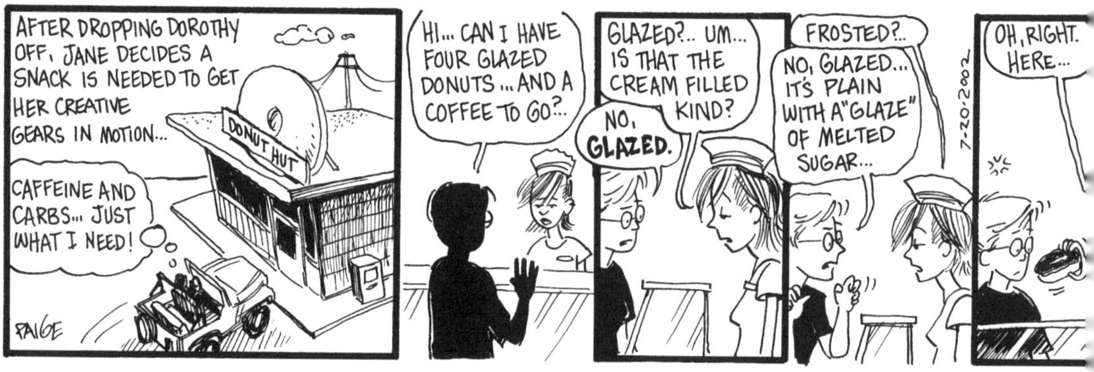
AFTER DROPPING DOROTHY OFF, JANE DECIDES A SNACK IS NEEDED TO GET HER CREATIVE GEARS IN MOTION...
DONUT HUT
CAFFEINE AND CARBS... JUST WHAT I NEED!
PAIGE
HI... CAN I HAVE FOUR GLAZED DONUTS... AND A COFFEE TO GO?..
GLAZED?.. UM... IS THAT THE CREAM FILLED KIND?
NO, **GLAZED.**
FROSTED?..
NO, GLAZED... IT'S PLAIN WITH A "GLAZE" OF MELTED SUGAR...
7-20-2002
OH, RIGHT. HERE...

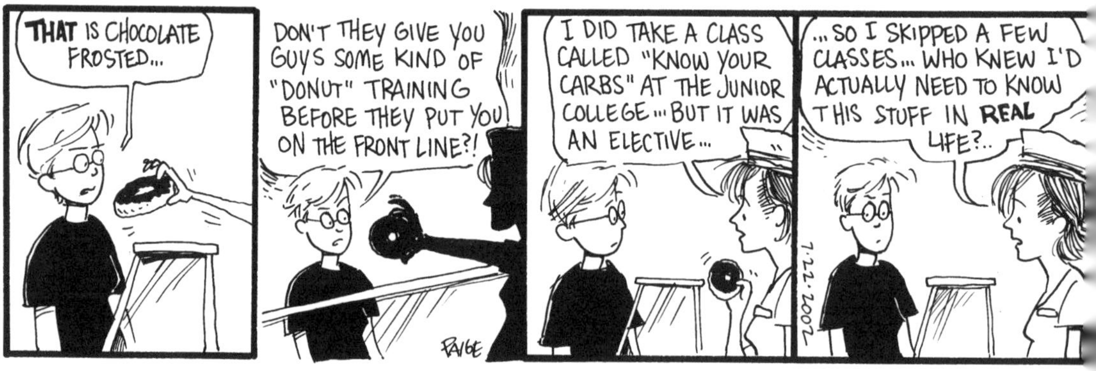
THAT IS CHOCOLATE FROSTED...
DON'T THEY GIVE YOU GUYS SOME KIND OF "DONUT" TRAINING BEFORE THEY PUT YOU ON THE FRONT LINE?!
PAIGE
I DID TAKE A CLASS CALLED "KNOW YOUR CARBS" AT THE JUNIOR COLLEGE... BUT IT WAS AN ELECTIVE...
7-22-2002
...SO I SKIPPED A FEW CLASSES... WHO KNEW I'D ACTUALLY NEED TO KNOW THIS STUFF IN **REAL** LIFE?..

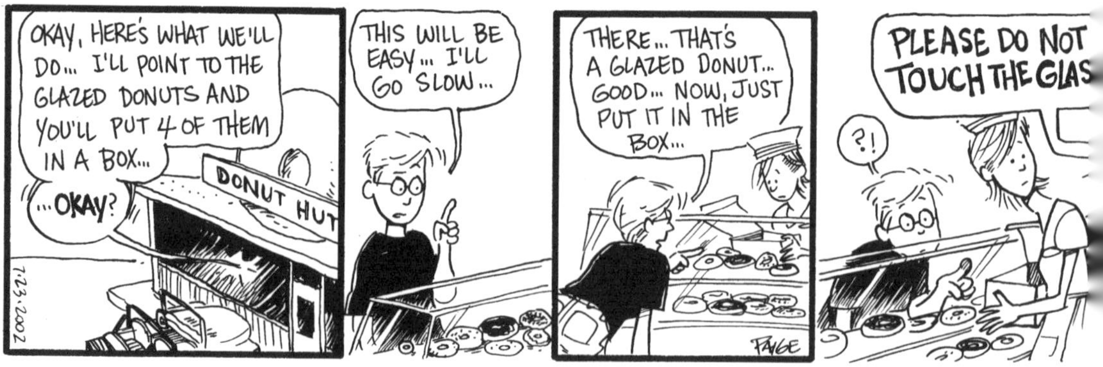
OKAY, HERE'S WHAT WE'LL DO... I'LL POINT TO THE GLAZED DONUTS AND YOU'LL PUT 4 OF THEM IN A BOX...
...**OKAY**?
DONUT HUT
7-23-2002
THIS WILL BE EASY... I'LL GO SLOW...
THERE... THAT'S A GLAZED DONUT... GOOD... NOW, JUST PUT IT IN THE BOX...
PAIGE
?!
PLEASE DO NOT TOUCH THE GLAS

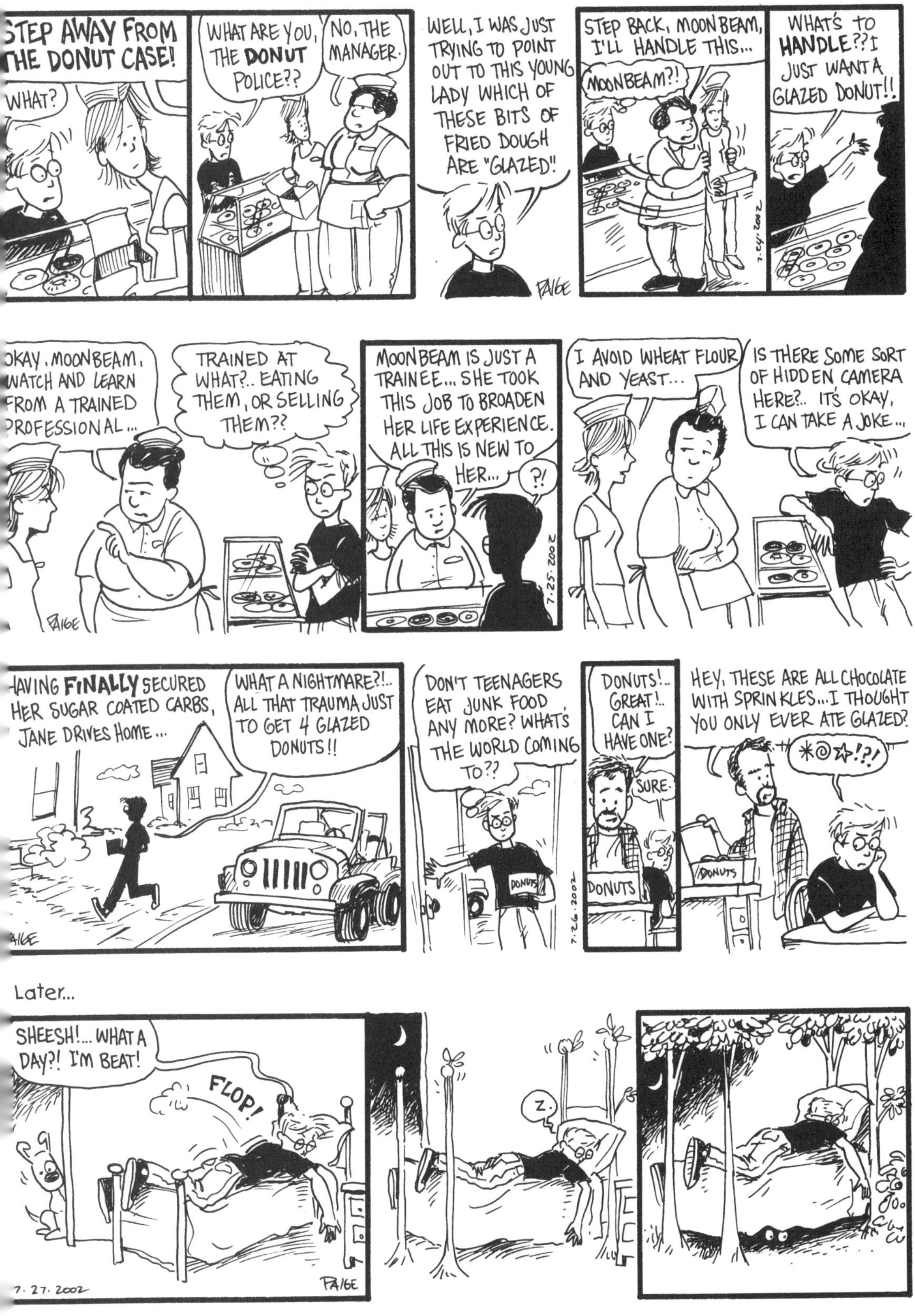
STEP AWAY FROM THE DONUT CASE!
WHAT?
WHAT ARE YOU, THE DONUT POLICE??
NO, THE MANAGER.
WELL, I WAS JUST TRYING TO POINT OUT TO THIS YOUNG LADY WHICH OF THESE BITS OF FRIED DOUGH ARE "GLAZED"!
PAIGE
STEP BACK, MOONBEAM, I'LL HANDLE THIS...
MOONBEAM?!
WHAT'S TO HANDLE?? I JUST WANT A GLAZED DONUT!!
7.24.2002
OKAY, MOONBEAM, WATCH AND LEARN FROM A TRAINED PROFESSIONAL...
TRAINED AT WHAT?.. EATING THEM, OR SELLING THEM??
PAIGE
MOONBEAM IS JUST A TRAINEE... SHE TOOK THIS JOB TO BROADEN HER LIFE EXPERIENCE. ALL THIS IS NEW TO HER...
?!
7.25.2002
I AVOID WHEAT FLOUR AND YEAST...
IS THERE SOME SORT OF HIDDEN CAMERA HERE?.. IT'S OKAY, I CAN TAKE A JOKE...
HAVING FINALLY SECURED HER SUGAR COATED CARBS, JANE DRIVES HOME...
WHAT A NIGHTMARE?!.. ALL THAT TRAUMA JUST TO GET 4 GLAZED DONUTS!!
PAIGE
DON'T TEENAGERS EAT JUNK FOOD ANY MORE? WHAT'S THE WORLD COMING TO??
DONUTS
7.26.2002
DONUTS!.. GREAT!.. CAN I HAVE ONE?
SURE.
DONUTS
HEY, THESE ARE ALL CHOCOLATE WITH SPRINKLES... I THOUGHT YOU ONLY EVER ATE GLAZED?
*@☆!?!
DONUTS
Later...
SHEESH!... WHAT A DAY?! I'M BEAT!
FLOP!
Z
7.27.2002
PAIGE

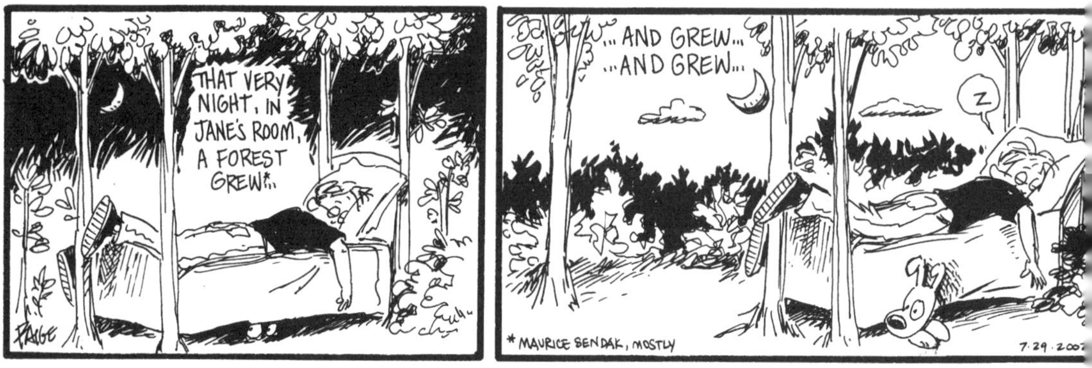
THAT VERY NIGHT, IN JANE'S ROOM, A FOREST GREW*...
PAIGE
... AND GREW... ...AND GREW...
Z
* MAURICE SENDAK, MOSTLY
7·29·200

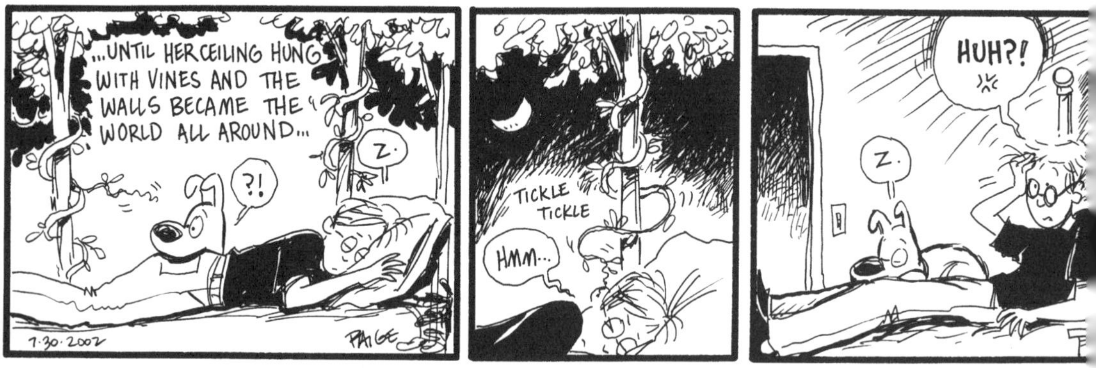
...UNTIL HER CEILING HUNG WITH VINES AND THE WALLS BECAME THE WORLD ALL AROUND...
?!
Z
7·30·2002
PAIGE
TICKLE TICKLE
HMM...
Z.
HUH?!

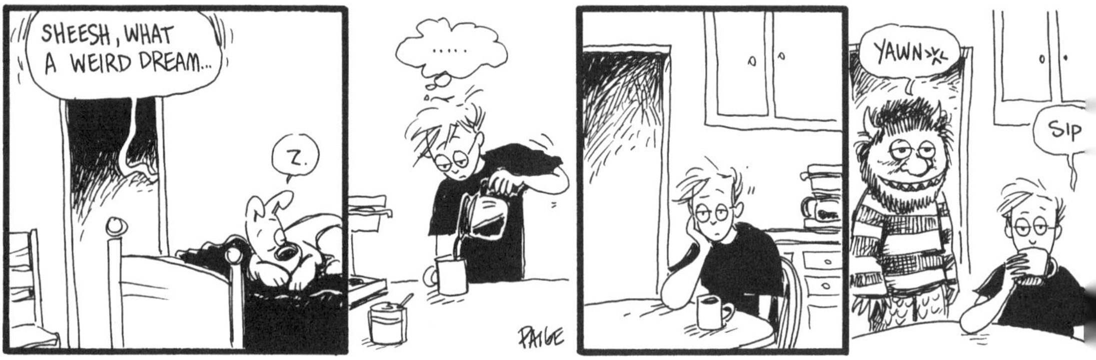
SHEESH, WHAT A WEIRD DREAM...
Z.
.....
PAIGE
YAWN
SIP

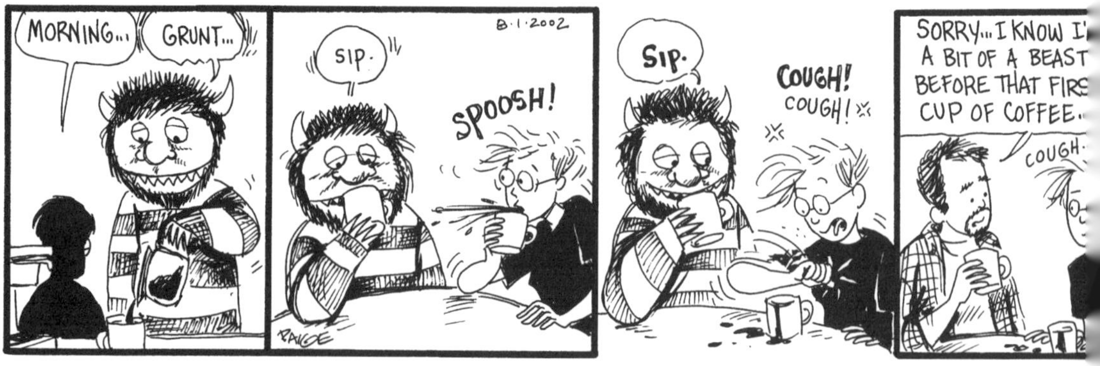
MORNING...
GRUNT...
8·1·2002
SIP.
SPOOSH!
PAIGE
SIP.
COUGH!
COUGH!
SORRY... I KNOW I
A BIT OF A BEAST
BEFORE THAT FIRS
CUP OF COFFEE..
COUGH

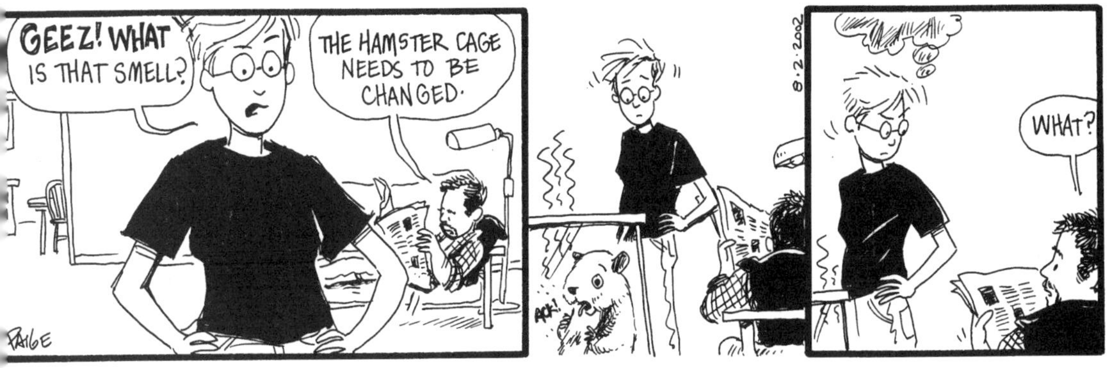
GEEZ! WHAT IS THAT SMELL?
THE HAMSTER CAGE NEEDS TO BE CHANGED.
PAIGE
ACK!
8·2·2002
WHAT?

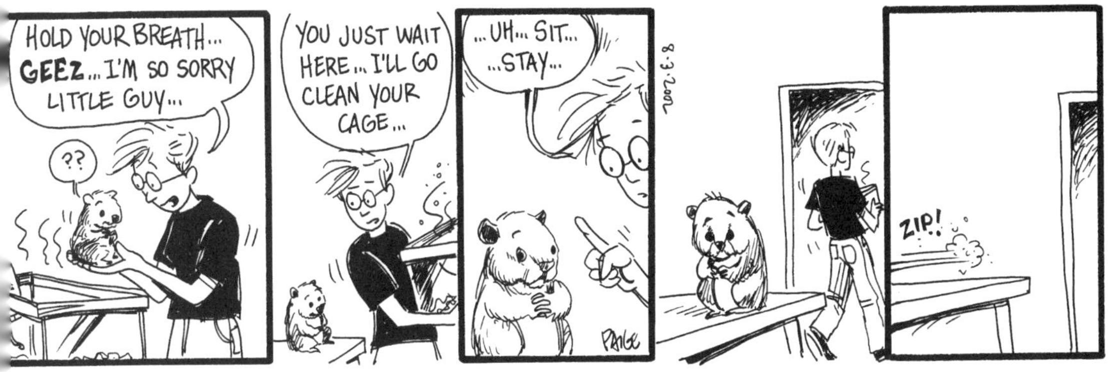
HOLD YOUR BREATH... GEEZ... I'M SO SORRY LITTLE GUY...
??
YOU JUST WAIT HERE... I'LL GO CLEAN YOUR CAGE...
...UH... SIT... ...STAY...
PAIGE
8·3·2002
ZIP!

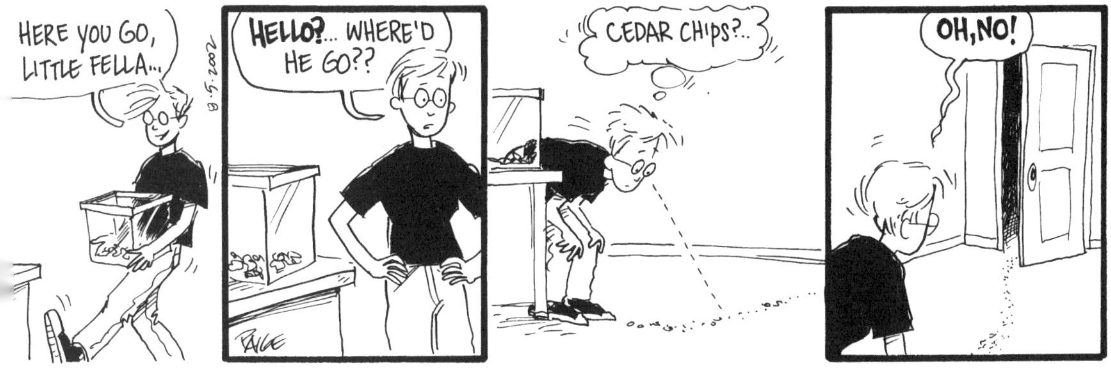
HERE YOU GO, LITTLE FELLA...
8·5·2002
HELLO?... WHERE'D HE GO??
PAIGE
CEDAR CHIPS?..
OH, NO!

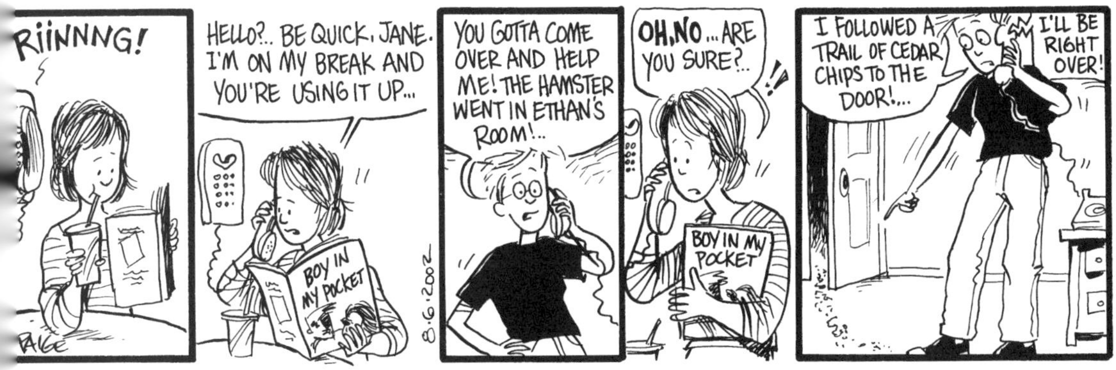
RIINNNG!
PAIGE
HELLO?.. BE QUICK, JANE. I'M ON MY BREAK AND YOU'RE USING IT UP...
BOY IN MY POCKET
8·6·2002
YOU GOTTA COME OVER AND HELP ME! THE HAMSTER WENT IN ETHAN'S ROOM!...
OH, NO... ARE YOU SURE?..
BOY IN MY POCKET
I FOLLOWED A TRAIL OF CEDAR CHIPS TO THE DOOR!...
I'LL BE RIGHT OVER!

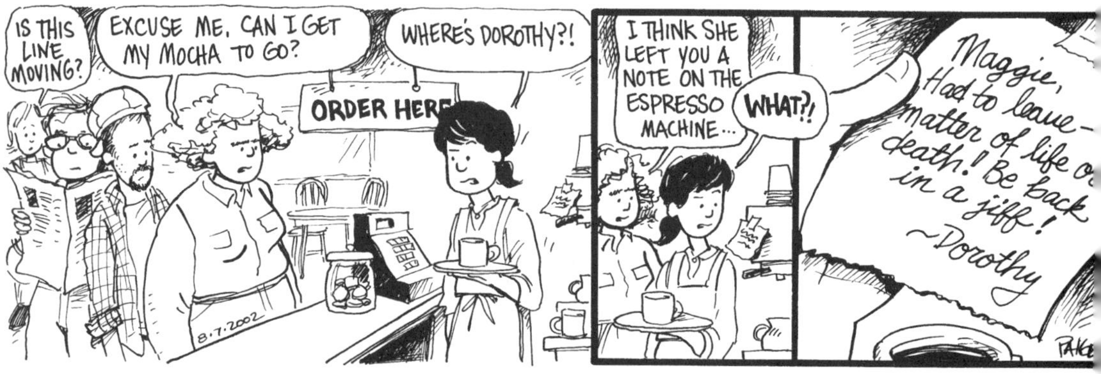
IS THIS LINE MOVING?
EXCUSE ME. CAN I GET MY MOCHA TO GO?
WHERE'S DOROTHY?!
ORDER HERE
8·7·2002
I THINK SHE LEFT YOU A NOTE ON THE ESPRESSO MACHINE...
WHAT?!
Maggie, Had to leave— matter of life o death! Be back in a jiff! ~Dorothy
PAGE

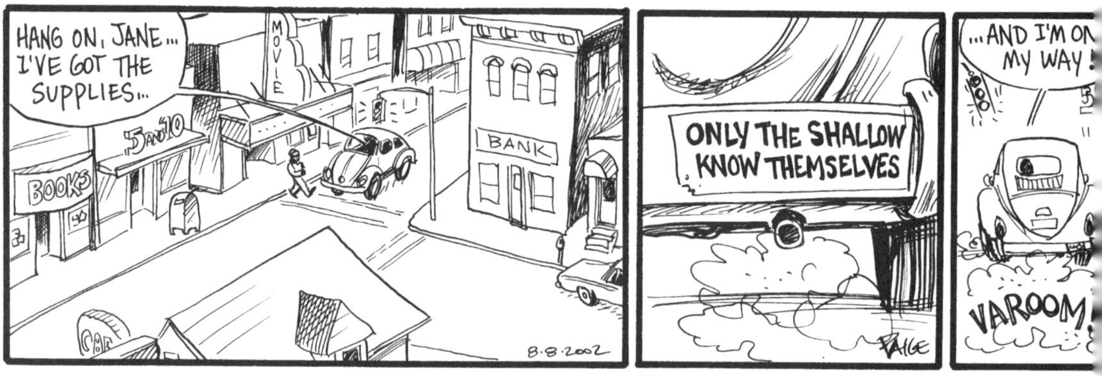
HANG ON, JANE... I'VE GOT THE SUPPLIES...
MOVIE
5 AND 10
BOOKS
BANK
8·8·2002
ONLY THE SHALLOW KNOW THEMSELVES
PAGE
...AND I'M O
MY WAY
VAROOM

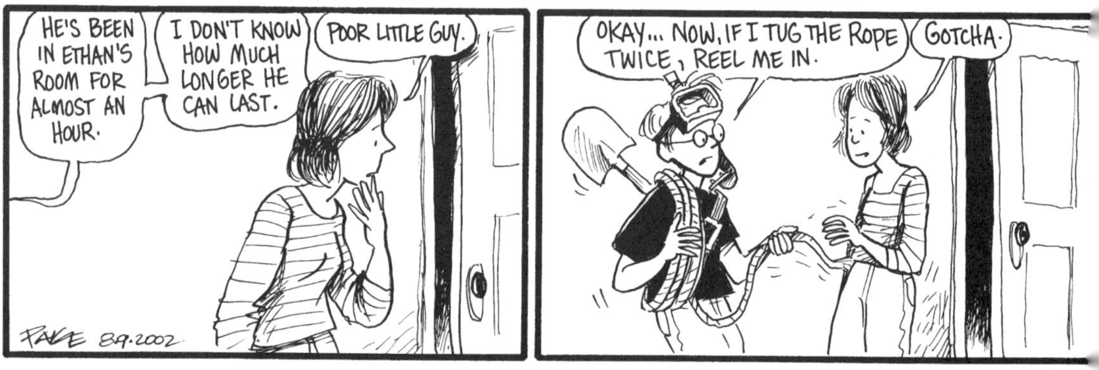
HE'S BEEN IN ETHAN'S ROOM FOR ALMOST AN HOUR.
I DON'T KNOW HOW MUCH LONGER HE CAN LAST.
POOR LITTLE GUY.
PAGE 8·9·2002
OKAY... NOW, IF I TUG THE ROPE TWICE, REEL ME IN.
GOTCHA.

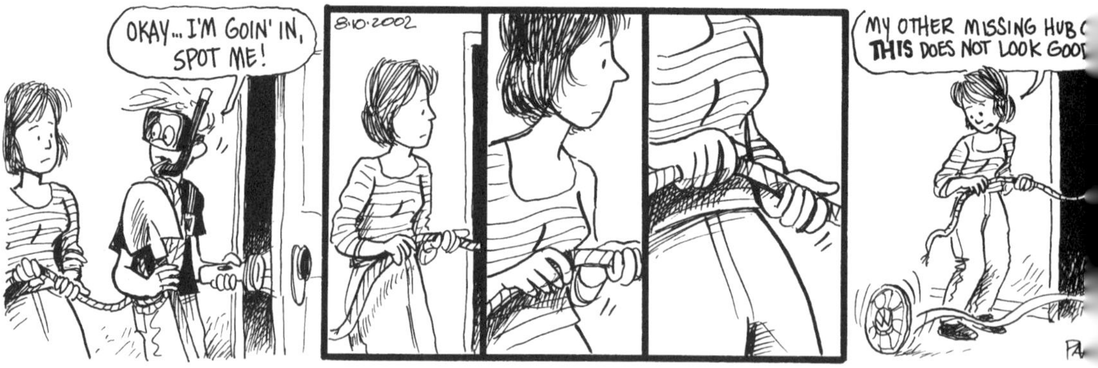
OKAY... I'M GOIN' IN, SPOT ME!
8·10·2002
MY OTHER MISSING HUB C
THIS DOES NOT LOOK GOOD

Chapter six

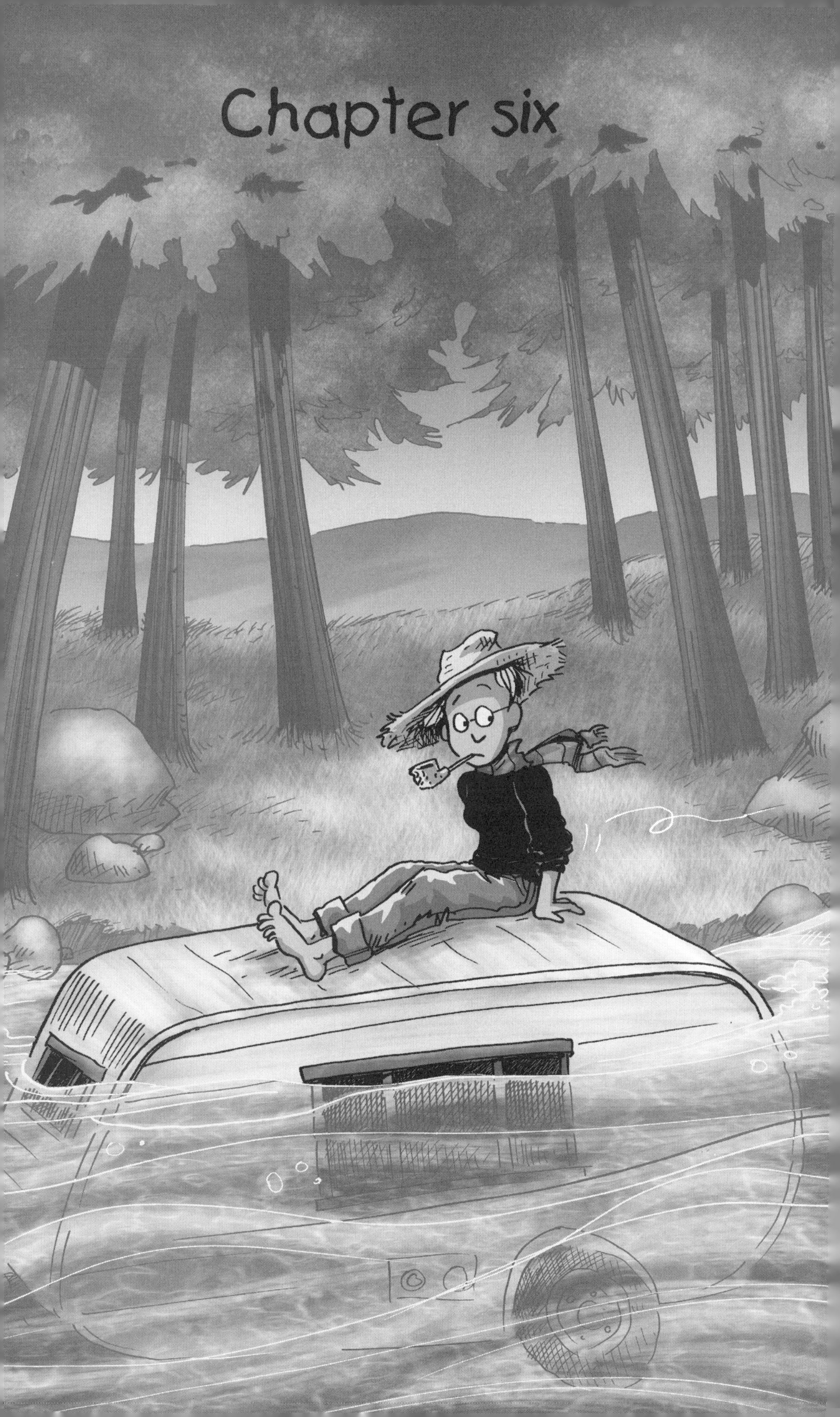

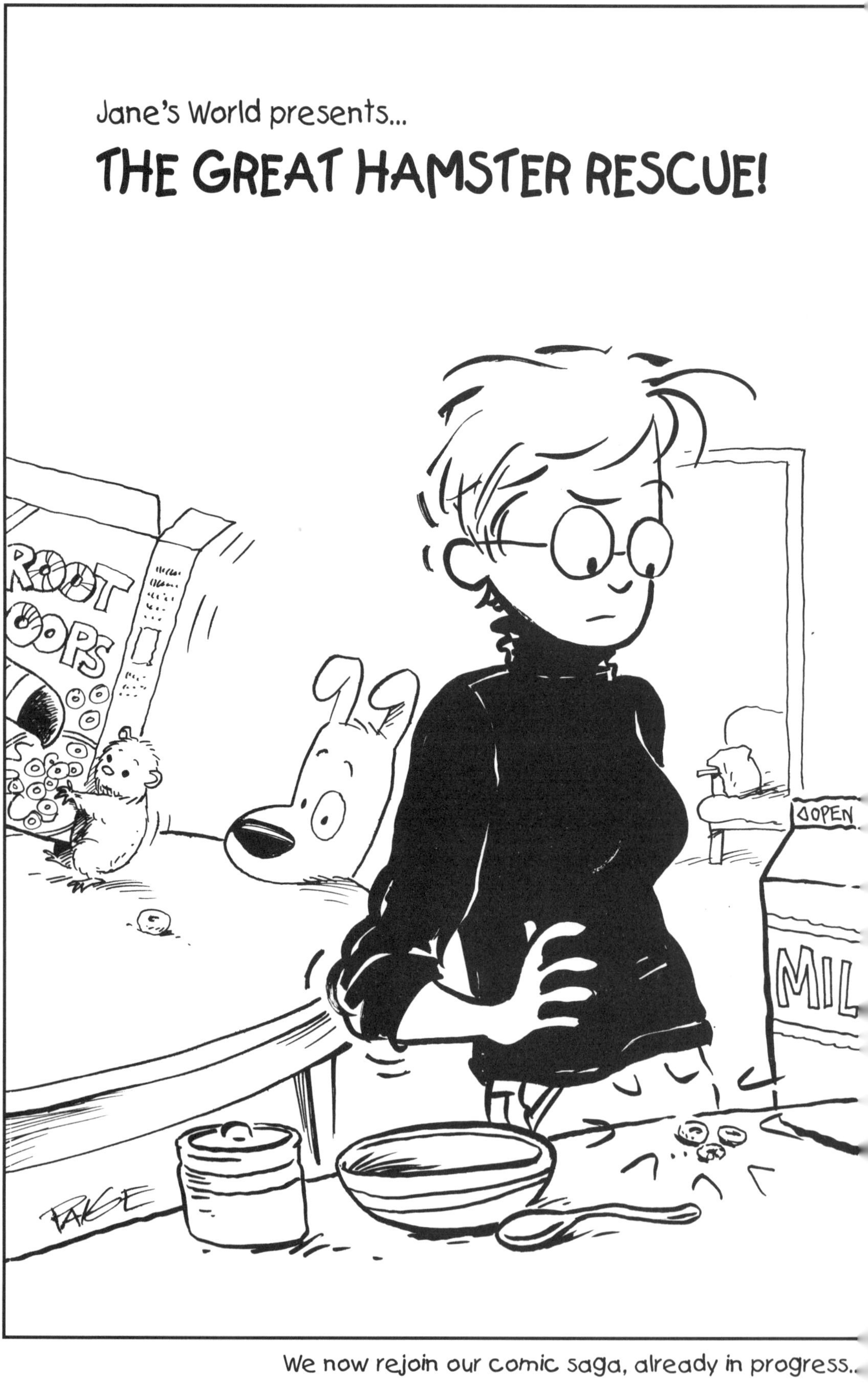
Jane's World presents...
THE GREAT HAMSTER RESCUE!
ROOT
OOPS
OPEN
MIL
PAGE

We now rejoin our comic saga, already in progress..

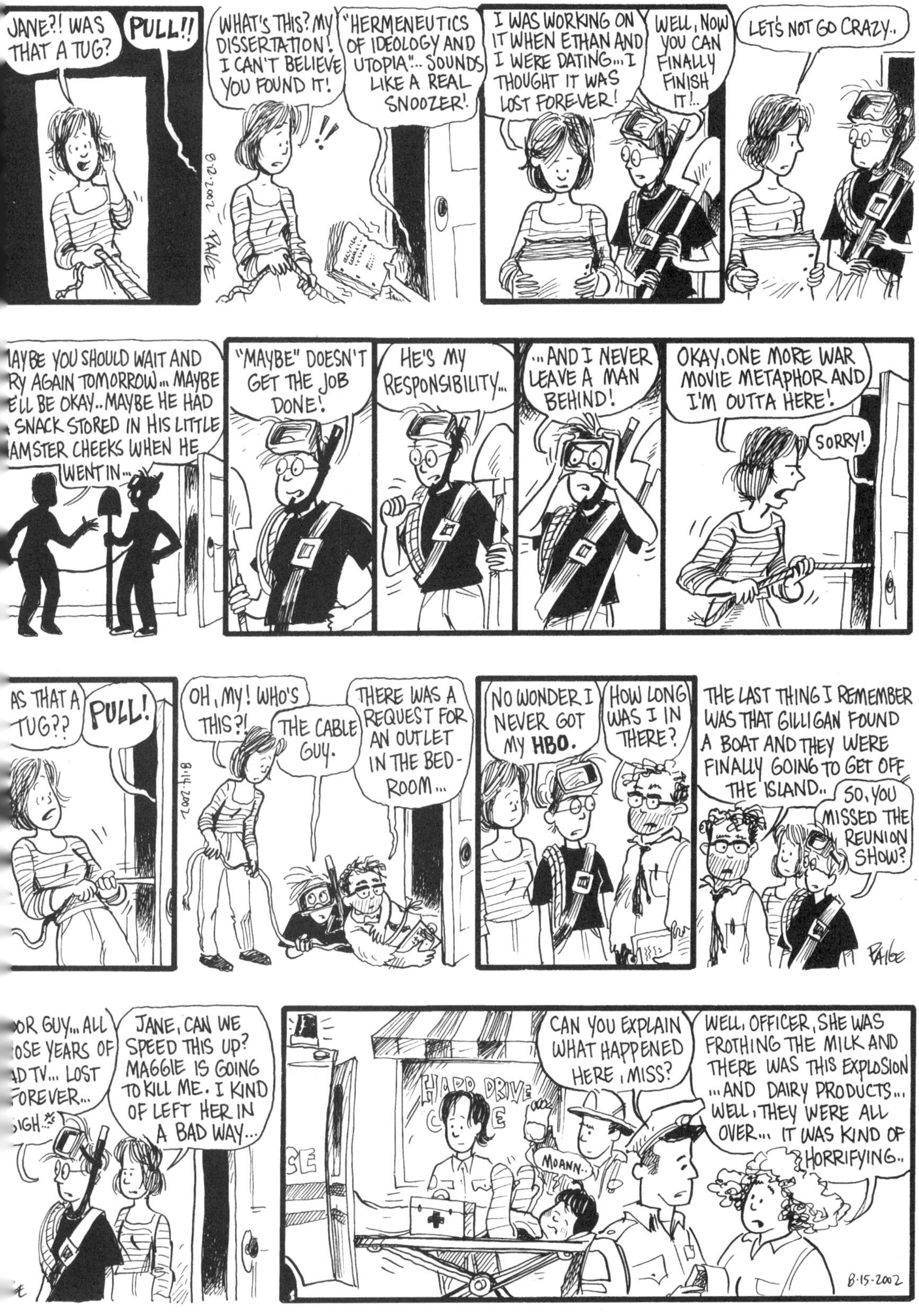

JANE?! WAS THAT A TUG?
PULL!!
8-12-2002
PAIGE
WHAT'S THIS? MY DISSERTATION! I CAN'T BELIEVE YOU FOUND IT!
"HERMENEUTICS OF IDEOLOGY AND UTOPIA"... SOUNDS LIKE A REAL SNOOZER!
I WAS WORKING ON IT WHEN ETHAN AND I WERE DATING... I THOUGHT IT WAS LOST FOREVER!
WELL, NOW YOU CAN FINALLY FINISH IT!...
LET'S NOT GO CRAZY..
IAYBE YOU SHOULD WAIT AND RY AGAIN TOMORROW... MAYBE E'LL BE OKAY.. MAYBE HE HAD SNACK STORED IN HIS LITTLE IAMSTER CHEEKS WHEN HE WENT IN...
"MAYBE" DOESN'T GET THE JOB DONE!
HE'S MY RESPONSIBILITY...
...AND I NEVER LEAVE A MAN BEHIND!
OKAY, ONE MORE WAR MOVIE METAPHOR AND I'M OUTTA HERE!
SORRY!
AS THAT A TUG??
PULL!
8-14-2002
OH, MY! WHO'S THIS?!
THE CABLE GUY.
THERE WAS A REQUEST FOR AN OUTLET IN THE BED-ROOM...
NO WONDER I NEVER GOT MY HBO.
HOW LONG WAS I IN THERE?
THE LAST THING I REMEMBER WAS THAT GILLIGAN FOUND A BOAT AND THEY WERE FINALLY GOING TO GET OFF THE ISLAND..
SO, YOU MISSED THE REUNION SHOW?
PAIGE
OR GUY... ALL OSE YEARS OF AD TV... LOST FOREVER... SIGH...
JANE, CAN WE SPEED THIS UP? MAGGIE IS GOING TO KILL ME. I KIND OF LEFT HER IN A BAD WAY...
CAN YOU EXPLAIN WHAT HAPPENED HERE, MISS?
WELL, OFFICER, SHE WAS FROTHING THE MILK AND THERE WAS THIS EXPLOSION ...AND DAIRY PRODUCTS... WELL, THEY WERE ALL OVER... IT WAS KIND OF HORRIFYING..
MOANN..
8-15-2002

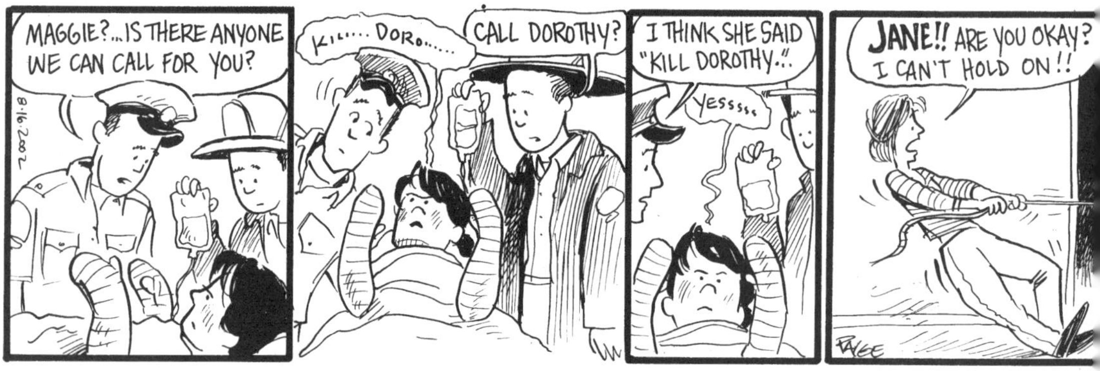
MAGGIE?...IS THERE ANYONE WE CAN CALL FOR YOU?
8.16.2002
KI..... DORO......
CALL DOROTHY?
I THINK SHE SAID "KILL DOROTHY."
YESSsss
JANE!! ARE YOU OKAY? I CAN'T HOLD ON!!

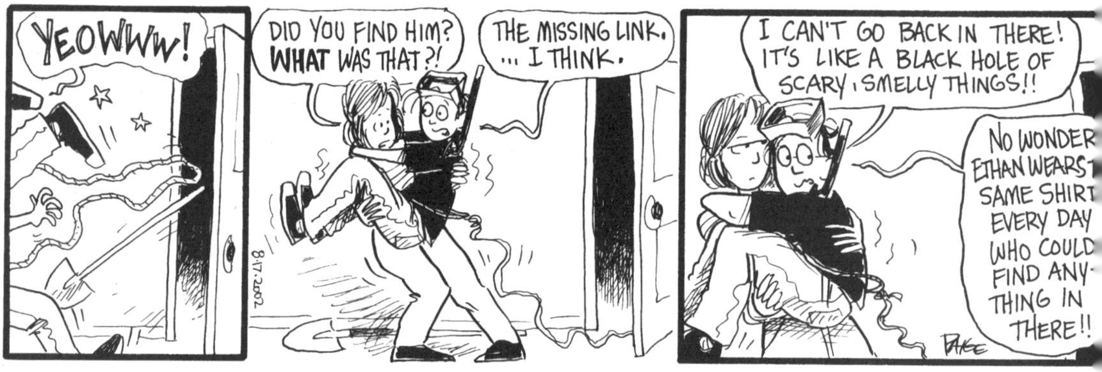
YEOWWW!
DID YOU FIND HIM? WHAT WAS THAT?!
THE MISSING LINK. ... I THINK.
8.17.2002
I CAN'T GO BACK IN THERE! IT'S LIKE A BLACK HOLE OF SCARY, SMELLY THINGS!!
NO WONDER ETHAN WEARS T SAME SHIRT EVERY DAY WHO COULD FIND ANY-THING IN THERE!!

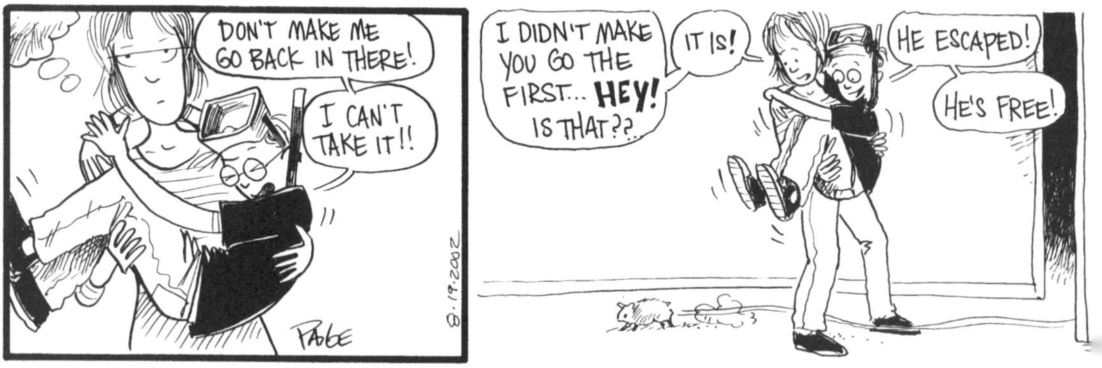
DON'T MAKE ME GO BACK IN THERE!
I CAN'T TAKE IT!!
8.19.2002
I DIDN'T MAKE YOU GO THE FIRST... HEY! IS THAT??
IT IS!
HE ESCAPED!
HE'S FREE!

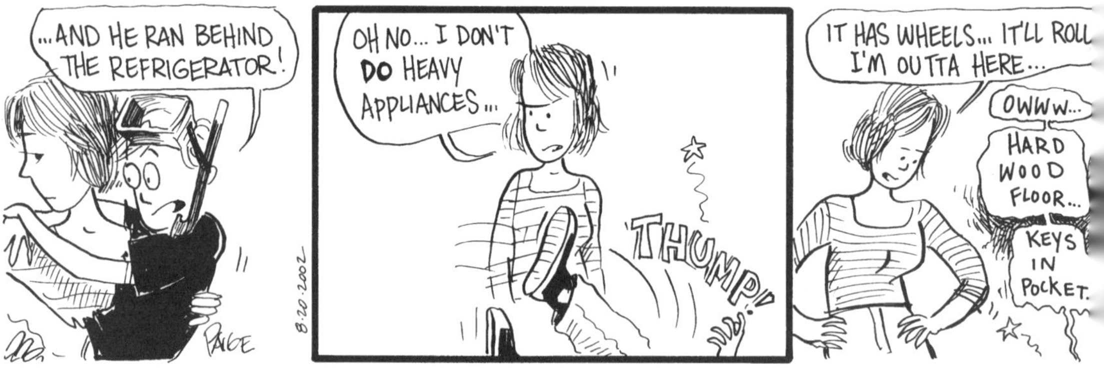
...AND HE RAN BEHIND THE REFRIGERATOR!
8.20.2002
OH NO... I DON'T DO HEAVY APPLIANCES...
THUMP!
IT HAS WHEELS... IT'LL ROLL I'M OUTTA HERE...
OWWW...
HARD WOOD FLOOR...
KEYS IN POCKET.

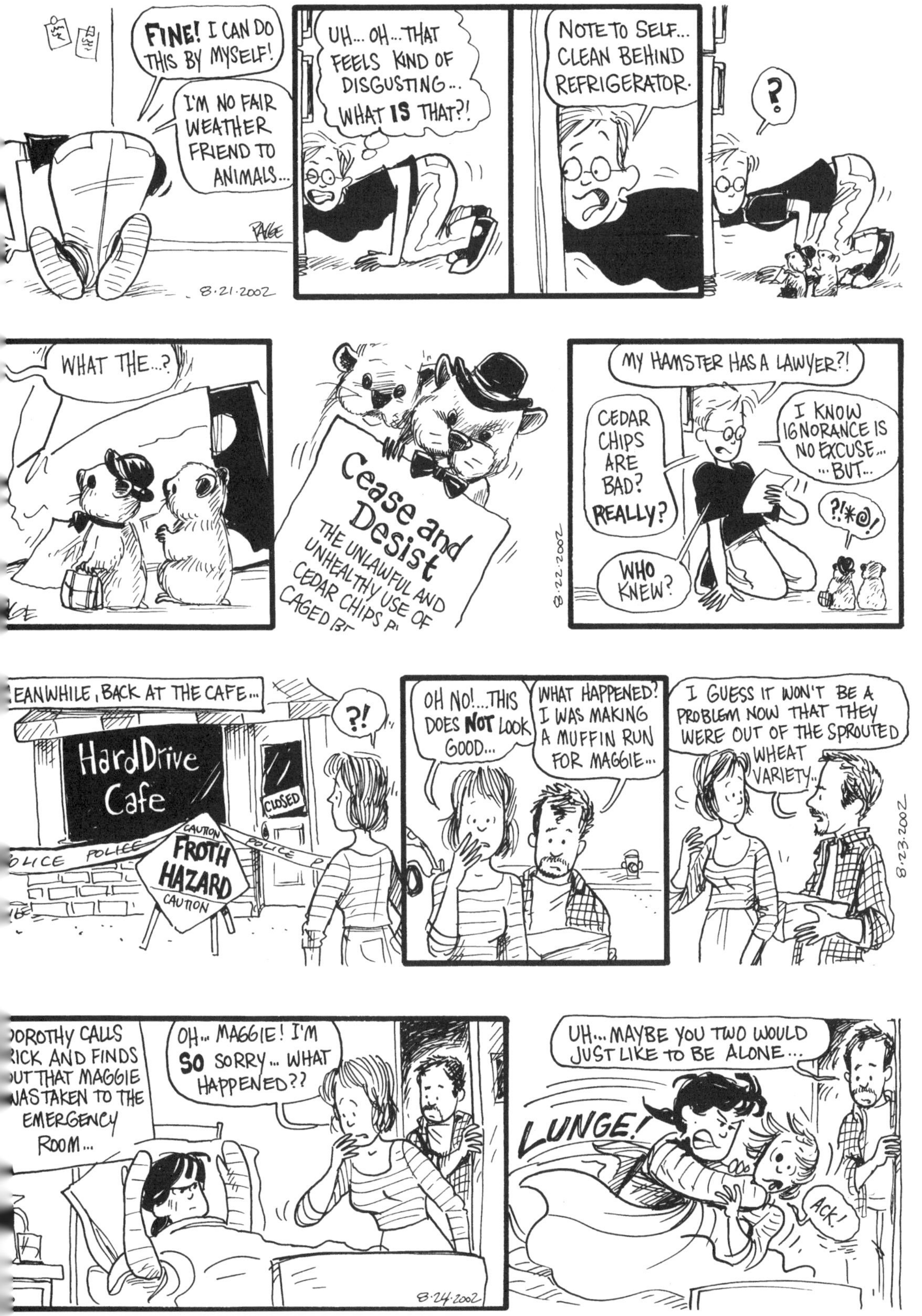
FINE! I CAN DO THIS BY MYSELF!
I'M NO FAIR WEATHER FRIEND TO ANIMALS...
PAIGE
8·21·2002
UH... OH... THAT FEELS KIND OF DISGUSTING... WHAT IS THAT?!
NOTE TO SELF... CLEAN BEHIND REFRIGERATOR.
?
WHAT THE...?
Cease and Desist
THE UNLAWFUL AND UNHEALTHY USE OF CEDAR CHIPS
8·22·2002
MY HAMSTER HAS A LAWYER?!
CEDAR CHIPS ARE BAD? REALLY?
I KNOW IGNORANCE IS NO EXCUSE... ...BUT...
?!*@!
WHO KNEW?
EANWHILE, BACK AT THE CAFE...
HardDrive Cafe
CLOSED
CAUTION FROTH HAZARD CAUTION
POLICE POLICE POLICE
?!
OH NO!...THIS DOES NOT LOOK GOOD...
WHAT HAPPENED? I WAS MAKING A MUFFIN RUN FOR MAGGIE...
I GUESS IT WON'T BE A PROBLEM NOW THAT THEY WERE OUT OF THE SPROUTED WHEAT VARIETY...
8·23·2002
OROTHY CALLS ICK AND FINDS UT THAT MAGGIE WAS TAKEN TO THE EMERGENCY ROOM...
OH... MAGGIE! I'M SO SORRY... WHAT HAPPENED??
8·24·2002
UH... MAYBE YOU TWO WOULD JUST LIKE TO BE ALONE...
LUNGE!
ACK!

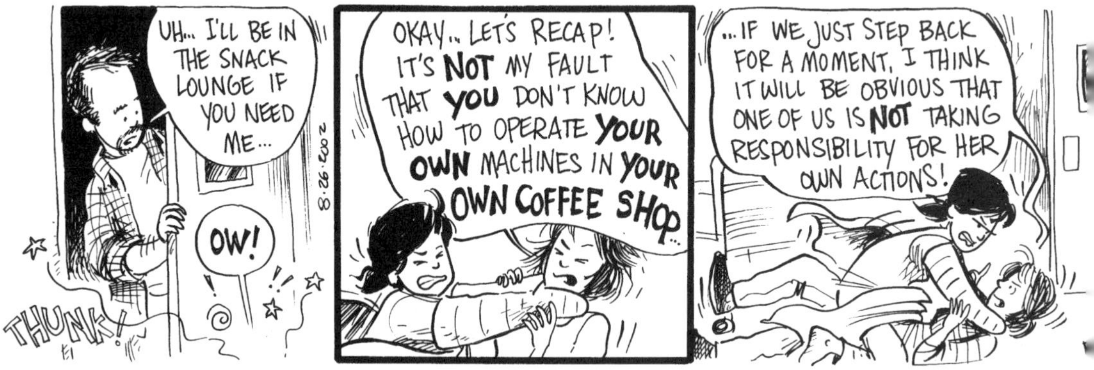
UH... I'LL BE IN THE SNACK LOUNGE IF YOU NEED ME...
THUNK!
OW!
8·26·2002
OKAY.. LET'S RECAP! IT'S NOT MY FAULT THAT YOU DON'T KNOW HOW TO OPERATE YOUR OWN MACHINES IN YOUR OWN COFFEE SHOP...
...IF WE JUST STEP BACK FOR A MOMENT, I THINK IT WILL BE OBVIOUS THAT ONE OF US IS NOT TAKING RESPONSIBILITY FOR HER OWN ACTIONS!

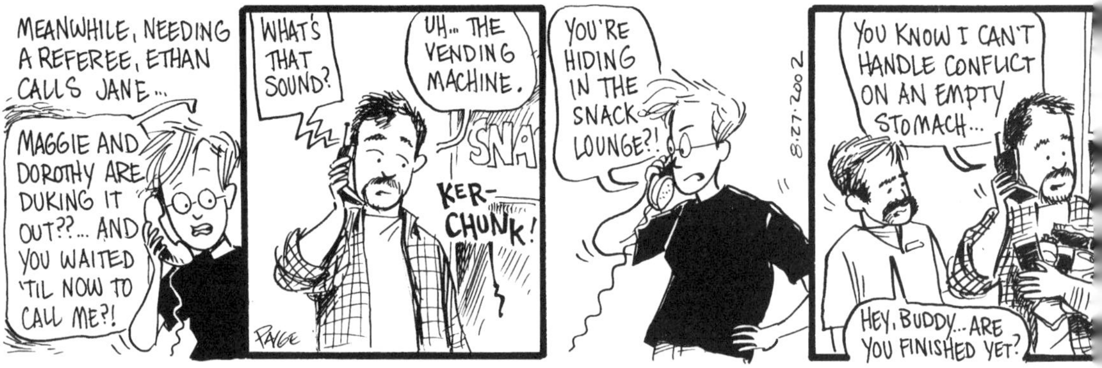
MEANWHILE, NEEDING A REFEREE, ETHAN CALLS JANE...
MAGGIE AND DOROTHY ARE DUKING IT OUT??... AND YOU WAITED 'TIL NOW TO CALL ME?!
WHAT'S THAT SOUND?
UH... THE VENDING MACHINE.
KER-CHUNK!
PAIGE
YOU'RE HIDING IN THE SNACK LOUNGE?!
8·27·2002
YOU KNOW I CAN'T HANDLE CONFLICT ON AN EMPTY STOMACH...
HEY, BUDDY... ARE YOU FINISHED YET?

Shortly...

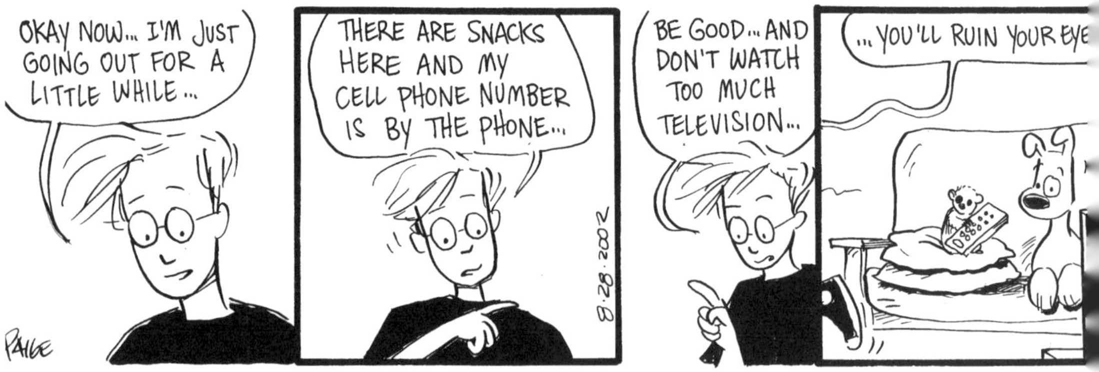
OKAY NOW... I'M JUST GOING OUT FOR A LITTLE WHILE...
PAIGE
THERE ARE SNACKS HERE AND MY CELL PHONE NUMBER IS BY THE PHONE...
8·28·2002
BE GOOD... AND DON'T WATCH TOO MUCH TELEVISION...
... YOU'LL RUIN YOUR EYE

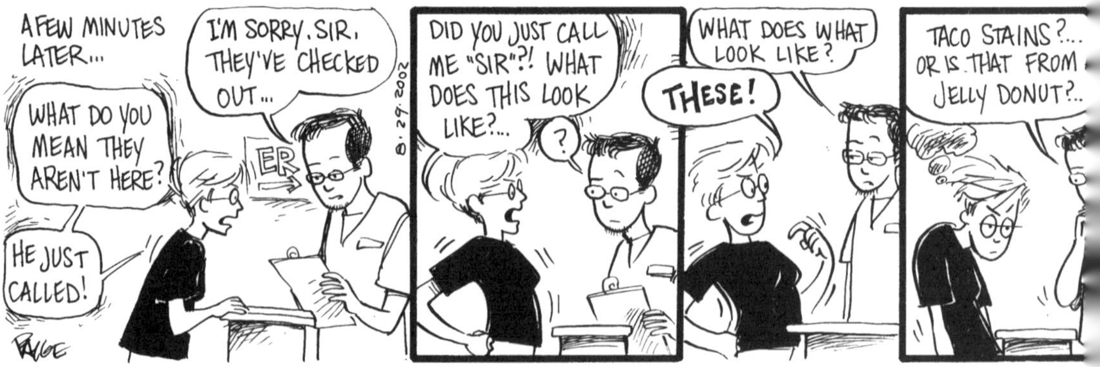
A FEW MINUTES LATER...
WHAT DO YOU MEAN THEY AREN'T HERE?
HE JUST CALLED!
I'M SORRY, SIR, THEY'VE CHECKED OUT...
ER
PAIGE
8·29·2002
DID YOU JUST CALL ME "SIR"?! WHAT DOES THIS LOOK LIKE?...
?
WHAT DOES WHAT LOOK LIKE?
THESE!
TACO STAINS?... OR IS THAT FROM JELLY DONUT?...

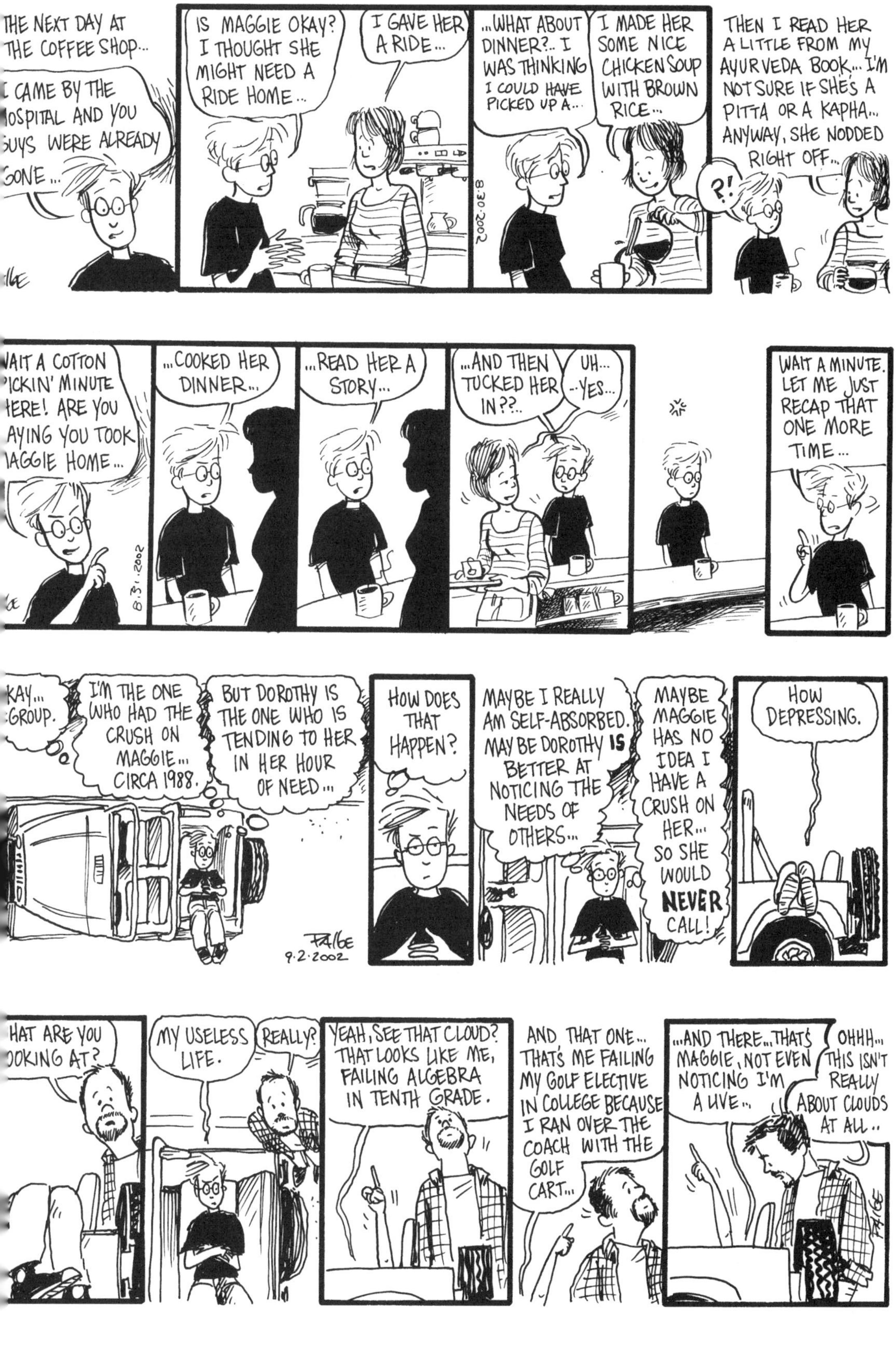

THE NEXT DAY AT THE COFFEE SHOP...
I CAME BY THE OSPITAL AND YOU UYS WERE ALREADY GONE...
IS MAGGIE OKAY? I THOUGHT SHE MIGHT NEED A RIDE HOME...
I GAVE HER A RIDE...
...WHAT ABOUT DINNER?.. I WAS THINKING I COULD HAVE PICKED UP A...
I MADE HER SOME NICE CHICKEN SOUP WITH BROWN RICE...
THEN I READ HER A LITTLE FROM MY AYURVEDA BOOK... I'M NOT SURE IF SHE'S A PITTA OR A KAPHA... ANYWAY, SHE NODDED RIGHT OFF...
?!
8.30.2002
VAIT A COTTON PICKIN' MINUTE HERE! ARE YOU AYING YOU TOOK MAGGIE HOME...
...COOKED HER DINNER...
...READ HER A STORY...
...AND THEN TUCKED HER IN??..
UH... ..YES...
WAIT A MINUTE. LET ME JUST RECAP THAT ONE MORE TIME...
8.31.2002
KAY... GROUP.
I'M THE ONE WHO HAD THE CRUSH ON MAGGIE... CIRCA 1988.
BUT DOROTHY IS THE ONE WHO IS TENDING TO HER IN HER HOUR OF NEED...
HOW DOES THAT HAPPEN?
MAYBE I REALLY AM SELF-ABSORBED. MAYBE DOROTHY IS BETTER AT NOTICING THE NEEDS OF OTHERS...
MAYBE MAGGIE HAS NO IDEA I HAVE A CRUSH ON HER... SO SHE WOULD NEVER CALL!
HOW DEPRESSING.
PAIGE
9.2.2002
HAT ARE YOU OOKING AT?
MY USELESS LIFE.
REALLY?
YEAH, SEE THAT CLOUD? THAT LOOKS LIKE ME, FAILING ALGEBRA IN TENTH GRADE.
AND THAT ONE... THAT'S ME FAILING MY GOLF ELECTIVE IN COLLEGE BECAUSE I RAN OVER THE COACH WITH THE GOLF CART...
...AND THERE... THAT'S MAGGIE, NOT EVEN NOTICING I'M ALIVE...
OHHH... THIS ISN'T REALLY ABOUT CLOUDS AT ALL..
PAIGE

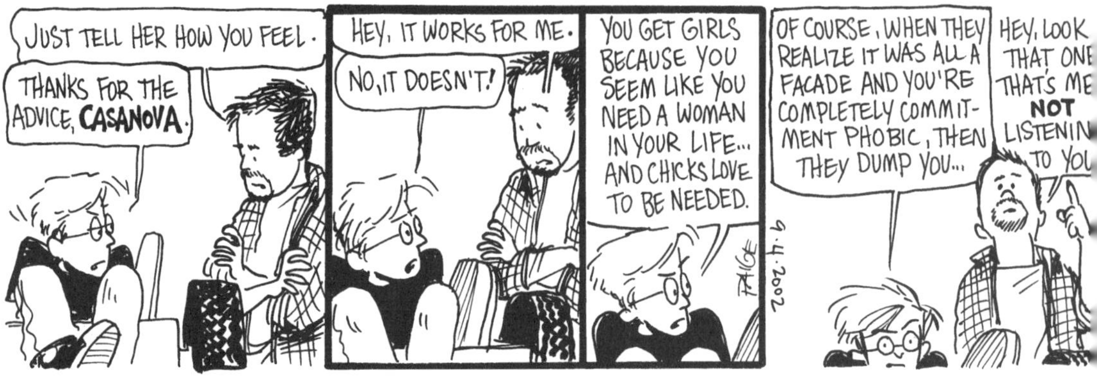
JUST TELL HER HOW YOU FEEL.
THANKS FOR THE ADVICE, CASANOVA.
HEY, IT WORKS FOR ME.
NO, IT DOESN'T!
YOU GET GIRLS BECAUSE YOU SEEM LIKE YOU NEED A WOMAN IN YOUR LIFE... AND CHICKS LOVE TO BE NEEDED.
PAIGE
9·4·2002
OF COURSE, WHEN THEY REALIZE IT WAS ALL A FACADE AND YOU'RE COMPLETELY COMMIT-MENT PHOBIC, THEN THEY DUMP YOU...
HEY, LOOK THAT ONE THAT'S ME NOT LISTENIN TO YOU

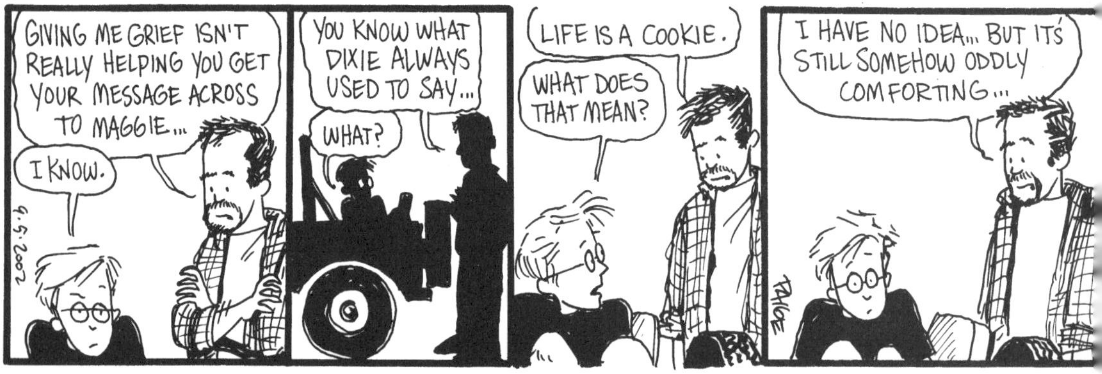
GIVING ME GRIEF ISN'T REALLY HELPING YOU GET YOUR MESSAGE ACROSS TO MAGGIE...
I KNOW.
9·5·2002
YOU KNOW WHAT DIXIE ALWAYS USED TO SAY...
WHAT?
LIFE IS A COOKIE.
WHAT DOES THAT MEAN?
I HAVE NO IDEA... BUT IT'S STILL SOMEHOW ODDLY COMFORTING...
PAIGE

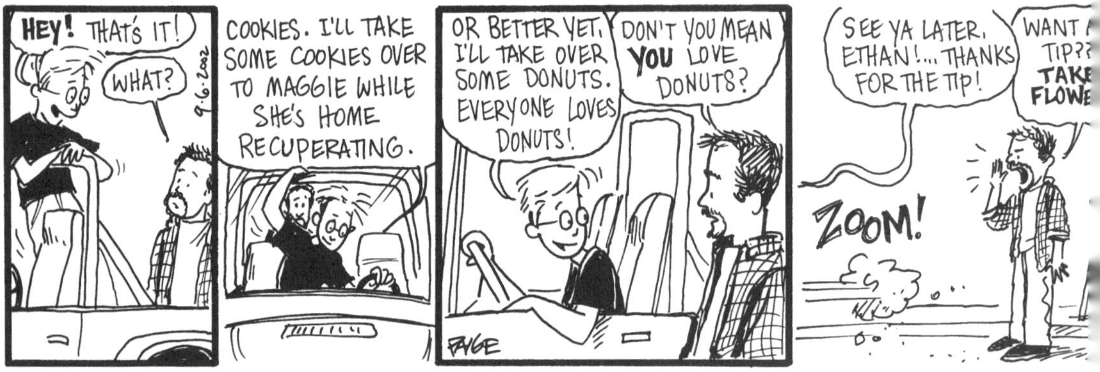
HEY! THAT'S IT!
WHAT?
9·6·2002
COOKIES. I'LL TAKE SOME COOKIES OVER TO MAGGIE WHILE SHE'S HOME RECUPERATING.
OR BETTER YET, I'LL TAKE OVER SOME DONUTS. EVERYONE LOVES DONUTS!
DON'T YOU MEAN YOU LOVE DONUTS?
PAIGE
SEE YA LATER, ETHAN!... THANKS FOR THE TIP!
WANT A TIP?? TAKE FLOWE
ZOOM!

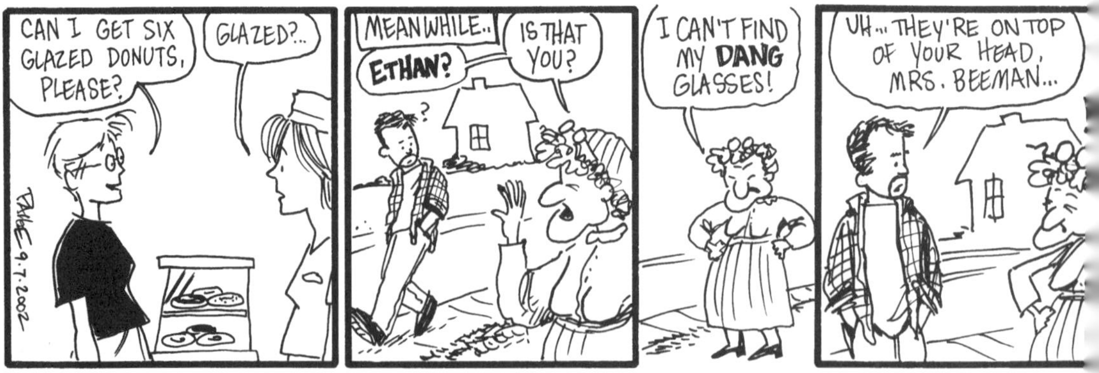
CAN I GET SIX GLAZED DONUTS, PLEASE?
GLAZED?...
PAIGE 9·7·2002
MEANWHILE..
ETHAN?
IS THAT YOU?
?
I CAN'T FIND MY DANG GLASSES!
UH... THEY'RE ON TOP OF YOUR HEAD, MRS. BEEMAN...

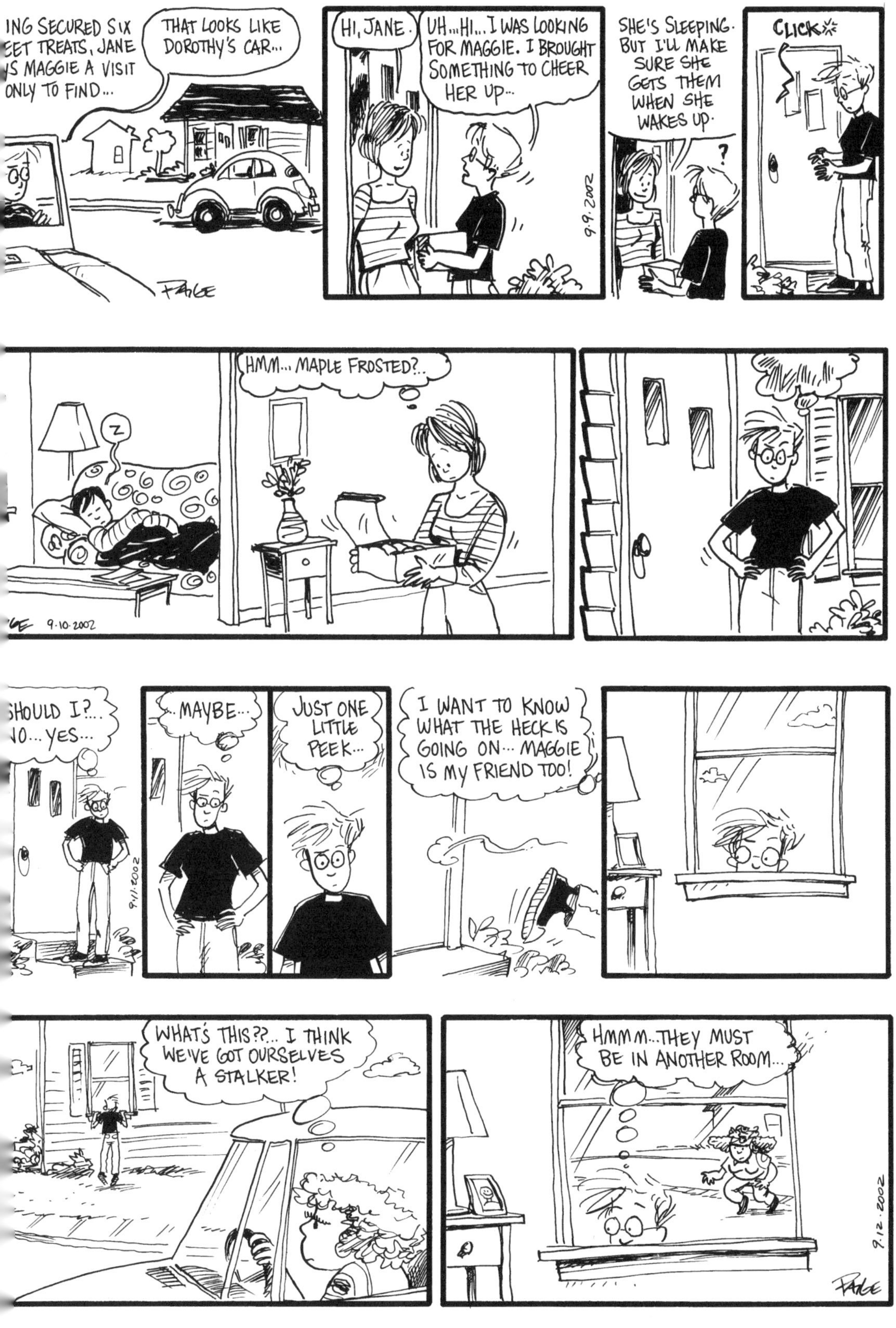
ING SECURED SIX
EET TREATS, JANE
VS MAGGIE A VISIT
ONLY TO FIND...
THAT LOOKS LIKE DOROTHY'S CAR...
PAIGE
HI, JANE.
UH...HI... I WAS LOOKING FOR MAGGIE. I BROUGHT SOMETHING TO CHEER HER UP...
9.9.2002
SHE'S SLEEPING. BUT I'LL MAKE SURE SHE GETS THEM WHEN SHE WAKES UP.
?
CLICK
Z
9.10.2002
HMM... MAPLE FROSTED?..
SHOULD I?...
NO... YES...
9.11.2002
...MAYBE...
JUST ONE LITTLE PEEK...
I WANT TO KNOW WHAT THE HECK IS GOING ON... MAGGIE IS MY FRIEND TOO!
WHAT'S THIS??... I THINK WE'VE GOT OURSELVES A STALKER!
HMMM...THEY MUST BE IN ANOTHER ROOM...
9.12.2002
PAIGE

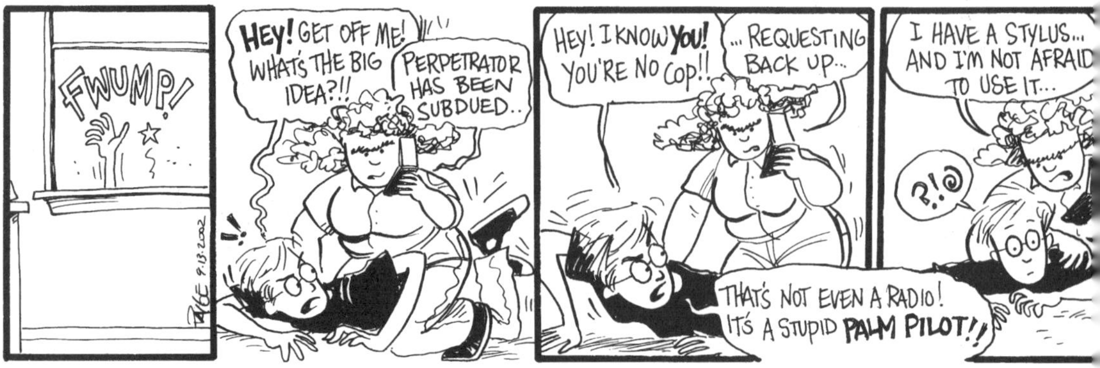
FWUMP!
HEY! GET OFF ME! WHAT'S THE BIG IDEA?!!
PERPETRATOR HAS BEEN SUBDUED...
PAIGE 9.13.2002
HEY! I KNOW YOU! YOU'RE NO COP!!
...REQUESTING BACK UP...
THAT'S NOT EVEN A RADIO! IT'S A STUPID PALM PILOT!!
I HAVE A STYLUS... AND I'M NOT AFRAID TO USE IT...
?!@

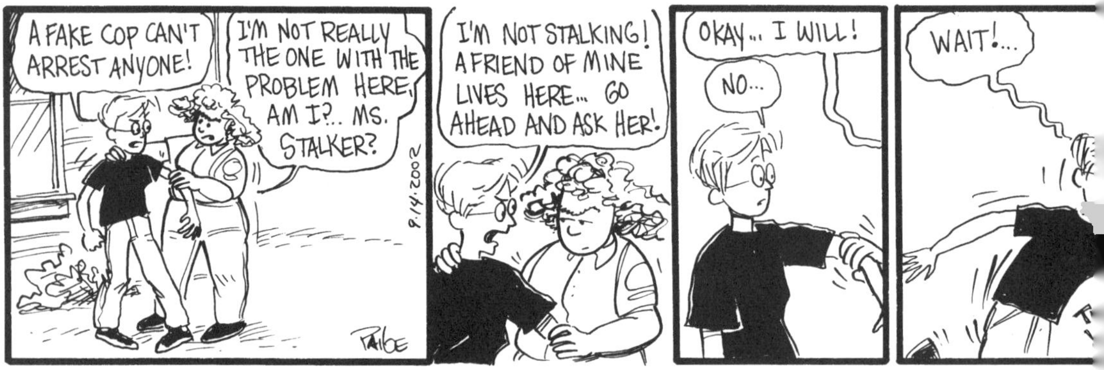
A FAKE COP CAN'T ARREST ANYONE!
I'M NOT REALLY THE ONE WITH THE PROBLEM HERE, AM I?.. MS. STALKER?
PAIGE
9.14.2002
I'M NOT STALKING! A FRIEND OF MINE LIVES HERE... GO AHEAD AND ASK HER!
OKAY... I WILL!
NO...
WAIT!...

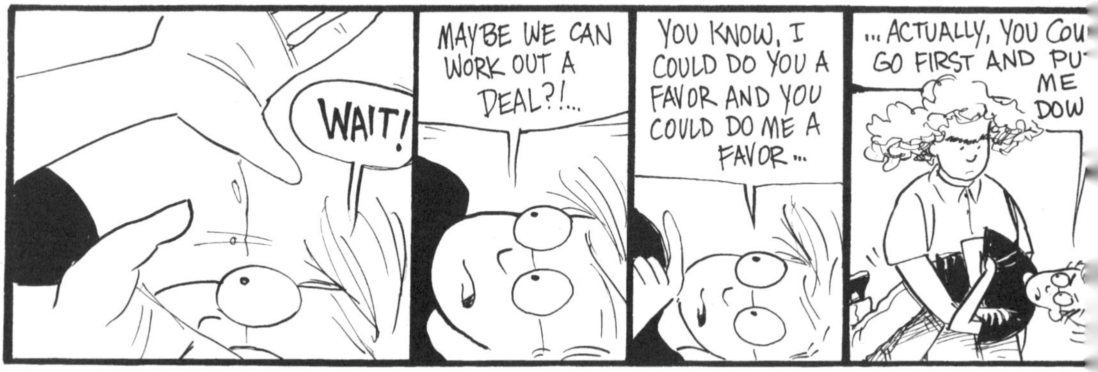
WAIT!
MAYBE WE CAN WORK OUT A DEAL?!...
YOU KNOW, I COULD DO YOU A FAVOR AND YOU COULD DO ME A FAVOR...

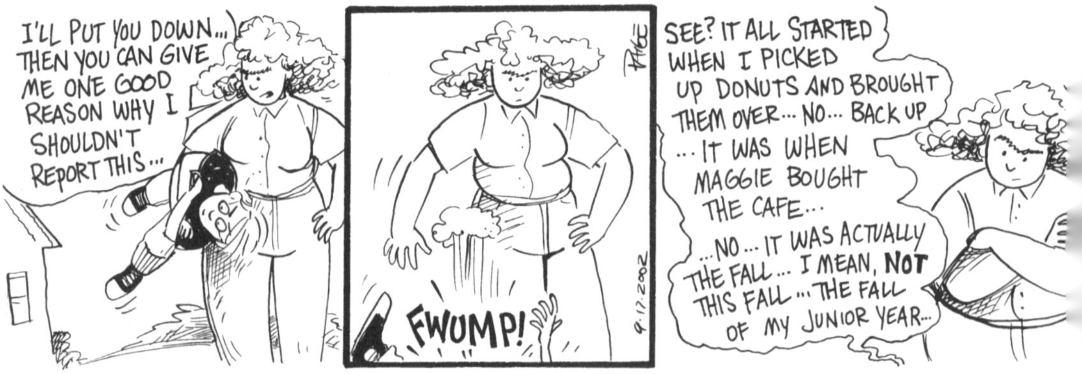
I'LL PUT YOU DOWN... THEN YOU CAN GIVE ME ONE GOOD REASON WHY I SHOULDN'T REPORT THIS...
PAIGE
FWUMP!
9.17.2002
SEE? IT ALL STARTED WHEN I PICKED UP DONUTS AND BROUGHT THEM OVER... NO... BACK UP ... IT WAS WHEN MAGGIE BOUGHT THE CAFE...
...NO... IT WAS ACTUALLY THE FALL... I MEAN, NOT THIS FALL... THE FALL OF MY JUNIOR YEAR...

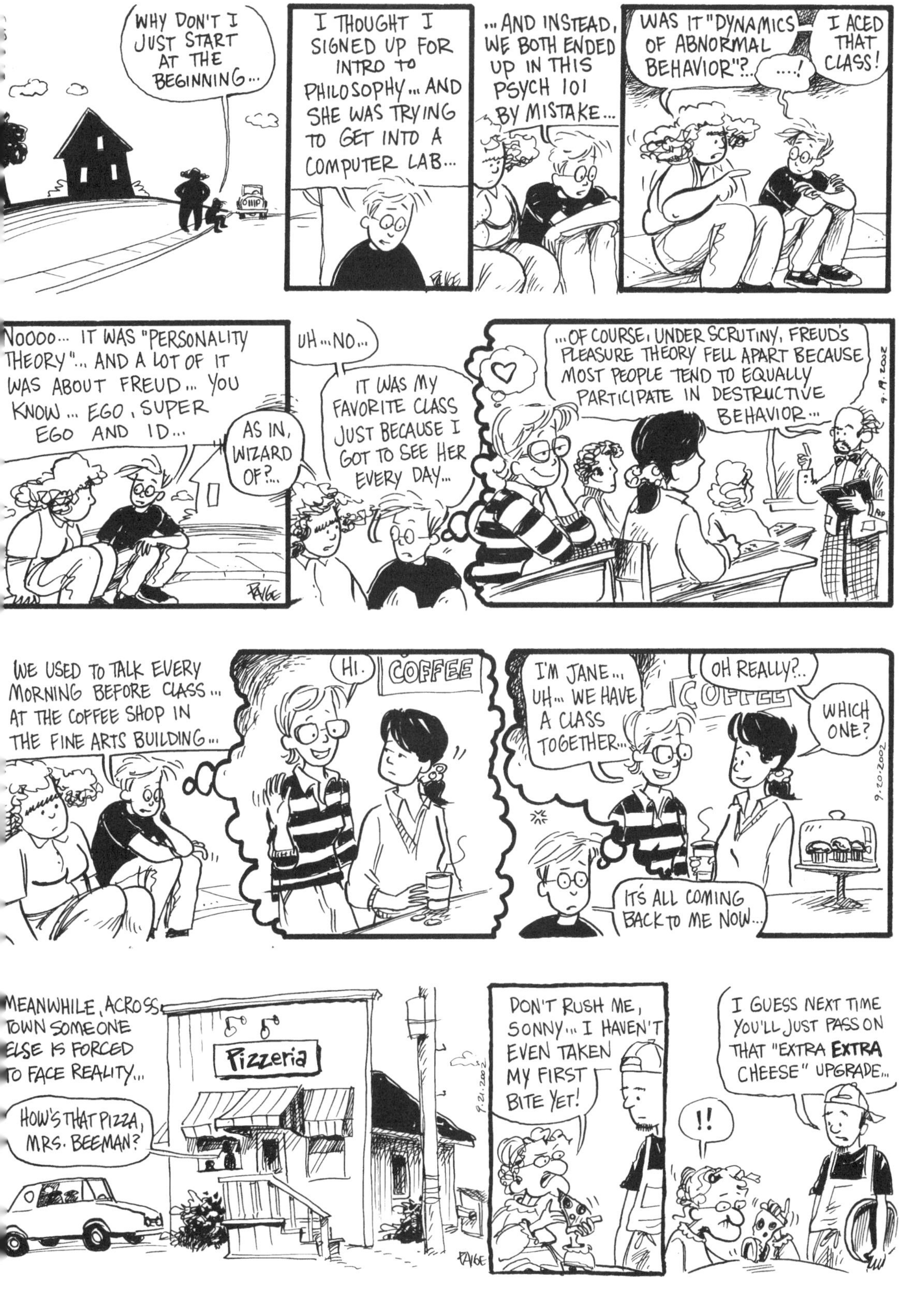
WHY DON'T I JUST START AT THE BEGINNING...
I THOUGHT I SIGNED UP FOR INTRO TO PHILOSOPHY... AND SHE WAS TRYING TO GET INTO A COMPUTER LAB...
...AND INSTEAD, WE BOTH ENDED UP IN THIS PSYCH 101 BY MISTAKE...
WAS IT "DYNAMICS OF ABNORMAL BEHAVIOR"?...
....!
I ACED THAT CLASS!
PAIGE
NOOOO... IT WAS "PERSONALITY THEORY"... AND A LOT OF IT WAS ABOUT FREUD... YOU KNOW... EGO, SUPER EGO AND ID...
AS IN, WIZARD OF?...
UH...NO...
IT WAS MY FAVORITE CLASS JUST BECAUSE I GOT TO SEE HER EVERY DAY...
...OF COURSE, UNDER SCRUTINY, FREUD'S PLEASURE THEORY FELL APART BECAUSE MOST PEOPLE TEND TO EQUALLY PARTICIPATE IN DESTRUCTIVE BEHAVIOR...
9.19.2002
PAIGE
WE USED TO TALK EVERY MORNING BEFORE CLASS... AT THE COFFEE SHOP IN THE FINE ARTS BUILDING...
HI.
COFFEE
I'M JANE... UH... WE HAVE A CLASS TOGETHER...
OH REALLY?..
WHICH ONE?
9.20.2002
IT'S ALL COMING BACK TO ME NOW...
MEANWHILE, ACROSS TOWN SOMEONE ELSE IS FORCED TO FACE REALITY...
Pizzeria
HOW'S THAT PIZZA, MRS. BEEMAN?
9.21.2002
PAIGE
DON'T RUSH ME, SONNY... I HAVEN'T EVEN TAKEN MY FIRST BITE YET!
!!
I GUESS NEXT TIME YOU'LL JUST PASS ON THAT "EXTRA EXTRA CHEESE" UPGRADE...

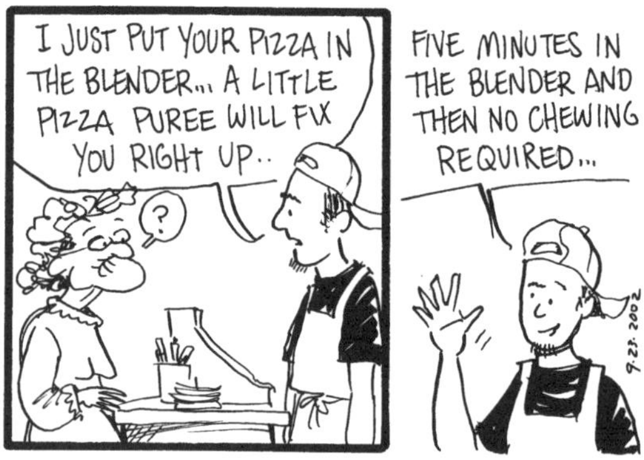
I JUST PUT YOUR PIZZA IN THE BLENDER... A LITTLE PIZZA PUREE WILL FIX YOU RIGHT UP..
?
FIVE MINUTES IN THE BLENDER AND THEN NO CHEWING REQUIRED...
9.23.2002

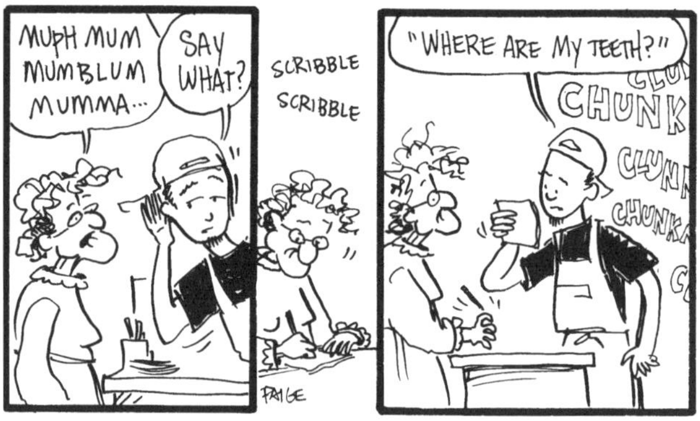
MUPH MUM MUMBLUM MUMMA...
SAY WHAT?
SCRIBBLE
SCRIBBLE
"WHERE ARE MY TEETH?"
CHUNK
PAIGE

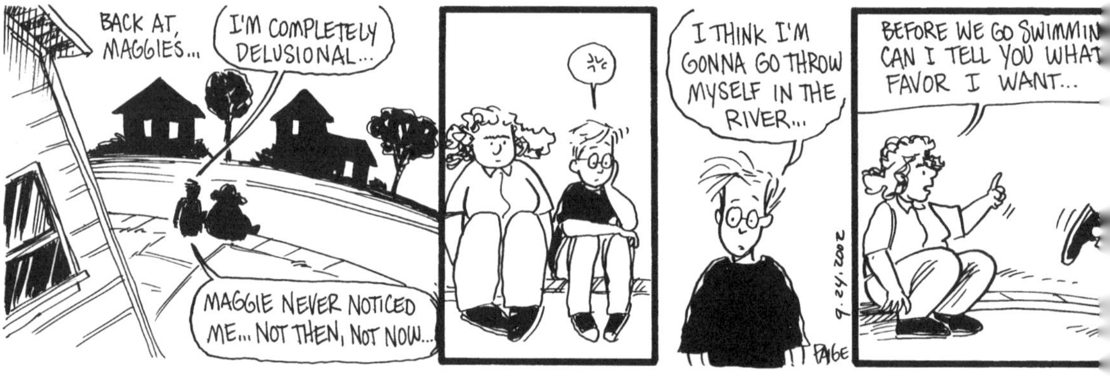
BACK AT, MAGGIE'S...
I'M COMPLETELY DELUSIONAL...
MAGGIE NEVER NOTICED ME... NOT THEN, NOT NOW...
I THINK I'M GONNA GO THROW MYSELF IN THE RIVER...
9.24.2002
PAIGE
BEFORE WE GO SWIMMIN
CAN I TELL YOU WHAT
FAVOR I WANT...

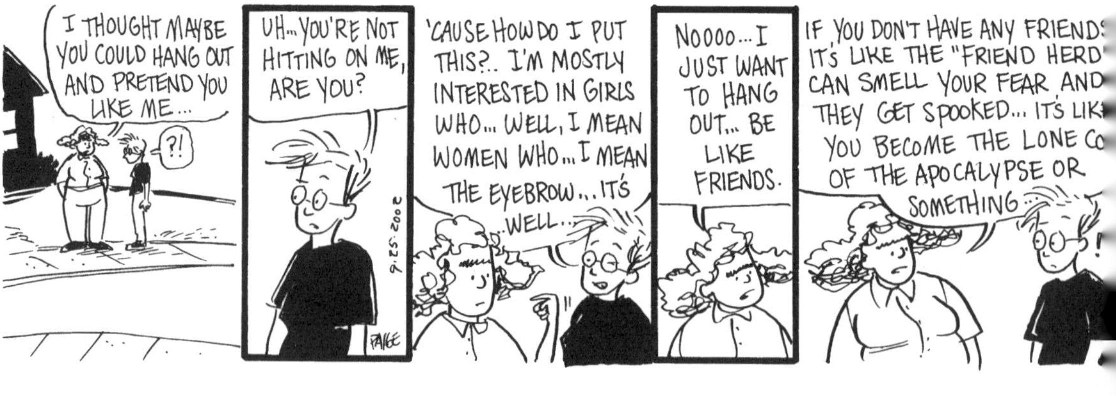
I THOUGHT MAYBE YOU COULD HANG OUT AND PRETEND YOU LIKE ME...
?!
UH... YOU'RE NOT HITTING ON ME, ARE YOU?
9.25.2002
PAIGE
'CAUSE HOW DO I PUT THIS?.. I'M MOSTLY INTERESTED IN GIRLS WHO... WELL, I MEAN WOMEN WHO... I MEAN THE EYEBROW... IT'S ...WELL...
NOOOO... I JUST WANT TO HANG OUT... BE LIKE FRIENDS.
IF YOU DON'T HAVE ANY FRIENDS
IT'S LIKE THE "FRIEND HERD"
CAN SMELL YOUR FEAR AND
THEY GET SPOOKED... IT'S LIK
YOU BECOME THE LONE C
OF THE APOCALYPSE OR
SOMETHING...

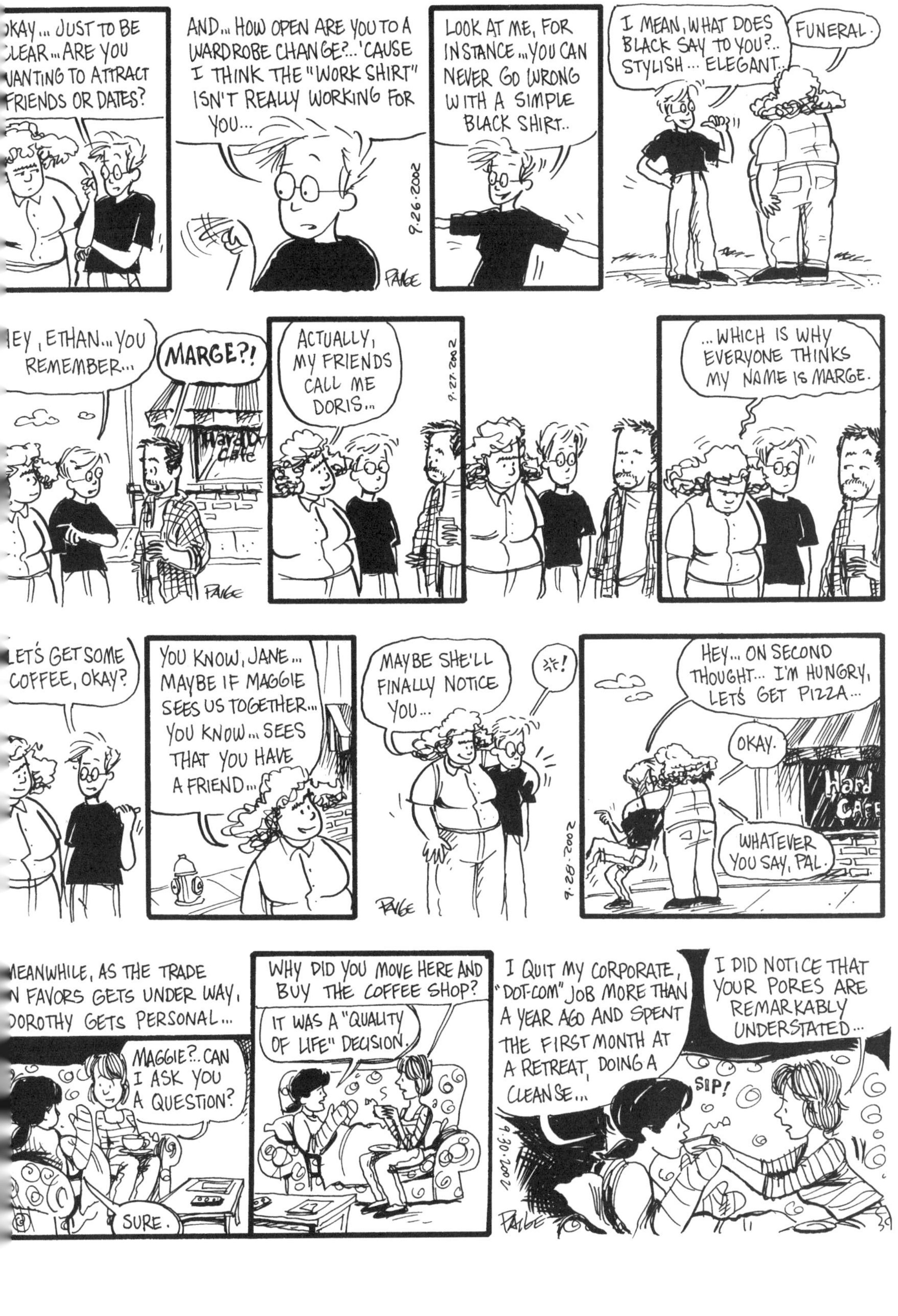

KAY... JUST TO BE LEAR... ARE YOU VANTING TO ATTRACT FRIENDS OR DATES?
AND... HOW OPEN ARE YOU TO A WARDROBE CHANGE?... 'CAUSE I THINK THE "WORK SHIRT" ISN'T REALLY WORKING FOR YOU...
9·26·2002
PAIGE
LOOK AT ME, FOR INSTANCE... YOU CAN NEVER GO WRONG WITH A SIMPLE BLACK SHIRT..
I MEAN, WHAT DOES BLACK SAY TO YOU?.. STYLISH... ELEGANT..
FUNERAL.
IEY, ETHAN... YOU REMEMBER...
MARGE?!
Hard Cafe
PAIGE
ACTUALLY, MY FRIENDS CALL ME DORIS...
9·27·2002
...WHICH IS WHY EVERYONE THINKS MY NAME IS MARGE.
LET'S GET SOME COFFEE, OKAY?
YOU KNOW, JANE... MAYBE IF MAGGIE SEES US TOGETHER... YOU KNOW... SEES THAT YOU HAVE A FRIEND...
MAYBE SHE'LL FINALLY NOTICE YOU...
!
PAIGE
HEY... ON SECOND THOUGHT... I'M HUNGRY, LET'S GET PIZZA...
OKAY.
Hard CAFE
WHATEVER YOU SAY, PAL.
9·28·2002
MEANWHILE, AS THE TRADE N FAVORS GETS UNDER WAY, DOROTHY GETS PERSONAL...
MAGGIE?.. CAN I ASK YOU A QUESTION?
SURE.
WHY DID YOU MOVE HERE AND BUY THE COFFEE SHOP?
IT WAS A "QUALITY OF LIFE" DECISION.
I QUIT MY CORPORATE, "DOT-COM" JOB MORE THAN A YEAR AGO AND SPENT THE FIRST MONTH AT A RETREAT, DOING A CLEANSE...
I DID NOTICE THAT YOUR PORES ARE REMARKABLY UNDERSTATED...
SIP!
9·30·2002
PAIGE

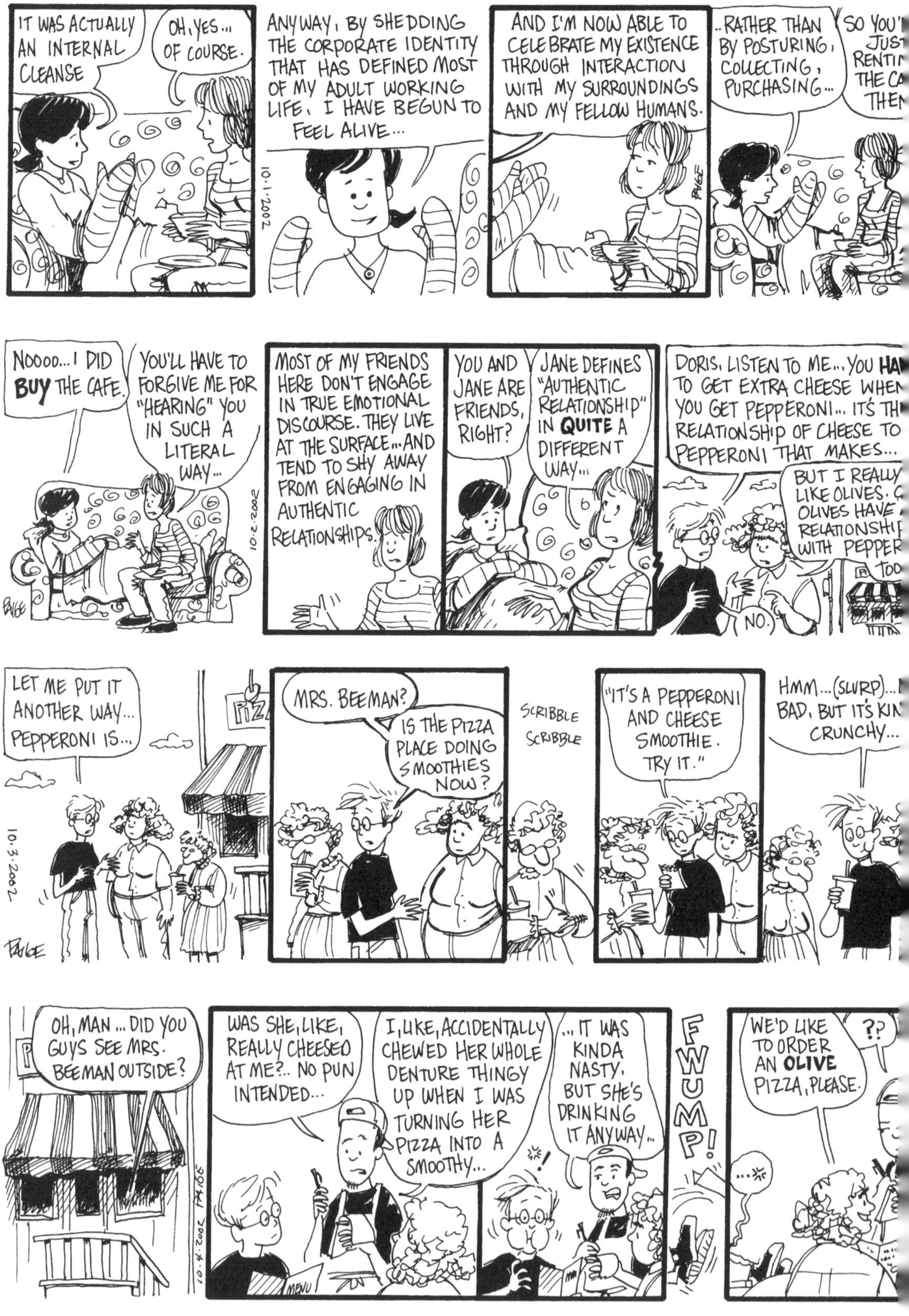
IT WAS ACTUALLY AN INTERNAL CLEANSE
OH, YES... OF COURSE.
ANYWAY, BY SHEDDING THE CORPORATE IDENTITY THAT HAS DEFINED MOST OF MY ADULT WORKING LIFE, I HAVE BEGUN TO FEEL ALIVE...
10.1.2002
AND I'M NOW ABLE TO CELEBRATE MY EXISTENCE THROUGH INTERACTION WITH MY SURROUNDINGS AND MY FELLOW HUMANS.
PAIGE
..RATHER THAN BY POSTURING, COLLECTING, PURCHASING...
SO YOU' JUST RENTI THE CA THEM
NOOOO... I DID **BUY** THE CAFE.
YOU'LL HAVE TO FORGIVE ME FOR "HEARING" YOU IN SUCH A LITERAL WAY...
PAIGE
10.2.2002
MOST OF MY FRIENDS HERE DON'T ENGAGE IN TRUE EMOTIONAL DISCOURSE. THEY LIVE AT THE SURFACE... AND TEND TO SHY AWAY FROM ENGAGING IN AUTHENTIC RELATIONSHIPS.
YOU AND JANE ARE FRIENDS, RIGHT?
JANE DEFINES "AUTHENTIC RELATIONSHIP" IN **QUITE** A DIFFERENT WAY...
DORIS, LISTEN TO ME... YOU **HA** TO GET EXTRA CHEESE WHEN YOU GET PEPPERONI... IT'S TH RELATIONSHIP OF CHEESE TO PEPPERONI THAT MAKES...
BUT I REALLY LIKE OLIVES. O OLIVES HAVE RELATIONSHIP WITH PEPPER TOO
NO.
LET ME PUT IT ANOTHER WAY... PEPPERONI IS...
10.3.2002
PAIGE
PIZ
MRS. BEEMAN?
IS THE PIZZA PLACE DOING SMOOTHIES NOW?
SCRIBBLE SCRIBBLE
"IT'S A PEPPERONI AND CHEESE SMOOTHIE. TRY IT."
HMM... (SLURP)... BAD, BUT IT'S KIN CRUNCHY...
OH, MAN... DID YOU GUYS SEE MRS. BEEMAN OUTSIDE?
WAS SHE, LIKE, REALLY CHEESED AT ME?.. NO PUN INTENDED...
I, LIKE, ACCIDENTALLY CHEWED HER WHOLE DENTURE THINGY UP WHEN I WAS TURNING HER PIZZA INTO A SMOOTHY...
MENU
10.4.2002 PAIGE
...IT WAS KINDA NASTY, BUT SHE'S DRINKING IT ANYWAY...
FWUMP!
WE'D LIKE TO ORDER AN **OLIVE** PIZZA, PLEASE.
??

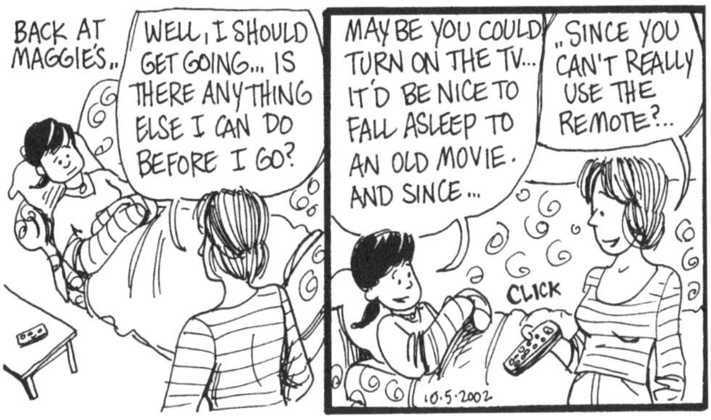
BACK AT MAGGIE'S..
WELL, I SHOULD GET GOING... IS THERE ANYTHING ELSE I CAN DO BEFORE I GO?
MAYBE YOU COULD TURN ON THE TV... IT'D BE NICE TO FALL ASLEEP TO AN OLD MOVIE. AND SINCE...
..SINCE YOU CAN'T REALLY USE THE REMOTE?..
CLICK
10.5.2002

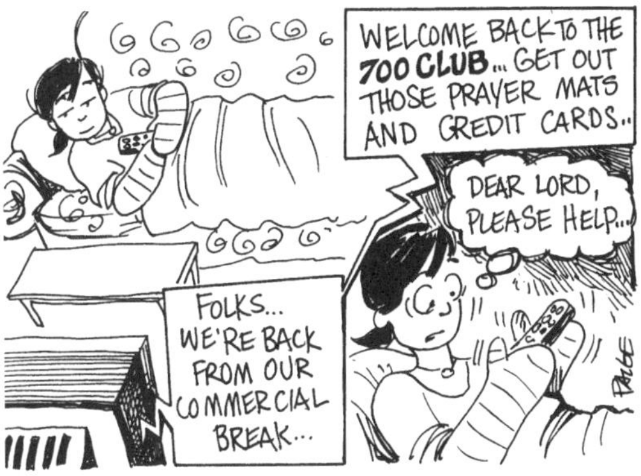
WELCOME BACK TO THE 700 CLUB... GET OUT THOSE PRAYER MATS AND CREDIT CARDS..
FOLKS... WE'RE BACK FROM OUR COMMERCIAL BREAK...
DEAR LORD, PLEASE HELP...
PAIGE

Meanwhile, at Jane's...

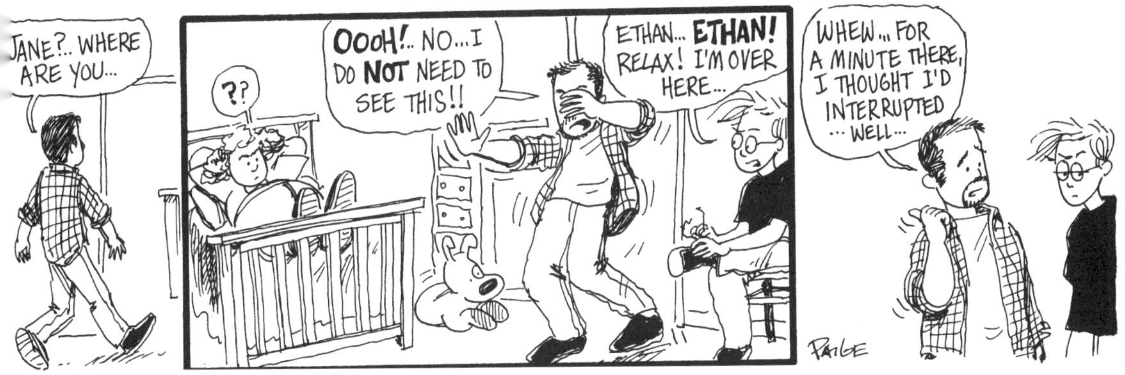
JANE?.. WHERE ARE YOU...
??
OOOH!.. NO...I DO NOT NEED TO SEE THIS!!
ETHAN... ETHAN! RELAX! I'M OVER HERE...
WHEW... FOR A MINUTE THERE, I THOUGHT I'D INTERRUPTED ... WELL...
PAIGE

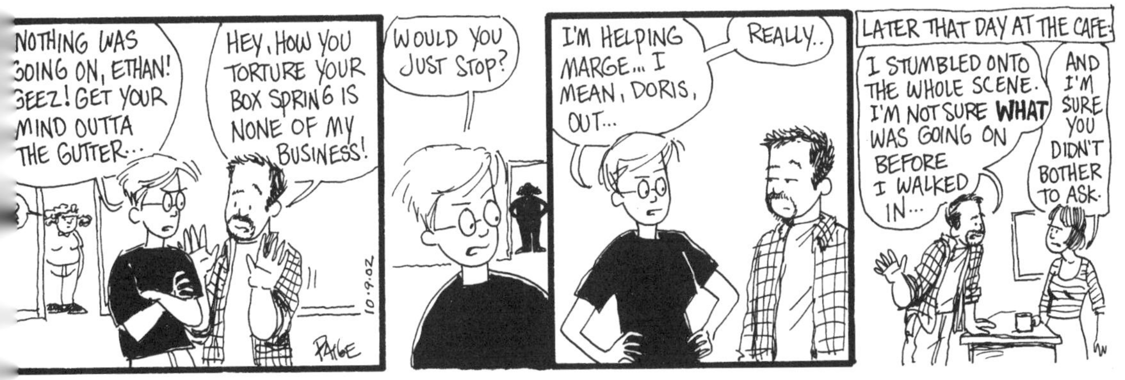
NOTHING WAS GOING ON, ETHAN! GEEZ! GET YOUR MIND OUTTA THE GUTTER...
HEY, HOW YOU TORTURE YOUR BOX SPRING IS NONE OF MY BUSINESS!
10.9.02
PAIGE
WOULD YOU JUST STOP?
I'M HELPING MARGE... I MEAN, DORIS, OUT...
REALLY..
LATER THAT DAY AT THE CAFE:
I STUMBLED ONTO THE WHOLE SCENE. I'M NOT SURE WHAT WAS GOING ON BEFORE I WALKED IN...
AND I'M SURE YOU DIDN'T BOTHER TO ASK.

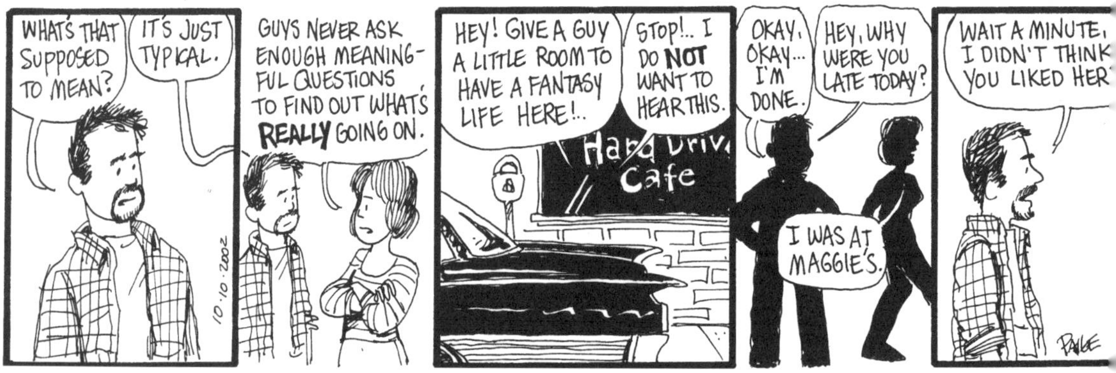
WHAT'S THAT SUPPOSED TO MEAN?
IT'S JUST TYPICAL.
GUYS NEVER ASK ENOUGH MEANINGFUL QUESTIONS TO FIND OUT WHAT'S REALLY GOING ON.
10·10·2002
HEY! GIVE A GUY A LITTLE ROOM TO HAVE A FANTASY LIFE HERE!..
STOP!.. I DO NOT WANT TO HEAR THIS.
OKAY, OKAY... I'M DONE.
HEY, WHY WERE YOU LATE TODAY?
I WAS AT MAGGIE'S.
WAIT A MINUTE, I DIDN'T THINK YOU LIKED HER

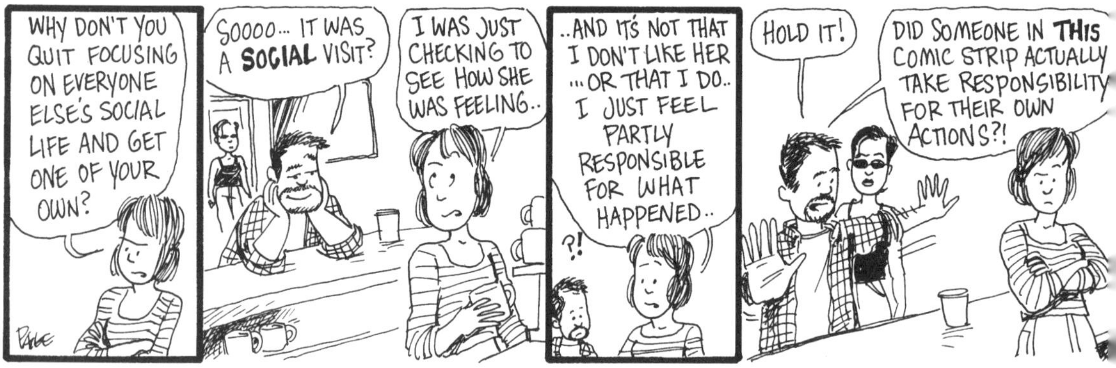
WHY DON'T YOU QUIT FOCUSING ON EVERYONE ELSE'S SOCIAL LIFE AND GET ONE OF YOUR OWN?
SOOOO... IT WAS A SOCIAL VISIT?
I WAS JUST CHECKING TO SEE HOW SHE WAS FEELING..
..AND IT'S NOT THAT I DON'T LIKE HER ...OR THAT I DO.. I JUST FEEL PARTLY RESPONSIBLE FOR WHAT HAPPENED..
?!
HOLD IT!
DID SOMEONE IN THIS COMIC STRIP ACTUALLY TAKE RESPONSIBILITY FOR THEIR OWN ACTIONS?!

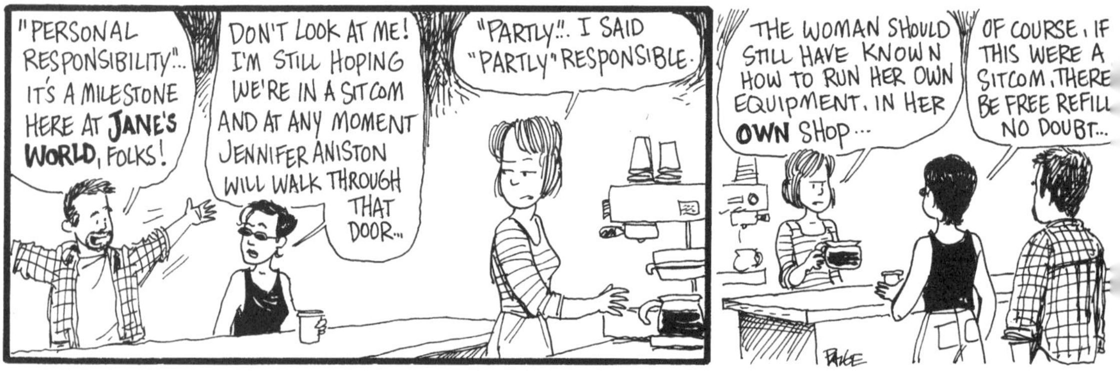
"PERSONAL RESPONSIBILITY"... IT'S A MILESTONE HERE AT JANE'S WORLD, FOLKS!
DON'T LOOK AT ME! I'M STILL HOPING WE'RE IN A SITCOM AND AT ANY MOMENT JENNIFER ANISTON WILL WALK THROUGH THAT DOOR...
"PARTLY"!.. I SAID "PARTLY" RESPONSIBLE.
THE WOMAN SHOULD STILL HAVE KNOWN HOW TO RUN HER OWN EQUIPMENT, IN HER OWN SHOP...
OF COURSE, IF THIS WERE A SITCOM, THERE BE FREE REFILL NO DOUBT...

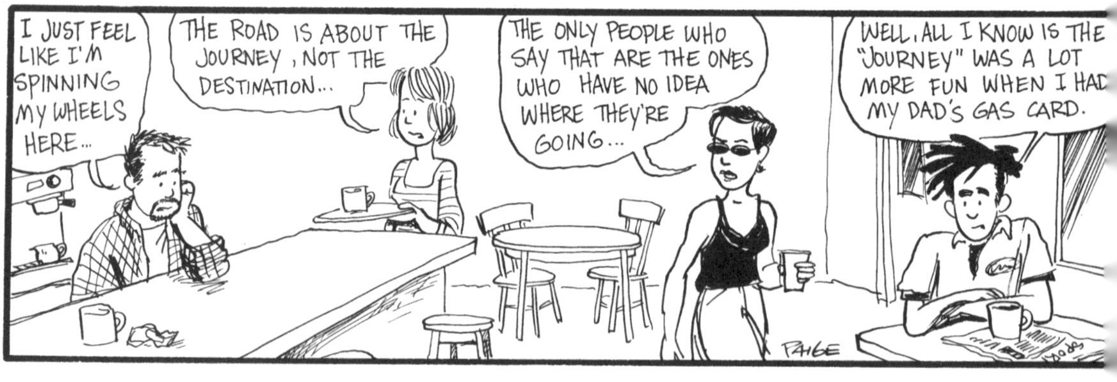
I JUST FEEL LIKE I'M SPINNING MY WHEELS HERE...
THE ROAD IS ABOUT THE JOURNEY, NOT THE DESTINATION...
THE ONLY PEOPLE WHO SAY THAT ARE THE ONES WHO HAVE NO IDEA WHERE THEY'RE GOING...
WELL, ALL I KNOW IS THE "JOURNEY" WAS A LOT MORE FUN WHEN I HAD MY DAD'S GAS CARD.

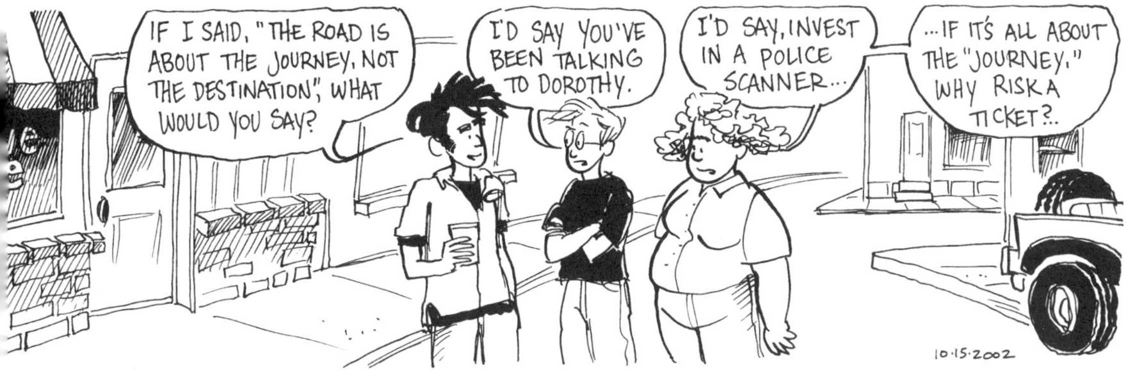
IF I SAID, "THE ROAD IS ABOUT THE JOURNEY, NOT THE DESTINATION", WHAT WOULD YOU SAY?
I'D SAY YOU'VE BEEN TALKING TO DOROTHY.
I'D SAY, INVEST IN A POLICE SCANNER...
...IF IT'S ALL ABOUT THE "JOURNEY," WHY RISK A TICKET?..
10·15·2002

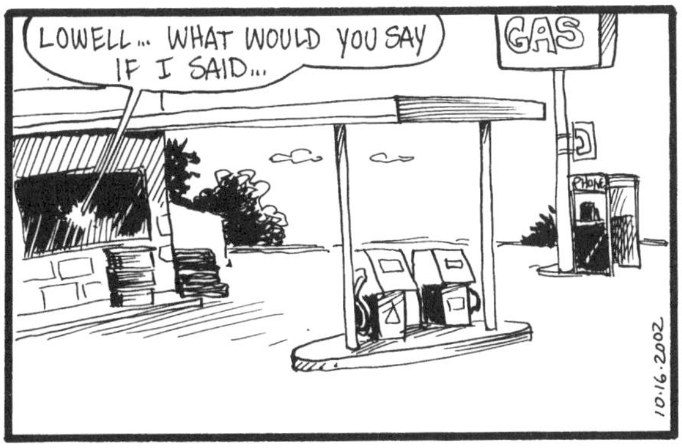
LOWELL... WHAT WOULD YOU SAY IF I SAID...
GAS
PHONE
10·16·2002

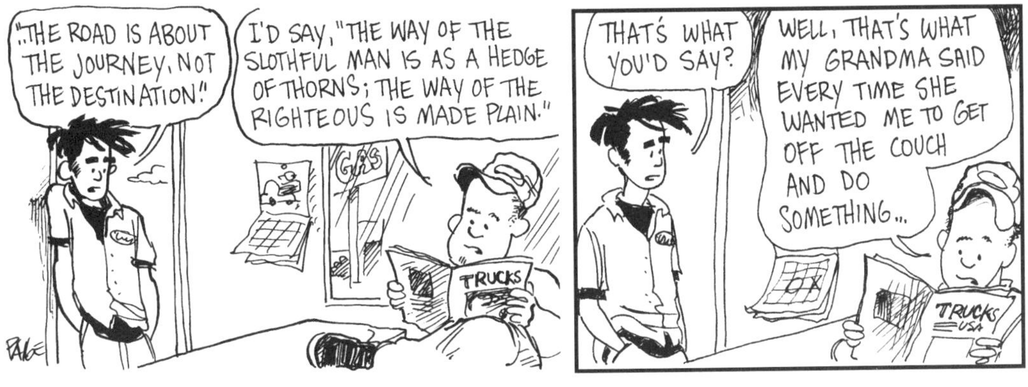
"..THE ROAD IS ABOUT THE JOURNEY, NOT THE DESTINATION!"
I'D SAY, "THE WAY OF THE SLOTHFUL MAN IS AS A HEDGE OF THORNS; THE WAY OF THE RIGHTEOUS IS MADE PLAIN."
GAS
TRUCKS
PAGE
THAT'S WHAT YOU'D SAY?
WELL, THAT'S WHAT MY GRANDMA SAID EVERY TIME SHE WANTED ME TO GET OFF THE COUCH AND DO SOMETHING...
TRUCKS USA

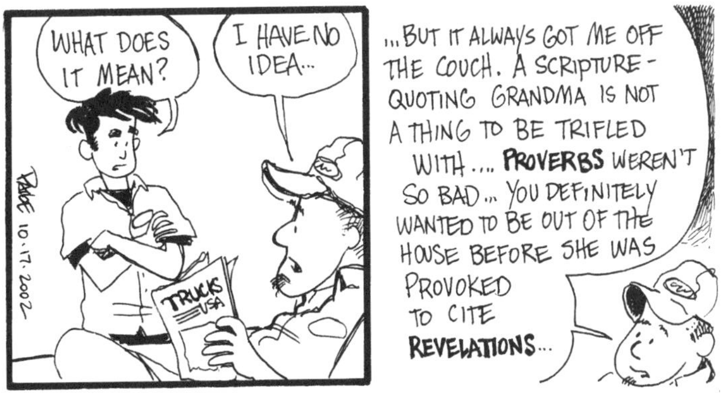
WHAT DOES IT MEAN?
I HAVE NO IDEA...
PAGE 10·17·2002
TRUCKS USA
...BUT IT ALWAYS GOT ME OFF THE COUCH. A SCRIPTURE-QUOTING GRANDMA IS NOT A THING TO BE TRIFLED WITH.... **PROVERBS** WEREN'T SO BAD... YOU DEFINITELY WANTED TO BE OUT OF THE HOUSE BEFORE SHE WAS PROVOKED TO CITE **REVELATIONS**...

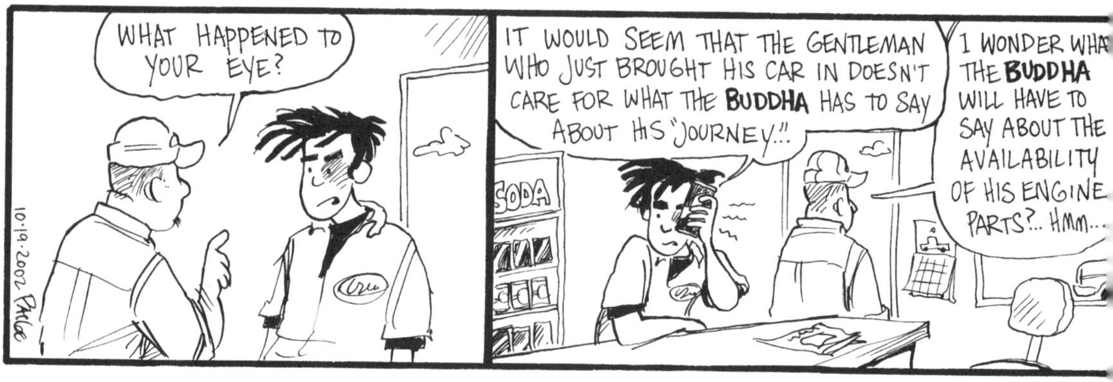
WHAT HAPPENED TO YOUR EYE?
10·19·2002
PAIGE
IT WOULD SEEM THAT THE GENTLEMAN WHO JUST BROUGHT HIS CAR IN DOESN'T CARE FOR WHAT THE **BUDDHA** HAS TO SAY ABOUT HIS "JOURNEY"!
SODA
I WONDER WHA THE **BUDDHA** WILL HAVE TO SAY ABOUT THE AVAILABILITY OF HIS ENGINE PARTS?.. HMM...

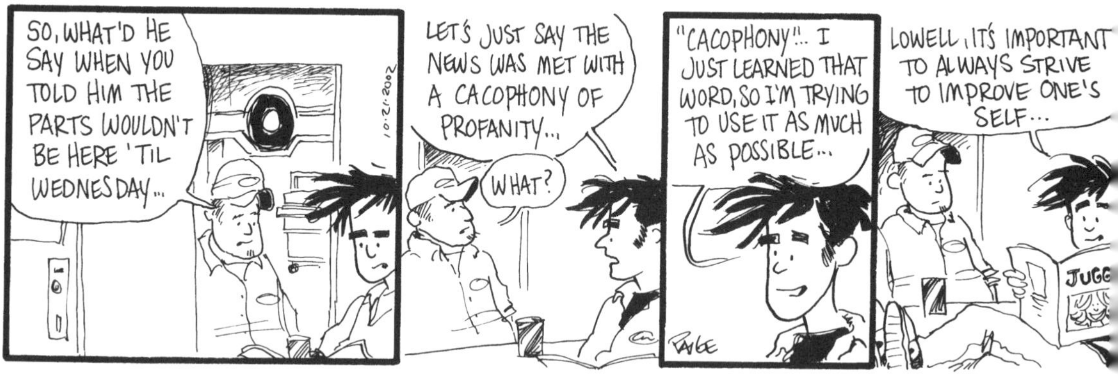
SO, WHAT'D HE SAY WHEN YOU TOLD HIM THE PARTS WOULDN'T BE HERE 'TIL WEDNESDAY...
10·21·2002
LET'S JUST SAY THE NEWS WAS MET WITH A CACOPHONY OF PROFANITY...
WHAT?
"CACOPHONY"!.. I JUST LEARNED THAT WORD, SO I'M TRYING TO USE IT AS MUCH AS POSSIBLE...
PAIGE
LOWELL, IT'S IMPORTANT TO ALWAYS STRIVE TO IMPROVE ONE'S SELF...
JUGG

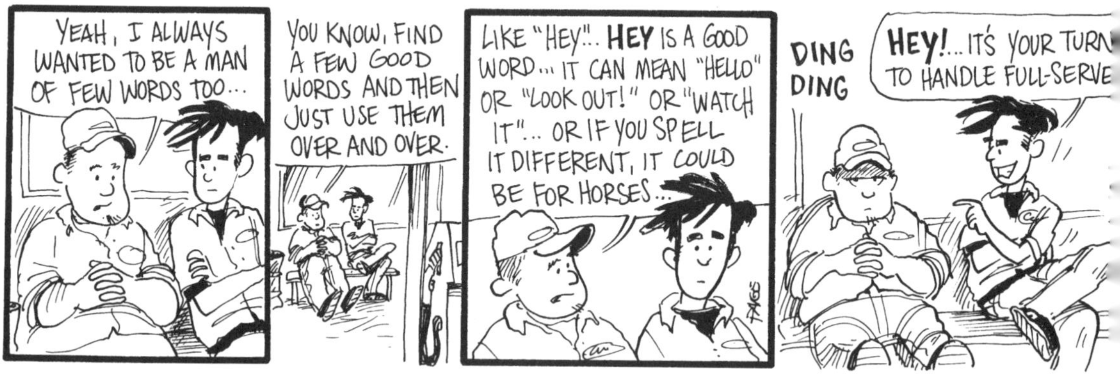
YEAH, I ALWAYS WANTED TO BE A MAN OF FEW WORDS TOO...
YOU KNOW, FIND A FEW GOOD WORDS AND THEN JUST USE THEM OVER AND OVER.
LIKE "HEY"!.. **HEY** IS A GOOD WORD... IT CAN MEAN "HELLO" OR "LOOK OUT!" OR "WATCH IT"... OR IF YOU SPELL IT DIFFERENT, IT COULD BE FOR HORSES...
PAIGE
DING DING
HEY!... IT'S YOUR TURN TO HANDLE FULL-SERVE

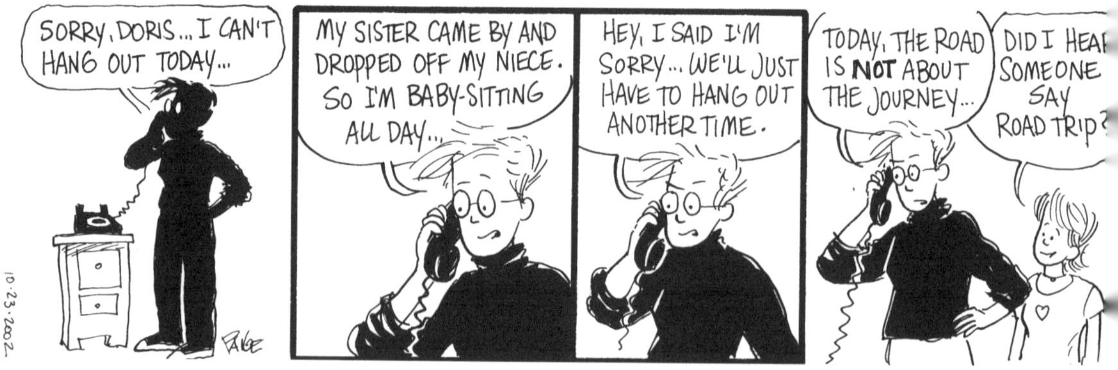
SORRY, DORIS... I CAN'T HANG OUT TODAY...
10·23·2002
PAIGE
MY SISTER CAME BY AND DROPPED OFF MY NIECE. SO I'M BABY-SITTING ALL DAY...
HEY, I SAID I'M SORRY... WE'LL JUST HAVE TO HANG OUT ANOTHER TIME.
TODAY, THE ROAD IS **NOT** ABOUT THE JOURNEY...
DID I HEAR SOMEONE SAY ROAD TRIP?

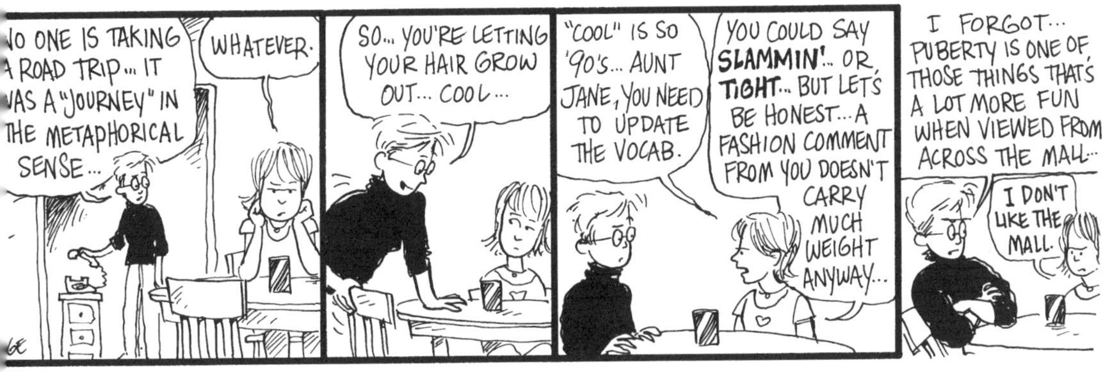
O ONE IS TAKING ROAD TRIP... IT AS A "JOURNEY" IN THE METAPHORICAL SENSE...
WHATEVER.
SO... YOU'RE LETTING YOUR HAIR GROW OUT... COOL...
"COOL" IS SO '90'S... AUNT JANE, YOU NEED TO UPDATE THE VOCAB.
YOU COULD SAY **SLAMMIN'**... OR **TIGHT**... BUT LET'S BE HONEST... A FASHION COMMENT FROM YOU DOESN'T CARRY MUCH WEIGHT ANYWAY...
I FORGOT... PUBERTY IS ONE OF THOSE THINGS THAT'S A LOT MORE FUN WHEN VIEWED FROM ACROSS THE MALL...
I DON'T LIKE THE MALL.

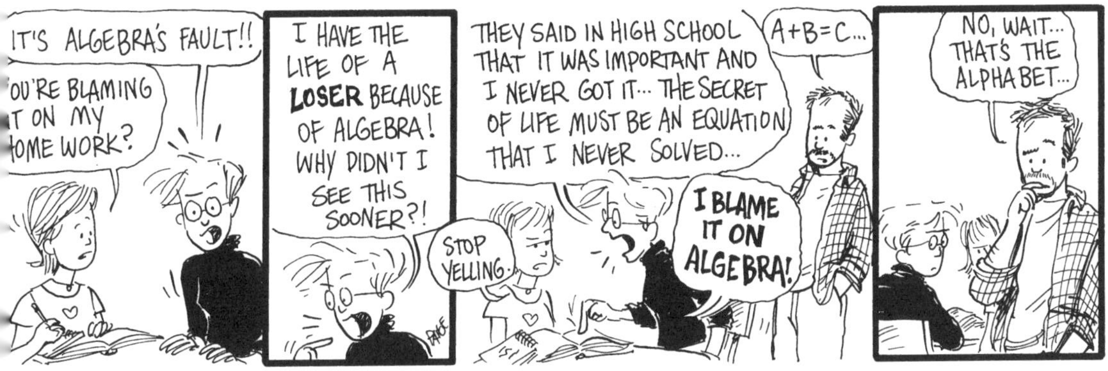
IT'S ALGEBRA'S FAULT!!
OU'RE BLAMING T ON MY OME WORK?
I HAVE THE LIFE OF A **LOSER** BECAUSE OF ALGEBRA! WHY DIDN'T I SEE THIS SOONER?!
THEY SAID IN HIGH SCHOOL THAT IT WAS IMPORTANT AND I NEVER GOT IT... THE SECRET OF LIFE MUST BE AN EQUATION THAT I NEVER SOLVED...
A+B=C...
STOP YELLING.
I BLAME IT ON ALGEBRA!
NO, WAIT... THAT'S THE ALPHABET...

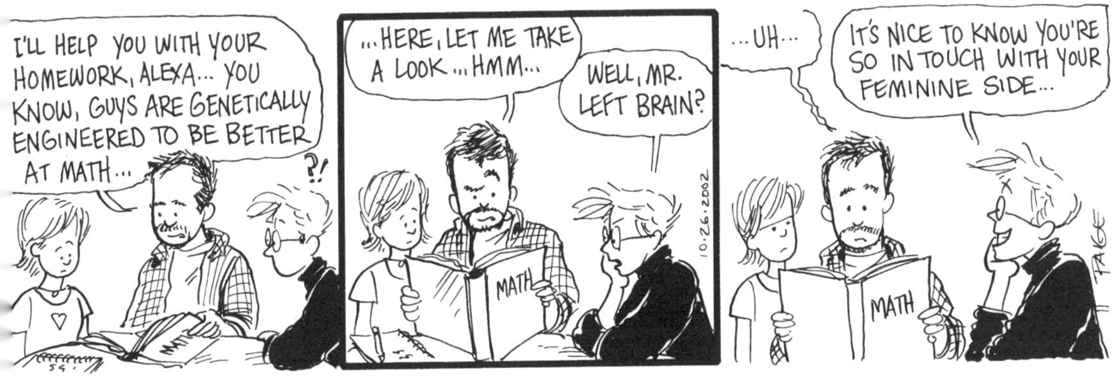
I'LL HELP YOU WITH YOUR HOMEWORK, ALEXA... YOU KNOW, GUYS ARE GENETICALLY ENGINEERED TO BE BETTER AT MATH...
?!
...HERE, LET ME TAKE A LOOK... HMM...
WELL, MR. LEFT BRAIN?
MATH
10.26.2002
...UH...
IT'S NICE TO KNOW YOU'RE SO IN TOUCH WITH YOUR FEMININE SIDE...
MATH

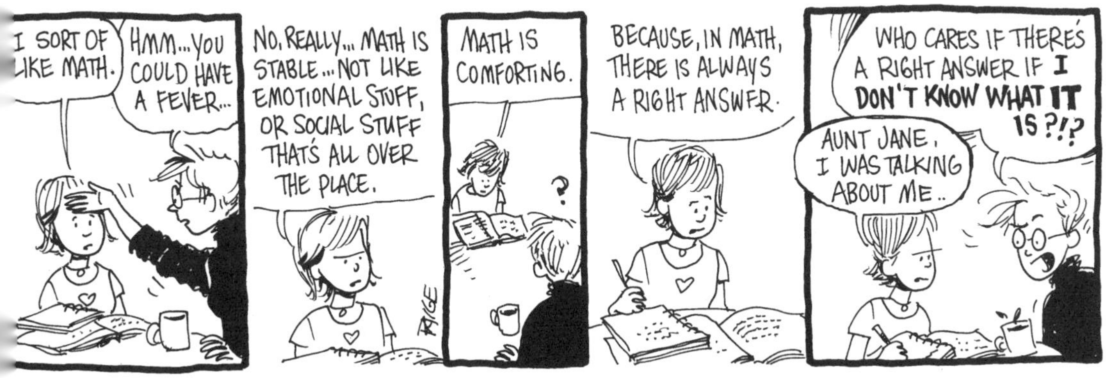
I SORT OF LIKE MATH.
HMM... YOU COULD HAVE A FEVER...
NO, REALLY... MATH IS STABLE... NOT LIKE EMOTIONAL STUFF, OR SOCIAL STUFF THAT'S ALL OVER THE PLACE.
MATH IS COMFORTING.
?
BECAUSE, IN MATH, THERE IS ALWAYS A RIGHT ANSWER.
WHO CARES IF THERE'S A RIGHT ANSWER IF **I DON'T KNOW WHAT IT IS?!?**
AUNT JANE, I WAS TALKING ABOUT ME..

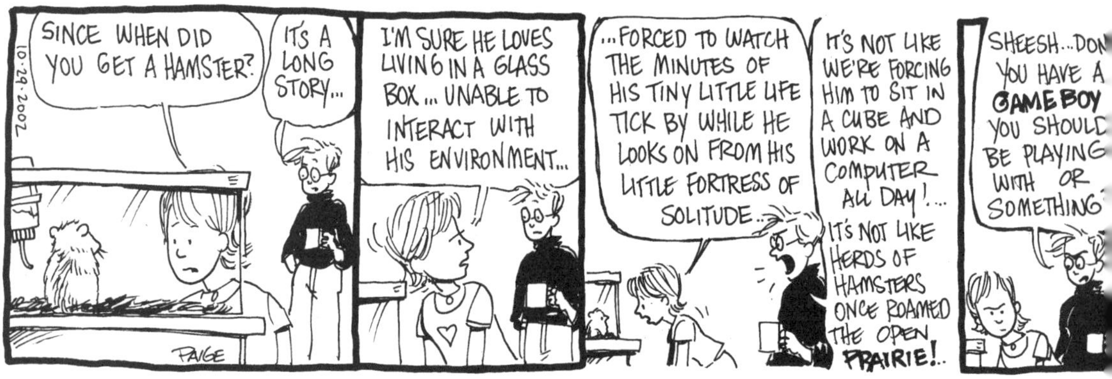
10·29·2002
SINCE WHEN DID YOU GET A HAMSTER?
IT'S A LONG STORY...
I'M SURE HE LOVES LIVING IN A GLASS BOX ... UNABLE TO INTERACT WITH HIS ENVIRONMENT...
...FORCED TO WATCH THE MINUTES OF HIS TINY LITTLE LIFE TICK BY WHILE HE LOOKS ON FROM HIS LITTLE FORTRESS OF SOLITUDE...
IT'S NOT LIKE WE'RE FORCING HIM TO SIT IN A CUBE AND WORK ON A COMPUTER ALL DAY!...
IT'S NOT LIKE HERDS OF HAMSTERS ONCE ROAMED THE OPEN PRAIRIE!..
SHEESH...DON
YOU HAVE A GAME BOY YOU SHOULD BE PLAYING WITH OR SOMETHING
PAIGE

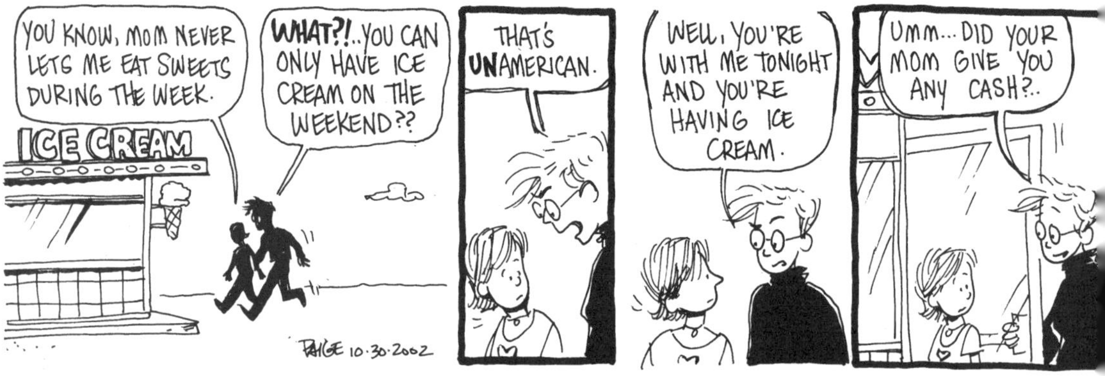
YOU KNOW, MOM NEVER LETS ME EAT SWEETS DURING THE WEEK.
WHAT?!..YOU CAN ONLY HAVE ICE CREAM ON THE WEEKEND??
ICE CREAM
PAIGE 10·30·2002
THAT'S UNAMERICAN.
WELL, YOU'RE WITH ME TONIGHT AND YOU'RE HAVING ICE CREAM.
UMM... DID YOUR MOM GIVE YOU ANY CASH?..

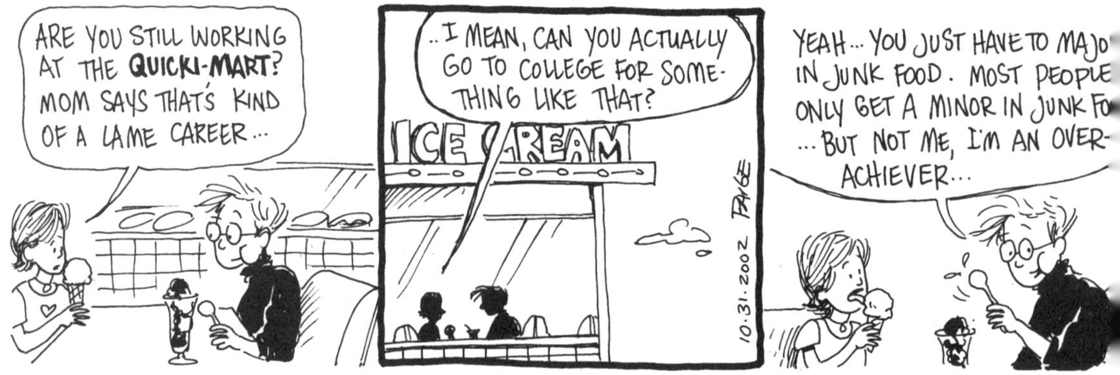
ARE YOU STILL WORKING AT THE QUICKI-MART? MOM SAYS THAT'S KIND OF A LAME CAREER...
..I MEAN, CAN YOU ACTUALLY GO TO COLLEGE FOR SOMETHING LIKE THAT?
ICE CREAM
PAIGE
10·31·2002
YEAH... YOU JUST HAVE TO MAJO
IN JUNK FOOD. MOST PEOPLE
ONLY GET A MINOR IN JUNK FO
...BUT NOT ME, I'M AN OVER-
ACHIEVER...

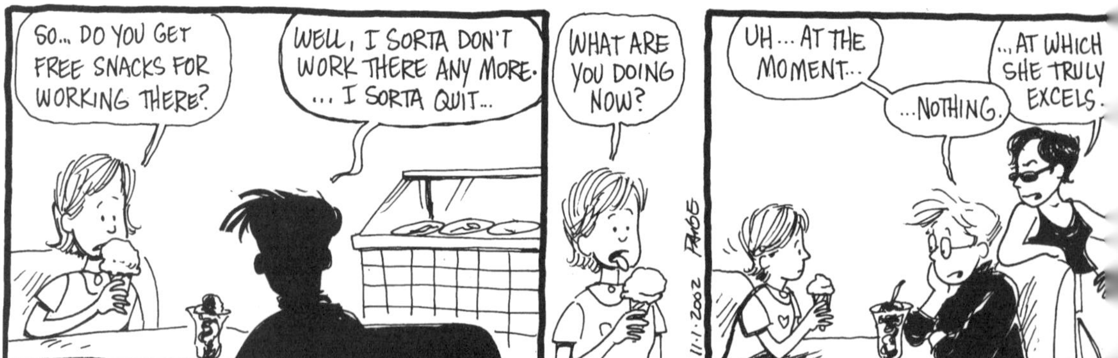
SO... DO YOU GET FREE SNACKS FOR WORKING THERE?
WELL, I SORTA DON'T WORK THERE ANY MORE. ... I SORTA QUIT...
WHAT ARE YOU DOING NOW?
PAIGE
11·1·2002
UH... AT THE MOMENT...
...NOTHING.
...AT WHICH SHE TRULY EXCELS.

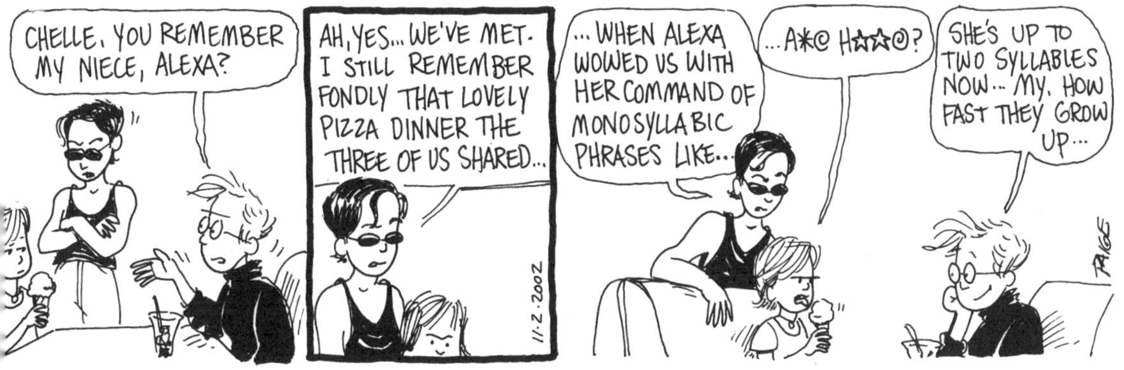
CHELLE, YOU REMEMBER MY NIECE, ALEXA?
AH, YES... WE'VE MET. I STILL REMEMBER FONDLY THAT LOVELY PIZZA DINNER THE THREE OF US SHARED...
11.2.2002
...WHEN ALEXA WOWED US WITH HER COMMAND OF MONOSYLLABIC PHRASES LIKE...
...A*@ H☆☆@?
SHE'S UP TO TWO SYLLABLES NOW... MY, HOW FAST THEY GROW UP...
PAIGE

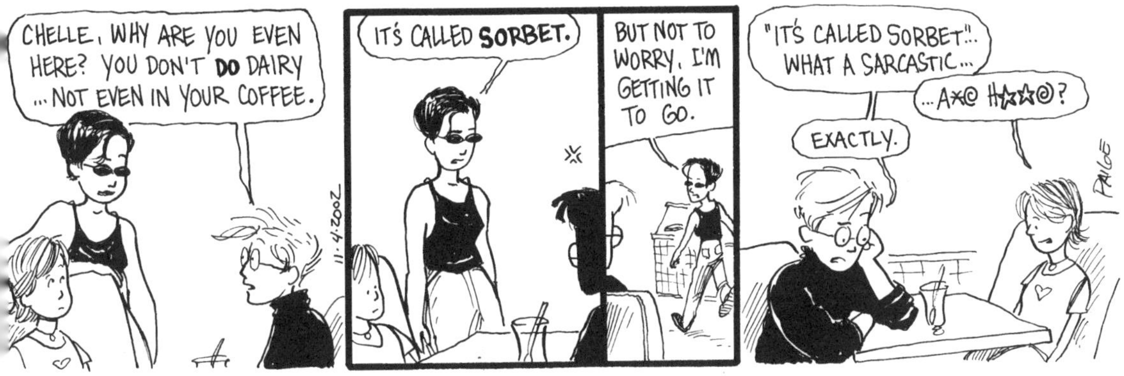
CHELLE, WHY ARE YOU EVEN HERE? YOU DON'T DO DAIRY ...NOT EVEN IN YOUR COFFEE.
11.4.2002
IT'S CALLED SORBET.
BUT NOT TO WORRY, I'M GETTING IT TO GO.
"IT'S CALLED SORBET"... WHAT A SARCASTIC...
...A*@ H☆☆@?
EXACTLY.
PAIGE

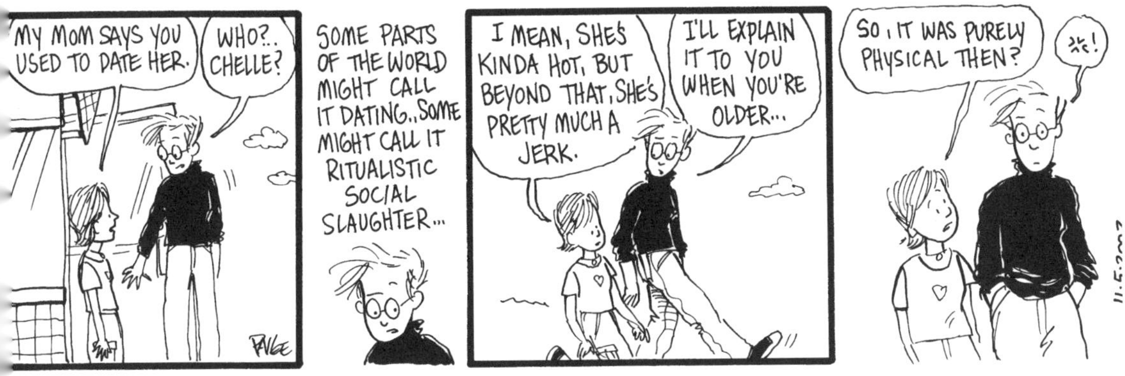
MY MOM SAYS YOU USED TO DATE HER.
WHO?.. CHELLE?
PAIGE
SOME PARTS OF THE WORLD MIGHT CALL IT DATING.. SOME MIGHT CALL IT RITUALISTIC SOCIAL SLAUGHTER...
I MEAN, SHE'S KINDA HOT, BUT BEYOND THAT, SHE'S PRETTY MUCH A JERK.
I'LL EXPLAIN IT TO YOU WHEN YOU'RE OLDER...
SO, IT WAS PURELY PHYSICAL THEN?
⁂!

Later...

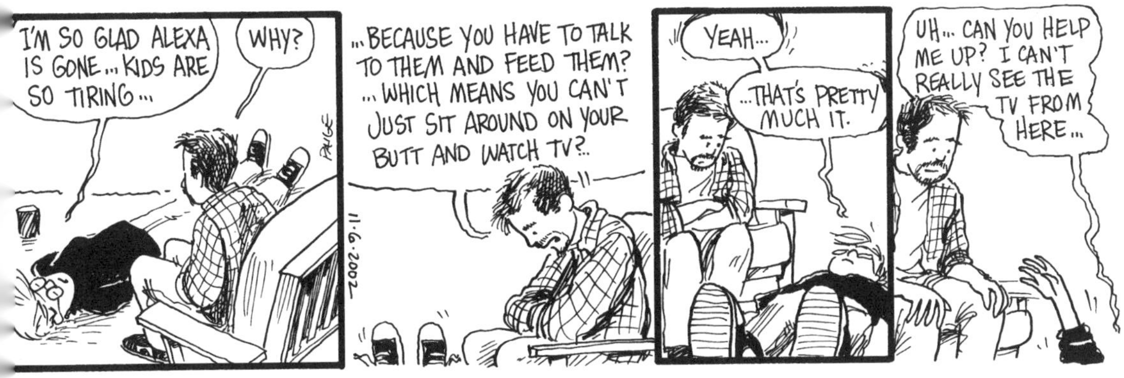
I'M SO GLAD ALEXA IS GONE... KIDS ARE SO TIRING...
WHY?
PAIGE
11.6.2002
...BECAUSE YOU HAVE TO TALK TO THEM AND FEED THEM? ...WHICH MEANS YOU CAN'T JUST SIT AROUND ON YOUR BUTT AND WATCH TV?..
YEAH...
...THAT'S PRETTY MUCH IT.
UH... CAN YOU HELP ME UP? I CAN'T REALLY SEE THE TV FROM HERE...

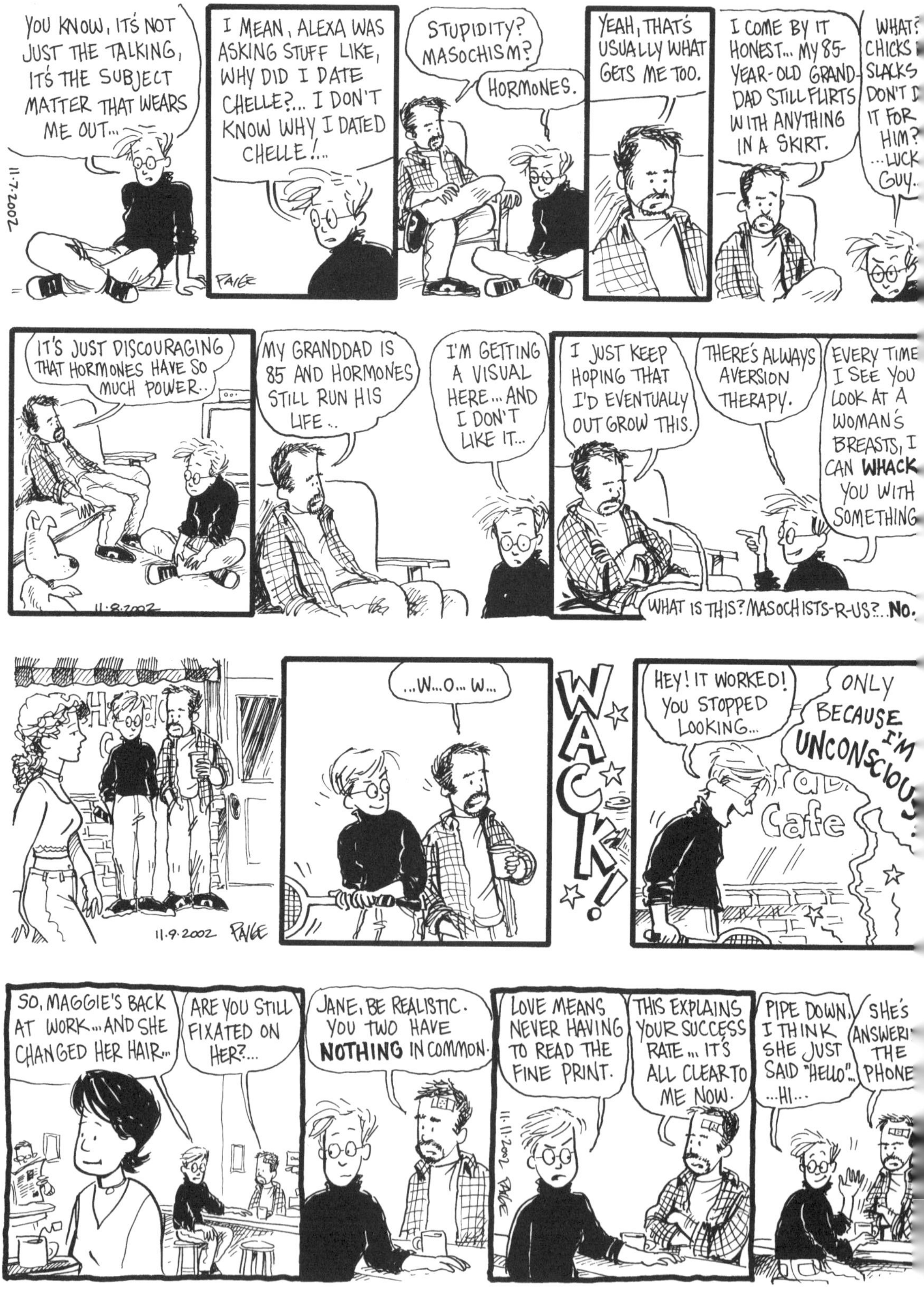
11·7·2002
YOU KNOW, IT'S NOT JUST THE TALKING, IT'S THE SUBJECT MATTER THAT WEARS ME OUT...
I MEAN, ALEXA WAS ASKING STUFF LIKE, WHY DID I DATE CHELLE?... I DON'T KNOW WHY I DATED CHELLE!...
PAIGE
STUPIDITY? MASOCHISM?
HORMONES.
YEAH, THAT'S USUALLY WHAT GETS ME TOO.
I COME BY IT HONEST... MY 85-YEAR-OLD GRAND-DAD STILL FLIRTS WITH ANYTHING IN A SKIRT.
WHAT? CHICKS SLACKS DON'T IT FOR HIM? ...LUCK GUY.
IT'S JUST DISCOURAGING THAT HORMONES HAVE SO MUCH POWER..
11·8·2002
MY GRANDDAD IS 85 AND HORMONES STILL RUN HIS LIFE..
I'M GETTING A VISUAL HERE... AND I DON'T LIKE IT...
I JUST KEEP HOPING THAT I'D EVENTUALLY OUTGROW THIS.
THERE'S ALWAYS AVERSION THERAPY.
EVERY TIME I SEE YOU LOOK AT A WOMAN'S BREASTS, I CAN WHACK YOU WITH SOMETHING
WHAT IS THIS? MASOCHISTS-R-US?... NO.
11·9·2002 PAIGE
...W...O... W...
WACK!
HEY! IT WORKED! YOU STOPPED LOOKING...
ONLY BECAUSE I'M UNCONSCIOUS
Cafe
SO, MAGGIE'S BACK AT WORK... AND SHE CHANGED HER HAIR...
ARE YOU STILL FIXATED ON HER?...
JANE, BE REALISTIC. YOU TWO HAVE NOTHING IN COMMON.
11·11·2002 PAIGE
LOVE MEANS NEVER HAVING TO READ THE FINE PRINT.
THIS EXPLAINS YOUR SUCCESS RATE... IT'S ALL CLEAR TO ME NOW.
PIPE DOWN, I THINK SHE JUST SAID "HELLO"... ...HI...
SHE'S ANSWERI THE PHONE

HEY... ISN'T THAT DORIS?
DON'T LOOK... MAYBE SHE WON'T SEE ME.
11.12.2002 PAIGE

AREN'T YOU GUYS LIKE PALS OR SOMETHING?
IT'S A LONG STORY... ANYWAY, I JUST NEED A BREAK.
SHE'S KINDA NEEDY, AND I'M... WELL, I'M...
HAVE YOU CONSIDERED AVERSION THERAPY?

HI, JANE... I SAW YOU FROM THE WINDOW.
OH... SORRY, DORIS. I DIDN'T SEE YOU...
BIG FAT LIAR
DORIS?! WHAT ARE YOU WEARING??
11.13.2002
PAIGE

DO YOU LIKE MY NEW TOP? IT'S KIND OF INVIGORATING...
IT'S KIND OF REVEALING! ...MAYBE YOU NEED A BIT MORE COVERAGE..
..HERE.........

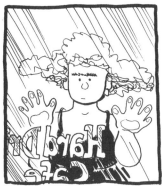

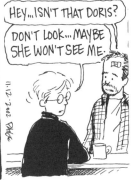

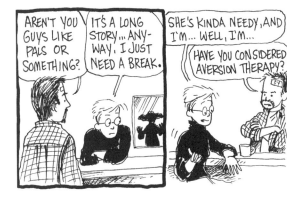

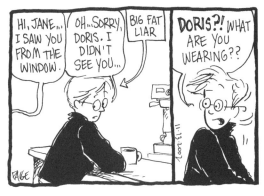

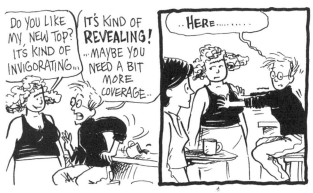

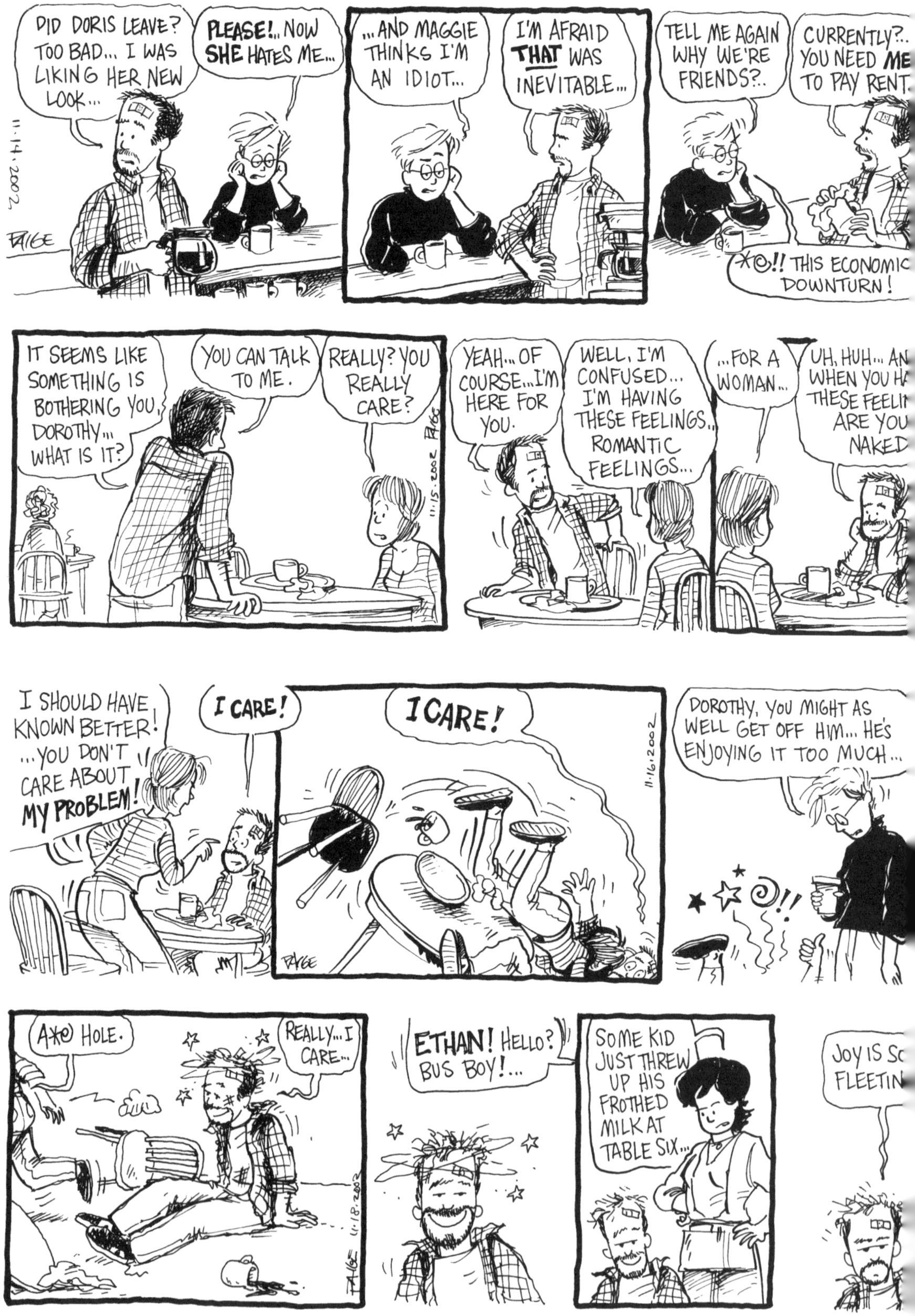

DID DORIS LEAVE? TOO BAD... I WAS LIKING HER NEW LOOK...
PLEASE!.. NOW SHE HATES ME...
...AND MAGGIE THINKS I'M AN IDIOT...
I'M AFRAID THAT WAS INEVITABLE...
TELL ME AGAIN WHY WE'RE FRIENDS?..
CURRENTLY?.. YOU NEED ME TO PAY RENT.
*@!! THIS ECONOMIC DOWNTURN!
11.14.2002
PAIGE
IT SEEMS LIKE SOMETHING IS BOTHERING YOU, DOROTHY... WHAT IS IT?
YOU CAN TALK TO ME.
REALLY? YOU REALLY CARE?
YEAH... OF COURSE...I'M HERE FOR YOU.
WELL, I'M CONFUSED... I'M HAVING THESE FEELINGS... ROMANTIC FEELINGS...
...FOR A WOMAN...
11.15.2002
I SHOULD HAVE KNOWN BETTER! ...YOU DON'T CARE ABOUT MY PROBLEM!
I CARE!
I CARE!
DOROTHY, YOU MIGHT AS WELL GET OFF HIM... HE'S ENJOYING IT TOO MUCH...
11.16.2002
A*@ HOLE.
REALLY... I CARE...
ETHAN! HELLO? BUS BOY!...
SOME KID JUST THREW UP HIS FROTHED MILK AT TABLE SIX...
11.18.2002

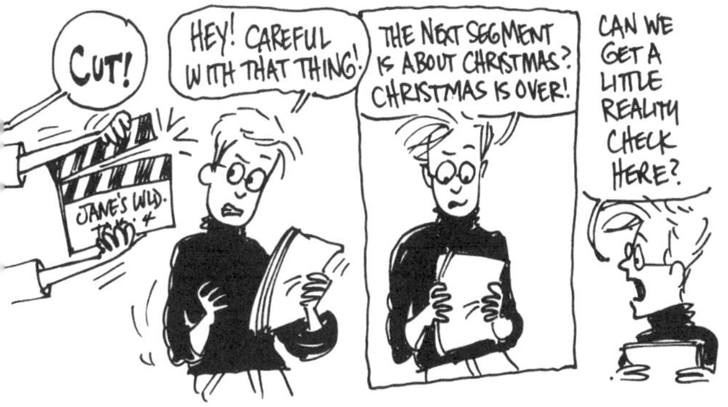
CUT!
HEY! CAREFUL WITH THAT THING!
THE NEXT SEGMENT IS ABOUT CHRISTMAS? CHRISTMAS IS OVER!
CAN WE GET A LITTLE REALITY CHECK HERE?

Author's note: Okay, while Ethan get's cleaned up a bit I'll explain the whole Christmas problem. It all has to do with pacing... Comic strip style pacing that is... See, I started this Christmas tale just before Christmas, but then I got sort of carried away with the storyline and since I can only get one tiny installment in per day... well, you can see how if you got carried away it would be easy to be wrapping up your Christmas tale in April. Sorry. So, do me a favor, suspend disbelief for a few more pages and just ride this out with us. Pretend Christmas lasted just a little bit longer...

Cartoon time isn't "real" time anyway, is it?... okay, folks... roll tape....

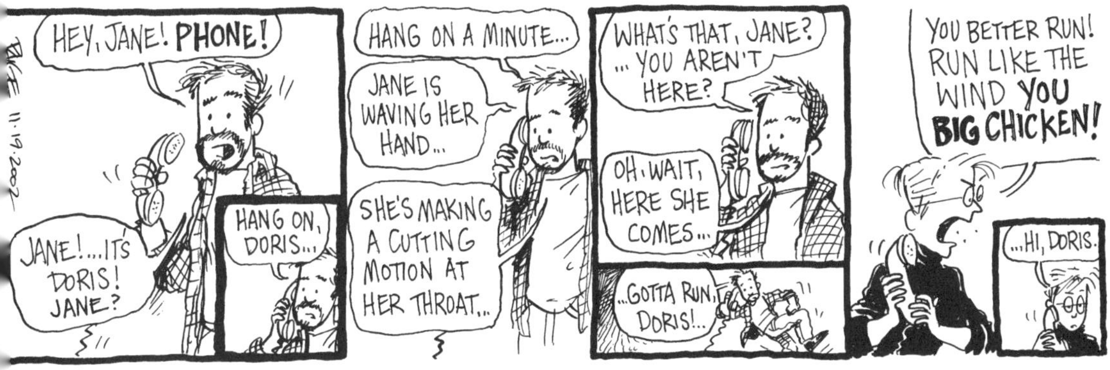
PAIGE 11.19.2002
HEY, JANE! **PHONE!**
JANE!...IT'S DORIS! JANE?
HANG ON, DORIS...
HANG ON A MINUTE...
JANE IS WAVING HER HAND...
SHE'S MAKING A CUTTING MOTION AT HER THROAT...
WHAT'S THAT, JANE? ...YOU AREN'T HERE?
OH, WAIT, HERE SHE COMES...
...GOTTA RUN, DORIS!...
YOU BETTER RUN! RUN LIKE THE WIND **YOU BIG CHICKEN!**
...HI, DORIS.

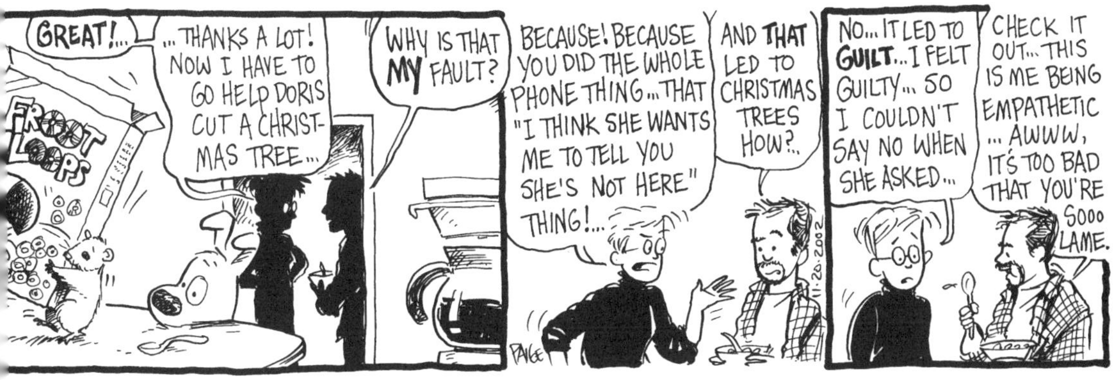
GREAT!...
...THANKS A LOT! NOW I HAVE TO GO HELP DORIS CUT A CHRIST-MAS TREE...
FROOT LOOPS
WHY IS THAT **MY** FAULT?
BECAUSE! BECAUSE YOU DID THE WHOLE PHONE THING... THAT "I THINK SHE WANTS ME TO TELL YOU SHE'S NOT HERE" THING!...
AND **THAT** LED TO CHRISTMAS TREES HOW?..
11.20.2002
NO... IT LED TO **GUILT**... I FELT GUILTY... SO I COULDN'T SAY NO WHEN SHE ASKED...
CHECK IT OUT... THIS IS ME BEING EMPATHETIC ... AWWW, IT'S TOO BAD THAT YOU'RE SOOO LAME.
PAIGE

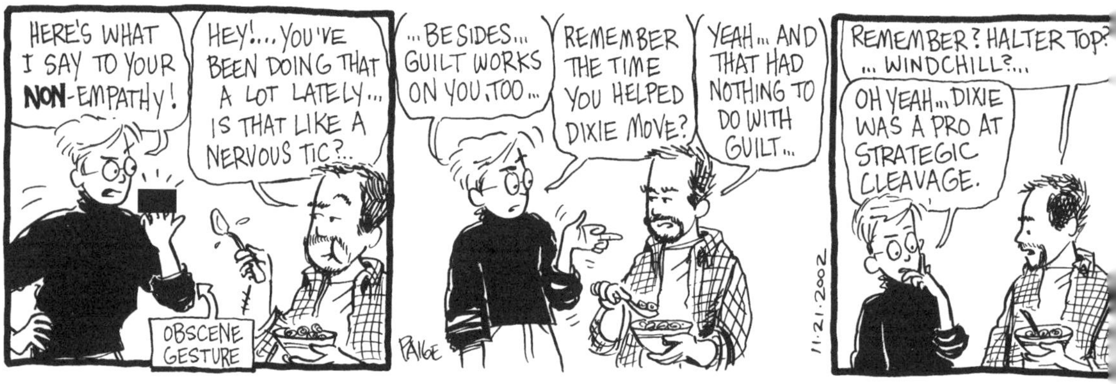
HERE'S WHAT I SAY TO YOUR NON-EMPATHY!
OBSCENE GESTURE
HEY!... YOU'VE BEEN DOING THAT A LOT LATELY... IS THAT LIKE A NERVOUS TIC?...
...BESIDES... GUILT WORKS ON YOU, TOO...
REMEMBER THE TIME YOU HELPED DIXIE MOVE?
YEAH... AND THAT HAD NOTHING TO DO WITH GUILT...
PAIGE
11·21·2002
REMEMBER? HALTER TOP? ... WINDCHILL?...
OH YEAH... DIXIE WAS A PRO AT STRATEGIC CLEAVAGE.

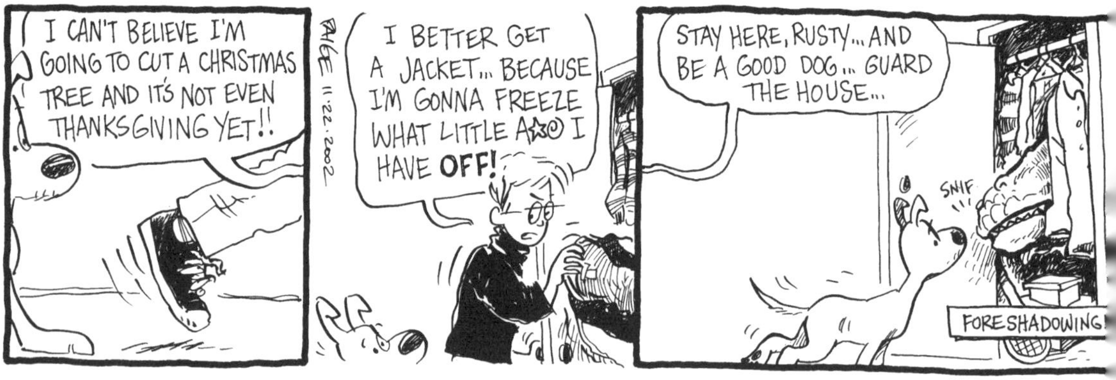
I CAN'T BELIEVE I'M GOING TO CUT A CHRISTMAS TREE AND IT'S NOT EVEN THANKSGIVING YET!!
PAIGE 11·22·2002
I BETTER GET A JACKET... BECAUSE I'M GONNA FREEZE WHAT LITTLE A☆◎ I HAVE OFF!
STAY HERE, RUSTY... AND BE A GOOD DOG... GUARD THE HOUSE...
SNIF
FORESHADOWING!

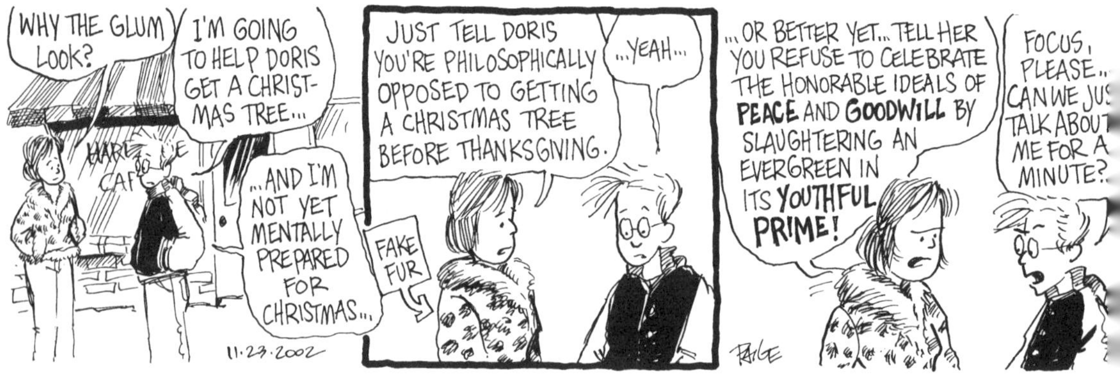
WHY THE GLUM LOOK?
I'M GOING TO HELP DORIS GET A CHRISTMAS TREE...
...AND I'M NOT YET MENTALLY PREPARED FOR CHRISTMAS...
11·23·2002
JUST TELL DORIS YOU'RE PHILOSOPHICALLY OPPOSED TO GETTING A CHRISTMAS TREE BEFORE THANKSGIVING.
...YEAH...
FAKE FUR
...OR BETTER YET... TELL HER YOU REFUSE TO CELEBRATE THE HONORABLE IDEALS OF PEACE AND GOODWILL BY SLAUGHTERING AN EVERGREEN IN ITS YOUTHFUL PRIME!
FOCUS, PLEASE... CAN WE JUS TALK ABOUT ME FOR A MINUTE?..
PAIGE

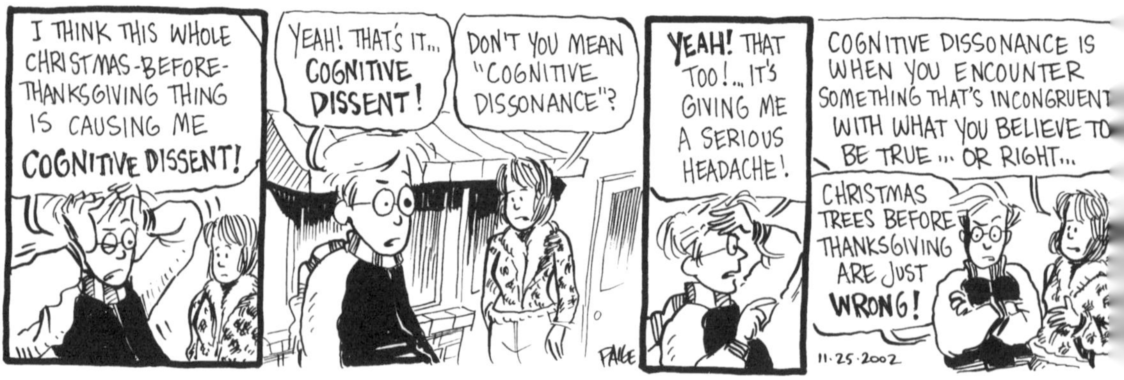
I THINK THIS WHOLE CHRISTMAS-BEFORE-THANKSGIVING THING IS CAUSING ME COGNITIVE DISSENT!
YEAH! THAT'S IT... COGNITIVE DISSENT!
DON'T YOU MEAN "COGNITIVE DISSONANCE"?
PAIGE
YEAH! THAT TOO!... IT'S GIVING ME A SERIOUS HEADACHE!
COGNITIVE DISSONANCE IS WHEN YOU ENCOUNTER SOMETHING THAT'S INCONGRUENT WITH WHAT YOU BELIEVE TO BE TRUE... OR RIGHT...
CHRISTMAS TREES BEFORE THANKSGIVING ARE JUST WRONG!
11·25·2002

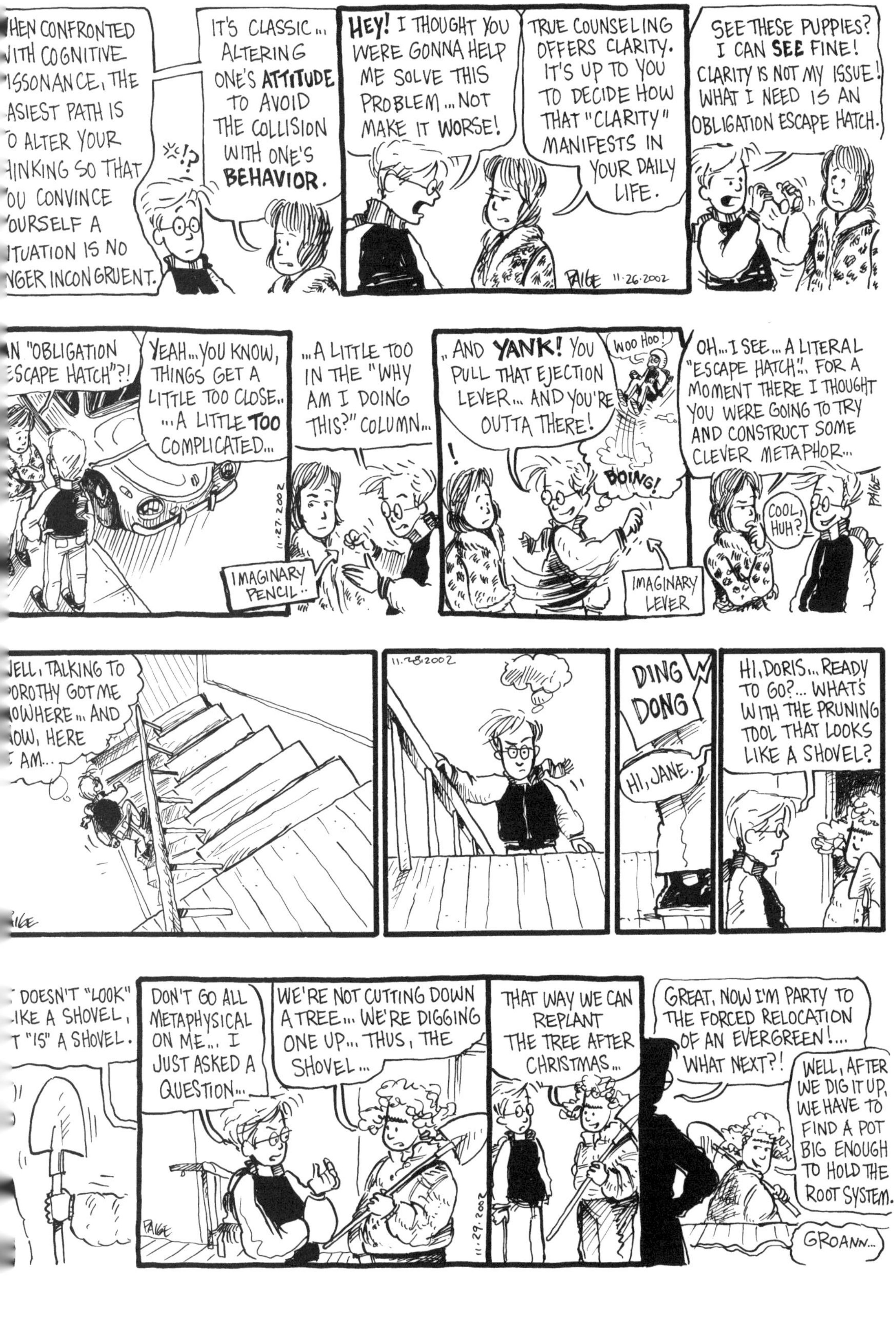
HEN CONFRONTED ITH COGNITIVE ISSONANCE, THE ASIEST PATH IS O ALTER YOUR HINKING SO THAT OU CONVINCE OURSELF A ITUATION IS NO NGER INCONGRUENT.
IT'S CLASSIC... ALTERING ONE'S ATTITUDE TO AVOID THE COLLISION WITH ONE'S BEHAVIOR.
!?
HEY! I THOUGHT YOU WERE GONNA HELP ME SOLVE THIS PROBLEM... NOT MAKE IT WORSE!
TRUE COUNSELING OFFERS CLARITY. IT'S UP TO YOU TO DECIDE HOW THAT "CLARITY" MANIFESTS IN YOUR DAILY LIFE.
PAIGE 11·26·2002
SEE THESE PUPPIES? I CAN SEE FINE! CLARITY IS NOT MY ISSUE! WHAT I NEED IS AN OBLIGATION ESCAPE HATCH.
N "OBLIGATION ESCAPE HATCH"?!
YEAH... YOU KNOW, THINGS GET A LITTLE TOO CLOSE.. ...A LITTLE TOO COMPLICATED...
11·27·2002
...A LITTLE TOO IN THE "WHY AM I DOING THIS?" COLUMN...
IMAGINARY PENCIL..
..AND YANK! YOU PULL THAT EJECTION LEVER... AND YOU'RE OUTTA THERE!
WOO HOO!
!
BOING!
IMAGINARY LEVER
OH... I SEE... A LITERAL "ESCAPE HATCH"... FOR A MOMENT THERE I THOUGHT YOU WERE GOING TO TRY AND CONSTRUCT SOME CLEVER METAPHOR...
COOL, HUH?
PAIGE
ELL, TALKING TO OROTHY GOT ME OWHERE... AND OW, HERE AM...
11·28·2002
DING DONG
HI, JANE.
HI, DORIS... READY TO GO?... WHAT'S WITH THE PRUNING TOOL THAT LOOKS LIKE A SHOVEL?
DOESN'T "LOOK" LIKE A SHOVEL, T "IS" A SHOVEL.
DON'T GO ALL METAPHYSICAL ON ME... I JUST ASKED A QUESTION...
PAIGE
WE'RE NOT CUTTING DOWN A TREE... WE'RE DIGGING ONE UP... THUS, THE SHOVEL...
THAT WAY WE CAN REPLANT THE TREE AFTER CHRISTMAS...
11·29·2002
GREAT, NOW I'M PARTY TO THE FORCED RELOCATION OF AN EVERGREEN!... WHAT NEXT?!
WELL, AFTER WE DIG IT UP, WE HAVE TO FIND A POT BIG ENOUGH TO HOLD THE ROOT SYSTEM.
GROANN...

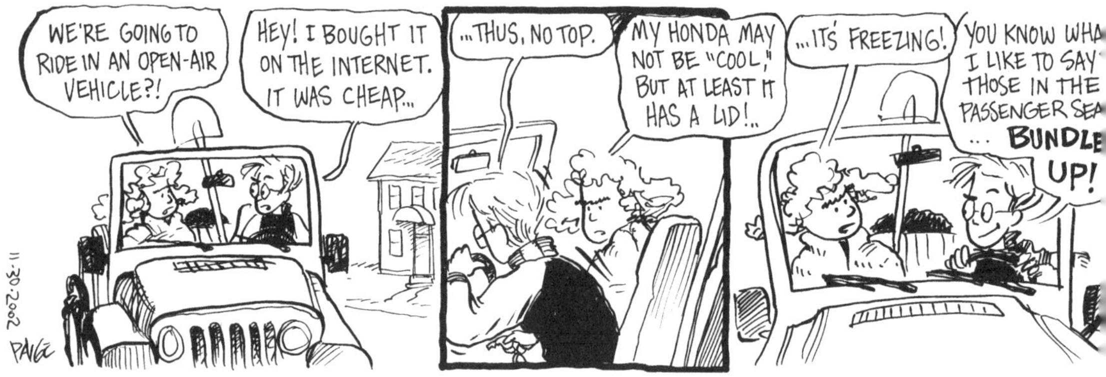
WE'RE GOING TO RIDE IN AN OPEN-AIR VEHICLE?!
HEY! I BOUGHT IT ON THE INTERNET. IT WAS CHEAP...
...THUS, NO TOP.
MY HONDA MAY NOT BE "COOL," BUT AT LEAST IT HAS A LID!..
...IT'S FREEZING!
YOU KNOW WHA I LIKE TO SAY THOSE IN THE PASSENGER SEA ... BUNDLE UP!
11·30·2002
PAIGE

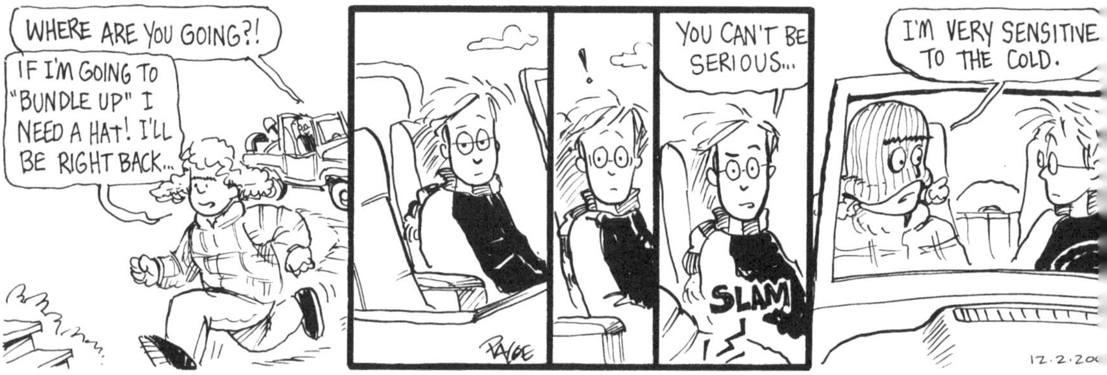
WHERE ARE YOU GOING?!
IF I'M GOING TO "BUNDLE UP" I NEED A HAT! I'LL BE RIGHT BACK...
!
YOU CAN'T BE SERIOUS...
SLAM
I'M VERY SENSITIVE TO THE COLD.
PAIGE
12·2·20

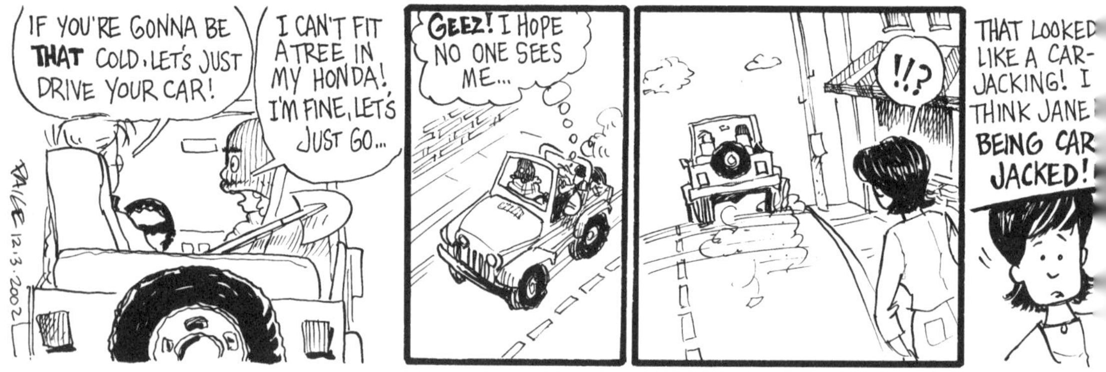
IF YOU'RE GONNA BE THAT COLD, LET'S JUST DRIVE YOUR CAR!
I CAN'T FIT A TREE IN MY HONDA! I'M FINE, LET'S JUST GO...
PAIGE 12·3·2002
GEEZ! I HOPE NO ONE SEES ME...
!!?
THAT LOOKED LIKE A CAR-JACKING! I THINK JANE BEING CAR JACKED!

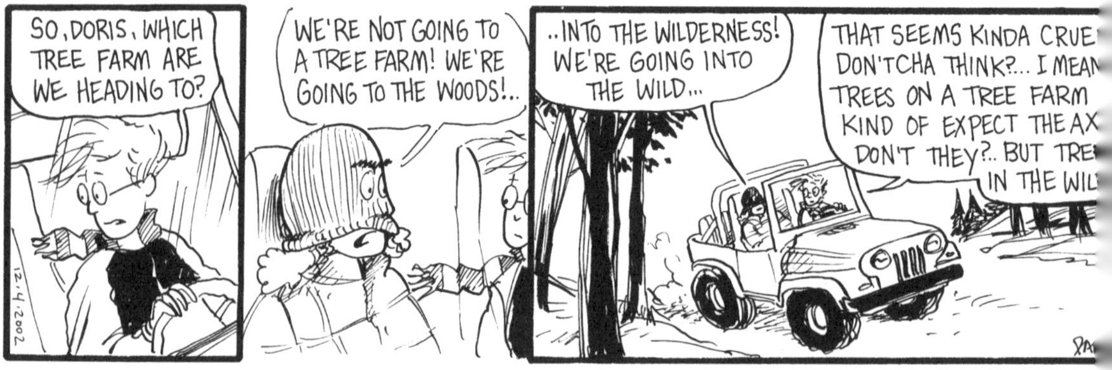
SO, DORIS, WHICH TREE FARM ARE WE HEADING TO?
12·4·2002
WE'RE NOT GOING TO A TREE FARM! WE'RE GOING TO THE WOODS!..
..INTO THE WILDERNESS! WE'RE GOING INTO THE WILD...
THAT SEEMS KINDA CRUE DON'TCHA THINK?... I MEAN TREES ON A TREE FARM KIND OF EXPECT THE AX DON'T THEY?.. BUT TRE IN THE WIL

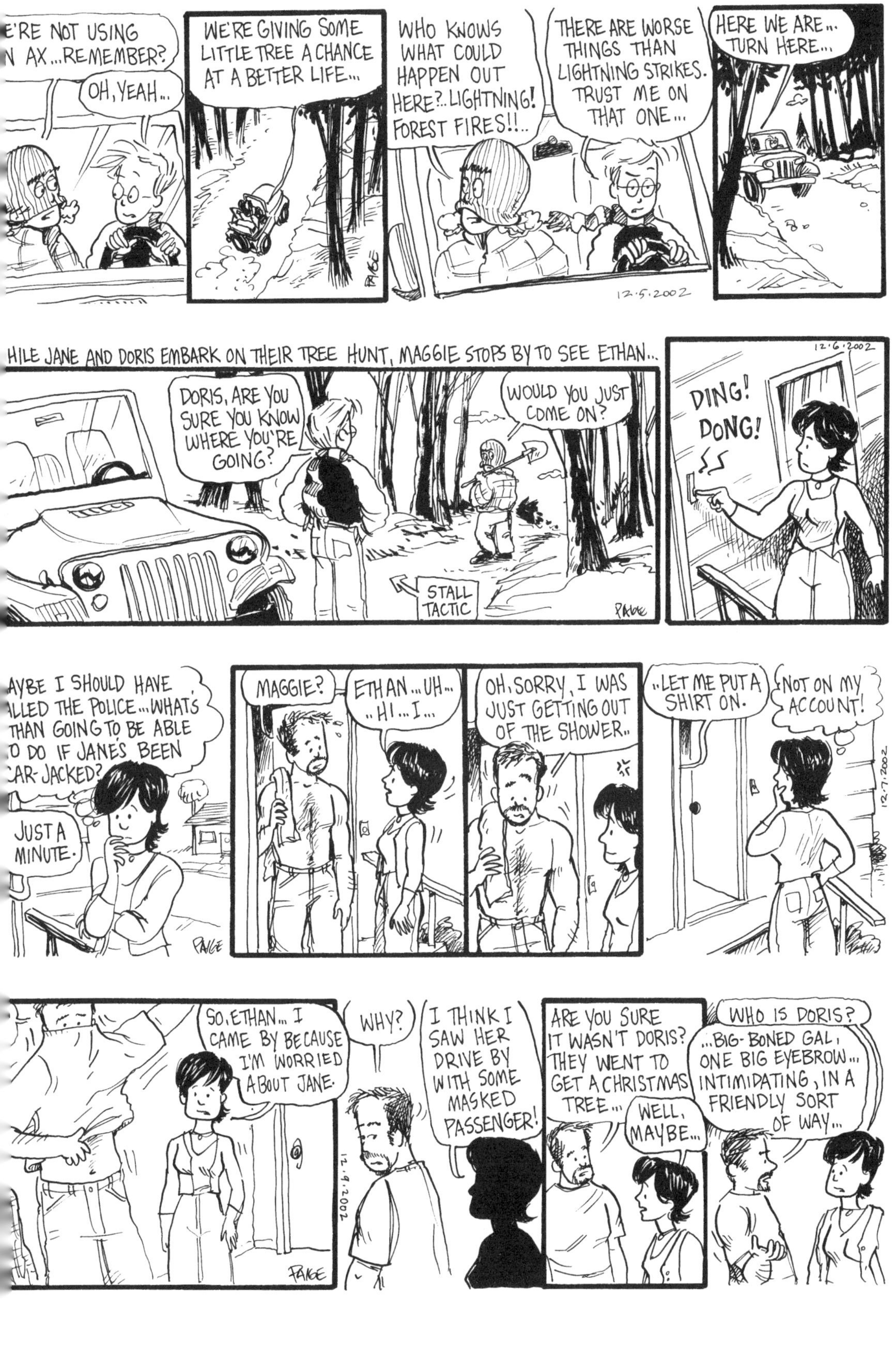
E'RE NOT USING
N AX...REMEMBER?
OH, YEAH...
WE'RE GIVING SOME LITTLE TREE A CHANCE AT A BETTER LIFE...
PAGE
WHO KNOWS WHAT COULD HAPPEN OUT HERE?.. LIGHTNING! FOREST FIRES!!...
THERE ARE WORSE THINGS THAN LIGHTNING STRIKES. TRUST ME ON THAT ONE...
12·5·2002
HERE WE ARE... TURN HERE...
HILE JANE AND DORIS EMBARK ON THEIR TREE HUNT, MAGGIE STOPS BY TO SEE ETHAN...
DORIS, ARE YOU SURE YOU KNOW WHERE YOU'RE GOING?
WOULD YOU JUST COME ON?
STALL TACTIC
PAGE
12·6·2002
DING! DONG!
AYBE I SHOULD HAVE
ALLED THE POLICE...WHAT'S
THAN GOING TO BE ABLE
O DO IF JANE'S BEEN
CAR-JACKED?
JUST A MINUTE.
PAGE
MAGGIE?
ETHAN...UH... ..HI...I...
OH, SORRY, I WAS JUST GETTING OUT OF THE SHOWER..
..LET ME PUT A SHIRT ON.
NOT ON MY ACCOUNT!
12·7·2002
SO, ETHAN... I CAME BY BECAUSE I'M WORRIED ABOUT JANE.
PAGE
12·9·2002
WHY?
I THINK I SAW HER DRIVE BY WITH SOME MASKED PASSENGER!
ARE YOU SURE IT WASN'T DORIS? THEY WENT TO GET A CHRISTMAS TREE...
WELL, MAYBE...
WHO IS DORIS?
...BIG-BONED GAL, ONE BIG EYEBROW... INTIMIDATING, IN A FRIENDLY SORT OF WAY...

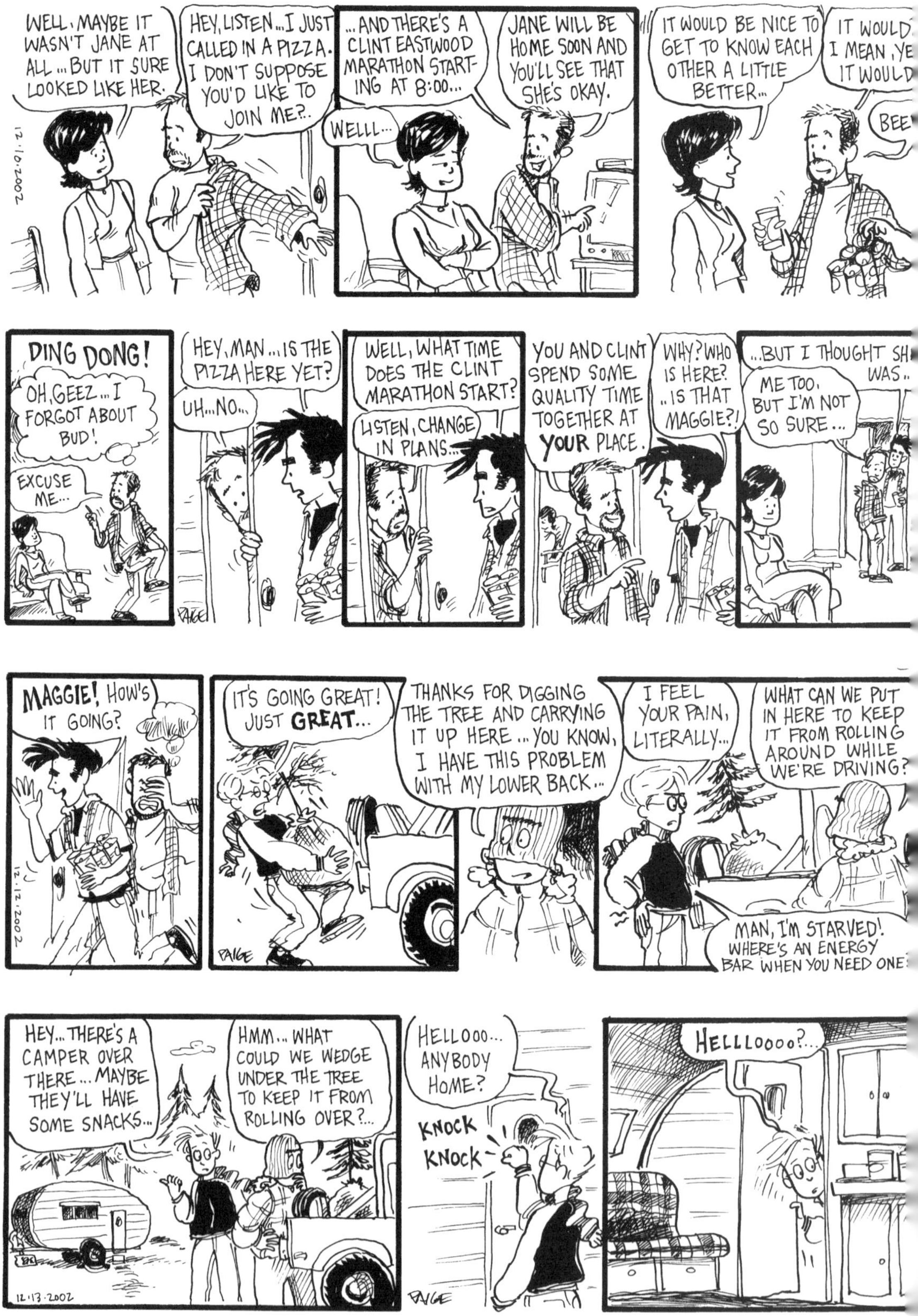
12.10.2002
WELL, MAYBE IT WASN'T JANE AT ALL ... BUT IT SURE LOOKED LIKE HER.
HEY, LISTEN ... I JUST CALLED IN A PIZZA. I DON'T SUPPOSE YOU'D LIKE TO JOIN ME?..
... AND THERE'S A CLINT EASTWOOD MARATHON STARTING AT 8:00...
WELLL...
JANE WILL BE HOME SOON AND YOU'LL SEE THAT SHE'S OKAY.
IT WOULD BE NICE TO GET TO KNOW EACH OTHER A LITTLE BETTER...
IT WOULD
I MEAN, YE
IT WOULD
BEE
DING DONG!
OH, GEEZ ... I FORGOT ABOUT BUD!
EXCUSE ME...
PAIGE
HEY, MAN ... IS THE PIZZA HERE YET?
UH... NO...
WELL, WHAT TIME DOES THE CLINT MARATHON START?
LISTEN, CHANGE IN PLANS...
YOU AND CLINT SPEND SOME QUALITY TIME TOGETHER AT YOUR PLACE.
WHY? WHO IS HERE? .. IS THAT MAGGIE?!
...BUT I THOUGHT SH
WAS..
ME TOO, BUT I'M NOT SO SURE...
12.12.2002
MAGGIE! HOW'S IT GOING?
IT'S GOING GREAT! JUST GREAT...
PAIGE
THANKS FOR DIGGING THE TREE AND CARRYING IT UP HERE ... YOU KNOW, I HAVE THIS PROBLEM WITH MY LOWER BACK...
I FEEL YOUR PAIN, LITERALLY...
WHAT CAN WE PUT IN HERE TO KEEP IT FROM ROLLING AROUND WHILE WE'RE DRIVING?
MAN, I'M STARVED! WHERE'S AN ENERGY BAR WHEN YOU NEED ONE?
12.13.2002
HEY... THERE'S A CAMPER OVER THERE... MAYBE THEY'LL HAVE SOME SNACKS...
HMM... WHAT COULD WE WEDGE UNDER THE TREE TO KEEP IT FROM ROLLING OVER?..
HELLOOO... ANYBODY HOME?
KNOCK KNOCK
PAIGE
HELLLOOOO?...

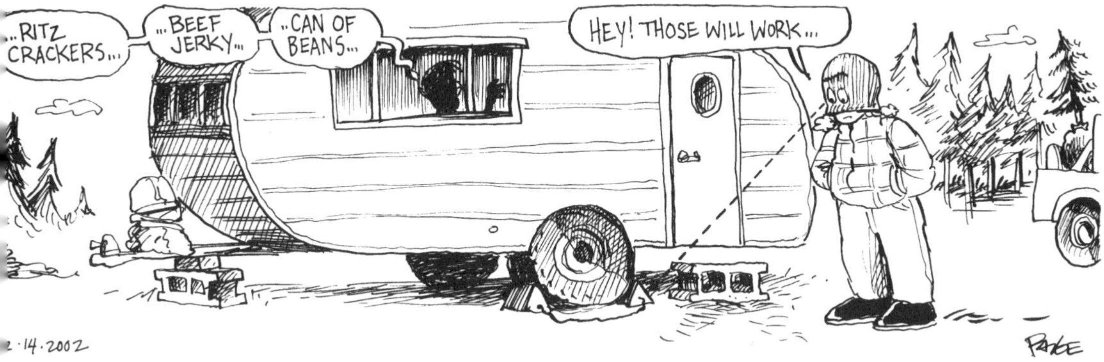
...RITZ CRACKERS...
...BEEF JERKY...
...CAN OF BEANS...
HEY! THOSE WILL WORK...
14·2002
PAIGE

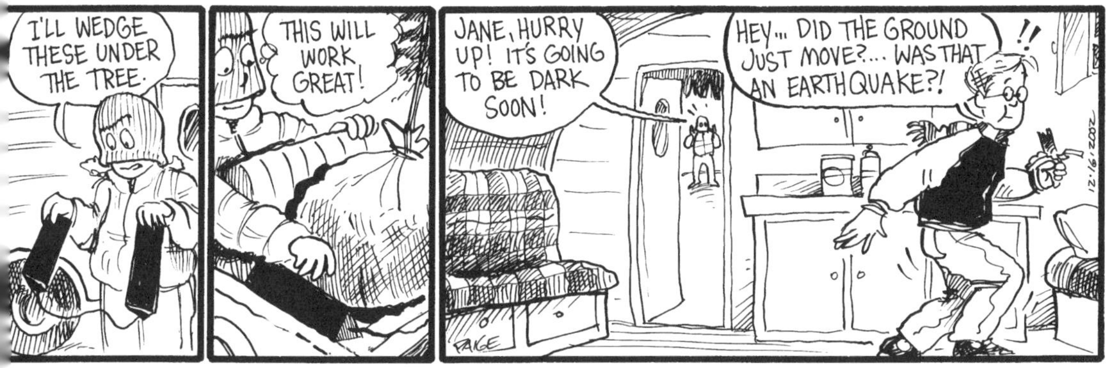
I'LL WEDGE THESE UNDER THE TREE.
THIS WILL WORK GREAT!
JANE, HURRY UP! IT'S GOING TO BE DARK SOON!
PAIGE
HEY... DID THE GROUND JUST MOVE?... WAS THAT AN EARTHQUAKE?!
!!
12·16·2002

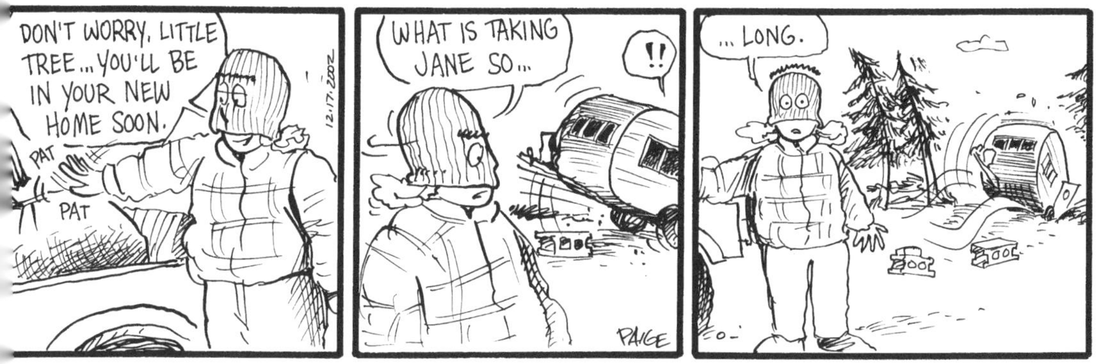
DON'T WORRY, LITTLE TREE... YOU'LL BE IN YOUR NEW HOME SOON.
PAT
PAT
12·17·2002
WHAT IS TAKING JANE SO...
!!
PAIGE
... LONG.

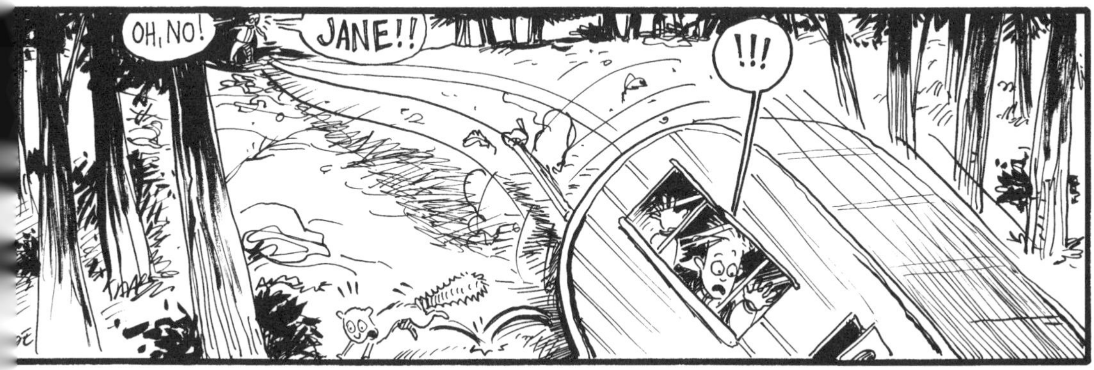
OH, NO!
JANE!!
!!!

To be continued!

SKETCHBOOK:

This is where I had planned to write about my "process"... you know, as an artist... but then I realized that I don't have much of one to write about.

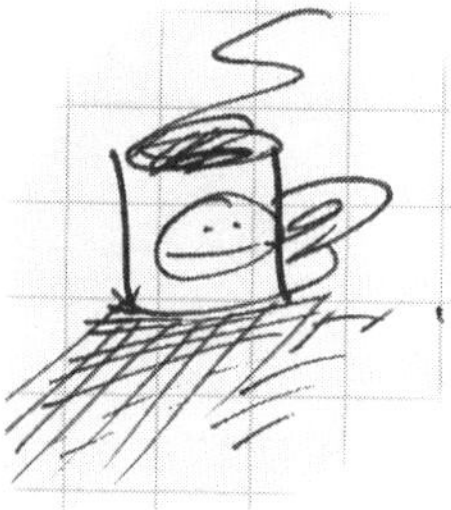

See, I have this day job, that's pretty time consuming, which means I'm always behind on my deadlines for ***Jane's World***, which means I get some of my best ideas in meetings, in the shower, while I'm sleeping or when I'm driving my car. None of this on-the-go "process" allows for much quality art, but I've decorated these pages with a few of the drawings anyway.

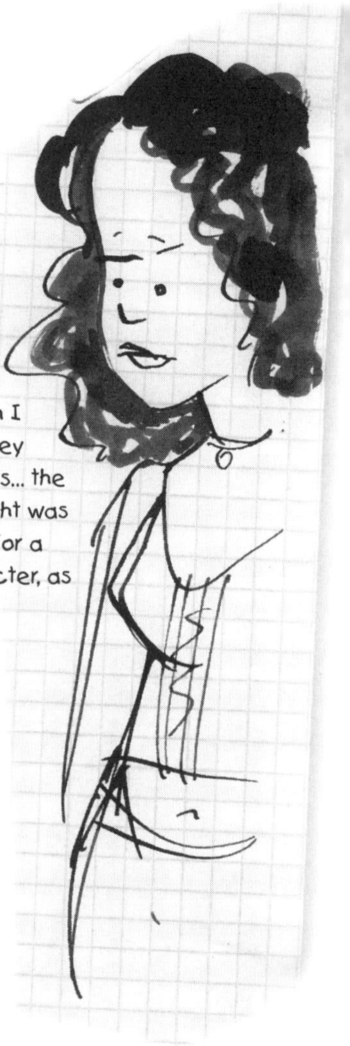

For some reason I draw lots of smiley mugs in meetings... the image on the right was a rough sketch for a potential character, as yet unnamed.

Some of my ideas go straight from post-it note to Bristol board, without much of a filter. Which is why, when I'm doing it right, the strip seems real.

Because real life doesn't have a filter.

Sometimes, the story arcs I like best are the ones that just jump out and onto the paper... somehow, if I don't over-think them and just let the characters act out their own lives, something magical happens and I feel like an innocent bystander... standing on the sideline, watching it happen.

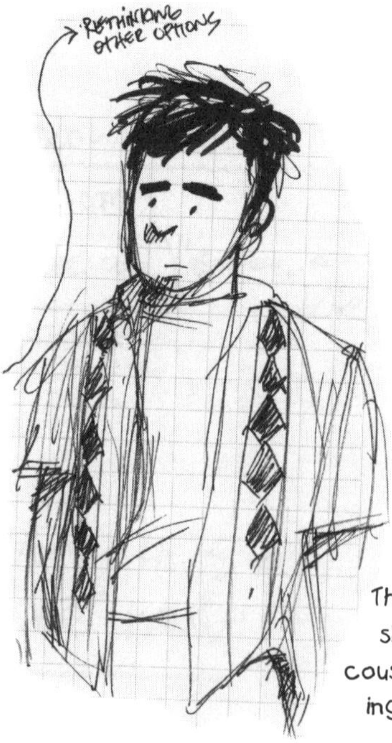
OTHER OPTIONS

This was a "first draft" sketch of Bud, Jane's cousin. I ended up making him a lot skinnier in the comic strip.

That may sound corny, but it's true. As my friend Terry Moore says, good characters are a gift.

Well, I feel pretty lucky to have been gifted with a cast of characters that just keep telling stories and as goofball as it sounds, I can't wait to see what'll happen next.

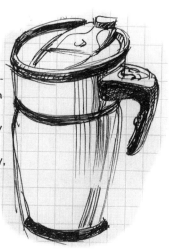

:e... What did I
ll you...another
etch of my cof-
e cup du jour in
me meeting
ere I obviously
' my mind won-
r. Unfortunately,
s was of no
e for a comic
ip idea.

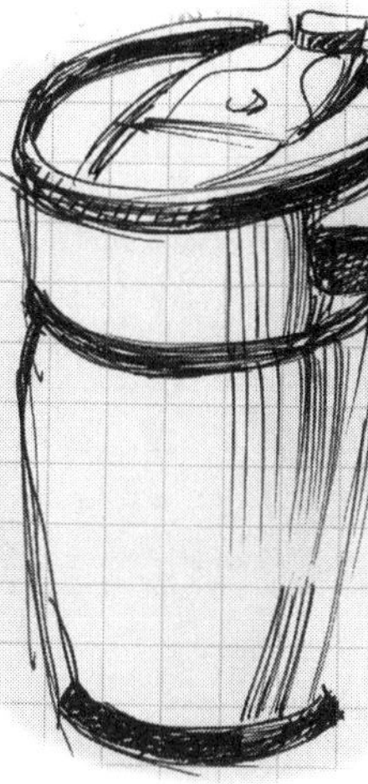

Before I came up with Rusty, as he looks now, I played around with some other "dog" looks. It's really hard to come up with a dog character that hasn't already been done. This particular sketch was modeled after one of my own dogs... a wiener dog.

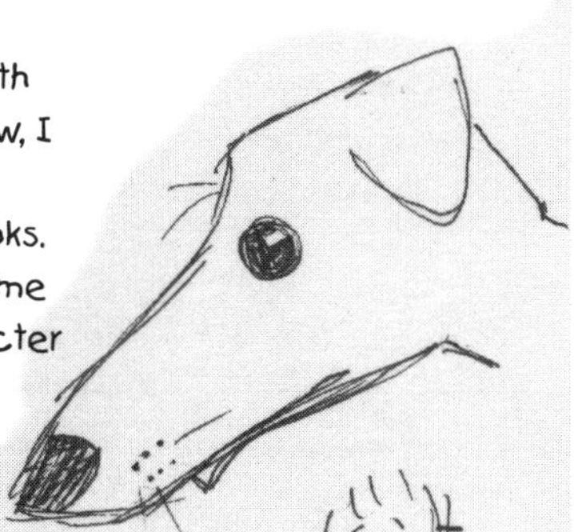

Here's an early couple of sketches for Jane's niece, Alexa.

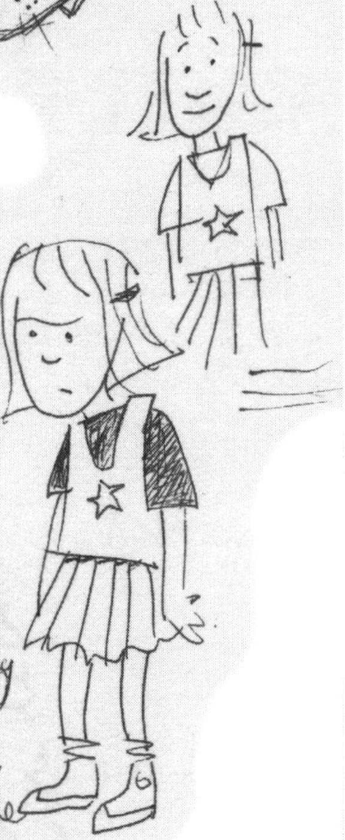

And some random note that refers to a much earlier story line.

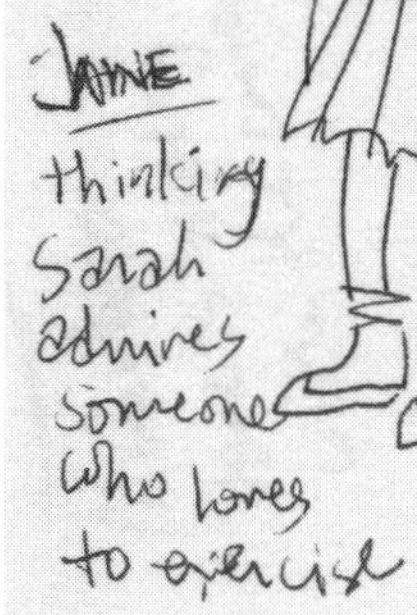
JANE
thinking
Sarah
admires
someone
who loves
to exercise

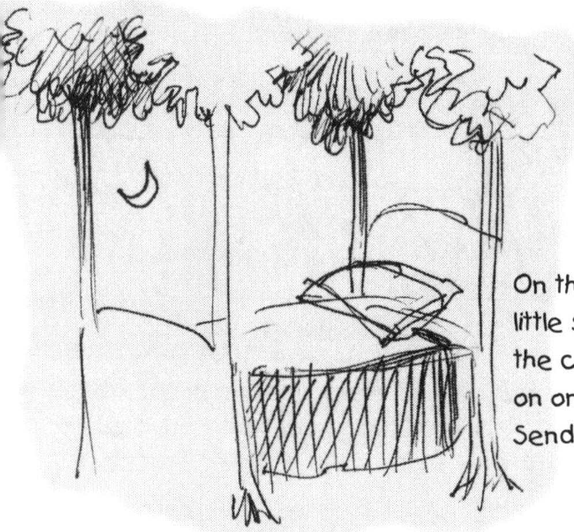

On the left was a little sketch for the comic based on one Maurice Sendak's stories.

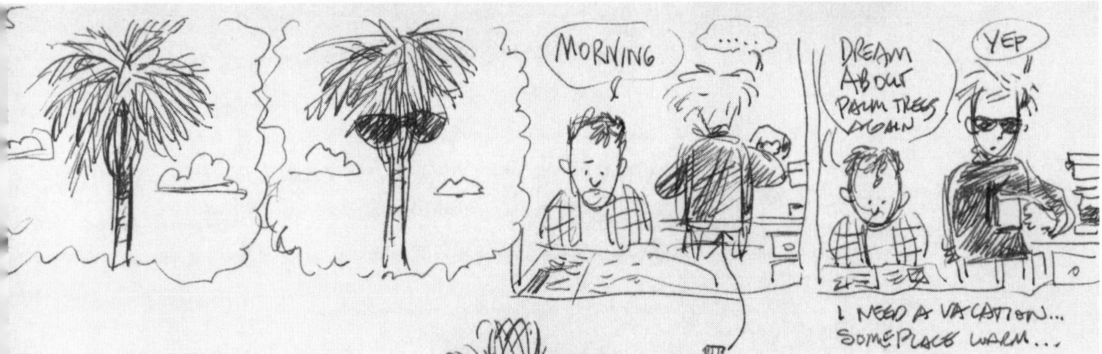
MORNING
...
DREAM ABOUT PALM TREES AGAIN
YEP
I NEED A VACATION... SOMEPLACE WARM...

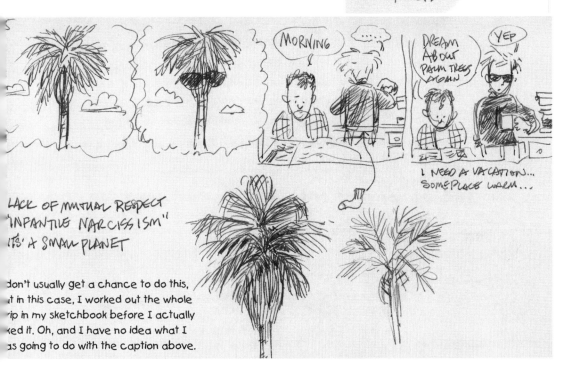

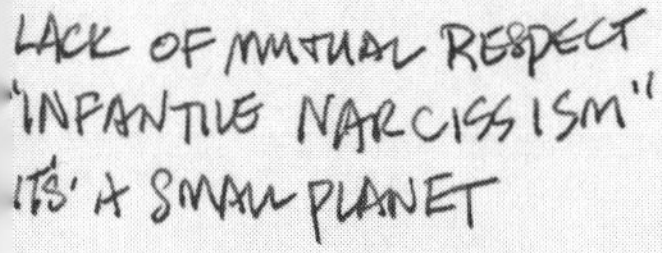
LACK OF MUTUAL RESPECT
"INFANTILE NARCISSISM"
IT'S A SMALL PLANET

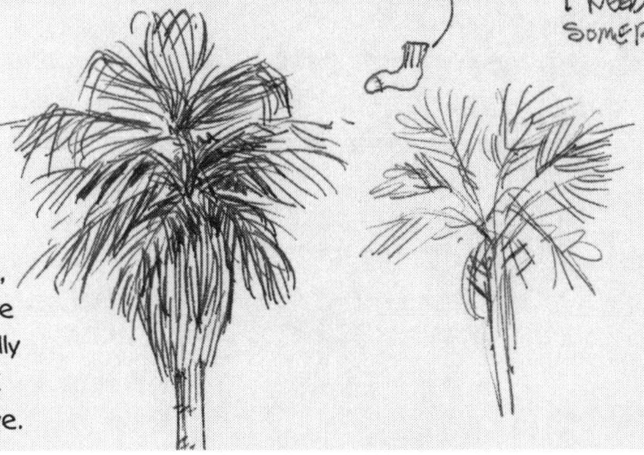

don't usually get a chance to do this,
it in this case, I worked out the whole
rip in my sketchbook before I actually
ked it. Oh, and I have no idea what I
as going to do with the caption above.

The two sections below were scanned, unfiltered, from my sketchbook. I really liked the drawing of Lowell on the bench... I don't think the final version had quite the spark that this first sketch did. That's the way it goes sometimes.

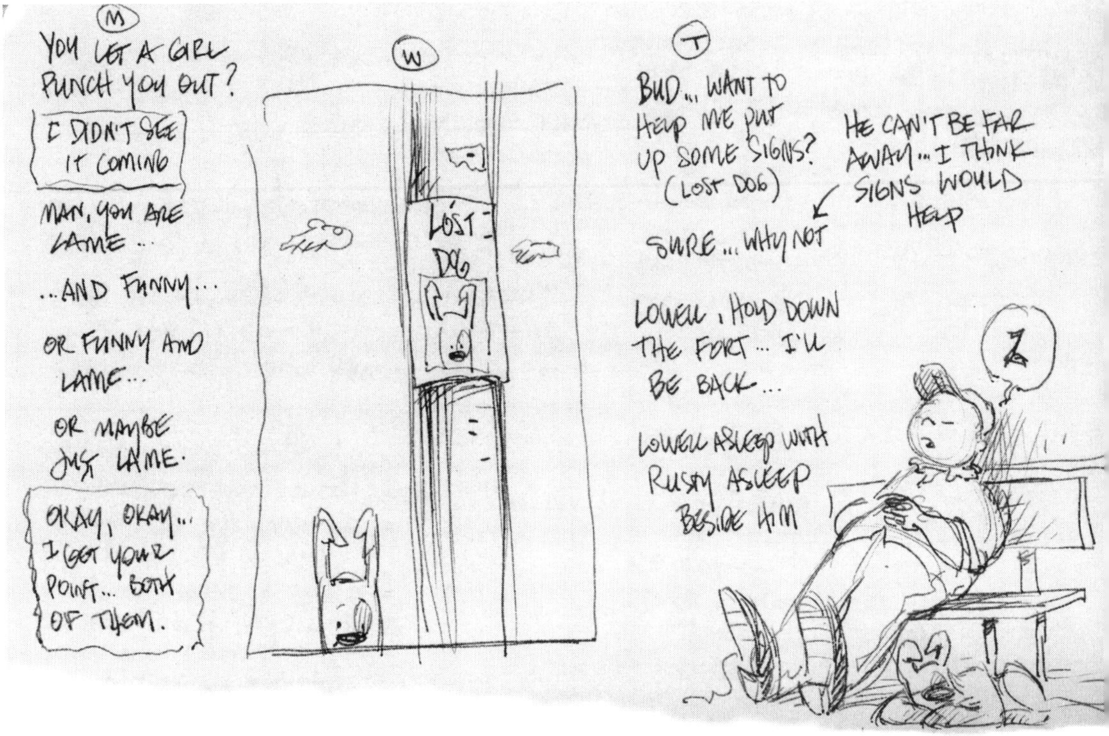
M
YOU LET A GIRL PUNCH YOU OUT?
I DIDN'T SEE IT COMING
MAN, YOU ARE LAME...
...AND FUNNY...
OR FUNNY AND LAME...
OR MAYBE JUST LAME.
OKAY, OKAY... I GET YOUR POINT... BOTH OF THEM.
W
LOST DOG
T
BUD... WANT TO HELP ME PUT UP SOME SIGNS? (LOST DOG)
HE CAN'T BE FAR AWAY... I THINK SIGNS WOULD HELP
SURE... WHY NOT
LOWELL, HOLD DOWN THE FORT... I'LL BE BACK...
LOWELL ASLEEP WITH RUSTY ASLEEP BESIDE HIM
Z

I used to have a hamster named Rufus when I was kid. More than once, under the cover of night, he escaped from his Habitrail and ran across my bed. It always freaked me out. I love hamsters... but in the dark, they can be kinda scary.

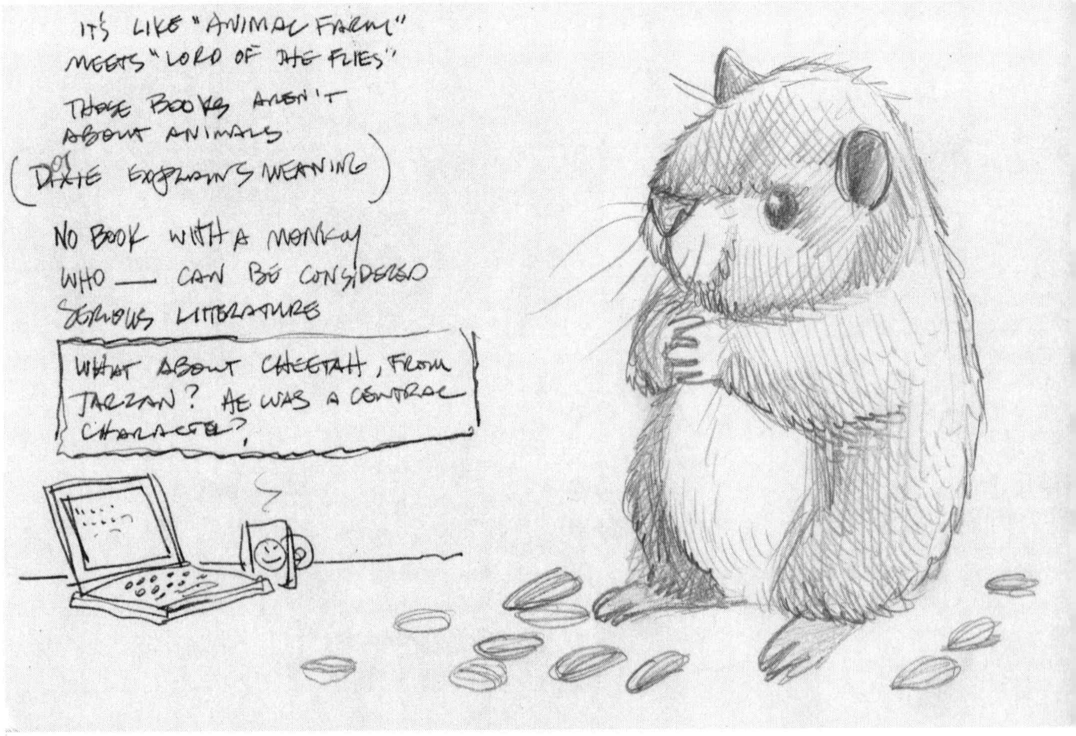
IT'S LIKE "ANIMAL FARM" MEETS "LORD OF THE FLIES"
THOSE BOOKS AREN'T ABOUT ANIMALS
(DIXIE EXPLAINS MEANING)
NO BOOK WITH A MONKEY WHO — CAN BE CONSIDERED SERIOUS LITERATURE
WHAT ABOUT CHEETAH, FROM TARZAN? HE WAS A CENTRAL CHARACTER?